THE **COMPLETE WORKS** OF **SWAMI VIVEKANANDA**

VOLUME VIII

Discovery Publisher

2019, Discovery Publisher

No part of this book may be reproduced in any form or by any electronic or mechanical means including information storage and retrieval systems, without permission in writing from the publisher.

Author: Swami Vivekananda

616 Corporate Way, Suite 2-4933
Valley Cottage, New York, 10989
www.discoverypublisher.com
edition@discoverypublisher.com
facebook.com/discoverypublisher
twitter.com/discoverypb

New York • Paris • Dublin • Tokyo • Hong Kong

TABLE OF CONTENTS

Lectures and Discourses — 3

- DISCOURSES ON JNANA-YOGA — 4
- I — 4
- II — 5
- III — 6
- IV — 8
- V — 9
- VI — 11
- VII — 12
- VIII — 14
- IX — 16
- SIX LESSONS ON RAJA-YOGA — 18
- FIRST LESSON — 18
- SECOND LESSON — 20
- THIRD LESSON — 22
- FOURTH LESSON — 23
- FIFTH LESSON — 23
- SIXTH LESSON — 24
- WOMEN OF INDIA — 25
- THE LECTURE — 25
- MY LIFE AND MISSION — 33
- DISCIPLESHIP — 41
- IS VEDANTA THE FUTURE RELIGION? — 48

Writings: Prose And Poems — 58

- THE STRUGGLE FOR EXPANSION — 60
- THE BIRTH OF RELIGION — 61
- FOUR PATHS OF YOGA — 62
- CYCLIC REST AND CHANGE — 64
- A PREFACE TO THE IMITATION OF CHRIST — 65
- AN INTERESTING CORRESPONDENCE — 66
- THOU BLESSED DREAM — 69
- LIGHT — 69
- THE LIVING GOD — 69
- TO AN EARLY VIOLET — 69
- TO MY OWN SOUL — 70
- THE DANCE OF SHIVA — 70
- SHIVA IN ECSTASY — 70
- TO SHRI KRISHNA — 70
- A HYMN TO SHRI RAMAKRISHNA — 70
- NO ONE TO BLAME — 71

Notes Of Class Talks And Lectures — 74

- NOTES OF CLASS TALKS — 76
- WHEN WILL CHRIST COME AGAIN? — 76
- THE DIFFERENCE BETWEEN MAN AND CHRIST — 76
- ARE CHRIST AND BUDDHA IDENTICAL? — 76
- SALVATION FROM SIN — 76
- COMING BACK TO THE DIVINE MOTHER — 77
- NO INDIVIDUALITY APART FROM GOD — 77
- MAN THE MAKER OF HIS DESTINY — 77

GOD: PERSONAL AND IMPERSONAL	79
THE DIVINE INCARNATION OR AVATARA	80
PRANAYAMA	80
WOMEN OF THE EAST	83
CONGRESS OF RELIGIOUS UNITY	83
THE LOVE OF GOD — I	83
THE LOVE OF GOD — II	84
INDIA	85
HINDUS AND CHRISTIANS	87
CHRISTIANITY IN INDIA	89
THE RELIGION OF LOVE	92
JNANA AND KARMA	93
THE CLAIMS OF VEDANTA ON THE MODERN WORLD	96
THE LAWS OF LIFE AND DEATH	97
THE REALITY AND THE SHADOW	98
WAY TO SALVATION	99
THE PEOPLE OF INDIA	100
I AM THAT I AM	101
UNITY	103
THE WORSHIP OF THE DIVINE MOTHER	104
THE ESSENCE OF RELIGION	105

Sayings and Utterances   110

SAYINGS AND UTTERANCES	112

Epistles - Fourth Series

I — SIR	124
II — SIR	124
III — SIR	124
IV — SIR	125
V — SIR	125
VI — DIWANJI SAHEB	125
VII — DIWANJI SAHEB	125
VIII — DIWANJI SAHEB	126
IX — DIWANJI SAHEB	126
X — HARIPADA	127
XI — ALASINGA	127
XII — DIWANJI SAHEB	128
XIII — DIWANJI SAHEB	128
XIV — DIWANJI SAHEB	129
XV — DIWANJI SAHEB	130
XVI — SISTERS	131
XVII — BABIES	132
XVIII — SISTER MARY	133
XIX — SISTER	133
XX — DIWANJI SAHEB	134
XXI — DEAR__	136
XXII — MOTHER	137
XXIII — SISTERS	138
XXIV — BABIES	138
XXV — SISTERS	139
XXVI — SISTER	140
XXVII — LEON	140
XXVIII — SISTER	140
XXIX — DIWANJI SAHEB	141
XXX — DIWANJI SAHEB	141
XXXI — MOTHER	141
XXXII — SISTER	142
XXXIII — DIWANJI SAHEB	142
XXXIV — DIWANJI	144
XXXV — SISTER	145
XXXVI — SISTER	145
XXXVII — SISTER	146
XXXVIII — MISS BELL	146
XXXIX — FRIEND	146
XL — FRIEND	146
XLI — FRIEND	147
XLII — BABIES	147
XLIII — ALASINGA	148
XLIV — JOE	148
XLV — SISTER	149
XLVI — SISTER	149
XLVII — SISTER	150
XLVIII — SISTER	151
IL — FRIEND	151
L — FRIEND	152
LI — FRIEND	153
LII — JOE JOE	154
LIII — KALI	154
LIV — JOE JOE	155
LV — JOE JOE	155
LVI — JOE JOE	156
LVII — FRIEND	156
LVIII — FRIEND	157
LIX — FRIEND	157
LX — BLESSED AND BELOVED	157
LXI — FRIEND	157
LXII — JOE JOE	158
LXIII — STURDY	158
LXIV — BLESSED AND BELOVED	159
LXV — SHARAT	160

LXVI — FRIEND	161
LXVII — SISTER	161
LXVIII — BLESSED AND BELOVED	162
LXIX — ALASINGA	162
LXX — BLESSED AND BELOVED	163
LXXI — BLESSED AND BELOVED	163
LXXI — BLESSED AND BELOVED	164
LXXII — SISTER	165
LXXIII — SISTERS	165
LXXIV — STURDY	165
LXXV — SISTERS	165
LXXVI — MARY	166
LXXVII — BABIES	166
LXXVIII — BLESSED AND BELOVED	167
LXXIX — BLESSED AND BELOVED	167
LXXX — DEAR__	168
LXXXI — GOODWIN	168
LXXXII — BLESSESD AND BELOVED	169
LXXXIII — BLESSED AND BELOVED	170
LXXXIV — FRIEND	171
LXXXV — SISTER	171
LXXXVI — JOE	172
LXXXVII — RAKHAL	173
LXXXVIII — MARY	173
LXXXIX — RAKHAL	174
XC — SHASHI	174
XCI — MISS NOBLE	175
XCII — RAKHAL	176
XCIII — SUDHIR	177
XCIV — MARIE	177
XCV — MISS NOBLE	178
XCVI — MISS NOBLE	179
XCVII — JOE JOE	179
XCVIII — RAKHAL	180
IC — MARIE	181
C — SHASHI	183
CI — SHASHI	183
CII — RAKHAL	184
CIII — RAKHAL	184
CIV — SHUDDHANANDA	185
CV — HARIPADA	186
CVI — MISS MACLEOD	186
CVII — RAKHAL	186
CVIII — SHASHI	187
CIX — RAKHAL	188
CX — MARGO	188
CXI — RAKHAL	189
CXII — RAKHAL	190
CXIII — MISS NOBLE	191
CXIV — RAKHAL	191
CXV — RAKHAL	191
CXVI — BABURAM	192
CXVII — RAKHAL	192
CXVIII — RAKHAL	193
CXIX — RAKHAL	193
CXX — SHIVANANDA	194
CXXI — RAJAJI	194
CXXII — SHASHI	194
CXXIII — MARY	196
CXXIV — SHASHI	197
CXXV — JOE JOE	197
CXXVI — RAKHAL	198
CXXVII — JOE JOE	198
CXXVIII — RAKHAL	199

CXXIX — STURDY	200
CXXX — RAKHAL	200
CXXXI — RAKHAL	201
CXXXII — MARY	201
CXXXIII — HARIPADA	202
CXXXIV — HARIPADA	203
CXXXV — JOE	203
CXXXVI — MARY	203
CXXXVII — STURDY	204
CXXXVIII — JOE	204
CXXXIX — MARIE	205
CXL — RAKHAL	206
CXLI — MOTHER	207
CXLII — STURDY	207
CXLIII — MARY	208
CXLIV — MARY	209
CXLV — OPTIMIST	209
CXLVI — STURDY	210
CXLVII — MRS. BULL	211
CXLVIII — RAKHAL	211
CXLIX — MARY	212
CL — BRAHMANANDA	212
CLI — DHIRA MATA	213
CLII — DHIRA MATA	213
CLIII — MARY	214
CLIV — DHIRA MATA	215
CLV — DHIRA MATA	216
CLVI — MARY	216
CLVII — MARY	217
CLVIII — DHIRA MATA	217
CLIX — DHIRA MATA	218
CLX — JOE	219
CLXI — RAKHAL	219
CLXII — MARY	220
CLXIII — DHIRA MATA	220
CLXIV — MARY	221
CLXV — MARY	221
CLXVI — HARIBHAI	222
CLXVII — JOE	222
CLXVIII — HARIBHAI	223
CLXIX — JOE	223
CLXX — DHIRA MATA	224
CLXXI — MARGOT	225
CLXXII — AMERICAN FRIEND	225
CLXXIII — DHIRA MATA	226
CLXXIV — JOE	226
CLXXV — AMERICAN FRIEND	227
CLXXVI — JOE	228
CLXXVII — MARY	228
CLXXVIII — MARY	229
CLXXIX — NIVEDITA	229
CLXXX — NIVEDITA	229
CLXXXI — MARY	230
CLXXXII — MARY	231
CLXXXIII — SISTER	231
CLXXXIV — TURIYANANDA	231
CLXXXV — JOE	232
CLXXXVI — JOE	232
CLXXXVII — TURIYANANDA	233
CLXXXVIII — DEAR__	233
CLXXXIX — HARI	233
CXC — JOHN FOX	234
CXCI — BROTHER HARI	234
CXCII — HARI	235
CXCIII — TURIYANANDA	235
CXCIV — MADEMOISELLE	236
CXCV — SISTER CHRISTINE	236
CXCVI — JOE	237
CXCVII — MOTHER	238

THE **COMPLETE WORKS** OF
SWAMI VIVEKANANDA

VOLUME VIII

LECTURES AND DISCOURSES

DISCOURSES ON JNANA-YOGA[1]

I

Om Tat Sat! To know the Om is to know the secret of the universe. The object of Jnana-Yoga is the same as that of Bhakti and Raja Yogas, but the method is different. This is the Yoga for the strong, for those who are neither mystical nor devotional, but rational. As the Bhakti-Yogi works his way to complete oneness with the Supreme through love and devotion, so the Jnana-yogi forces his way to the realisation of God by the power of pure reason. He must be prepared to throw away all old idols, all old beliefs and superstitions, all desire for this world or another, and be determined only to find freedom. Without Jnana (knowledge) liberation cannot be ours. It consists in knowing what we really are, that we are beyond fear, beyond birth, beyond death. The highest good is the realisation of the Self. It is beyond sense, beyond thought. The real "I" cannot be grasped. It is the eternal subject and can never become the object of knowledge, because knowledge is only of the related, not of the Absolute. All sense-knowledge is limitation, it is an endless chain of cause and effect. This world is a relative world, a shadow of the real; still, being the plane of equipoise where happiness and misery are about evenly balanced, it is the only plane where man can realise his true Self and know that he is Brahman.

This world is "the evolution of nature and the manifestation of God". It is our interpretation of Brahman or the Absolute, seen through the veil of Maya or appearance. The world is not zero, it has a certain reality; it only appears because Brahman is .

How shall we know the knower? The Vedanta says, "We are It, but can never know It, because It can never become the object of knowledge." Modern science also says that It cannot be known. We can, however, have glimpses of It from time to time.

---

1. These were originally recorded by a prominent American disciple of the Swami, Miss S.E. Waldo. Swami Saradananda, while he was in America (1896), copied them out from her notebook — Ed.

When the delusion of this world is once broken, it will come back to us, but no longer will it hold any reality for us. We shall know it as a mirage. To reach behind the mirage is the aim of all religions. That man and God are one is the constant teaching of the Vedas, but only few are able to penetrate behind the veil and reach the realisation of this truth.

The first thing to be got rid of by him who would be a Jnani is fear. Fear is one of our worst enemies. Next, believe in nothing until you know it. Constantly tell yourself, "I am not the body, I am not the mind, I am not thought, I am not even consciousness; I am the Atman." When you can throw away all, only the true Self will remain. The Jnani's meditation is of two sorts: (1) to deny and think away everything we are not; (2) to insist upon what we really are — the Atman, the One Self — existence, Knowledge, and Bliss. The true rationalist must go on and fearlessly follow his reason to its farthest limits. It will not answer to stop anywhere on the road. When we begin to deny, all must go until we reach what cannot be thrown away or denied, which is the real "I". That "I" is the witness of the universe, it is unchangeable, eternal, infinite. Now, layer after layer of ignorance covers it from our eyes, but it remains ever the same.

Two birds sat on one tree. The bird at the top was calm, majestic, beautiful, perfect. The lower bird was always hopping from twig to twig, now eating sweet fruits and being happy, now eating bitter fruits and being miserable. One day, when he had eaten a fruit more bitter than usual, he glanced up at the calm majestic upper bird and thought, "How I would like to be like him!" and he hopped up a little way towards him. Soon he forgot all about his desire to be like the upper bird, and went on as before, eating sweet and bitter fruits and being happy and miserable. Again he looked up, again he went up a little nearer to the calm and majestic upper bird. Many times was this repeated until at last he drew very near the upper bird; the brilliancy of his plumage dazzled him, seemed to absorb him, and finally, to his wonder and surprise, he found there was only one bird — he was the upper bird all the time and had but just found it out. Man is like that lower bird, but if he perseveres in his efforts to rise to the highest ideal he can conceive of, he too will find that he was the Self all the time and the other was but a dream. To separate ourselves utterly from matter and all belief in its reality is true Jnana. The Jnani must keep ever in his mind the "Om Tat Sat", that is, Om the only real existence. Abstract unity is the foundation of Jnana-yoga. This is called Advaitism ("without dualism or dvaitism"). This is the corner-stone of the Vedanta philosophy, the Alpha and the Omega. "Brahman alone is true, all else is false and I am Brahman." Only by telling ourselves this until we make it a part of our very being, can we rise beyond all duality, beyond both good and evil, pleasure and pain, joy and sorrow, and know ourselves as the One, eternal, unchanging, infinite — the "One without a second".

The Jnana-yogi must be as intense as the narrowest sectarian, yet as broad as the heavens. He must absolutely control his mind, be able to be a Buddhist or a Christian, to have the power to consciously divide himself into all these different ideas and yet hold fast to the eternal harmony. Constant drill alone can enable us to get this control. All variations are in the One, but we must learn not to identify ourselves with what we do, and to hear nothing, see nothing, talk of nothing but the thing in hand. We must put in our whole soul and be intense. Day and night tell yourself, "I am He, I am He."

II

The greatest teacher of the Vedanta philosophy was Shankaracharya. By solid reasoning he extracted from the Vedas the truths of Vedanta, and on them built up the wonderful system of Jnana that is taught in his commentaries. He unified all the conflicting descriptions of Brahman and showed that there is only one Infinite Reality. He showed too that as man can only travel slowly on the upward road, all the varied presentations are needed to suit his varying capacity. We find something akin to this in the teachings of Jesus, which he evidently adapted to the different abilities of his hearers. First he taught them of a Father in heaven and to pray to Him. Next he rose a step higher and told them, "I am the vine, you are the branches", and lastly he gave them the highest truth: "I and my Father are one", and "The Kingdom of Heaven is within you." Shankara taught that three things were the great gifts of God: (1) human body, (2) thirst after God, and (3) a teacher who can show us the light. When these three great gifts are ours, we may know that our redemption is at hand. Only knowledge can free and save us, but with knowledge must go virtue.

The essence of Vedanta is that there is but one Being and that every soul is that Being in full, not a part of that Being. All the sun is reflected in each dew-drop. Appearing in time, space and causality, this Being is man, as we know him, but behind all appearance is the one Reality. Unselfishness is the denial of the lower or apparent self. We have to free ourselves from this miserable dream that we are these bodies. We must know the truth, "I am He". We are not drops to fall into the ocean and be lost; each one is the whole, infinite ocean, and will know it when released from the fetters of illusion. Infinity cannot be divided, the "One without a second" can have no second, all is that One. This knowledge will come to all, but we should struggle to attain it now, because until we have it, we cannot really give mankind the best help. The Jivanmukta ('the living free' or one who knows) alone is able to give real love, real charity, real truth, and it is truth alone that makes us free. Desire makes slaves of us, it is an insatiable tyrant and gives its victims no rest; but the Jivanmukta has conquered all desire by rising to the knowledge that he is the One and there is nothing left to wish for.

The mind brings before us all our delusions — body, sex, creed, caste, bondage; so we have to tell the truth to the mind incessantly, until it is made to realise it. Our real nature is all bliss, and all the pleasure we know is but a reflection, an atom, of that bliss we get from touching our real nature. That is beyond both pleasure and pain. It is the "witness" of the universe, the unchanging reader before whom turn the leaves of the book of life.

Through practice comes Yoga, through Yoga comes knowledge, through knowledge love, and through love bliss. "Me and mine" is a superstition; we have lived in it so long that it is well-nigh impossible to shake it off. Still we must get rid of it if we would rise to the highest. We must be bright and cheerful, long faces do not make religion. Religion should be the most joyful thing in the world, because it is the best. Asceticism cannot make us holy. Why should a man who loves God and who is pure be sorrowful? He should be like a happy child, be truly a child of God. The essential thing in religion is making the heart pure; the Kingdom of Heaven is within us, but only the pure in heart can see the King. While we think of the world, it is only the world for us; but let us come to it with the feeling that the world is God, and we shall have God. This should be our thought towards everyone and everything — parents, children, husbands, wives, friends, and enemies. Think how it would change the whole universe for us if we could consciously fill it with God! See nothing but God! All sorrow, all struggle, all pain would be for ever lost to us!

Jnana is "creedlessness", but that does not mean that it despises creeds. It only means that a stage above and beyond creeds has been gained. The Jnani seeks not to destroy, but to help all. As all rivers roll their waters into the sea and become one, so all creeds should lead to Jnana and become one.

The reality of everything depends upon Brahman, and only as we really grasp this truth, have we any reality. When we cease to see any differences, then we know that "I and the Father are One".

Jnana is taught very clearly by Krishna in the Bhagavad-gita. This great poem is held to be the Crown jewel of all Indian literature. It is a kind of commentary on the Vedas. It shows us that our battle for spirituality must be fought out in this life; so we must not flee from it, but rather compel it to give us all that it holds. As the Gita typifies this struggle for higher things, it is highly poetical to lay the scene in a battlefield. Krishna in the guise of a charioteer to Arjuna, leader of one of the opposing armies, urges him not to be sorrowful, not to fear death, since he knows he is immortal, that nothing which changes can be in the real nature of man. Through chapter after chapter, Krishna teaches the higher truths of philosophy and religion to Arjuna. It is these teachings which make this poem so wonderful; practically the whole of the Vedanta philosophy is included in them. The Vedas teach that the soul is infinite and in no way affected by the death of the body. The soul is a circle whose circumference is nowhere, but whose centre is in some body. Death (so-called) is but a change of centre. God is a circle whose circumference is nowhere and whose centre is everywhere, and when we can get out of the narrow centre of body, we shall realise God — our true Self.

The present is only a line of demarcation between the past and the future; so we cannot rationally say that we care only for the present, as it has no existence apart from the past and the future. It is all one complete whole, the idea of time being merely a condition imposed upon us by the form of our understanding.

III

Jnana teaches that the world should be given up, but not on that account to be abandoned. To be in the world, but not of it, is the true test of the Sannyasin. This idea of renunciation has been in some form common to nearly all religions. Jnana demands that we look upon all alike, that we see only "sameness". Praise and blame, good and bad, even heat and cold, must be equally acceptable to us. In India there are many holy men of whom this is literally true. They wander on the snow-clad heights of the Himalayas or over the burning desert sands, entirely unclothed and apparently entirely unconscious of any difference in temperature.

We have first of all to give up this superstition of body; we are not the body. Next must go the further superstition that we are mind. We are not mind; it is but the "silken body", not any part of the soul. The mere word "body", applied to nearly all things, includes something common among all bodies. This is existence .

Our bodies are symbols of thought behind, and the thoughts themselves are in their turn symbols of something behind them, that is, the one Real

Existence, the Soul of our soul, the Self of the universe, the Life of our life, our true Self. As long as we believe ourselves to be even the least different from God, fear remains with us; but when we know ourselves to be the One, fear goes: of what can we be afraid? By sheer force of will the Jnani rises beyond body, beyond mind, making this universe zero. Thus he destroys Avidya and knows his true Self, the Atman. Happiness and misery are only in the senses, they cannot touch our real Self. The soul is beyond time, space, and causality — therefore unlimited, omnipresent.

The Jnani has to come out of all forms, to get beyond all rules and books, and be his own book. Bound by forms, we crystallise and die. Still the Jnani must never condemn those who cannot yet rise above forms. He must never even think of another, "I am holier than thou".

These are the marks of the true Jnana-yogi: (1) He desires nothing, save to know. (2) All his senses are under perfect restraint; he suffers everything without murmuring, equally content if his bed be the bare ground under the open sky, or if he is lodged in a king's palace. He shuns no suffering, he stands and bears it — he has given up all but the Self. (3) He knows that all but the One is unreal. (4) He has an intense desire for freedom. With a strong will, he fixes his mind on higher things and so attains to peace. If we know not peace, what are we more than the brutes? He does everything for others — for the Lord — giving up all fruits of work and looking for no result, either here or hereafter. What can the universe give us more than our own soul? Possessing that, we possess all. The Vedas teach that the Atman, or Self, is the One Undivided Existence. It is beyond mind, memory, thought, or even consciousness as we know it. From it are all things. It is that through which (or because of which) we see, hear, feel, and think. The goal of the universe is to realise oneness with the "Om" or One Existence. The Jnani has to be free from all forms; he is neither a Hindu, a Buddhist, nor a Christian, but he is all three. All action is renounced, given up to the Lord; then no action has power to bind. The Jnani is a tremendous rationalist; he denies everything. He tells himself day and night, "There are no beliefs, no sacred words, no heaven, no hell, no creed, no church — there is only Atman." When everything has been thrown away until what cannot be thrown away is reached, that is the Self. The Jnani takes nothing for granted; he analyses by pure reason and force of will, until he reaches Nirvana which is the extinction of all relativity. No description or even conception of this state is possible. Jnana is never to be judged by any earthly result. Be not like the vulture which soars almost beyond sight, but which is ever ready to swoop downwards at the sight of a bit of carrion. Ask not for healing, or longevity, or prosperity, ask only to be free.

We are "Existence, Knowledge, Bliss" (Sachchidananda). Existence is the last generalisation in the universe; so we exist, we know it; and bliss is the natural result of existence without alloy. Now and then we know a moment of supreme bliss, when we ask nothing, give nothing, and know nothing but bliss. Then it passes and we again see the panorama of the universe going on before us and we know it is but a "mosaic work set upon God, who is the background of all things". When we return to earth and see the Absolute as relative, we see Sachchidananda as Trinity — father, Son, Holy Ghost. Sat = the creating principle; Chit = the guiding principle; Ananda = the realising principle, which joins us again to the One. No one can know "existence" (Sat) except through "knowledge" (Chit), and hence the force of the saying of Jesus, No man can see the Father save through the Son. The Vedanta teaches that Nirvana can be attained here and now, that we do not have to wait for death to reach it. Nirvana is the realisation of the Self, and after having once, if only for an instant, known this, never again can one be deluded by the mirage of personality. Having eyes, we must see the apparent; but all the time we know it for what it is, we have found out its true nature. It is the "screen" that hides the Self which is unchanging. The screen opens and we find the Self behind it — all change is in the screen. In the saint the screen is thin and the Reality can almost shine through; but in the sinner it is thick, and we are apt to lose sight of the truth that the Atman is there, as well as behind the saint.

All reasoning ends only in finding Unity; so we first use analysis, then synthesis. In the world of science, the forces are gradually narrowed down in the search for one underlying force. When physical science can perfectly grasp the final unity, it will have reached an end, for reaching unity we find rest. Knowledge is final.

Religion, the most precious of all sciences, long ago discovered that final unity, to reach which is the object of Jnana-yoga. There is but one Self in the universe, of which all lower selves are but manifestations. The Self, however, is infinitely more than all of its manifestations. All is the Self or Brahman. The saint, the sinner, the lamb, the tiger, even the murderer, as far as they have any reality, can be nothing else, because there is nothing else. "That which exists is One, sages call It variously." Nothing can be higher than this knowledge, and in those purified by Yoga it comes in flashes to the soul. The more one has been purified and prepared by Yoga and meditation, the clearer are these flashes of realisation. This was dis-

covered 4,000 years ago, but has not yet become the property of the race; it is still the property of some individuals only.

IV

All men, so-called, are not yet really human beings. Every one has to judge of this world through his own mind. The higher understanding is extremely difficult. The concrete is more to most people than the abstract. As an illustration of this, a story is told of two men in Bombay — one a Hindu and the other a Jain — who were playing chess in the house of a rich merchant of Bombay. The house was near the sea, the game long; the ebb and flow of the tide under the balcony where they sat attracted the attention of the players. One explained it by a legend that the gods in their play threw the water into a great pit and then threw it out again. The other said: No, the gods draw it up to the top of a high mountain to use it, and then when they have done with it, they throw it down again. A young student present began to laugh at them and said, "Do you not know that the attraction of the moon causes the tides?" At this, both men turned on him in a fury and inquired if he thought they were fools. Did he suppose that they believed the moon had any ropes to pull up the tides, or that it could reach so far? They utterly refused to accept any such foolish explanation. At this juncture the host entered the room and was appealed to by both parties. He was an educated man and of course knew the truth, but seeing plainly the impossibility of making the chess-players understand it, he made a sign to the student and then proceeded to give an explanation of the tides that proved eminently satisfactory to his ignorant hearers. "You must know", he told them, "that afar off in the middle of the ocean, there is a huge mountain of sponge — you have both seen sponge, and know what

I mean. This mountain of sponge absorbs a great deal of the water and then the sea falls; by and by the gods come down and dance on the mountain and their weight squeezes all the water out and the sea rises again. This, gentlemen, is the cause of the tides, and you can easily see for yourselves how reasonable and simple is this explanation." The two men who ridiculed the power of the moon to cause the tides, found nothing incredible in a mountain of sponge, danced upon by the gods! The gods were real to them, and they had actually seen sponge; what was more likely than their joint effect upon the sea! "Comfort" is no test of truth; on the contrary, truth is often far from being "comfortable". If one intends to really find truth, one must not cling to comfort. It is hard to let all go, but the Jnani must do it. He must become pure, kill out all desires and cease to identify himself with the body. Then and then only, the higher truth can shine in his soul. Sacrifice is necessary, and this immolation of the lower self is the underlying truth that has made sacrifice a part of all religions. All the propitiatory offerings to the gods were but dimly understood types of the only sacrifice that is of any real value, the surrender of the apparent self, through which alone we can realise the higher Self, the Atman. The Jnani must not try to preserve the body, nor even wish to do so. He must be strong and follow truth, though the universe fall. Those who follow "fads" can never do this. It is a life-work, nay, the work of a hundred lives! Only the few dare to realise the God within, to renounce heaven and Personal God and all hope of reward. A firm will is needed to do this; to be even vacillating is a sign of tremendous weakness. Man always is perfect, or he never could become so; but he had to realise it. If man were bound by external causes, he could only be mortal. Immortality can only be true of the unconditioned. Nothing can act on the Atman — the idea is pure delusion; but man must identify himself with that, not with body or mind. Let him know that he is the witness of the universe, then he can enjoy the beauty of the wonderful panorama passing before him. Let him even tell himself, "I am the universe, I am Brahman." When man really identifies himself with the One, the Atman, everything is possible to him and all matter becomes his servant. As Shri Ramakrishna has said: After the butter is churned, it can be put in water or milk and will never mix with either; so when man has once realised the Self, he can no more be contaminated by the world. "From a balloon, no minor distinctions are visible, so when man rises high enough, he will not see good and evil people." "Once the pot is burned, no more can it be shaped; so with the mind that has once touched the Lord and has had a baptism of fire, no more can it be changed." Philosophy in Sanskrit means "clear vision", and religion is practical philosophy. Mere theoretic, speculative philosophy is not much regarded in India. There is no church, no creed, no dogma. The two great divisions are the "Dvaitists" and the "Advaitists". The former say, "The way to salvation is through the mercy of God; the law of causation, once set in motion, can never be broken; only God, who is not bound by this law, by His mercy helps us to break it". The latter say, "Behind all this nature is something that is free; and finding that which is beyond all law gets us freedom; and freedom is salvation." Dualism is only one phase, Advaitism goes to the ultimate. To become pure is the shortest path to freedom. Only that is ours which we earn. No authority can save us, no beliefs. If there is a God, all can find Him. No one needs to be told it is warm; each one can discover it for himself. So it should be with God. He should be a fact in the consciousness of all men. The Hindus do not recognise "sin", as it is understood by the Western mind. Evil deeds are not "sins", we are not offending some Ruler in committing these; we are simply injuring ourselves, and we must suffer the penalty. It is not a sin to put one's finger in the fire, but he who does so will surely suffer just as much as if it were. All deeds produce certain results, and "every deed returns to the doer". "Trinitarianism" is an advance on "Unitarianism" (which is dualism, God and man for ever separate). The first step upwards is when we recognise ourselves as the children of God; the last step is when we realise ourselves as the One, the Atman.

V

The question why there cannot be eternal bodies is in itself illogical, as "body" is a term applied to a certain combination of elements, changeable and in its very nature impermanent. When we are not passing through changes, we will not have bodies (so-called). "Matter" beyond the limit of time, space, and causality will not be matter at all. Time and space exist only in us, we are the one Permanent Being. All forms are transitory, that is why all religions say, "God has no form". Menander was a Greco-bactrian king. He was converted to Buddhism about 150 B.C. by one of the Buddhist missionary monks and was called by them "Milinda". He asked a young monk, his teacher, "Can a perfect man (such as Buddha) be in error or make mistakes?" The young monk's answer was : The perfect man can remain in ignorance of minor matters not in his experience, but he can never be in error as to what his insight has actually realised. He is perfect here and now. He knows the whole mystery, the Essence of the universe, but he may not know the mere external variation through which that Essence is manifested in time and space. He knows the clay itself, but has not had experience of every shape it may be wrought into. The perfect man knows the Soul itself, but not every form and combination of its manifestation. He would have to attain more relative knowledge just as we do, though on account of his immense power, he would learn it far more quickly.

The tremendous "search-light" of a perfectly controlled mind, when thrown on any subject, would rapidly reduce it to possession. It is very important to understand this, because it saves so much foolish explanation as to how a Buddha or a Jesus could be mistaken in ordinary relative Knowledge, as we well know they were. The disciples should not be blamed as having put down the sayings erroneously. It is humbug to say that one thing is true and another untrue in their statements. Accept the whole account, or reject it. How can we pick out the true from the false?

If a thing happens once, it can happen again. If any human being has ever realised perfection, we too can do so. If we cannot become perfect here and now, we never can in any state or heaven or condition we may imagine. If Jesus Christ was not perfect, then the religion bearing his name falls to the ground. If he was perfect, then we too can become perfect. The perfect man does not reason or "know", as we count "knowing", for all our knowledge is mere comparison, and there is no comparison, no classification, possible in the Absolute. Instinct is less liable to error than reason, but reason is higher and leads to intuition, which is higher still. Knowledge is the parent of intuition, which like instinct, is also unerring, but on a higher plane. There are three grades of manifestation in living beings: (1) subconscious — mechanical, unerring; (2) conscious — knowing, erring; (3) superconscious — intuitional, unerring; and these are illustrated in an animal, man, and God. For the man who has become perfect, nothing remains but to apply his understanding. He lives only to help the world, desiring nothing for himself. What distinguishes is negative — the positive is ever wider and wider. What we have in common is the widest of all, and that is "Being". "Law is a mental shorthand to explain a series of phenomena"; but law as an entity, so to speak, does not exist. We use the word to express the regular succession of certain occurrences in the phenomenal world. We must not let law become a superstition, a something inevitable, to which we must submit. Error must accompany reason, but the very struggle to conquer error makes us gods. Disease is the struggle of nature to cast out something wrong; so sin is the struggle of the divine in us to throw off the animal. We must "sin" (that is, make mistakes) in order to rise to Godhood.

Do not pity anyone. Look upon all as your equal, cleanse yourself of the primal sin of inequality. We are all equal and must not think, "I am good and you are bad, and I am trying to reclaim you". Equality is the sign of the free. Jesus came to publicans and sinners and lived with them. He never set himself on a pedestal. Only sinners see sin. See not man, see only the Lord. We manufacture our own heaven and can make a heaven even in hell. Sinners are only to be found in hell, and as long as we see them around us, we are there ourselves. Spirit is not in time, nor in space. Realise "I am Existence Absolute, Knowledge Absolute, Bliss Absolute — i am He, I am He". Be glad at birth, be glad at death, rejoice always in the love of God. Get rid of the bondage of body; we have become slaves to it and learnt to hug our chains and love our slavery; so much so that we long to perpetuate it, and go on with "body" "body" for ever. Do not cling to the idea of "body", do not look for a future existence in any way like this one; do not love or want the body, even of those dear to us. This life is our teacher, and dying only makes room to begin over again. Body is our schoolmaster, but to commit suicide is folly, it is only killing the "schoolmaster". Another will take his place. So until we have learnt to transcend the body, we must have it, and losing one, will get another. Still we must not identify ourselves with the body, but look upon it only as an instrument to be used in reaching perfection. Hanuman, the devotee of Rama, summed up his philosophy in these words: When I identify myself with the body, O Lord, I am Thy creature, eternally separate from Thee. When I identify myself with the soul, I am a spark of that Divine Fire which Thou art. But when I identify myself with the Atman, I and Thou art one.

Therefore the Jnani strives to realise the Self and nothing else.

VI

Thought is all important, for "what we become". There was once a Sannyasin, a holy man, who sat under a tree and taught the people. He drank milk, and ate only fruit, and made endless "Pranayamas", and felt himself to be very holy. In the same village lived an evil woman. Every day the Sannyasin went and warned her that her wickedness would lead her to hell. The poor woman, unable to change her method of life which was her only means of livelihood, was still much moved by the terrible future depicted by the Sannyasin. She wept and prayed to the Lord, begging Him to forgive her because she could not help herself. By and by both the holy man and the evil woman died. The angels came and bore her to heaven, while the demons claimed the soul of the Sannyasin. "Why is this!" he exclaimed, "have I not lived a most holy life, and preached holiness to everybody? Why should I be taken to hell while this wicked woman is taken to heaven?" "Because," answered the demons, "while she was forced to commit unholy acts, her mind was always fixed on the Lord and she sought deliverance, which has now come to her. But you, on the contrary, while you performed only holy acts, had your mind always fixed on the wickedness of others. You saw only sin, and thought only of sin, so now you have to go to that place where only sin is." The moral of the story is obvious: The outer life avails little. The heart must be pure and the pure heart sees only good, never evil. We should never try to be guardians of mankind, or to stand on a pedestal as saints reforming sinners. Let us rather purify ourselves, and the result must be that in so doing we shall help others.

Physics is bounded on both sides by metaphysics. So it is with reason — it starts from non-reason and ends with non-reason. If we push inquiry far enough in the world of perception, we must reach a plane beyond perception. Reason is really stored up and classified perception, preserved by memory. We can never imagine or reason beyond our sense-perceptions. Nothing beyond reason can be an object of sense-knowledge. We feel the limited character of reason, yet it does bring us to a plane where we get a glimpse of something beyond. The question then arises: Has man an instrument that transcends reason? It is very probable that in man there is a power to reach beyond reason; in fact the saints in all ages assert the existence of this power in themselves. But it is impossible in the very nature of things to translate spiritual ideas and perceptions into the language of reason; and these saints, each and all, have declared their inability to make known their spiritual experiences. Language can, of course, supply no words for them, so that it can only be asserted that these are actual experiences and can be had by all. Only in that way can they become known, but they can never be described. Religion is the science which learns the transcendental in nature through the transcendental in man. We know as yet but little of man, consequently but little of the universe. When we know more of man, we shall probably know more of the universe. Man is the epitome of all things and all knowledge is in him. Only for the infinitesimal portion of the universe, which comes into sense-perception, are we able to find a reason; never can we give the reason for any fundamental principle. Giving a reason for a thing is simply to classify it and put it in a pigeon-hole of the mind. When we meet a new fact, we at once strive to put it in some existing category and the attempt to do this is to reason. When we succeed in placing the fact, it gives a certain amount of satisfaction, but we can never go beyond the physical plane in this classification. That man can transcend the limits of the senses is the emphatic testimony of all past ages. The Upanishads told 5,000 years ago that the realisation of God could never be had through the senses. So far, modern agnosticism agrees, but the Vedas go further than the negative side and assert in the plainest terms that man can and does transcend this sense-bound, frozen universe. He can, as it were, find a hole in the ice, through which he can pass and reach the whole ocean of life. Only by so transcending the world of sense, can he reach his true Self and realise what he really is.

Jnana is never sense-knowledge. We cannot know Brahman, but we are Brahman, the whole of It, not a piece. The unextended can never be divided. The apparent variety is but the reflection seen in time and space, as we see the sun reflected in a million dewdrops, though we know that the sun itself is one and not many. In Jnana we have to lose sight of the variety and see only the Unity. Here there is no subject, no object, no knowing, no thou or he or I, only the one, absolute Unity. We are this all the time; once free,

ever free. Man is not bound by the law of causation. Pain and misery are not in man, they are but as the passing cloud throwing its shadow over the sun, but the cloud passes, the sun is unchanged; and so it is with man. He is not born, he does not die, he is not in time and space. These ideas are mere reflections of the mind, but we mistake them for the reality and so lose sight of the glorious truth they obscure. Time is but the method of our thinking, but we are the eternally present tense. Good and evil have existence only in relation to us. One cannot be had without the other, because neither has meaning or existence apart from the other. As long as we recognise duality, or separate God and man, so long we must see good and evil. Only by going to the centre, by unifying ourselves with God can we escape the delusions of the senses. When we let go the eternal fever of desire, the endless thirst that gives us no rest, when we have for ever quenched desire, we shall escape both good and evil, because we shall have transcended both. The satisfaction of desire only increases it, as oil poured on fire but makes it burn more fiercely. The further from the centre, the faster goes the wheel, the less the rest. Draw near the centre, check desire, stamp it out, let the false self go, then our vision will clear and we shall see God. Only through renunciation of this life and of all life to come (heaven etc.), can we reach the point where we stand firmly on the true Self. While we hope for anything, desire still rules us. Be for one moment really "hopeless", and the mist will clear. For what to hope when one is the all of existence? The secret of Jnana is to give up all and be sufficient unto ourselves. Say "not", and you become "not"; say "is", and you become "is". Worship the Self within, naught else exists. All that binds us is Maya — delusion.

VII

The Self is the condition of all in the universe, but It can never be conditioned. As soon as we know that we are It, we are free. As mortals we are not and never can be free. Free mortality is a contradiction in terms, for mortality implies change, and only the changeless can be free. The Atman alone is free, and that is our real essence. We feel this inner freedom; in spite of all theories, all beliefs, we know it, and every action proves that we know it. The will is not free, its apparent freedom is but a reflection from the Real. If the world were only an endless chain of cause and effect, where could one stand to help it? There must needs be a piece of dry land for the rescuer to stand on, else how can he drag anyone out of the rushing stream and save him from drowning? Even the fanatic who cries "I am a worm", thinks that he is on the way to become a saint. He sees the saint even in the worm.

There are two ends or aims of human life, real knowing (Vijnana) and bliss. Without freedom, these two are impossible. They are the touchstone of all life. We should feel the Eternal Unity so much, that we should weep for all sinners, knowing that it is we who are sinning. The eternal law is self-sacrifice, not self-assertion. What self to assert when all is one? There are no "rights", all is love. The great truths that Jesus taught have never been lived. Let us try his method and see if the world will not be saved. The contrary method has nearly destroyed it. Selflessness only, not selfishness, can solve the question. The idea of "right" is a limitation; there is really no "mine" and "thine", for I am thou and thou art I. We have "responsibility", not "rights". We should say, "I am the universe", not "I am John" or "I am Mary". These limitations are all delusions and are what holds us in bondage, for as soon as I think, "I am John", I want exclusive possession of certain things and begin to say "me and mine", and continually make new distinctions in so doing. So our bondage goes on increasing with every fresh distinction, and we get further and further away from the central Unity, the undivided Infinite. There is only one Individual, and each of us is That. Oneness alone is love and fearlessness; separation leads us to hatred and fear. Oneness fulfils the law. Here, on earth, we strive to enclose little spaces and exclude outsiders, but we cannot do that in the sky, though that is what sectarian religion tries to do when it says, "Only this way leads to salvation, all others are wrong". Our aim should be to wipe out these little enclosures to widen the boundaries until they are lost sight of, and to realise that all religions lead to God. This little puny self must be sacrificed. This is the truth symbolised by baptism into a new life, the death of the old man, the birth of the new — the perishing of the false self, the realisation of the Atman, the one Self of the universe.

The two great divisions of the Vedas are Karma Kanda — the portion pertaining to doing or work, and Jnana Kanda — the portion treating of knowing, true knowledge. In the Vedas we can find the whole process of the growth of religious ideas. This is because when a higher truth was reached, the lower perception that led to it, was still preserved. This was done, because the sages realised that the world of creation being eternal, there would always be those who needed the first steps to knowledge, that the highest philosophy, while open to all, could never be grasped by all. In nearly every other religion, only the last or highest realisation of truth has been preserved, with the natural consequence that the older ideas were lost, while the newer ones were only understood by the few and gradually came to have no meaning for the many. We see this result illustrated in the growing revolt against old traditions and authorities.

Instead of accepting them, the man of today boldly challenges them to give reasons for their claims, to make clear the grounds upon which they demand acceptance. Much in Christianity is the mere application of new names and meanings to old pagan beliefs and customs. If the old sources had been preserved and the reasons for the transitions fully explained, many things would have been clearer. The Vedas preserved the old ideas and this fact necessitated huge commentaries to explain them and why they were kept. It also led to many superstitions, through clinging to old forms after all sense of their meaning had been lost. In many ceremonials, words are repeated which have survived from a now forgotten language and to which no real meaning can now be attached. The idea of evolution was to be found in the Vedas long before the Christian era; but until Darwin said it was true, it was regarded as a mere Hindu superstition.

All external forms of prayer and worship are included in the Karma Kanda. These are good when performed in a spirit of unselfishness and not allowed to degenerate into mere formality. They purify the heart. The Karma-yogi wants everyone to be saved before himself. His only salvation is to help others to salvation. "To serve Krishna's servants is the highest worship." One great saint prayed, "Let me go to hell with the sins of the whole world, but let the world be saved." This true worship leads to intense self-sacrifice. It is told of one sage that he was willing to give all his virtues to his dog, that it might go to heaven, because it had long been faithful to him, while he himself was content to go to hell.

The Jnana Kanda teaches that knowledge alone can save, in other words, that he must become "wise unto salvation". Knowledge is first objective, the Knower knowing Himself. The Self, the only subject, is in manifestation seeking only to know Itself. The better the mirror, the better reflection it can give; so man is the best mirror, and the purer the man, the more clearly he can reflect God. Man makes the mistake of separating himself from God and identifying himself with the body. This mistake arises through Maya, which is not exactly delusion but might be said to be seeing the real as something else and not as it is. This identifying of ourselves with the body leads to inequality, which inevitably leads to struggle and jealousy, and so long as we see inequality, we can never know happiness. "Ignorance and inequality are the two sources of all misery", says Jnana.

When man has been sufficiently buffeted by the world, he awakes to a desire for freedom; and searching for means of escape from the dreary round of earthly existence, he seeks knowledge, learns what he really is, and is free. After that he looks at the world as a huge machine, but takes good care to keep his fingers out of the wheels. Duty ceases for him who is free; what power can constrain the free being? He does good, because it is his nature, not because any fancied duty commands it. This does not apply to those who are still in the bondage of the senses. Only for him, who has transcended the lower self, is this freedom. He stands on his own soul, obeys no law; he is free and perfect. He has undone the old superstitions and got out of the wheel. Nature is but the mirror of our own selves. There is a limit to the working power of human beings, but no limit to desire; so we strive to get hold of the working powers of others and enjoy the fruits of their labours, escaping work ourselves. Inventing machinery to work for us can never increase well-being, for in gratifying desire, we only find it, and then we want more and more without end. Dying, still filled with ungratified desires, we have to be born again and again in the vain search for satisfaction. "Eight Millions of bodies have we had, before we reached the human", say the Hindus. Jnana says, "Kill desire and so get rid of it". That is the only way. Cast out all causation and realise the Atman. Only freedom can produce true morality. If there were only an endless chain of cause and effect, Nirvana could not be. It is extinction of the seeming self, bound by this chain. That is what constitutes freedom, to get beyond causality.

Our true nature is good, it is free, the pure being that can never be or do wrong. When we read God with our eyes and minds, we call Him this or that; but in reality there is but One, all variations are our interpretations of that One. We become nothing; we regain our true Self. Buddha's summary of misery as the outcome of "ignorance and caste" (inequality) has been adopted by the Vedantists, because it is the best ever made. It manifests the wonderful insight of this greatest among men. Let us then be brave and sincere: whatever path we follow with devotion, must take us to freedom. Once lay hold of one link of the chain and the whole must come after it by degrees. Water the root of the tree and the whole tree is watered. It is of little advantage to waste time to water each leaf. In other words, seek the Lord and getting Him we get all. Churches, doctrines, forms — these are merely the hedges to protect the tender plant of religion; but later on they must all be broken down, that the little plant may become a tree. So the various religious sects, Bibles, Vedas, and scriptures are just "tubs" for the little plant; but it has to get out of the tub and fill the world.

We must learn to feel ourselves as much in the sun, in the stars, as here. Spirit is beyond all time and space; every eye seeing is my eye; every mouth praising the Lord is my mouth; every sinner is I. We are confined nowhere, we are not body. The universe is our body. We are just the pure crystal reflecting all, but itself

ever the same. We are magicians waving magic wands and creating scenes before us at will, but we have to go behind appearances and know the Self. This world is like water in a kettle, beginning to boil; first a bubble comes, then another, then many until all is in ebullition and passes away in steam. The great teachers are like the bubbles as they begin — here one, there one; but in the end every creature has to be a bubble and escape. Creation, ever new, will bring new water and go through the process all over again. Buddha and Christ are the two greatest "bubbles" the world has known. They were great souls who having realised freedom helped others to escape. Neither was perfect, but they are to be judged by their virtues, never by their defects. Jesus fell short, because he did not always live up to his own highest ideal; and above all, because he did not give woman an equal place with man. Woman did everything for him, yet not one was made an apostle. This was doubtless owing to his Semitic origin. The great Aryans, Buddha among the rest, have always put woman in an equal position with man. For them sex in religion did not exist. In the Vedas and Upanishads, women taught the highest truths and received the same veneration as men.

VIII

Both happiness and misery are chains, the one golden, the other iron; but both are equally strong to bind us and hold us back from realising our true nature. The Atman knows neither happiness nor misery. These are mere "states", and states must ever change. The nature of the soul is bliss and peace unchanging. We have not to get it; we have it; let us wash away the dross from our eyes and see it. We must stand ever on the Self and look with perfect calmness upon all the panorama of the world. It is but baby's play and ought never to disturb us. If the mind is pleased by praise, it will be pained by blame. All pleasures of the senses or even of the mind are evanescent, but within ourselves is the one true unrelated pleasure, dependent on nothing outside. "The pleasure of the Self is what the world calls religion." The more our bliss is within, the more spiritual we are. Let us not depend upon the world for pleasure.

Some poor fishwives, overtaken by a violent storm, found refuge in the garden of a rich man. He received them kindly, fed them, and left them to rest in a summer-house, surrounded by exquisite flowers which filled all the air with their rich perfume. The women lay down in this sweet-smelling paradise, but could not sleep. They missed something out of their lives and could not be happy without it. At last one of the women arose and went to the place where they had left their fish baskets, brought them to the summer-house, and then once more happy in the familiar smell, they were all soon sound asleep.

Let not the world be our "fish basket" which we have to depend upon for enjoyment. This is Tamasika, or being bound by the lowest of the three qualities (or Gunas). Next higher come the egotistical who talk always about "I", "I". Sometimes they do good work and may become spiritual. These are Rajasika or active. Highest come the introspective nature (Sattvika), those who live only in the Self. These three qualities are in every human being in varying proportions, and different ones predominate at different times. We must strive to overcome Tamas with Rajas and then to submerge both in Sattva.

Creation is not a "making" of something, it is the struggle to regain equilibrium, as when atoms of cork are thrown to the bottom of a pail of water: they rush to the top singly and in clusters, and when all have reached the top and equilibrium has been regained, all motion or "life" ceases. So with creation; if equilibrium were reached, all change would cease and life, so-called, would end. Life must be accompanied with evil, for when the balance is regained, the world must end, as sameness and destruction are one. There is no possibility of ever having pleasure without pain, or good without evil, for living itself is just the lost equilibrium. What we want is freedom, not life, nor pleasure, nor good. Creation is eternal, without beginning, without end, the ever moving ripple in an infinite lake. There are yet unreached depths and others where stillness has been regained, but the ripple is ever progressing, the struggle to regain the balance is eternal. Life and death are but different names for the same fact, they are the two sides of one coin. Both are Maya, the inexplicable state of striving at one point to live and a moment later to die. Beyond all this is the true nature, the Atman. We enter into creation, and then, for us, it becomes living. Things are dead in themselves, only we give them life, and then, like fools, we turn round and are afraid of them or enjoy them! The world is neither true nor untrue, it is the shadow of truth. "Imagination is the gilded shadow of truth", says the poet. The internal universe, the Real, is infinitely greater than the external one, which is but the shadowy projection of the true one. When we see the "rope", we do not see the "serpent", and when the "serpent" is, the "rope" is not. Both cannot exist at the same time; so while we see the world we do not realise the Self, it is only an intellectual concept. In the realisation of Brahman, the personal "I" and all sense of the world is lost. The Light does not know the darkness, because it has no existence in the light; so Brahman is all. While we recognise a God, it is really only the Self that we have separated from ourselves and worship as outside of us; but all the time it is our own true Self, the one and only God. The nature of the brute is to remain where he is, of man to seek good and avoid evil, of God to neither seek nor avoid, but just to be blissful eternally. Let us be Gods, let us make our hearts like an ocean, to go beyond all the trifles of the world and see it only as a picture. We can then enjoy it without being in any way affected by it. Why look for good in the world, what can we find there? The best it has to offer is only as if children playing in a mud puddle found a few glass beads. They lose them again and have to begin the search anew. Infinite strength is religion and God. We are only souls if we are free, there is immortality only if we are free, there is God only if He is free.

Until we give up the world manufactured by the ego, never can we enter the Kingdom of Heaven. None ever did, none ever will. To give up the world is to utterly forget the ego, to know it not at all, living in the body but not being ruled by it. This rascal ego must be obliterated. Power to help mankind is with the silent ones who only live and love and withdraw their own personality entirely. They never say "me" or "mine", they are only blessed in being the instruments to help others. They are wholly identified with God, asking nothing and not consciously doing anything. They are the true Jivanmuktas — the absolutely selfless, their little personality thoroughly blown away, ambition non-existent. They are all principle, with no personality. The more we sink the "little self", the more God comes. Let us get rid of the little "I" and let only the great "I" live in us. Our best work and our greatest influence is when we are without a thought of self. It is the "desireless" who bring great results to pass. Bless men when they revile you. Think how much good they are doing by helping to stamp out the false ego. Hold fast to the real Self, think only pure thoughts, and you will accomplish more than a regiment of mere preachers. Out of purity and silence comes the word of power.

IX

Expression is necessarily degeneration, because spirit can only be expressed by the "letter", and as St. Paul said, "the letter killeth". Life cannot be in the "letter" which is only a reflection. Yet, principle must be clothed in matter to be "known". We lose sight of the Real in the covering and come to consider that as the Real, instead of as the symbol. This is an almost universal mistake. Every great Teacher knows this and tries to guard against it; but humanity, in general, is prone to worship the seen rather than the unseen. This is why a succession of prophets have come to the world to point again and again to the principle behind the personality and to give it a new covering suited to the times. Truth remains ever unchanged, but it can only be presented in a "form"; so from time to time a new "form" or expression is given to Truth, as the progress of mankind makes them ready to receive it. When we free ourselves from name and form, especially when we no longer need a body of any kind, good or bad, coarse or fine, then only do we escape from bondage. "Eternal progression" would be eternal bondage. We must get beyond all differentiation and reach eternal "sameness" or homogeneity or Brahman. The Atman is the unity of all personalities and is unchangeable, the "One without a second". It is not life, but it is coined into life. It is beyond life and death and good and bad. It is the Absolute Unity. Dare to seek Truth even through hell. Freedom can never be true of name and form, of the related. No form can say, "I am free as a form." Not until all idea of form is lost, does freedom come. If our freedom hurts others, we are not free there. We must not hurt others. While real perception is only one, relative perceptions must be many. The fountain of all knowledge is in every one of us — in the ant as in the highest angel. Real religion is one; all quarrel is with the forms, the symbols, the "illustrations". The millennium exists already for those who find it. The truth is, we have lost ourselves and think the world to be lost. "Fool! Hearest not thou? In thine own heart, day and night, is singing that Eternal Music — sachchidananda, Soham, Soham, (Existence, Knowledge, and Bliss, I am He, I am He)!"

To try to think without a phantasm is to try to make the impossible possible. Each thought has two parts — the thinking and the word, and we must have both. Neither idealists nor materialists are able to explain the world; to do that, we must take both idea and expression. All knowledge is of the reflected as we can only see our own faces reflected in a mirror. So no one can know his Self or Brahman; but each is that Self and must see it reflected in order to make it an object of knowledge.

This seeing the illustrations of the unseen Principle is what leads to idolatry — so-called. The range of idols is wider than is usually supposed. They range from wood and stone to great personalities as Jesus or Buddha. The introduction of idols into India was the result of Buddha's constantly inveighing against a Personal God. The Vedas knew them not, but the reaction against the loss of God as Creator and Friend led to making idols of the great teachers, and Buddha himself became an idol and is worshipped as such by millions of people. Violent attempts at reform always end in retarding true reform. To worship is inherent in every man's nature; only the highest philosophy can rise to pure abstraction. So man will ever personify his God in order to worship Him. This is very good, as long as the symbol, be it what it may, is worshipped as a symbol of the Divinity behind and not in and for itself. Above all, we need to free ourselves from the superstition of believing because "it is in the books". To try to make everything — science, religion, philosophy, and all — conform to what any book says, is a most horrible tyranny. Book-worship is the worst form of idolatry. There was once a stag, proud and free, and he talked in a lordly fashion to his child, "Look at me, see my powerful horns! With one thrust I can kill a man; it is a fine thing to be a stag!" Just then the sound of the huntsman's bugle was heard in the distance, and the stag precipitately fled, followed by his wondering child. When they had reached a place of safety, he inquired, "Why do you fly before man, O my father, when you are so strong and brave?" The stag answered, "My child, I know I am strong and powerful, but when I hear that sound, something seizes me and makes me fly whether I will or no." So with us. We hear the "bugle sound" of the laws laid down in the books, habits and old superstitions lay hold of us; and before we know it, we are fast bound and forget our real nature which is freedom.

Knowledge exists eternally. The man who discovers a spiritual truth is what we call "inspired", and what he brings to the world is revelation. But revelation too is eternal and is not to be crystallised as final and then blindly followed. Revelation may come to any man who has fitted himself to receive it. Perfect purity is the most essential thing, for only "the pure in heart shall see God". Man is the highest being that exists and this is the greatest world, for here can man realise freedom. The highest concept we can have of God is man. Every attribute we give Him belongs also to man, only in a lesser degree. When we rise higher and want to get out of this concept of God, we have to get out of the body, out of mind and imagination, and leave this world out of sight. When we rise to be the absolute, we are no longer in the world — all is Subject, without object.

Man is the apex of the only "world" we can ever know. Those who have attained "sameness" or perfection, are said to be "living in God". All hatred is "killing the self by the self"; therefore, love is the law of life. To rise to this is to be perfect; but the more "perfect" we are, the less work can we do. The Sattvika see and know that all this world is mere child's play and do not trouble themselves about that. We are not much disturbed when we see two puppies fighting and biting each other. We know it is not a serious matter. The perfect one knows that this world is Maya. Life is called Samsara — it is the result of the conflicting forces acting upon us. Materialism says, "The voice of freedom is a delusion." Idealism says, "The voice that tells of bondage is but a dream." Vedanta says, "We are free and not free at the same time." That means that we are never free on the earthly plane, but ever free on the spiritual side. The Self is beyond both freedom and bondage. We are Brahman, we are immortal knowledge beyond the senses, we are Bliss Absolute.

SIX LESSONS ON RAJA-YOGA[1]

Raja-Yoga is as much a science as any in the world. It is an analysis of the mind, a gathering of the facts of the supersensuous world and so building up the spiritual world. All the great spiritual teachers the world has known said, "I see and I know." Jesus, Paul, and Peter all claimed actual perception of the spiritual truths they taught.

This perception is obtained by Yoga.

Neither memory nor consciousness can be the limitation of existence. There is a superconscious state. Both it and the unconscious state are sensationless, but with a vast difference between them — the difference between ignorance and knowledge. Present Yoga as an appeal to reason, as a science.

Concentration of the mind is the source of all knowledge.

Yoga teaches us to make matter our slave, as it ought to be. Yoga means "yoke", "to join", that is, to join the soul of man with the supreme Soul or God.

The mind acts in and under consciousness. What we call consciousness is only one link in the infinite chain that is our nature.

This "I" of ours covers just a little consciousness and a vast amount of unconsciousness, while over it, and mostly unknown to it, is the superconscious plane.

Through faithful practice, layer after layer of the mind opens before us, and each reveals new facts to us. We see as it were new worlds created before us, new powers are put into our hands, but we must not stop by the way or allow ourselves to be dazzled by these "beads of glass" when the mine of diamonds lies before us.

God alone is our goal. Failing to reach God, we die.

Three things are necessary to the student who wishes to succeed. First. Give up all ideas of enjoyment in this world and the next, care only for God and Truth. We are here to know truth, not for enjoyment. Leave that to brutes who enjoy as we never can. Man is a thinking being and must struggle on until he conquers death, until he sees the light. He must not spend himself in vain talking that bears no fruit. Worship of society and popular opinion is idolatry. The soul has no sex, no country, no place, no time.

Second. Intense desire to know Truth and God. Be eager for them, long for them, as a drowning man longs for breath. Want only God, take nothing else, let not "seeming" cheat you any longer. Turn from all and seek only God.

Third. The six trainings: First — restraining the mind from going outward. Second — restraining the senses. Third — turning the mind inward. Fourth — suffering everything without murmuring. Fifth — fastening the mind to one idea. Take the subject before you and think it out; never leave it. Do not count time. Sixth — think constantly of your real nature. Get rid of superstition. Do not hypnotise yourself into a belief in your own inferiority. Day and night tell yourself what you really are, until you realise (actually realise) your oneness with God.

Without these disciplines, no results can be gained.

We can be conscious of the Absolute, but we can never express It. The moment we try to express It, we limit It and It ceases to be Absolute.

We have to go beyond sense limit and transcend even reason, and we have the power to do this.

After practising the first lesson in breathing a week, the pupil reports to the teacher.

FIRST LESSON

This is a lesson seeking to bring out the individuality. Each individuality must be cultivated. All will meet at the centre. "Imagination is the door to inspiration and the basis of all thought." All prophets, poets, and discoverers have had great imaginative

---

1. These lessons are composed of notes of class talks given by Swami Vivekananda to an intimate audience in the house of Mrs. Sara C. Bull, a devoted American disciple, and were preserved by her and finally printed in 1913 for private circulation — Ed.

power. The explanation of nature is in us; the stone falls outside, but gravitation is in us, not outside. Those who stuff themselves, those who starve themselves, those who sleep too much, those who sleep too little, cannot become Yogis. Ignorance, fickleness, jealousy, laziness, and excessive attachment are the great enemies to success in Yoga practice. The three great requisites are:

First. Purity, physical and mental; all uncleanness, all that would draw the mind down, must be abandoned.

Second. Patience: At first there will be wonderful manifestations, but they will all cease. This is the hardest period, but hold fast; in the end the gain is sure if you have patience.

Third. Perseverance: Persevere through thick and thin, through health and sickness, never miss a day in practice.

The best time for practice is the junction of day and night, the calmest time in the tides of our bodies, the zero point between two states. If this cannot be done, practise upon rising and going to bed. Great personal cleanliness is necessary — a daily bath.

After bathing, sit down and hold the seat firm, that is, imagine that you sit as firm as a rock, that nothing can move you. Hold the head and shoulders and the hips in a straight line, keeping the spinal column free; all action is along it, and it must not be impaired.

Begin with your toes and think of each part of your body as perfect; picture it so in your mind, touching each part if you prefer to do so. Pass upward bit by bit until you reach the head, thinking of each as perfect, lacking nothing. Then think of the whole as perfect, an instrument given to you by God to enable you to attain Truth, the vessel in which you are to cross the ocean and reach the shores of eternal truth. When this has been done, take a long breath through both nostrils, throw it out again, and then hold it out as long as you comfortably can. Take four such breaths, then breathe naturally and pray for illumination. "I meditate on the glory of that being who created this universe; may he illuminate my mind." Sit and meditate on this ten or fifteen minutes.

Tell your experiences to no one but your Guru.

Talk as little as possible.

Keep your thoughts on virtue; what we think we tend to become.

Holy meditation helps to burn out all mental impurities. All who are not Yogis are slaves; bond after bond must be broken to make us free.

All can find the reality beyond. If God is true, we must feel him as a fact, and if there is a soul, we ought to be able to see it and feel it.

The only way to find if there be a soul is to be something which is not the body.

The Yogis class our organs under two chief heads: organs of sense and organs of motion, or knowledge and action.

The internal organ or mind has four aspects. First — manas, the cogitating or thinking faculty, which is usually almost entirely wasted, because uncontrolled; properly governed, it is a wonderful power. Second — buddhi, the will (sometimes called the intellect). Third — ahamkara, the self-conscious egotism (from Aham). Fourth — chitta, the substance in and through which all the faculties act, the floor of the mind as it were; or the sea in which the various faculties are waves.

Yoga is the science by which we stop Chitta from assuming, or becoming transformed into, several faculties. As the reflection of the moon on the sea is broken or blurred by the waves, so is the reflection of the Atman, the true Self, broken by the mental waves. Only when the sea is stilled to mirror-like calmness, can the reflection of the moon be seen, and only when the "mind-stuff", the Chitta is controlled to absolute calmness, is the Self to be recognised.

The mind is not the body, though it is matter in a finer form. It is not eternally bound by the body. This is proved as we get occasionally loosened from it. We can learn to do this at will by controlling the senses.

When we can do that fully, we shall control the

universe, because our world is only what the senses bring us. Freedom is the test of the higher being. Spiritual life begins when you have loosened yourself from the control of the senses. He whose senses rule him is worldly — is a slave.

If we could entirely stop our mind-stuff from breaking into waves, it would put an end to our bodies. For millions of years we have worked so hard to manufacture these bodies that in the struggle we have forgotten our real purpose in getting them, which was to become perfect. We have grown to think that body-making is the end of our efforts. This is Maya. We must break this delusion and return to our original aim and realise we are not the body, it is our servant.

Learn to take the mind out and to see that it is separate from the body. We endow the body with sensation and life and then think it is alive and real. We have worn it so long that we forget that it is not identical with us. Yoga is to help us put off our body when we please and see it as our servant, our instrument, not our ruler. Controlling the mental powers is the first great aim in Yoga practices. The second is concentrating them in full force upon any subject.

You cannot be a Yogi if you talk much.

SECOND LESSON

This Yoga is known as the eightfold Yoga, because it is divided into eight principal parts. These are:

First — Yama. This is most important and has to govern the whole life; it has five divisions:

- 1st. Not injuring any being by thought, word, or deed.
- 2nd. Non-covetousness in thought, word, or deed.
- 3rd. Perfect chastity in thought, word, or deed.
- 4th. Perfect truthfulness in thought, word, or deed.
- 5th. Non-receiving of gifts.

Second — Niyama. The bodily care, bathing daily, dietary, etc.

Third — Asana, posture. Hips, shoulders, and head must be held straight, leaving the spine free.

Fourth — pranayama, restraining the breath (in order to get control of the Prana or vital force).

Fifth — Pratyahara, turning the mind inward and restraining it from going outward, revolving the matter in the mind in order to understand it.

Sixth — Dharana, concentration on one subject.

Seventh — Dhyana, meditation.

Eighth — Samadhi, illumination, the aim of all our efforts.

Yama and Niyama are for lifelong practice. As for the others, we do as the leech does, not leave one blade of grass before firmly grasping another. In other words, we have thoroughly to understand and practise one step before taking another.

The subject of this lesson is Pranayama, or controlling the Prana. In Raja-Yoga breathing enters the psychic plane and brings us to the spiritual. It is the fly-wheel of the whole bodily system. It acts first upon the lungs, the lungs act on the heart, the heart acts upon the circulation, this in turn upon the brain, and the brain upon the mind. The will can produce an outside sensation, and the outside sensation can arouse the will. Our wills are weak; we do not realise their power, we are so much bound up in matter. Most of our action is from outside in. Outside nature throws us off our balance, and we cannot (as we ought) throw nature off her balance. This is all wrong; the stronger power is really within.

The great saints and teachers were those who had conquered this world of thought within themselves and so spake with power. The story[1] of the minister confined in a high tower, who was released through the efforts of his wife who brought him a beetle, honey, a silken thread, a cord, and a rope, illustrates the way we gain control of our mind by using first the physical regulation of the breath as the silken thread. That enables us to lay hold on one power after another until the rope of concentration delivers us from the prison of the body and we are free. Reaching freedom, we can discard the means used to bring us there.

---

1. For the story see *Complete Works of Swami Vivekananda*, Vol. I, p. 143.

Pranayama has three parts:
- 1st. Puraka — inhaling
- 2nd. Kumbhaka — restraining
- 3rd. Rechaka — exhaling

There are two currents passing through the brain and circulating down the sides of the spine, crossing at the base and returning to the brain. One of these currents, called the "sun" (Pingala), starts from the left hemisphere of the brain, crosses at the base of the brain to the right side of the spine, and recrosses at the base of the spine, like one-half of the figure eight.

The other current, the "moon" (Ida), reverses this action and completes this figure eight. Of course, the lower part is much longer than the upper. These currents flow day and night and make deposits of the great life forces at different points, commonly known as "plexuses"; but we are rarely conscious of them. By concentration we can learn to feel them and trace them over all parts of the body. These "sun" and "moon" currents are intimately connected with breathing, and by regulating this we get control of the body.

In the Katha Upanishad the body is described as the chariot, the mind is the reins, the intellect is the charioteer, the senses are the horses, and the objects of the senses their road. The self is the rider, seated in the chariot. Unless the rider has understanding and can make the charioteer control his horses, he can never attain the goal; but the senses, like vicious steeds, will drag him where they please and may even destroy him. These two currents are the great "check rein" in the hands of the charioteer, and he must get control of this to control the horses. We have to get the power to become moral; until we do that, we cannot control our actions. Yoga alone enables us to carry into practice the teachings of morality. To become moral is the object of Yoga. All great teachers were Yogis and controlled every current. The Yogis arrest these currents at the base of the spine and force them through the centre of the spinal column. They then become the current of knowledge, which only exists in the Yogi.

Second Lesson in Breathing: One method is not for all. This breathing must be done with rhythmic regularity, and the easiest way is by counting; as that is purely mechanical, we repeat the sacred word "Om" a certain number of times instead.

The process of Pranayama is as follows: Close the right nostril with the thumb and then slowly inhale through the left nostril, repeating the word "Om" four times.

Then firmly close both nostrils by placing the forefinger on the left one and hold the breath in, mentally repeating "Om" eight times.

Then, removing the thumb from the right nostril, exhale slowly through that, repeating "Om" four times.

As you close the exhalation, draw in the abdomen forcibly to expel all the air from the lungs. Then slowly inhale through the right nostril, keeping the left one closed, repeating "Om" four times. Next close the right nostril with the thumb and hold the breath while repeating "Om" eight times. Then unclose the left nostril and slowly exhale, repeating "Om" four times, drawing in the abdomen as before. Repeat this whole operation twice at each sitting, that is, making four Pranayamas, two for each nostril. Before taking your seat it is well to begin with prayer.

This needs to be practised a week; then gradually increase the duration of breathing, keeping the same ratio, that is, if you repeat "Om" six times at inhalation, then do the same at exhalation and twelve times during Kumbhaka. These exercises will make us more spiritual, more pure, more holy. Do not be led aside into any byways or seek after power. Love is the only power that stays by us and increases. He who seeks to come to God through Raja-yoga must be strong mentally, physically, morally, and spiritually. Take every step in that light.

Of hundreds of thousands only one soul will say, "I will go beyond, and I will penetrate to God." Few can face the truth; but to accomplish anything, we must be willing to die for Truth.

THIRD LESSON

Kundalini: Realise the soul not as matter, but as it is. We are thinking of the soul as body, but we must separate it from sense and thought. Then alone can we know we are immortal. Change implies the duality of cause and effect, and all that changes must be mortal. This proves that the body cannot be immortal, nor can the mind, because both are constantly changing. Only the unchangeable can be immortal, because there is nothing to act upon it.

We do not become it, we are it; but we have to clear away the veil of ignorance that hides the truth from us. The body is objectified thought. The "sun" and "moon" currents bring energy to all parts of the body. The surplus energy is stored at certain points (plexuses) along the spinal column commonly known as nerve centres.

These currents are not to be found in dead bodies and can only be traced in a healthy organism.

The Yogi has an advantage; for he is able not only to feel them, but actually to see them. They are luminous in his life, and so are the great nerve centres.

There is conscious as well as unconscious action. The Yogis possess a third kind, the superconscious, which in all countries and in all ages has been the source of all religious knowledge. The superconscious state makes no mistakes, but whereas the action of the instinct would be purely mechanical, the former is beyond consciousness.

It has been called inspiration, but the Yogi says, "This faculty is in every human being, and eventually all will enjoy it."

We must give a new direction to the "sun" and "moon" currents and open for them a new passage through the centre of the spinal cord. When we succeed in bringing the currents through this passage called "Sushumna", up to the brain, we are for the time being separated entirely from the body.

The nerve centre at the base of the spine near the sacrum is most important. It is the seat of the generative substance of the sexual energy and is symbolised by the Yogi as a triangle containing a tiny serpent coiled up in it. This sleeping serpent is called Kundalini, and to raise this Kundalini is the whole object of Raja-yoga.

The great sexual force, raised from animal action and sent upward to the great dynamo of the human system, the brain, and there stored up, becomes Ojas or spiritual force. All good thought, all prayer, resolves a part of that animal energy into Ojas and helps to give us spiritual power. This Ojas is the real man and in human beings alone is it possible for this storage of Ojas to be accomplished. One in whom the whole animal sex force has been transformed into Ojas is a god. He speaks with power, and his words regenerate the world.

The Yogi pictures this serpent as being slowly lifted from stage to stage until the highest, the pineal gland, is reached. No man or woman can be really spiritual until the sexual energy, the highest power possessed by man, has been converted into Ojas.

No force can be created; it can only be directed. Therefore we must learn to control the grand powers that are already in our hands and by will power make them spiritual instead of merely animal. Thus it is clearly seen that chastity is the corner-stone of all morality and of all religion. In Raja-yoga especially, absolute chastity in thought, word, and deed is a sine qua non. The same laws apply to the married and the single. If one wastes the most potent forces of one's being, one cannot become spiritual.

All history teaches us that the great seers of all ages were either monks and ascetics or those who had given up married life; only the pure in life can see God.

Just before making the Pranayama, endeavour to visualise the triangle. Close your eyes and picture it vividly in your imagination. See it surrounded by flames and with the serpent coiled in the middle. When you can clearly see the Kundalini, place it in imagination at the base of the spine, and when restraining the breath in Kumbhaka, throw it forcibly down on the head of the serpent to awaken it. The more powerful the imagination, the more quickly will the real result be attained and the Kundalini be awakened. Until it does, imagine it does: try to feel the currents and try to force them through the

Sushumna. This hastens their action.

FOURTH LESSON

Before we can control the mind we must study it.

We have to seize this unstable mind and drag it from its wanderings and fix it on one idea. Over and over again this must be done. By power of will we must get hold of the mind and make it stop and reflect upon the glory of God.

The easiest way to get hold of the mind is to sit quiet and let it drift where it will for a while. Hold fast to the idea, "I am the witness watching my mind drifting. The mind is not I." Then see it think as if it were a thing entirely apart from yourself. Identify yourself with God, never with matter or with the mind.

Picture the mind as a calm lake stretched before you and the thoughts that come and go as bubbles rising and breaking on its surface. Make no effort to control the thoughts, but watch them and follow them in imagination as they float away. This will gradually lessen the circles. For the mind ranges over wide circles of thought and those circles widen out into ever-increasing circles, as in a pond when we throw a stone into it. We want to reverse the process and starting with a huge circle make it narrower until at last we can fix the mind on one point and make it stay there. Hold to the idea, "I am not the mind, I see that I am thinking, I am watching my mind act", and each day the identification of yourself with thought and feeling will grow less, until at last you can entirely separate yourself from the mind and actually know it to be apart from yourself.

When this is done, the mind is your servant to control as you will. The first stage of being a Yogi is to go beyond the senses. When the mind is conquered, he has reached the highest stage.

Live alone as much as possible. The seat should be of comfortable height; put first a grass mat, then a skin (fur), next a silken cover. It is better that the seat has no back and it must stand firm.

Thoughts being pictures, we should not create them. We have to exclude all thought from the mind and make it a blank; as fast as a thought comes we have to banish it. To be able to accomplish this, we must transcend matter and go beyond our body. The whole life of man is really an effort to do this.

Each soul has its own meaning: In our nature these two things are connected.

The highest ideal we have is God. Meditate on Him. We cannot know the Knower, but we are He.

Seeing evil, we are creating it. What we are, we see outside, for the world is our mirror. This little body is a little mirror we have created, but the whole universe is our body. We must think this all the time; then we shall know that we cannot die or hurt another, because he is our own. We are birthless and deathless and we ought only to love. "This whole universe is my body; all health, all happiness is mine, because all is in the universe." Say, "I am the universe." We finally learn that all action is from us to the mirror.

Although we appear as little waves, the whole sea is at our back, and we are one with it. No wave can exist of itself.

Imagination properly employed is our greatest friend; it goes beyond reason and is the only light that takes us everywhere.

Inspiration is from within and we have to inspire ourselves by our own higher faculties.

FIFTH LESSON

Pratyahara and Dharana: Krishna says, "All who seek me by whatever means will reach me", "All must reach me." Pratyahara is a gathering toward, an attempt to get hold of the mind and focus it on the desired object. The first step is to let the mind drift; watch it; see what it thinks; be only the witness. Mind is not soul or spirit. It is only matter in a finer form, and we own it and can learn to manipulate it through the nerve energies.

The body is the objective view of what we call mind (subjective). We, the Self, are beyond both body and mind; we are "Atman", the eternal, unchangeable witness. The body is crystallised thought.

When the breath is flowing through the left nostril, it is the time for rest; when through the right, for work; and when through both, the time to meditate. When we are calm and breathing equally through both nostrils, we are in the right condition for quiet meditation. It is no use trying to concentrate at first. Control of thought will come of itself.

After sufficient practice of closing the nostrils with the thumb and forefinger, we shall be able to do it by the power of will, through thought alone.

Pranayama is now to be slightly changed. If the student has the name of his "Ishta" (Chosen Ideal), he should use that instead of "Om" during inhalation and exhalation, and use the word "Hum" (pronounced Hoom) during Kumbhaka.

Throw the restrained breath forcibly down on the head of the Kundalini at each repetition of the word Hum and imagine that this awakens her. Identify yourself only with God. After a while thoughts will announce their coming, and we shall learn the way they begin and be aware of what we are going to think, just as on this plane we can look out and see a person coming. This stage is reached when we have learnt to separate ourselves from our minds and see ourselves as one and thought as something apart. Do not let the thoughts grasp you; stand aside, and they will die away.

Follow these holy thoughts; go with them; and when they melt away, you will find the feet of the Omnipotent God. This is the superconscious state; when the idea melts, follow it and melt with it.

Haloes are symbols of inner light and can be seen by the Yogi. Sometimes we may see a face as if surrounded by flames and in them read the character and judge without erring. We may have our Ishta come to us as a vision, and this symbol will be the one upon which we can rest easily and fully concentrate our minds.

We can imagine through all the senses, but we do so mostly through the eyes. Even imagination is half material. In other words, we cannot think without a phantasm. But since animals appear to think, yet have no words, it is probable that there is no inseparable connection between thought and images.

Try to keep up the imagination in Yoga, being careful to keep it pure and holy. We all have our peculiarities in the way of imaginative power; follow the way most natural to you; it will be the easiest.

We are the results of all reincarnations through Karma: "One lamp lighted from another", says the Buddhist — different lamps, but the same light.

Be cheerful, be brave, bathe daily, have patience, purity, and perseverance, then you will become a Yogi in truth. Never try to hurry, and if the higher powers come, remember that they are but side-paths. Do not let them tempt you from the main road; put them aside and hold fast to your only true aim — god. Seek only the Eternal, finding which we are at rest for ever; having the all, nothing is left to strive for, and we are for ever in free and perfect existence — existence absolute, Knowledge absolute, Bliss absolute.

SIXTH LESSON

Sushumna: It is very useful to meditate on the Sushumna. You may have a vision of it come to you, and this is the best way. Then meditate for a long time on that. It is a very fine, very brilliant thread, this living passage through the spinal cord, this way of salvation through which we have to make the Kundalini rise.

In the language of the Yogi, the Sushumna has its ends in two lotuses, the lower lotus surrounding the triangle of the Kundalini and the top one in the brain surrounding the pineal gland; between these two are four other lotuses, stages on the way:

- 6th. Pineal Gland.
- 5th. Between the Eyes.
- 4th. Bottom of the Throat.
- 3rd. Level with the Heart.
- 2nd. Opposite the Navel.
- 1st. Base of Spine.

We must awaken the Kundalini, then slowly raise it from one lotus to another till the brain is reached. Each stage corresponds to a new layer of the mind.

WOMEN OF INDIA

Delivered at the Shakespeare Club House, in Pasadena, California, on January 18, 1900.

Swami Vivekananda: "Some persons desire to ask questions about Hindu Philosophy before the lecture and to question in general about India after the lecture; but the chief difficulty is I do not know what I am to lecture on. I would be very glad to lecture on any subject, either on Hindu Philosophy or on anything concerning the race, its history, or its literature. If you, ladies and gentlemen, will suggest anything, I would be very glad."

Questioner: "I would like to ask, Swami, what special principle in Hindu Philosophy you would have us Americans, who are a very practical people, adopt, and what that would do for us beyond what Christianity can do."

Swami Vivekananda: "That is very difficult for me to decide; it rests upon you. If you find anything which you think you ought to adopt, and which will be helpful, you should take that. You see I am not a missionary, and I am not going about converting people to my idea. My principle is that all such ideas are good and great, so that some of your ideas may suit some people in India, and some of our ideas may suit some people here; so ideas must be cast abroad, all over the world."

Questioner: "We would like to know the result of your philosophy; has your philosophy and religion lifted your women above our women?"

Swami Vivekananda: "You see, that is a very invidious question: I like our women and your women too."

Questioner: "Well, will you tell us about your women, their customs and education, and the position they hold in the family?"

Swami Vivekananda: "Oh, yes, those things I would be very glad to tell you. So you want to know about Indian women tonight, and not philosophy and other things?"

The Lecture

I must begin by saying that you may have to bear with me a good deal, because I belong to an Order of people who never marry; so my knowledge of women in all their relations, as mother, as wife, as daughter and sister, must necessarily not be so complete as it may be with other men. And then, India, I must remember, is a vast continent, not merely a country, and is inhabited by many different races. The nations of Europe are nearer to each other, more similar to each other, than the races in India. You may get just a rough idea of it if I tell you that there are eight different languages in all India. Different languages — not dialects — each having a literature of its own. The Hindi language, alone, is spoken by 100,000,000 people; the Bengali by about 60,000,000, and so on. Then, again, the four northern Indian languages differ more from the southern Indian languages than any two European languages from each other. They are entirely different, as much different as your language differs from the Japanese, so that you will be astonished to know, when I go to southern India, unless I meet some people who can talk Sanskrit, I have to speak to them in English. Furthermore, these various races differ from each other in manners, customs, food, dress, and in their methods of thought.

Then, again, there is caste. Each caste has become, as it were, a separate racial element. If a man lives long enough in India, he will be able to tell from the features what caste a man belongs to. Then, between castes, the manners and customs are different. And all these castes are exclusive; that is to say, they would meet socially, but they would not eat or drink together, nor intermarry. In those things they remain separate. They would meet and be friends to each other, but there it would end.

Although I have more opportunity than many other men to know women in general, from my position and my occupation as a preacher, continuously travelling from one place to another and coming in contact with all grades of society —(and women, even in northern India, where they do not appear before men, in many places would break this law for religion and would come to hear us preach and talk to us)— still it would be hazardous on my part to assert that I know everything about the women of India.

So I will try to place before you the ideal. In each nation, man or woman represents an ideal consciously or unconsciously being worked out. The individual is the external expression of an ideal to be embodied. The collection of such individuals is the nation, which also represents a great ideal; towards that it is moving. And, therefore, it is rightly assumed that to understand a nation you must first understand its ideal, for each nation refuses to be judged by any other standard than its own.

All growth, progress, well-being, or degradation is but relative. It refers to a certain standard, and each man to be understood has to be referred to that standard of his perfection. You see this more markedly in nations: what one nation thinks good might not be so regarded by another nation. Cousin-marriage is quite permissible in this country. Now, in India, it is illegal; not only so, it would be classed with the most horrible incest. Widow-marriage is perfectly legitimate in this country. Among the higher castes in India it would be the greatest degradation for a woman to marry twice. So, you see, we work through such different ideas that to judge one people by the other's standard would be neither just nor practicable. Therefore we must know what the ideal is that a nation has raised before itself. When speaking of different nations, we start with a general idea that there is one code of ethics and the same kind of ideals for all races; practically, however, when we come to judge of others, we think what is good for us must be good for everybody; what we do is the right thing, what we do not do, of course in others would be outrageous. I do not mean to say this as a criticism, but just to bring the truth home. When I hear Western women denounce the confining of the feet of Chinese ladies, they never seem to think of the corsets which are doing far more injury to the race. This is just one example; for you must know that cramping the feet does not do one-millionth part of the injury to the human form that the corset has done and is doing — when every organ is displaced and the spine is curved like a serpent. When measurements are taken, you can note the curvatures. I do not mean that as a criticism but just to point out to you the situation, that as you stand aghast at women of other races, thinking that you are supreme, the very reason that they do not adopt your manners and customs shows that they also stand aghast at you.

Therefore there is some misunderstanding on both sides. There is a common platform, a common ground of understanding, a common humanity, which must be the basis of our work. We ought to find out that complete and perfect human nature which is working only in parts, here and there. It has not been given to one man to have everything in perfection. You have a part to play; I, in my humble way, another; here is one who plays a little part; there, another. The perfection is the combination of all these parts. Just as with individuals, so with races. Each race has a part to play; each race has one side of human nature to develop. And we have to take all these together; and, possibly in the distant future, some race will arise in which all these marvellous individual race perfections, attained by the different races, will come together and form a new race, the like of which the world has not yet dreamed. Beyond saying that, I have no criticism to offer about anybody. I have travelled not a little in my life; I have kept my eyes open; and the more I go about the more my mouth is closed. I have no criticism to offer.

Now, the ideal woman in India is the mother, the mother first, and the mother last. The word woman calls up to the mind of the Hindu, motherhood; and God is called Mother. As children, every day, when we are boys, we have to go early in the morning with a little cup of water and place it before the mother, and mother dips her toe into it and we drink it.

In the West, the woman is wife. The idea of womanhood is concentrated there — as the wife. To the ordinary man in India, the whole force of womanhood is concentrated in motherhood. In the Western home, the wife rules. In an Indian home, the mother rules. If a mother comes into a Western home, she has to be subordinate to the wife; to the wife belongs the home. A mother always lives in our homes: the wife must be subordinate to her. See all the difference of ideas.

Now, I only suggest comparisons; I would state facts so that we may compare the two sides. Make this comparison. If you ask, "What is an Indian woman as wife?", the Indian asks, "Where is the American woman as mother? What is she, the all-glorious, who gave me this body? What is she who kept me in her body for nine months? Where is she who would give me twenty times her life, if I had need? Where is she whose love never dies, however wicked, however vile I am? Where is she, in comparison with her, who goes to the divorce court the moment I treat her a little badly? O American woman! where is she?" I will not find her in your country. I have not found the son who thinks mother is first. When we die, even then, we do not want our wives and our children to take her place. Our mother!— we want to die with our head on her lap once more, if we die before her. Where is she? Is woman a name to be coupled with the physical body only? Ay! the Hindu mind fears all those ideals which say that the flesh must cling unto the flesh. No, no! Woman! thou shalt not be coupled with anything connected with the flesh. The name has been called holy once and for ever, for what name is there which no lust can ever approach, no carnality ever come near, than the one word mother? That is the ideal in India.

I belong to an Order very much like what you have in the Mendicant Friars of the Catholic Church; that is to say, we have to go about without very much in the way of dress and beg from door to door, live thereby, preach to people when they want it, sleep where we can get a place — that way we have to follow. And the rule is that the members of this Order have to call every woman "mother"; to every woman and little girl we have to say "mother"; that is the custom. Coming to the West, that old habit remained and I would say to ladies, "Yes, mother", and they are horrified. I could not understand why they should be horrified. Later on, I discovered the reason: because that would mean that they are old. The ideal of womanhood in India is motherhood — that marvellous, unselfish, all-suffering, ever-forgiving mother. The wife walks behind — the shadow. She must imitate the life of the mother; that is her duty. But the mother is the ideal of love; she rules the family, she possesses the family. It is the father in India who thrashes the child and spanks when there is something done by the child, and always the mother puts herself between the father and the child. You see it is just the opposite here. It has become the mother's business to spank the children in this country, and poor father comes in between. You see, ideals are different. I do not mean this as any criticism. It is all good — this what you do; but our way is what we have been taught for ages. You never hear of a mother cursing the child; she is forgiving, always forgiving. Instead of "Our Father in Heaven", we say "Mother" all the time; that idea and that word are ever associated in the Hindu mind with Infinite Love, the mother's love being the nearest approach to God's love in this mortal world of ours. "Mother, O Mother, be merciful; I am wicked! Many children have been wicked, but there never was a wicked mother"— so says the great saint Ramprasad.

There she is — the Hindu mother. The son's wife comes in as her daughter; just as the mother's own daughter married and went out, so her son married and brought in another daughter, and she has to fall in line under the government of the queen of queens, of his mother. Even I, who never married, belonging to an Order that never marries, would be disgusted if my wife, supposing I had married, dared to displease my mother. I would be disgusted. Why? Do I not worship my mother? Why should not her daughter-in-law? Whom I worship, why not she? Who is she, then, that would try to ride over my head and govern my mother? She has to wait till her womanhood is fulfilled; and the one thing that fulfils womanhood, that is womanliness in woman, is motherhood. Wait till she becomes a mother; then she will have the same right. That, according to the Hindu mind, is the great mission of woman — to become a mother. But oh, how different! Oh, how different! My father and mother fasted and prayed, for years and years, so that I would be born. They pray for every child before it is born. Says our great law-giver, Manu, giving the definition of an Aryan, "He is the Aryan, who is born through prayer". Every child not born through prayer is illegitimate, according to the great law-giver. The child must be prayed for. Those children that come with curses, that slip into the world, just in a moment of inadvertence, because that could not be prevented — what can we expect of such progeny? Mothers of America, think of that! Think in the heart of your hearts, are you ready to be women? Not any question of race or country, or that false sentiment of national pride. Who dares to be proud in this mortal life of ours, in this world of woes and miseries? What are we before this infinite force of God? But I ask you the question tonight: Do you all pray for the children to come? Are you thankful to be mothers, or not? Do you think that you are sanctified by motherhood, or not? Ask that of your minds. If you do not, your marriage is a lie, your womanhood is false, your education is superstition, and your children, if they come without prayer, will prove a curse to humanity.

See the different ideals now coming before us. From motherhood comes tremendous responsibility. There is the basis, start from that. Well, why is mother to be worshipped so much? Because our books teach that it is the pre-natal influence that gives the impetus to the child for good or evil. Go to a hundred thousand colleges, read a million books, associate with all the learned men of the world — better off you are when born with the right stamp. You are born for good or evil. The child is a born god or a born demon; that is what the books say. Education and all these things come afterwards — are a mere bagatelle. You are what you are born. Born unhealthful, how many drug stores, swallowed wholesale, will keep you well all through your life? How many people of good, healthy lives were born of weak parents, were born of sickly, blood-poisoned parents? How many? None — none. We come with a tremendous impetus for good or evil: born demons or born gods. Education or other things are a bagatelle.

Thus say our books: direct the pre-natal influence.

Why should mother be worshipped? Because she made herself pure. She underwent harsh penances sometimes to keep herself as pure as purity can be. For, mind you, no woman in India thinks of giving up her body to any man; it is her own. The English, as a reform, have introduced at present what they call "Restitution of conjugal rights", but no Indian would take advantage of it. When a man comes in physical contact with his wife, the circumstances she controls through what prayers and through what vows! For that which brings forth the child is the holiest symbol of God himself. It is the greatest prayer between man and wife, the prayer that is going to bring into the world another soul fraught with a tremendous power for good or for evil. Is it a joke? Is it a simple nervous satisfaction? Is it a brute enjoyment of the body? Says the Hindu: no, a thousand times, no!

But then, following that, there comes in another idea. The idea we started with was that the ideal is the love for the mother — herself all-suffering, all-forbearing. The worship that is accorded to the mother has its fountain-head there. She was a saint to bring me into the world; she kept her body pure, her mind pure, her food pure, her clothes pure, her imagination pure, for years, because I would be born. Because she did that, she deserves worship. And what follows? Linked with motherhood is wifehood.

You Western people are individualistic. I want to do this thing because I like it; I will elbow every one. Why? Because I like to. I want my own satisfaction, so I marry this woman. Why? Because I like her. This woman marries me. Why? Because she likes me. There it ends. She and I are the only two persons in the whole, infinite world; and I marry her and she marries me — nobody else is injured, nobody else responsible.

Your Johns and your Janes may go into the forest and there they may live their lives; but when they have to live in society, their marriage means a tremendous amount of good or evil to us. Their children may be veritable demons — burning, murdering, robbing, stealing, drinking, hideous, vile.

So what is the basis of the Indian's social order? It is the caste law. I am born for the caste, I live for the caste. I do not mean myself, because, having joined an Order, we are outside. I mean those that live in civil society. Born in the caste, the whole life must be lived according to caste regulation. In other words, in the present-day language of your country, the Western man is born individualistic, while the Hindu is socialistic — entirely socialistic. Now, then, the books say: if I allow you freedom to go about and marry any woman you like, and the woman to marry any man she likes, what happens? You fall in love; the father of the woman was, perchance, a lunatic or a consumptive. The girl falls in love with the face of a man whose father was a roaring drunkard. What says the law then? The law lays down that all these marriages would be illegal. The children of drunkards, consumptives, lunatics, etc., shall not be married. The deformed, humpbacked, crazy, idiotic — no marriage for them, absolutely none, says the law.

But the Mohammedan comes from Arabia, and he has his own Arabian law; so the Arabian desert law has been forced upon us. The Englishman comes with his law; he forces it upon us, so far as he can. We are conquered. He says, "Tomorrow I will marry your sister". What can we do? Our law says, those that are born of the same family, though a hundred degrees distant, must not marry, that is illegitimate, it would deteriorate or make the race sterile. That must not be, and there it stops. So I have no voice in my marriage, nor my sister. It is the caste that determines all that.

We are married sometimes when children. Why? Because the caste says: if they have to be married anyway without their consent, it is better that they are married very early, before they have developed this love: if they are allowed to grow up apart, the boy may like some other girl, and the girl some other boy, and then something evil will happen; and so, says the caste, stop it there. I do not care whether my sister is deformed, or good-looking, or bad-looking: she is my sister, and that is enough; he is my brother, and that is all I need to know. So they will love each other. You may say, "Oh! they lose a great deal of enjoyment — those exquisite emotions of a man falling in love with a woman and a woman falling in love with a man. This is a sort of tame thing, loving each other like brothers and sisters, as though they have to." So be it; but the Hindu says, "We are socialistic. For the sake of one man's or woman's exquisite pleasure we do not want to load misery on hundreds of others."

There they are — married. The wife comes home with her husband; that is called the second marriage. Marriage at an early age is considered the first marriage, and they grow up separately with women and with their parents. When they are grown, there is a second ceremony performed, called a second marriage. And then they live together, but under the same roof with his mother and father. When she becomes a mother, she takes her place in turn as queen of the family group.

Now comes another peculiar Indian institution. I have just told you that in the first two or three castes the widows are not allowed to marry. They cannot, even if they would. Of course, it is a hardship on many. There is no denying that not all the widows like it very much, because non-marrying entails upon them the life of a student. That is to say, a student must not eat meat or fish, nor drink wine, nor dress except in white clothes, and so on; there are many regulations. We are a nation of monks — always making penance, and we like it. Now, you see, a woman never drinks wine or eats meat. It was a hardship on us when we were students, but not on the girls. Our women would feel degraded at the idea of eating meat. Men eat meat sometimes in some castes; women never. Still, not being allowed to marry must be a hardship to many; I am sure of that.

But we must go back to the idea; they are intensely socialistic. In the higher castes of every country you will find the statistics show that the number of women is always much larger than the number of men. Why? Because in the higher castes, for generation after generation, the women lead an easy life. They "neither toil nor spin, yet Solomon in all his glory was not arrayed like one of them". And the poor boys, they die like flies. The girl has a cat's nine lives, they say in India. You will read in the statistics that they outnumber the boys in a very short time, except now when they are taking to work quite as hard as the boys. The number of girls in the higher castes is much larger than in the lower. Conditions are quite opposite in the lower castes. There they all work hard; women a little harder, sometimes, because they have to do the domestic work. But, mind you, I never would have thought of that, but one of your American travellers, Mark Twain, writes this about India: "In spite of all that Western critics have said of Hindu customs, I never saw a woman harnessed to a plough with a cow or to a cart with a dog, as is done in some European countries. I saw no woman or girl at work in the fields in India. On both sides and ahead (of the railway train) brown-bodied naked men and boys are ploughing in the fields. But not a woman. In these two hours I have not seen a woman or a girl working in the fields. In India, even the lowest caste never does any hard work. They generally have an easy lot compared to the same class in other nations; and as to ploughing, they never do it."

Now, there you are. Among the lower classes the number of men is larger than the number of women; and what would you naturally expect? A woman gets more chances of marriage, the number of men being larger.

Relative to such questions as to widows not marrying: among the first two castes, the number of women is disproportionately large, and here is a dilemma. Either you have a non-marriageable widow problem and misery, or the non-husband-getting young lady problem. To face the widow problem, or the old maid problem? There you are; either of the two. Now, go back again to the idea that the Indian mind is socialistic. It says, "Now look here! we take the widow problem as the lesser one." Why? "Because they have had their chance; they have been married. If they have lost their chance, at any rate they have had one. Sit down, be quiet, and consider these poor girls — they have not had one chance of marriage." Lord bless you! I remember once in Oxford Street, it was after ten o'clock, and all those ladies coming there, hundreds and thousands of them shopping; and some man, an American, looks around, and he says, "My Lord! how many of them will ever get husbands, I wonder!" So the Indian mind said to the widows, "Well, you have had your chance, and now we are very, very sorry that such mishaps have come to you, but we cannot help it; others are waiting."

Then religion comes into the question; the Hindu religion comes in as a comfort. For, mind you, our religion teaches that marriage is something bad, it is only for the weak. The very spiritual man or woman would not marry at all. So the religious woman says, "Well, the Lord has given me a better chance. What is the use of marrying? Thank God, worship God, what is the use of my loving man?" Of course, all of them cannot put their mind on God. Some find it simply impossible. They have to suffer; but the other poor people, they should not suffer for them. Now I leave this to your judgment; but that is their idea in India.

Next we come to woman as daughter. The great difficulty in the Indian household is the daughter. The daughter and caste combined ruin the poor Hindu, because, you see, she must marry in the same caste, and even inside the caste exactly in the same order; and so the poor man sometimes has to make himself a beggar to get his daughter married. The father of the boy demands a very high price for his son, and this poor man sometimes has to sell everything just to get a husband for his daughter. The great difficulty of the Hindu's life is the daughter. And, curiously enough, the word daughter in Sanskrit is "duhita". The real derivation is that, in ancient times, the daughter of the family was accustomed to milk the cows, and so the word "duhita" comes from "duh", to milk; and the word "daughter" really means a milkmaid. Later on, they found a new meaning to that word "duhita", the milkmaid — she who milks away all the milk of the family. That is the second meaning.

These are the different relations held by our Indian women. As I have told you, the mother is the greatest in position, the wife is next, and the daughter comes after them. It is a most intricate and complicated series of gradation. No foreigner can understand it, even if he lives there for years. For instance, we have three forms of the personal pronoun; they are a sort of verbs in our language. One is very respectful, one is middling, and the lowest is just like thou and thee. To children and servants the last is addressed. The middling one is used with equals. You see, these are to be applied in all the intricate relations of life. For example, to my elder sister I always throughout my life use the pronoun apani, but she never does in speaking to me; she says tumi to me. She should not, even by mistake, say apani to me, because that would mean a curse. Love, the love toward those that are superior, should always be expressed in that form of language. That is the custom. Similarly I would never dare address my elder sister or elder brother, much less my mother or father, as tu or tum or tumi. As to calling our mother and father by name, why, we would never do that. Before I knew the customs of this country, I received such a shock when the son, in a very refined family, got up and called the mother by name! However, I got used to that. That is the custom of the country. But with us, we never pronounce the name of our parents when they are present. It is always in the third person plural, even before them.

Thus we see the most complicated mesh-work in the social life of our men and our women and in our degree of relationship. We do not speak to our wives before our elders; it is only when we are alone or when inferiors are present. If I were married, I would speak to my wife before my younger sister, my nephews or nieces; but not before my elder sister or parents. I cannot talk to my sisters about their husbands at all. The idea is, we are a monastic race. The whole social organisation has that one idea before it. Marriage is thought of as something impure, something lower. Therefore the subject of love would never be talked of. I cannot read a novel before my sister, or my brothers, or my mother, or even before others. I close the book.

Then again, eating and drinking is all in the same category. We do not eat before superiors. Our women never eat before men, except they be the children or inferiors. The wife would die rather than, as she says, "munch" before her husband. Sometimes, for instance, brothers and sisters may eat together; and if I and my sister are eating, and the husband comes to the door, my sister stops, and the poor husband flies out.

These are the customs peculiar to the country. A few of these I note in different countries also. As I never married myself, I am not perfect in all my knowledge about the wife. Mother, sisters — i know what they are; and other people's wives I saw; from that I gather what I have told you.

As to education and culture, it all depends upon the man. That is to say, where the men are highly cultured, there the women are; where the men are not, women are not. Now, from the oldest times, you know, the primary education, according to the old Hindu customs, belongs to the village system. All the land from time immemorial was nationalised, as you say — belonged to the Government. There never is any private right in land. The revenue in India comes from the land, because every man holds so much land from the Government. This land is held in common by a community, it may be five, ten, twenty, or a hundred families. They govern the whole of the land, pay a certain amount of revenue to the Government, maintain a physician, a village schoolmaster, and so on.

Those of you who have read Herbert Spencer remember what he calls the "monastery system" of education that was tried in Europe and which in some parts proved a success; that is, there is one schoolmaster, whom the village keeps. These primary schools are very rudimentary, because our methods are so simple. Each boy brings a little mat; and his paper, to begin with, is palm leaves. Palm leaves first, paper is too costly. Each boy spreads his little mat and sits upon it, brings out his inkstand and his books and begins to write. A little arithmetic, some Sanskrit grammar, a little of language and accounts — these are taught in the primary school.

A little book on ethics, taught by an old man, we learnt by heart, and I remember one of the lessons: "For the good of a village, a man ought to give up his family;

For the good of a country, he ought to give up his

village;

For the good of humanity, he may give up his country;

For the good of the world, everything."

Such verses are there in the books. We get them by heart, and they are explained by teacher and pupil. These things we learn, both boys and girls together. Later on, the education differs. The old Sanskrit universities are mainly composed of boys. The girls very rarely go up to those universities; but there are a few exceptions.

In these modern days there is a greater impetus towards higher education on the European lines, and the trend of opinion is strong towards women getting this higher education. Of course, there are some people in India who do not want it, but those who do want it carried the day. It is a strange fact that Oxford and Cambridge are closed to women today, so are Harvard and Yale; but Calcutta University opened its doors to women more than twenty years ago. I remember that the year I graduated, several girls came out and graduated — the same standard, the same course, the same in everything as the boys; and they did very well indeed. And our religion does not prevent a woman being educated at all. In this way the girl should be educated; even thus she should be trained; and in the old books we find that the universities were equally resorted to by both girls and boys, but later the education of the whole nation was neglected. What can you expect under foreign rule? The foreign conqueror is not there to do good to us; he wants his money. I studied hard for twelve years and became a graduate of Calcutta University; now I can scarcely make $5.00 a month in my country. Would you believe it? It is actually a fact. So these educational institutions of foreigners are simply to get a lot of useful, practical slaves for a little money — to turn out a host of clerks, postmasters, telegraph operators, and so on. There it is.

As a result, education for both boys and girls is neglected, entirely neglected. There are a great many things that should be done in that land; but you must always remember, if you will kindly excuse me and permit me to use one of your own proverbs, "What is sauce for the goose is sauce for the gander." Your foreign born ladies are always crying over the hardships of the Hindu woman, and never care for the hardships of the Hindu man. They are all weeping salt tears. But who are the little girls married to? Some one, when told that they are all married to old men, asked, "And what do the young men do? What! are all the girls married to old men, only to old men?" We are born old — perhaps all the men there.

The ideal of the Indian race is freedom of the soul. This world is nothing. It is a vision, a dream. This life is one of many millions like it. The whole of this nature is Maya, is phantasm, a pest house of phantasms. That is the philosophy. Babies smile at life and think it so beautiful and good, but in a few years they will have to revert to where they began. They began life crying, and they will leave it crying. Nations in the vigour of their youth think that they can do anything and everything: "We are the gods of the earth. We are the chosen people." They think that God Almighty has given them a charter to rule over all the world, to advance His plans, to do anything they like, to turn the world upside down. They have a charter to rob, murder, kill; God has given them this, and they do that because they are only babes. So empire after empire has arisen — glorious, resplendent — now vanished away — gone, nobody knows where; it may have been stupendous in its ruin.

As a drop of water upon a lotus leaf tumbles about and falls in a moment, even so is this mortal life. Everywhere we turn are ruins. Where the forest stands today was once the mighty empire with huge cities. That is the dominant idea, the tone, the colour of the Indian mind. We know, you Western people have the youthful blood coursing through your veins. We know that nations, like men, have their day. Where is Greece? Where is Rome? Where that mighty Spaniard of the other day? Who knows through it all what becomes of India? Thus they are born, and thus they die; they rise and fall. The Hindu as a child knows of the Mogul invader whose cohorts no power on earth could stop, who has left in your language the terrible word "Tartar". The Hindu has learnt his lesson. He does not want to prattle, like the babes of today. Western people, say what you have to say. This is your day. Onward, go on, babes; have your prattle out. This is the day of the babies, to prattle. We have learnt our lesson and are quiet. You have a little wealth today, and you look down upon us. Well, this is your day. Prattle, babes, prattle — this is the Hindu's attitude.

The Lord of Lords is not to be attained by much frothy speech. The Lord of Lords is not to be attained even by the powers of the intellect. He is not gained by much power of conquest. That man who knows the secret source of things and that everything else is evanescent, unto him He, the Lord, comes; unto none else. India has learnt her lesson through ages and ages of experience. She has turned her face towards Him. She has made many mistakes; loads and loads of rubbish are heaped upon the race. Never mind; what of that? What is the clearing of rubbish, the cleaning of cities, and all that? Does that give life? Those that have fine institutions, they die. And what of institutions, those tinplate Western institutions, made in five days and broken on the sixth? One of these little handful nations cannot keep alive for two centuries together. And our institutions have stood the test of ages. Says the Hindu, "Yes, we have buried all the old nations of the earth and stand here to bury all the new races also, because our ideal is not this world, but the other. Just as your ideal is, so shall you be. If your ideal is mortal, if your ideal is of this earth, so shalt thou be. If your ideal is matter, matter shalt thou be. Behold! Our ideal is the Spirit. That alone exists, nothing else exists; and like Him, we live for ever."

MY LIFE AND MISSION

Delivered at the Shakespeare Club of Pasadena, California, on January 27, 1900.

Now, ladies and gentlemen, the subject for this morning was to have been the Vedanta Philosophy. That subject itself is interesting, but rather dry and very vast.

Meanwhile, I have been asked by your president and some of the ladies and gentlemen here to tell them something about my work and what I have been doing. It may be interesting to some here, but not so much so to me. In fact, I do not quite know how to tell it to you, for this will have been the first time in my life that I have spoken on that subject.

Now, to understand what I have been trying to do, in my small way, I will take you, in imagination, to India. We have not time to go into all the details and all the ramifications of the subject; nor is it possible for you to understand all the complexities in a foreign race in this short time. Suffice it to say, I will at least try to give you a little picture of what India is like.

It is like a gigantic building all tumbled down in ruins. At first sight, then, there is little hope. It is a nation gone and ruined. But you wait and study, then you see something beyond that. The truth is that so long as the principle, the ideal, of which the outer man is the expression, is not hurt or destroyed, the man lives, and there is hope for that man. If your coat is stolen twenty times, that is no reason why you should be destroyed. You can get a new coat. The coat is unessential. The fact that a rich man is robbed does not hurt the vitality of the man, does not mean death. The man will survive.

Standing on this principle, we look in and we see — what? India is no longer a political power; it is an enslaved race. Indians have no say, no voice in their own government; they are three hundred millions of slaves — nothing more! The average income of a man in India is two shillings a month. The common state of the vast mass of the people is starvation, so that, with the least decrease in income, millions die.

A little famine means death. So there, too, when I look on that side of India, I see ruin — hopeless ruin.

But we find that the Indian race never stood for wealth. Although they acquired immense wealth, perhaps more than any other nation ever acquired, yet the nation did not stand for wealth. It was a powerful race for ages, yet we find that that nation never stood for power, never went out of the country to conquer. Quite content within their own boundaries, they never fought anybody. The Indian nation never stood for imperial glory. Wealth and power, then, were not the ideals of the race.

What then? Whether they were wrong or right — that is not the question we discuss — that nation, among all the children of men, has believed, and believed intensely, that this life is not real. The real is God; and they must cling unto that God through thick and thin. In the midst of their degradation, religion came first. The Hindu man drinks religiously, sleeps religiously, walks religiously, marries religiously, robs religiously.

Did you ever see such a country? If you want to get up a gang of robbers, the leader will have to preach some sort of religion, then formulate some bogus metaphysics, and say that this method is the clearest and quickest way to get God. Then he finds a following, otherwise not. That shows that the vitality of the race, the mission of the race is religion; and because that has not been touched, therefore that race lives.

See Rome. Rome's mission was imperial power, expansion. And so soon as that was touched, Rome fell to pieces, passed out. The mission of Greece was intellect, as soon as that was touched, why, Greece passed out. So in modern times, Spain and all these modern countries. Each nation has a mission for the world. So long as that mission is not hurt, that nation lives, despite every difficulty. But as soon as its mission is destroyed, the nation collapses.

Now, that vitality of India has not been touched yet. They have not given up that, and it is still strong — in spite of all their superstitions. Hideous superstitions are there, most revolting some of them. Never mind. The national life-current is still there — the mission of the race.

The Indian nation never will be a powerful conquering people — never. They will never be a great political power; that is not their business, that is not the note India has to play in the great harmony of nations. But what has she to play? God, and God alone. She clings unto that like grim death. Still there is hope there.

So, then, after your analysis, you come to the conclusion that all these things, all this poverty and misery, are of no consequence — the man is living still, and therefore there is hope.

Well! You see religious activities going on all through the country. I do not recall a year that has not given birth to several new sects in India. The stronger the current, the more the whirlpools and eddies. Sects are not signs of decay, they are a sign of life. Let sects multiply, till the time comes when every one of us is a sect, each individual. We need not quarrel about that.

Now, take your country. (I do not mean any criticism). Here the social laws, the political formation — everything is made to facilitate man's journey in this life. He may live very happily so long as he is on this earth. Look at your streets — how clean! Your beautiful cities! And in how many ways a man can make money! How many channels to get enjoyment in this life! But, if a man here should say, "Now look here, I shall sit down under this tree and meditate; I do not want to work", why, he would have to go to jail. See! There would be no chance for him at all. None. A man can live in this society only if he falls in line. He has to join in this rush for the enjoyment of good in this life, or he dies.

Now let us go back to India. There, if a man says, "I shall go and sit on the top of that mountain and look at the tip of my nose all the rest of my days", everybody says, "Go, and Godspeed to you!" He need not speak a word. Somebody brings him a little cloth, and he is all right. But if a man says, "Behold, I am going to enjoy a little of this life", every door is closed to him.

I say that the ideas of both countries are unjust. I see no reason why a man here should not sit down and look at the tip of his nose if he likes. Why should everybody here do just what the majority does? I see no reason.

Nor why, in India, a man should not have the goods of this life and make money. But you see how those vast millions are forced to accept the opposite point of view by tyranny. This is the tyranny of the sages. This is the tyranny of the great, tyranny of the spiritual, tyranny of the intellectual, tyranny of the wise. And the tyranny of the wise, mind you, is much more powerful than the tyranny of the ignorant. The wise, the intellectual, when they take to forcing their opinions upon others, know a hundred thousand ways to make bonds and barriers which it is not in the power of the ignorant to break.

Now, I say that this thing has got to stop. There is no use in sacrificing millions and millions of people to produce one spiritual giant. If it is possible to make a society where the spiritual giant will be produced and all the rest of the people will be happy as well, that is good; but if the millions have to be ground down, that is unjust. Better that the one great man should suffer for the salvation of the world.

In every nation you will have to work through their methods. To every man you will have to speak in his own language. Now, in England or in America, if you want to preach religion to them, you will have to work through political methods — make organisations, societies, with voting, balloting, a president, and so on, because that is the language, the method of the Western race. On the other hand, if you want to speak of politics in India, you must speak through the language of religion. You will have to tell them something like this: "The man who cleans his house every morning will acquire such and such an amount of merit, he will go to heaven, or he comes to God." Unless you put it that way, they will not listen to you. It is a question of language. The thing done is the same. But with every race, you will have to speak their language in order to reach their hearts. And that is quite just. We need not fret about that.

In the Order to which I belong we are called Sannyasins. The word means "a man who has renounced". This is a very, very, very ancient Order. Even Buddha, who was 560 years before Christ, belonged to that Order. He was one of the reformers of his Order. That was all. So ancient! You find it mentioned away back in the Vedas, the oldest book in the world. In old India there was the regulation that every man and woman, towards the end of their lives, must get out of social life altogether and think of nothing except God and their own salvation. This was to get ready for the great event — death. So old people used to become Sannyasins in those early days. Later on, young people began to give up the world. And young people are active. They could not sit down under a tree and think all the time of their own death, so they went about preaching and starting sects, and so on. Thus, Buddha, being young, started that great reform. Had he been an old man, he would have looked at the tip of his nose and died quietly.

The Order is not a church, and the people who join the Order are not priests. There is an absolute difference between the priests and the Sannyasins. In India, priesthood, like every other business in a social life, is a hereditary profession. A priest's son will become a priest, just as a carpenter's son will be a carpenter, or a blacksmith's son a blacksmith. The priest must always be married. The Hindu does not think a man is complete unless he has a wife. An unmarried man has no right to perform religious ceremonies.

The Sannyasins do not possess property, and they do not marry. Beyond that there is no organisation. The only bond that is there is the bond between the teacher and the taught — and that is peculiar to India. The teacher is not a man who comes just to teach me, and I pay him so much, and there it ends. In India it is really like an adoption. The teacher is more than my own father, and I am truly his child, his son in every respect. I owe him obedience and reverence first, before my own father even; because, they say, the father gave me this body, but he showed me the way to salvation, he is greater than father. And we carry this love, this respect for our teacher all our lives. And that is the only organisation that exists. I adopt my disciples. Sometimes the teacher will be a young man and the disciple a very old man. But never mind, he is the son, and he calls me "Father", and I have to address him as my son, my daughter, and so on.

Now, I happened to get an old man to teach me, and he was very peculiar. He did not go much for intellectual scholarship, scarcely studied books; but when he was a boy he was seized with the tremendous idea of getting truth direct. First he tried by studying his own religion. Then he got the idea that he must get the truth of other religions; and with that idea he joined all the sects, one after another. For the time being he did exactly what they told him to do — lived with the devotees of these different sects in turn, until interpenetrated with the particular ideal of that sect. After a few years he would go to another sect. When he had gone through with all that, he came to the conclusion that they were all good. He had no criticism to offer to any one; they are all so many paths leading to the same goal. And then he said, "That is a glorious thing, that there should be so many paths, because if there were only one path, perhaps it would suit only an individual man. The more the number of paths, the more the chance for every one of us to know the truth. If I cannot be taught in one language, I will try another, and so on". Thus his benediction was for every religion.

Now, all the ideas that I preach are only an attempt to echo his ideas. Nothing is mine originally except the wicked ones, everything I say which is false and wicked. But every word that I have ever uttered which is true and good is simply an attempt to echo his voice. Read his life by Prof. Max Muller[1].

Well, there at his feet I conceived these ideas — there with some other young men. I was just a boy. I went there when I was about sixteen. Some of the other boys were still younger, some a little older — about a dozen or more. And together we conceived that this ideal had to be spread. And not only spread, but made practical. That is to say, we must show the spirituality of the Hindus, the mercifulness of the Buddhists, the activity of the Christians, the brotherhood of the Mohammedans, by our practical lives. "We shall start a universal religion now and here," we said, "we will not wait".

Our teacher was an old man who would never touch a coin with his hands. He took just the little food offered, just so many yards of cotton cloth, no more. He could never be induced to take any other gift. With all these marvellous ideas, he was strict, because that made him free. The monk in India is the friend of the prince today, dines with him; and tomorrow he is with the beggar, sleeps under a tree. He must come into contact with everyone, must always move about. As the saying is, "The rolling stone gathers no moss". The last fourteen years of my life, I have never been for three months at a time in any one place — continually rolling. So do we all.

Now, this handful of boys got hold of these ideas, and all the practical results that sprang out of these ideas. Universal religion, great sympathy for the poor, and all that are very good in theory, but one must practise.

Then came the sad day when our old teacher died. We nursed him the best we could. We had no friends. Who would listen to a few boys, with their crank notions? Nobody. At least, in India, boys are nobodies. Just think of it — a dozen boys, telling people vast, big ideas, saying they are determined to work these ideas out in life. Why, everybody laughed. From laughter it became serious; it became persecution. Why, the parents of the boys came to feel like spanking every one of us. And the more we were derided, the more determined we became.

Then came a terrible time — for me personally and for all the other boys as well. But to me came such misfortune! On the one side was my mother, my brothers. My father died at that time, and we were left poor. Oh, very poor, almost starving all the time! I was the only hope of the family, the only one who could do anything to help them. I had to stand between my two worlds. On the one hand, I would have to see my mother and brothers starve unto death; on the other, I had believed

---
1. *Ramakrishna: His Life and Sayings*, first published in London in 1896. Reprinted in 1951 by Advaita Ashrama.

that this man's ideas were for the good of India and the world, and had to be preached and worked out. And so the fight went on in my mind for days and months. Sometimes I would pray for five or six days and nights together without stopping. Oh, the agony of those days! I was living in hell! The natural affections of my boy's heart drawing me to my family — i could not bear to see those who were the nearest and dearest to me suffering. On the other hand, nobody to sympathise with me. Who would sympathise with the imaginations of a boy — imaginations that caused so much suffering to others? Who would sympathise with me? None — except one.

That one's sympathy brought blessing and hope. She was a woman. Our teacher, this great monk, was married when he was a boy and she a mere child. When he became a young man, and all this religious zeal was upon him, she came to see him. Although they had been married for long, they had not seen very much of each other until they were grown up. Then he said to his wife, "Behold, I am your husband; you have a right to this body. But I cannot live the sex life, although I have married you. I leave it to your judgment". And she wept and said, "God speed you! The Lord bless you! Am I the woman to degrade you? If I can, I will help you. Go on in your work".

That was the woman. The husband went on and became a monk in his own way; and from a distance the wife went on helping as much as she could. And later, when the man had become a great spiritual giant, she came — really, she was the first disciple — and she spent the rest of her life taking care of the body of this man. He never knew whether he was living or dying, or anything. Sometimes, when talking, he would get so excited that if he sat on live charcoals, he did not know it. Live charcoals! Forgetting all about his body, all the time.

Well, that lady, his wife, was the only one who sympathised with the idea of those boys. But she was powerless. She was poorer than we were. Never mind! We plunged into the breach. I believed, as I was living, that these ideas were going to rationalise India and bring better days to many lands and foreign races. With that belief, came the realisation that it is better that a few persons suffer than that such ideas should die out of the world. What if a mother or two brothers die? It is a sacrifice. Let it be done. No great thing can be done without sacrifice. The heart must be plucked out and the bleeding heart placed upon the altar. Then great things are done. Is there any other way? None have found it. I appeal to each one of you, to those who have accomplished any great thing. Oh, how much it has cost! What agony! What torture! What terrible suffering is behind every deed of success in every life! You know that, all of you.

And thus we went on, that band of boys. The only thing we got from those around us was a kick and a curse — that was all. Of course, we had to beg from door to door for our food: got hips and haws — the refuse of everything — a piece of bread here and there. We got hold of a broken-down old house, with hissing cobras living underneath; and because that was the cheapest, we went into that house and lived there.

Thus we went on for some years, in the meanwhile making excursions all over India, trying to bring about the idea gradually. Ten years were spent without a ray of light! Ten more years! A thousand times despondency came; but there was one thing always to keep us hopeful — the tremendous faithfulness to each other, the tremendous love between us. I have got a hundred men and women around me; if I become the devil himself tomorrow, they will say, "Here we are still! We will never give you up!" That is a great blessing. In happiness, in misery, in famine, in pain, in the grave, in heaven, or in hell who never gives me up is my friend. Is such friendship a joke? A man may have salvation through such friendship. That brings salvation if we can love like that. If we have that faithfulness, why, there is the essence of all concentration. You need not worship any gods in the world if you have that faith, that strength, that love. And that was there with us all throughout that hard time. That was there. That made us go from the Himalayas to Cape Comorin, from the Indus to the Brahmaputra.

This band of boys began to travel about. Gradually we began to draw attention: ninety per cent was antagonism, very little of it was helpful. For we had one fault: we were boys — in poverty and with all the roughness of boys. He who has to make his own way in life is a bit rough, he has not much time to be smooth and suave and polite —"my lady and my gentleman", and all that. You have seen that in life, always. He is a rough diamond, he has not much polish, he is a jewel in an indifferent casket.

And there we were. "No compromise!" was the watchword. "This is the ideal, and this has got to be carried out. If we meet the king, though we die, we must give him a bit of our minds; if the peasant, the same". Naturally, we met with antagonism.

But, mind you, this is life's experience; if you really want the good of others, the whole universe may stand against you and cannot hurt you. It must crumble before your power of the Lord Himself in you if you are sincere and really unselfish. And those boys were that.

They came as children, pure and fresh from the hands of nature. Said our Master: I want to offer at the altar of the Lord only those flowers that have not even been smelled, fruits that have not been touched with the fingers. The words of the great man sustained us all. For he saw through the future life of those boys that he collected from the streets of Calcutta, so to say. People used to laugh at him when he said, "You will see — this boy, that boy, what he becomes". His faith was unalterable: "Mother showed it to me. I may be weak, but when She says this is so — she can never make mistakes — it must be so."

So things went on and on for ten years without any light, but with my health breaking all the time. It tells on the body in the long run: sometimes one meal at nine in the evening, another time a meal at eight in the morning, another after two days, another after three days — and always the poorest and roughest thing. Who is going to give to the beggar the good things he has? And then, they have not much in India. And most of the time walking, climbing snow peaks, sometimes ten miles of hard mountain climbing, just to get a meal. They eat unleavened bread in India, and sometimes they have it stored away for twenty or thirty days, until it is harder than bricks; and then they will give a square of that. I would have to go from house to house to collect sufficient for one meal. And then the bread was so hard, it made my mouth bleed to eat it. Literally, you can break your teeth on that bread. Then I would put it in a pot and pour over it water from the river. For months and months I existed that way — of course it was telling on the health.

Then I thought, I have tried India: it is time for me to try another country. At that time your Parliament of Religions was to be held, and someone was to be sent from India. I was just a vagabond, but I said, "If you send me, I am going. I have not much to lose, and I do not care if I lose that." It was very difficult to find the money, but after a long struggle they got together just enough to pay for my passage — and I came. Came one or two months earlier, so that I found myself drifting about in the streets here, without knowing anybody.

But finally the Parliament of Religions opened, and I met kind friends, who helped me right along. I worked a little, collected funds, started two papers, and so on. After that I went over to England and worked there. At the same time I carried on the work for India in America too.

My plan for India, as it has been developed and centralised, is this: I have told you of our lives as monks there, how we go from door to door, so that religion is brought to everybody without charge, except, perhaps, a broken piece of bread. That is why you see the lowest of the low in India holding the most exalted religious ideas. It is all through the work of these monks. But ask a man, "Who are the English?"— he does not know. He says perhaps, "They are the children of those giants they speak of in those books, are they not?" "Who governs you?" "We do not know." "What is the government?" They do not know. But they know philosophy. It is a practical want of intellectual education about life on this earth they suffer from. These millions and millions of people are ready for life beyond this world — is not that enough for them? Certainly not. They must have a better piece of bread and a better piece of rag on their bodies. The great question is: How to get that better bread and better rag for these sunken millions.

First, I must tell you, there is great hope for them, because, you see, they are the gentlest people on earth. Not that they are timid. When they want to fight, they fight like demons. The best soldiers the English have are recruited from the peasantry of India. Death is a thing of no importance to them. Their attitude is "Twenty times I have died before, and I shall die many times after this. What of that?" They never turn back. They are not given to much emotion, but they make very good fighters.

Their instinct, however, is to plough. If you rob them, murder them, tax them, do anything to them, they will be quiet and gentle, so long as you leave them free to practise their religion. They never interfere with the religion of others. "Leave us liberty to worship our gods, and take everything else!" That is their attitude. When the English touch them there, trouble starts. That was the real cause of the 1857 Mutiny — they would not bear religious repression. The great Mohammedan governments were simply blown up because they touched the Indians' religion.

But aside from that, they are very peaceful, very quiet, very gentle, and, above all, not given to vice. The absence of any strong drink, oh, it makes them infinitely superior to the mobs of any other country. You cannot compare the decency of life among the poor in India with life in the slums here. A slum means poverty, but poverty does not mean sin, indecency, and vice in India. In other countries, the opportunities are such that only the indecent and the lazy need be poor. There is no reason for poverty unless one is a fool or a blackguard — the sort who want city life and all its luxuries. They will not go into the country. They say, "We are here with all the fun, and you must give us bread". But that is not the case in India, where the poor fellows work hard from morning to sunset, and somebody else takes the bread out of their hands, and their children go hungry. Notwithstanding the millions of tons of wheat raised in India, scarcely a grain passes the mouth of a peasant. He lives upon the poorest corn, which you would not feed to your canary-birds.

Now there is no reason why they should suffer such distress — these people; oh, so pure and good! We hear so much talk about the sunken millions and the degraded women of India — but none come to our help. What do they say? They say, "You can only be helped, you can only be good by ceasing to be what you are. It is useless to help Hindus." These people do not know the history of races. There will be no more India if they change their religion and their institutions, because that is the vitality of that race. It will disappear; so, really, you will have nobody to help.

Then there is the other great point to learn: that you can never help really. What can we do for each other? You are growing in your own life, I am growing in my own. It is possible that I can give you a push in your life, knowing that, in the long run, all roads lead to Rome. It is a steady growth. No national civilisation is perfect yet. Give that civilisation a push, and it will arrive at its own goal: do not strive to change it. Take away a nation's institutions, customs, and manners, and what will be left? They hold the nation together.

But here comes the very learned foreign man, and he says, "Look here; you give up all those institutions and customs of thousands of years, and take my tomfool tinpot and be happy". This is all nonsense.

We will have to help each other, but we have to go one step farther: the first thing is to become unselfish in help. "If you do just what I tell you to do, I will help you; otherwise not." Is that help?

And so, if the Hindus want to help you spiritually, there will be no question of limitations: perfect unselfishness. I give, and there it ends. It is gone from me. My mind, my powers, my everything that I have to give, is given: given with the idea to give, and no more. I have seen many times people who have robbed half the world, and they gave $20,000 "to convert the heathen".

What for? For the benefit of the heathen, or for their own souls? Just think of that.

And the Nemesis of crime is working. We men

try to hoodwink our own eyes. But inside the heart, He has remained, the real Self. He never forgets. We can never delude Him. His eyes will never be hoodwinked. Whenever there is any impulse of real charity, it tells, though it be at the end of a thousand years. Obstructed, it yet wakens once more to burst like a thunderbolt. And every impulse where the motive is selfish, self-seeking — though it may be launched forth with all the newspapers blazoning, all the mobs standing and cheering — it fails to reach the mark.

I am not taking pride in this. But, mark you, I have told the story of that group of boys. Today there is not a village, not a man, not a woman in India that does not know their work and bless them. There is not a famine in the land where these boys do not plunge in and try to work and rescue as many as they can. And that strikes to the heart. The people come to know it. So help whenever you can, but mind what your motive is. If it is selfish, it will neither benefit those you help, nor yourself. If it is unselfish, it will bring blessings upon them to whom it is given, and infinite blessings upon you, sure as you are living. The Lord can never be hoodwinked. The law of Karma can never be hoodwinked.

Well then, my plans are, therefore, to reach these masses of India. Suppose you start schools all over India for the poor, still you cannot educate them. How can you? The boy of four years would better go to the plough or to work, than to your school. He cannot go to your school. It is impossible. Self-preservation is the first instinct. But if the mountain does not go to Mohammed, then Mohammed can come to the mountain. Why should not education go from door to door, say I. If a ploughman's boy cannot come to education, why not meet him at the plough, at the factory, just wherever he is? Go along with him, like his shadow. But there are these hundreds and thousands of monks, educating the people on the spiritual plane; why not let these men do the same work on the intellectual plane? Why should they not talk to the masses a little about history — about many things? The ears are the best educators. The best principles in our lives were those which we heard from our mothers through our ears.

Books came much later. Book-learning is nothing. Through the ears we get the best formative principles. Then, as they get more and more interested, they may come to your books too. First, let it roll on and on — that is my idea.

Well, I must tell you that I am not a very great believer in monastic systems. They have great merits, and also great defects. There should be a perfect balance between the monastics and the householders. But monasticism has absorbed all the power in India. We represent the greatest power. The monk is greater than the prince. There is no reigning sovereign in India who dares to sit down when the "yellow cloth" is there. He gives up his seat and stands. Now, that is bad, so much power, even in the hands of good men — although these monastics have been the bulwark of the people. They stand between the priestcraft and knowledge. They are the centres of knowledge and reform. They are just what the prophets were among the Jews. The prophets were always preaching against the priests, trying to throw out superstitions. So are they in India. But all the same so much power is not good there; better methods should be worked out. But you can only work in the line of least resistance. The whole national soul there is upon monasticism. You go to India and preach any religion as a householder: the Hindu people will turn back and go out. If you have given up the world, however, they say, "He is good, he has given up the world. He is a sincere man, he wants to do what he preaches." What I mean to say is this, that it represents a tremendous power. What we can do is just to transform it, give it another form. This tremendous power in the hands of the roving Sannyasins of India has got to be transformed, and it will raise the masses up.

Now, you see, we have brought the plan down nicely on paper; but I have taken it, at the same time, from the regions of idealism. So far the plan was loose and idealistic. As years went on, it became more and more condensed and accurate; I began to see by actual working its defects, and all that.

What did I discover in its working on the material plane? First, there must be centres to educate these monks in the method of education. For instance,

I send one of my men, and he goes about with a camera: he has to be taught in those things himself. In India, you will find every man is quite illiterate, and that teaching requires tremendous centres. And what does all that mean? Money. From the idealistic plane you come to everyday work. Well, I have worked hard, four years in your country, and two in England. And I am very thankful that some friends came to the rescue. One who is here today with you is amongst them. There are American friends and English friends who went over with me to India, and there has been a very rude beginning. Some English people came and joined the orders. One poor man worked hard and died in India. There are an Englishman and an Englishwoman who have retired; they have some means of their own, and they have started a centre in the Himalayas, educating the children. I have given them one of the papers I have started — a copy you will find there on the table — the Awakened India. And there they are instructing and working among the people. I have another centre in Calcutta. Of course, all great movements must proceed from the capital. For what is a capital? It is the heart of a nation. All the blood comes into the heart and thence it is distributed; so all the wealth, all the ideas, all the education, all spirituality will converge towards the capital and spread from it.

I am glad to tell you I have made a rude beginning. But the same work I want to do, on parallel lines, for women. And my principle is: each one helps himself. My help is from a distance. There are Indian women, English women, and I hope American women will come to take up the task. As soon as they have begun, I wash my hands of it. No man shall dictate to a woman; nor a woman to a man. Each one is independent. What bondage there may be is only that of love. Women will work out their own destinies — much better, too, than men can ever do for them. All the mischief to women has come because men undertook to shape the destiny of women. And I do not want to start with any initial mistake. One little mistake made then will go on multiplying; and if you succeed, in the long run that mistake will have assumed gigantic proportions and become hard to correct. So, if I made this mistake of employing men to work out this women's part of the work, why, women will never get rid of that — it will have become a custom. But I have got an opportunity. I told you of the lady who was my Master's wife. We have all great respect for her. She never dictates to us. So it is quite safe.

That part has to be accomplished.

DISCIPLESHIP

Delivered in San Francisco, on March 29, 1900.

My subject is "Discipleship". I do not know how you will take what I have to say. It will be rather difficult for you to accept it — the ideals of teachers and disciples in this country vary so much from those in ours. An old proverb of India comes to my mind: "There are hundreds of thousands of teachers, but it is hard to find one disciple." It seems to be true. The one important thing in the attainment of spirituality is the attitude of the pupil. When the right attitude is there, illumination comes easily.

What does the disciple need in order to receive the truth? The great sages say that to attain truth takes but the twinkling of an eye — it is just a question of knowing — the dream breaks. How long does it take? In a second the dream is gone. When the illusion vanishes, how long does it take? Just the twinkling of an eye. When I know the truth, nothing happens except that the falsehood vanishes away: I took the rope for the snake, and now I see it is the rope. It is only a question of half a second and the whole thing is done. Thou art That. Thou art the Reality. How long does it take to know this? If we are God and always have been so, not to know this is most astonishing. To know this is the only natural thing. It should not take ages to find out what we have always been and what we now are.

Yet it seems difficult to realise this self-evident truth. Ages and ages pass before we begin to catch a faint glimpse of it. God is life; God is truth. We write about this; we feel in our inmost heart that this is so, that everything else than God is nothing — here today, gone tomorrow. And yet most of us remain the same all through life. We cling to untruth, and we turn our back upon truth. We do not want to attain truth. We do not want anyone to break our dream. You see, the teachers are not wanted. Who wants to learn? But if anyone wants to realise the truth and overcome illusion, if he wants to receive the truth from a teacher, he must be a true disciple.

It is not easy to be a disciple; great preparations are necessary; many conditions have to be fulfilled. Four principal conditions are laid down by the Vedantists.

The first condition is that the student who wants to know the truth must give up all desires for gain in this world or in the life to come.

The truth is not what we see. What we see is not truth as long as any desire creeps into the mind. God is true, and the world is not true. So long as there is in the heart the least desire for the world, truth will not come. Let the world fall to ruin around my ears: I do not care. So with the next life; I do not care to go to heaven. What is heaven? Only the continuation of this earth. We would be better and the little foolish dreams we are dreaming would break sooner if there were no heaven, no continuation of this silly life on earth. By going to heaven we only prolong the miserable illusions.

What do you gain in heaven? You become gods, drink nectar, and get rheumatism. There is less misery there than on earth, but also less truth. The very rich can understand truth much less than the poorer people. "It is easier for a camel to go through the eye of a needle, than for a rich man to enter into the kingdom of God." The rich man has no time to think of anything beyond his wealth and power, his comforts and indulgences. The rich rarely become religious. Why? Because they think, if they become religious, they will have no more fun in life. In the same way, there is very little chance to become spiritual in heaven; there is too much comfort and enjoyment there — the dwellers in heaven are disinclined to give up their fun.

They say there will be no more weeping in heaven. I do not trust the man who never weeps; he has a big block of granite where the heart should be. It is evident that the heavenly people have not much sympathy. There are vast masses of them over there, and we are miserable creatures suffering in this horrible place. They could pull us all out of it; but they do not. They do not weep. There is no sorrow or misery there; therefore they do not care for anyone's misery. They drink their nectar, dances go on; beautiful wives and all that.

Going beyond these things, the disciple should say, "I do not care for anything in this life nor for all the heavens that have ever existed — i do not care to go to any of them. I do not want the sense-life in any form — this identification of myself with the body — as I feel now, 'I am this body — this huge mass of flesh.' This is what I feel I am. I refuse to believe that."

The world and the heavens, all these are bound up with the senses. You do not care for the earth if you do not have any senses. Heaven also is the world. Earth, heaven, and all that is between have but one name — earth.

Therefore the disciple, knowing the past and the present and thinking of the future, knowing what prosperity means, what happiness means, gives up all these and seeks to know the truth and truth alone. This is the first condition.

The second condition is that the disciple must be able to control the internal and the external senses and must be established in several other spiritual virtues.

The external senses are the visible organs situated in different parts of the body; the internal senses are intangible. We have the external eyes, ears, nose, and so on; and we have the corresponding internal senses. We are continually at the beck and call of both these groups of senses. Corresponding to the senses are sense-objects. If any sense-objects are near by, the senses compel us to perceive them; we have no choice or independence. There is the big nose. A little fragrance is there; I have to smell it. If there were a bad odour, I would say to myself,

"Do not smell it"; but nature says, "Smell", and I smell it. Just think what we have become! We have bound ourselves. I have eyes. Anything going on, good or bad, I must see. It is the same with hearing. If anyone speaks unpleasantly to me, I must hear it. My sense of hearing compels me to do so, and how miserable I feel! Curse or praise — man has got to hear. I have seen many deaf people who do not usually hear, but anything about themselves they always hear!

All these senses, external and internal, must be under the disciple's control. By hard practice he has to arrive at the stage where he can assert his mind against the senses, against the commands of nature. He should be able to say to his mind, "You are mine; I order you, do not see or hear anything", and the mind will not see or hear anything — no form or sound will react on the mind. In that state the mind has become free of the domination of the senses, has become separated from them. No longer is it attached to the senses and the body. The external things cannot order the mind now; the mind refuses to attach itself to them. Beautiful fragrance is there. The disciple says to the mind, "Do not smell", and the mind does not perceive the fragrance. When you have arrived at that point, you are just beginning to be a disciple. That is why when everybody says, "I know the truth", I say, "If you know the truth, you must have self-control; and if you have control of yourself, show it by controlling these organs."

Next, the mind must be made to quiet down. It is rushing about. Just as I sit down to meditate, all the vilest subjects in the world come up. The whole thing is nauseating. Why should the mind think thoughts I do not want it to think? I am as it were a slave to the mind. No spiritual knowledge is possible so long as the mind is restless and out of control. The disciple has to learn to control the mind. Yes, it is the function of the mind to think. But it must not think if the disciple does not want it to; it must stop thinking when he commands it to. To qualify as a disciple, this state of the mind is very necessary.

Also, the disciple must have great power of endurance. Life seems comfortable; and you find the mind behaves well when everything is going well with you. But if something goes wrong, your mind loses its balance. That is not good. Bear all evil and misery without one murmur of hurt, without one thought of unhappiness, resistance, remedy, or retaliation. That is true endurance; and that you must acquire.

Good and evil there always are in the world. Many forget there is any evil — at least they try to forget; and when evil comes upon them, they are overwhelmed by it and feel bitter. There are others who deny that there is any evil at all and consider everything good. That also is a weakness; that also proceeds from a fear of evil. If something is evil-smelling, why sprinkle it with rose water and call it fragrant? Yes, there are good and evil in the world — god has put evil in the world. But you do not have to whitewash Him. Why there is evil is none of your business. Please have faith and keep quiet.

When my Master, Shri Ramakrishna fell ill, a Brahmin suggested to him that he apply his tremendous mental power to cure himself. He said that if my Master would only concentrate his mind on the diseased part of the body, it would heal. Shri Ramakrishna answered, "What! Bring down the mind that I've given to God to this little body!" He refused to think of body and illness. His mind was continually conscious of God; it was dedicated to Him utterly. He would not use it for any other purpose.

This craving for health, wealth, long life, and the like — the so-called good — is nothing but an illusion. To devote the mind to them in order to secure them only strengthens the delusion. We have these dreams and illusions in life, and we want to have more of them in the life to come, in heaven. More and more illusion. Resist not evil. Face it! You are higher than evil.

There is this misery in the world — it has to be suffered by someone. You cannot act without making evil for somebody. And when you seek worldly good, you only avoid an evil which must be suffered by somebody else. Everyone is trying to put it on someone else's shoulders. The disciple says, "Let the miseries of the world come to me; I shall endure them all. Let others go free."

Remember the man on the cross. He could have brought legions of angels to victory; but he did not resist. He pitied those who crucified him. He endured every humiliation and suffering. He took the burden of all upon himself: "Come unto me, all ye that labour and are heavy laden, and I will give you rest." Such is true endurance. How very high he was above this life, so high that we cannot understand it, we slaves! No sooner does a man slap me in the face than my hand hits back: bang, it goes! How can I understand the greatness and blessedness of the Glorified One? How can I see the glory of it?

But I will not drag the ideal down. I feel I am the body, resisting evil. If I get a headache, I go all over the world to have it cured; I drink two thousand bottles of medicine. How can I understand these marvellous minds? I can see the ideal, but how much of that ideal? None of this consciousness of the body, of the little self, of its pleasures and pains, its hurts and comforts, none of these can reach that atmosphere. By thinking only of the spirit and keeping the mind out of matter all the time, I can catch a glimpse of that ideal. Material thought and forms of the sense-world have no place in that ideal. Take them off and put the mind upon the spirit. Forget your life and death, your pains and pleasures, your name and fame, and realise that you are neither body nor mind but the pure spirit.

When I say "I", I mean this spirit. Close your eyes and see what picture appears when you think of your "I". Is it the picture of your body that comes, or of your mental nature? If so, you have not realised your true "I" yet. The time will come, however, when as soon as you say "I" you will see the universe, the Infinite Being. Then you will have realised your true Self and found that you are infinite. That is the truth: you are the spirit, you are not matter. There is such a thing as illusion — in it one thing is taken for another: matter is taken for spirit, this body for soul. That is the tremendous illusion. It has to go.

The next qualification is that the disciple must have faith in the Guru (teacher). In the West the teacher simply gives intellectual knowledge; that is all. The relationship with the teacher is the greatest in life. My dearest and nearest relative in life is my Guru; next, my mother; then my father. My first reverence is to the Guru. If my father says, "Do this", and my Guru says, "Do not do this", I do not do it. The Guru frees my soul. The father and mother give me this body; but the Guru gives me rebirth in the soul.

We have certain peculiar beliefs. One of these is that there are some souls, a few exceptional ones, who are already free and who will be born here for the good of the world, to help the world. They are free already; they do not care for their own salvation — they want to help others. They do not require to be taught anything. From their childhood they know everything; they may speak the highest truth even when they are babies six months old.

Upon these free souls depends the spiritual growth of mankind. They are like the first lamps from which other lamps are lighted. True, the light is in everyone, but in most men it is hidden. The great souls are shining lights from the beginning. Those who come in contact with them have as it were their own lamps lighted. By this the first lamp does not lose anything; yet it communicates its light to other lamps. A million lamps are lighted; but the first lamp goes on shining with undiminished light. The first lamp is the Guru, and the lamp that is lighted from it is the disciple. The second in turn becomes the Guru, and so on. These great ones whom you call Incarnations of God are mighty spiritual giants. They come and set in motion a tremendous spiritual current by transmitting their power to their immediate disciples and through them to generation after generation of disciples.

A bishop in the Christian Church, by the laying on of hands, claims to transmit the power which he is supposed to have received from the preceding bishops. The bishop says that Jesus Christ transmitted his power to his immediate disciples and they to others, and that that is how the Christ's power has come to him. We hold that every one of us, not bishops only, ought to have such power. There is no reason why each of you cannot be a vehicle of the mighty current of spirituality.

But first you must find a teacher, a true teacher, and you must remember that he is not just a man. You may get a teacher in the body; but the real teacher is not in the body; he is not the physical man — he is not as he appears to your eyes. It may be the teacher will come to you as a human being, and you will receive the power from him. Sometimes he will come in a dream and transmit things to the world. The power of the teacher may come to us in many ways. But for us ordinary mortals the teacher must come, and our preparation must go on till he comes.

We attend lectures and read books, argue and reason about God and soul, religion and salvation. These are not spirituality, because spirituality does not exist in books or theories or in philosophies. It is not in learning or reasoning, but in actual inner growth. Even parrots can learn things by heart and repeat them. If you become learned, what of it? Asses can carry whole libraries. So when real light will come, there will be no more of this learning from books — no book-learning. The man who cannot write even his own name can be perfectly religious, and the man with all the libraries of the world in his head may fail to be. Learning is not a condition of spiritual growth; scholarship is not a condition. The touch of the Guru, the transmittal of spiritual energy, will quicken your heart. Then will begin the growth. That is the real baptism by fire. No more stopping. You go on and go on.

Some years ago one of your Christian teachers, a friend of mine, said, "You believe in Christ?" "Yes," I answered, "but perhaps with a little more reverence." "Then why don't you be baptised?" How could I be baptised? By whom? Where is the man who can give true baptism? What is baptism? Is it sprinkling some water over you, or dipping you in water, while muttering formulas?

Baptism is the direct introduction into the life of the spirit. If you receive the real baptism, you know you are not the body but the spirit. Give me that baptism if you can. If not, you are not Christians. Even after the so-called baptism which you received, you have remained the same. What is the sense of merely saying you have been baptised in the name of the Christ? Mere talk, talk — ever disturbing the world with your foolishness! "Ever steeped in the darkness of ignorance, yet considering themselves wise and learned, the fools go round and round, staggering to and fro like the blind led by the blind."[1] Therefore do not say you are Christians, do not brag about baptism and things of that sort.

Of course there is true baptism — there was baptism in the beginning when the Christ came to the earth and taught. The illumined souls, the great ones that come to the earth from time to time, have the power to reveal the Supernal Vision to us. This is true baptism. You see, before the formulas and ceremonies of every religion, there exists the germ of universal truth. In course of time this truth becomes forgotten; it becomes as it were strangled by forms and ceremonies. The forms remain — we find there the casket with the spirit all gone. You have the form of baptism, but few can evoke the living spirit of baptism. The form will not suffice. If we want to gain the living knowledge of the living truth, we have to be truly initiated into it. That is the ideal.

The Guru must teach me and lead me into light, make me a link in that chain of which he himself is a link. The man in the street cannot claim to be a Guru. The Guru must be a man who has known, has actually realised the Divine truth, has perceived himself as the spirit. A mere talker cannot be the Guru. A talkative fool like me can talk much, but cannot be the Guru. A true Guru will tell the disciple, "Go and sin no more"; and no more can he sin, no more has the person the power to sin.

I have seen such men in this life. I have read the Bible and all such books; they are wonderful. But the living power you cannot find in the books. The power that can transform life in a moment can be found only in the living illumined souls, those shining lights who appear among us from time to time. They alone are fit to be Gurus. You and I are only hollow talk-talk, not teachers. We are disturbing

---

1. Katha Upanishad, I.ii.5.

the world more by talking, making bad vibrations. We hope and pray and struggle on, and the day will come when we shall arrive at the truth, and we shall not have to speak. "The teacher was a boy of sixteen; he taught a man of eighty. Silence was the method of the teacher; and the doubts of the disciple vanished for ever."[2] That is the Guru. Just think, if you find such a man, what faith and love you ought to have for that person! Why, he is God Himself, nothing less than that! That is why Christ's disciples worshipped him as God. The disciple must worship the Guru as God Himself. All a man can know is the living God, God as embodied in man, until he himself has realised God. How else would he know God?

Here is a man in America, born nineteen hundred years after Christ, who does not even belong to the same race as Christ, the Jewish race. He has not seen Jesus or his family. He says, "Jesus was God. If you do not believe it, you will go to hell". We can understand how the disciples believed it — that Christ was God; he was their Guru, and they must have believed he was God. But what has this American got to do with the man born nineteen hundred years ago? This young man tells me that I do not believe in Jesus and therefore I shall have to go to hell. What does he know of Jesus? He is fit for a lunatic asylum. This kind of belief will not do. He will have to find his Guru.

Jesus may be born again, may come to you. Then, if you worship him as God, you are all right. We must all wait till the Guru comes, and the Guru must be worshipped as God. He is God, he is nothing less than that. As you look at him, the Guru gradually melts away and what is left? The Guru picture gives place to God Himself. The Guru is the bright mask which God wears in order to come to us. As we look steadily on, gradually the mask falls off and God is revealed. "I bow to the Guru who is the embodiment of the Bliss Divine, the personification of the highest knowledge and the giver of the greatest beatitude, who is pure, perfect, one without a second, eternal, beyond pleasure and pain, beyond all thought and all qualification, transcendental". Such is in reality the Guru. No wonder the disciple looks upon him as God Himself and trusts him, reveres him, obeys him, follows him unquestioningly. This is the relation between the Guru and the disciple.

The next condition the disciple must fulfil is to conceive an extreme desire to be free.

We are like moths plunging into the flaming fire, knowing that it will burn us, knowing that the senses only burn us, that they only enhance desire. "Desire is never satiated by enjoyment; enjoyment only increases desire as butter fed into fire increases the fire."[3] Desire is increased by desire. Knowing all this, people still plunge into it all the time. Life after life they have been going after the objects of desire, suffering extremely in consequence, yet they cannot give up desire. Even religion, which should rescue them from this terrible bondage of desire, they have made a means of satisfying desire. Rarely do they ask God to free them from bondage to the body and senses, from slavery to desires. Instead, they pray to Him for health and prosperity, for long life: "O God, cure my headache, give me some money or something!"

The circle of vision has become so narrow, so degraded, so beastly, so animal! None is desiring anything beyond this body. Oh, the terrible degradation, the terrible misery of it! What little flesh, the five senses, the stomach! What is the world but a combination of stomach and sex? Look at millions of men and women — that is what they are living for. Take these away from them and they will find their life empty, meaningless, and intolerable. Such are we. And such is our mind; it is continually hankering for ways and means to satisfy the hunger of the stomach and sex. All the time this is going on. There is also endless suffering; these desires of the body bring only momentary satisfaction and endless suffering. It is like drinking a cup of which the surface layer is nectar, while underneath all is poison. But we still hanker for all these things.

What can be done? Renunciation of the senses and desires is the only way out of this misery. If you want to be spiritual, you must renounce. This is the

---

2. Dakshinamurti-stotram, 12 (adapted).

3. Bhagavata, IX.xix.14.

real test. Give up the world — this nonsense of the senses. There is only one real desire: to know what is true, to be spiritual. No more materialism, no more this egoism, I must become spiritual. Strong, intense must be the desire. If a man's hands and feet were so tied that he could not move and then if a burning piece of charcoal were placed on his body, he would struggle with all his power to throw it off. When I shall have that sort of extreme desire, that restless struggle, to throw off this burning world, then the time will have come for me to glimpse the Divine Truth.

Look at me. If I lose my little pocketbook with two or three dollars in it, I go twenty times into the house to find that pocketbook. The anxiety, the worry, and the struggle! If one of you crosses me, I remember it twenty years, I cannot forgive and forget it. For the little things of the senses I can struggle like that. Who is there that struggles for God that way? "Children forget everything in their play. The young are mad after the enjoyment of the senses; they do not care for anything else. The old are brooding over their past misdeeds" (Shankara). They are thinking of their past enjoyments — old men that cannot have any enjoyment. Chewing the cud — that is the best they can do. None crave for the Lord in the same intense spirit with which they crave for the things of the senses.

They all say that God is the Truth, the only thing that really exists; that spirit alone is, not matter. Yet the things they seek of God are rarely spirit. They ask always for material things. In their prayers spirit is not separated from matter. Degradation — that is what religion has turned out to be. The whole thing is becoming sham. And the years are rolling on and nothing spiritual is being attained. But man should hunger for one thing alone, the spirit, because spirit alone exists. That is the ideal. If you cannot attain it now, say, "I cannot do it; that is the ideal, I know, but I cannot follow it yet." But that is not what you do. You degrade religion to your low level and seek matter in the name of spirit. You are all atheists. You do not believe in anything except the senses. "So-and-so said such-and-such — there may be something in it. Let us try and have the fun. Possibly some benefit will come; possibly my broken leg will get straight."

Miserable are the diseased people; they are great worshippers of the Lord, for they hope that if they pray to Him He will heal them. Not that that is altogether bad — if such prayers are honest and if they remember that that is not religion. Shri Krishna says in the Gita (VII.16), "Four classes of people worship Me: the distressed, the seeker of material things, the inquirer, and the knower of truth." People who are in distress approach God for relief. If they are ill, they worship Him to be healed; if they lose their wealth, they pray to Him to get it back. There are other people who ask Him for all kinds of things, because they are full of desires — name, fame, wealth, position and so on. They will say, "O Virgin Mary, I will make an offering to you if I get what I want. If you are successful in granting my prayer, I will worship God and give you a part of everything." Men not so material as that, but still with no faith in God, feel inclined to know about Him. They study philosophies, read scriptures, listen to lectures, and so on. They are the inquirers. The last class are those who worship God and know Him. All these four classes of people are good, not bad. All of them worship Him.

But we are trying to be disciples. Our sole concern is to know the highest truth. Our goal is the loftiest. We have said big words to ourselves — absolute realisation and all that. Let us measure up to the words. Let us worship the spirit in spirit, standing on spirit. Let the foundation be spirit, the middle spirit, the culmination spirit. There will be no world anywhere. Let it go and whirl into space — who cares? Stand thou in the spirit! That is the goal. We know we cannot reach it yet. Never mind. Do not despair, and do not drag the ideal down. The important thing is: how much less you think of the body, of yourself as matter — as dead, dull, insentient matter; how much more you think of yourself as shining immortal being. The more you think of yourself as shining immortal spirit, the more eager you will be to be absolutely free of matter, body, and senses. This is the intense desire to be free.

The fourth and last condition of discipleship is

the discrimination of the real from the unreal. There is only one thing that is real — god. All the time the mind must be drawn to Him, dedicated to Him. God exists, nothing else exists, everything else comes and goes. Any desire for the world is illusion, because the world is unreal. More and more the mind must become conscious of God alone, until everything else appears as it really is — unreal.

These are the four conditions which one who wants to be a disciple must fulfil; without fulfilling them he will not be able to come in contact with the true Guru. And even if he is fortunate enough to find him, he will not be quickened by the power that the Guru may transmit. There cannot be any compromising of these conditions. With the fulfilment of these conditions — with all these preparations — the lotus of the disciple's heart will open, and the bee shall come. Then the disciple knows that the Guru was within the body, within himself. He opens out. He realises. He crosses the ocean of life, goes beyond. He crosses this terrible ocean: and in mercy, without a thought of gain or praise, he in his turn helps others to cross.

IS VEDANTA THE FUTURE RELIGION?

Delivered in San Francisco on April 8, 1900.

Those of you who have been attending my lectures for the last month or so must, by this time, be familiar with the ideas contained in the Vedanta philosophy. Vedanta is the most ancient religion of the world; but it can never be said to have become popular. Therefore the question "Is it going to be the religion of the future?" is very difficult to answer.

At the start, I may tell you that I do not know whether it will ever be the religion of the vast majority of men. Will it ever be able to take hold of one whole nation such as the United States of America? Possibly it may. However, that is the question we want to discuss this afternoon.

I shall begin by telling you what Vedanta is not, and then I shall tell you what it is. But you must remember that, with all its emphasis on impersonal principles, Vedanta is not antagonistic to anything, though it does not compromise or give up the truths which it considers fundamental.

You all know that certain things are necessary to make a religion. First of all, there is the book. The power of the book is simply marvellous! Whatever it be, the book is the centre round which human allegiance gathers. Not one religion is living today but has a book. With all its rationalism and tall talk, humanity still clings to the books. In your country every attempt to start a religion without a book has failed. In India sects rise with great success, but within a few years they die down, because there is no book behind them. So in every other country.

Study the rise and fall of the Unitarian movement. It represents the best thought of your nation. Why should it not have spread like the Methodist, Baptist, and other Christian denominations? Because there was no book. On the other hand, think of the Jews. A handful of men, driven from one country to another, still hold together, because they have a book. Think of the Parsees — only a hundred thousand in the world. About a million are all that remain of the Jains in India. And do you know that these handfuls of Parsees and Jains still keep on just because of their books? The religions that are living at the present day — every one of them has a book.

The second requisite, to make a religion, is veneration for some person. He is worshipped either as the Lord of the world or as the great Teacher. Men must worship some embodied man! They must have the Incarnation or the prophet or the great leader. You find it in every religion today. Hindus and Christians — they have Incarnations: Buddhists, Mohammedans, and Jews have prophets. But it is all about the same — all their veneration twines round some person or persons.

The third requisite seems to be that a religion, to be strong and sure of itself, must believe that it alone is the truth; otherwise it cannot influence people.

Liberalism dies because it is dry, because it cannot rouse fanaticism in the human mind, because it cannot bring out hatred for everything except itself. That is why liberalism is bound to go down again and again. It can influence only small numbers of people. The reason is not hard to see. Liberalism tries to make us unselfish. But we do not want to be unselfish — we see no immediate gain in unselfishness; we gain more by being selfish. We accept liberalism as long as we are poor, have nothing. The moment we acquire money and power, we turn very conservative. The poor man is a democrat. When he becomes rich, he becomes an aristocrat. In religion, too, human nature acts in the same way.

A prophet arises, promises all kinds of rewards to those who will follow him and eternal doom to those who will not. Thus he makes his ideas spread. All existent religions that are spreading are tremendously fanatic. The more a sect hates other sects, the greater is its success and the more people it draws into its fold. My conclusion, after travelling over a good part of the world and living with many races, and in view of the conditions prevailing in the world, is that the present state of things is going to continue, in spite of much talk of universal brotherhood.

Vedanta does not believe in any of these teachings. First, it does not believe in a book — that is the difficulty to start with. It denies the authority of any book over any other book. It denies emphatically that any one book can contain all the truths about God, soul, the ultimate reality. Those of you who have read the Upanishads remember that they say again and again, "Not by the reading of books can we realise the Self."

Second, it finds veneration for some particular person still more difficult to uphold. Those of you who are students of Vedanta — by Vedanta is always meant the Upanishads — know that this is the only religion that does not cling to any person. Not one man or woman has ever become the object of worship among the Vedantins. It cannot be. A man is no more worthy of worship than any bird, any worm. We are all brothers. The difference is only in degree. I am exactly the same as the lowest worm. You see how very little room there is in Vedanta for any man to stand ahead of us and for us to go and worship him — he dragging us on and we being saved by him. Vedanta does not give you that. No book, no man to worship, nothing.

A still greater difficulty is about God. You want to be democratic in this country. It is the democratic God that Vedanta teaches.

You have a government, but the government is impersonal. Yours is not an autocratic government, and yet it is more powerful than any monarchy in the world. Nobody seems to understand that the real power, the real life, the real strength is in the unseen, the impersonal, the nobody. As a mere person separated from others, you are nothing, but as an impersonal unit of the nation that rules itself, you are tremendous. You are all one in the government — you are a tremendous power. But where exactly is the power? Each man is the power. There is no king. I see everybody equally the same. I have not to take off my hat and bow low to anyone. Yet there is a tremendous power in each man.

Vedanta is just that. Its God is not the monarch sitting on a throne, entirely apart. There are those who like their God that way — a God to be feared and propitiated. They burn candles and crawl in the dust before Him. They want a king to rule them — they believe in a king in heaven to rule them all. The king is gone from this country at least. Where is the king of heaven now? Just where the earthly king is. In this country the king has entered every one of you. You are all kings in this country. So with the religion of Vedanta. You are all Gods. One God is not sufficient. You are all Gods, says the Vedanta.

This makes Vedanta very difficult. It does not teach the old idea of God at all. In place of that God who sat above the clouds and managed the affairs of the world without asking our permission, who created us out of nothing just because He liked it and made us undergo all this misery just because He liked it, Vedanta teaches the God that is in everyone, has become everyone and everything. His majesty the king has gone from this country; the Kingdom of Heaven went from Vedanta hundreds of years ago.

India cannot give up his majesty the king of

the earth — that is why Vedanta cannot become the religion of India. There is a chance of Vedanta becoming the religion of your country because of democracy. But it can become so only if you can and do clearly understand it, if you become real men and women, not people with vague ideas and superstitions in your brains, and if you want to be truly spiritual, since Vedanta is concerned only with spirituality.

What is the idea of God in heaven? Materialism. The Vedantic idea is the infinite principle of God embodied in every one of us. God sitting up on a cloud! Think of the utter blasphemy of it! It is materialism — downright materialism. When babies think this way, it may be all right, but when grown-up men try to teach such things, it is downright disgusting — that is what it is. It is all matter, all body idea, the gross idea, the sense idea. Every bit of it is clay and nothing but clay. Is that religion? It is no more religion than is the Mumbo Jumbo "religion" of Africa. God is spirit and He should be worshipped in spirit and in truth. Does spirit live only in heaven? What is spirit? We are all spirit. Why is it we do not realise it? What makes you different from me? Body and nothing else. Forget the body, and all is spirit.

These are what Vedanta has not to give. No book. No man to be singled out from the rest of mankind —"You are worms, and we are the Lord God!"— none of that. If you are the Lord God, I also am the Lord God. So Vedanta knows no sin. There are mistakes but no sin; and in the long run everything is going to be all right. No Satan — none of this nonsense. Vedanta believes in only one sin, only one in the world, and it is this: the moment you think you are a sinner or anybody is a sinner, that is sin. From that follows every other mistake or what is usually called sin. There have been many mistakes in our lives. But we are going on. Glory be unto us that we have made mistakes! Take a long look at your past life. If your present condition is good, it has been caused by all the past mistakes as well as successes. Glory be unto success! Glory be unto mistakes! Do not look back upon what has been done. Go ahead!

You see, Vedanta proposes no sin nor sinner. No God to be afraid of. He is the one being of whom we shall never be afraid, because He is our own Self. There is only one being of whom you cannot possibly be afraid; He is that. Then is not he really the most superstitious person who has fear of God? There may be someone who is afraid of his shadow; but even he is not afraid of himself. God is man's very Self. He is that one being whom you can never possibly fear. What is all this nonsense, the fear of the Lord entering into a man, making him tremble and so on? Lord bless us that we are not all in the lunatic asylum! But if most of us are not lunatics, why should we invent such ideas as fear of God? Lord Buddha said that the whole human race is lunatic, more or less. It is perfectly true, it seems.

No book, no person, no Personal God. All these must go. Again, the senses must go. We cannot be bound to the senses. At present we are tied down — like persons dying of cold in the glaciers. They feel such a strong desire to sleep, and when their friends try to wake them, warning them of death, they say, "Let me die, I want to sleep." We all cling to the little things of the senses, even if we are ruined thereby: we forget there are much greater things.

There is a Hindu legend that the Lord was once incarnated on earth as a pig. He had a pig mate and in course of time several little pigs were born to Him. He was very happy with His family, living in the mire, squealing with joy, forgetting His divine glory and lordship. The gods became exceedingly concerned and came to the earth to beg Him to give up the pig body and return to heaven. But the Lord would have none of that; He drove them away. He said He was very happy and did not want to be disturbed. Seeing no other course, the gods destroyed the pig body of the Lord. At once He regained His divine majesty and was astonished that He could have found any joy in being a pig.

People behave in the same way. Whenever they hear of the Impersonal God, they say, "What will become of my individuality?— my individuality will go!" Next time that thought comes, remember the pig, and then think what an infinite mine of happiness you have, each one of you. How pleased you are with your present condition! But when you realise what you truly are, you will be astonished that you were unwilling to give up your sense-life. What is there in your personality? It is any better than that pig life? And this you do not want to give up! Lord bless us all!

What does Vedanta teach us? In the first place, it teaches that you need not even go out of yourself to know the truth. All the past and all the future are here in the present. No man ever saw the past. Did any one of you see the past? When you think you are knowing the past, you only imagine the past in the present moment. To see the future, you would have to bring it down to the present, which is the only reality — the rest is imagination. This present is all that is. There is only the One. All is here right now. One moment in infinite time is quite as complete and all-inclusive as every other moment. All that is and was and will be is here in the present. Let anybody try to imagine anything outside of it — he will not succeed.

What religion can paint a heaven which is not like this earth? And it is all art, only this art is being made known to us gradually. We, with five senses, look upon this world and find it gross, having colour, form, sound, and the like. Suppose I develop an electric sense — all will change. Suppose my senses grow finer — you will all appear changed. If I change, you change. If I go beyond the power of the senses, you will appear as spirit and God. Things are not what they seem.

We shall understand this by and by, and then see it: all the heavens — everything — are here, now, and they really are nothing but appearances on the Divine Presence. This Presence is much greater than all the earths and heavens. People think that this world is bad and imagine that heaven is somewhere else. This world is not bad. It is God Himself if you know it. It is a hard thing even to understand, harder than to believe. The murderer who is going to be hanged tomorrow is all God, perfect God. It is very hard to understand, surely; but it can be understood.

Therefore Vedanta formulates, not universal brotherhood, but universal oneness. I am the same as any other man, as any animal — good, bad, anything. It is one body, one mind, one soul throughout. Spirit never dies. There is no death anywhere, not even for the body. Not even the mind dies. How can even the body die? One leaf may fall — does the tree die? The universe is my body. See how it continues. All minds are mine. With all feet I walk. Through all mouths I speak. In everybody I reside.

Why can I not feel it? Because of that individuality, that piggishness. You have become bound up with this mind and can only be here, not there. What is immortality? How few reply, "It is this very existence of ours!" Most people think this is all mortal and dead — that God is not here, that they will become immortal by going to heaven. They imagine that they will see God after death. But if they do not see Him here and now, they will not see Him after death. Though they all believe in immortality, they do not know that immortality is not gained by dying and going to heaven, but by giving up this piggish individuality, by not tying ourselves down to one little body. Immortality is knowing ourselves as one with all, living in all bodies, perceiving through all minds. We are bound to feel in other bodies than this one. We are bound to feel in other bodies. What is sympathy? Is there any limit to this sympathy, this feeling in our bodies? It is quite possible that the time will come when I shall feel through the whole universe.

What is the gain? The pig body is hard to give up; we are sorry to lose the enjoyment of our one little pig body! Vedanta does not say, "Give it up": it says, "Transcend it". No need of asceticism — better would be the enjoyment of two bodies, better three, living in more bodies than one! When I can enjoy through the whole universe, the whole universe is my body.

There are many who feel horrified when they hear these teachings. They do not like to be told that they are not just little pig bodies, created by a tyrant God. I tell them, "Come up!" They say they are born in sin — they cannot come up except through someone's grace. I say, "You are Divine! They answer, "You blasphemer, how dare you speak so? How can a miserable creature be God? We are sinners!" I get very much discouraged at times, you know. Hundreds of men and women tell me, "If there is no hell, how can there be any religion?" If these people go to hell of their own will, who can prevent them?

Whatever you dream and think of, you create. If it is hell, you die and see hell. If it is evil and Satan, you get a Satan. If ghosts, you get ghosts. Whatever you think, that you become. If you have to think, think good thoughts, great thoughts. This taking for granted that you are weak little worms! By declaring we are weak, we become weak, we do not become better. Suppose we put out the light, close the windows, and call the room dark. Think of the nonsense! What good does it do me to say I am a sinner? If I am in the dark, let me light a lamp. The whole thing is gone. Yet how curious is the nature of men! Though always conscious that the universal mind is behind their life, they think more of Satan, of darkness and lies. You tell them the truth — they do not see it; they like darkness better.

This forms the one great question asked by Vedanta: Why are people so afraid? The answer is that they have made themselves helpless and dependent on others. We are so lazy, we do not want to do anything for ourselves. We want a Personal God, a saviour or a prophet to do everything for us. The very rich man never walks, always goes in the carriage; but in the course of years, he wakes up one day paralysed all over. Then he begins to feel that the way he had lived was not good after all. No man can walk for me. Every time one did, it was to my injury. If everything is done for a man by another, he will lose the use of his own limbs. Anything we do ourselves, that is the only thing we do. Anything that is done for us by another never can be ours. You cannot learn spiritual truths from my lectures. If you have learnt anything, I was only the spark that brought it out, made it flash. That is all the prophets and teachers can do. All this running after help is foolishness.

You know, there are bullock carts in India. Usually two bulls are harnessed to a cart, and sometimes a sheaf of straw is dangled at the tip of the pole, a little in front of the animals but beyond their reach. The bulls try continually to feed upon the straw, but never succeed. This is exactly how we are helped! We think we are going to get security, strength, wisdom, happiness from the outside. We always hope but never realise our hope. Never does any help come from the outside.

There is no help for man. None ever was, none is, and none will be. Why should there be? Are you not men and women? Are the lords of the earth to be helped by others? Are you not ashamed? You will be helped when you are reduced to dust. But you are spirit. Pull yourself out of difficulties by yourself! Save yourself by yourself! There is none to help you — never was. To think that there is, is sweet delusion. It comes to no good.

There came a Christian to me once and said, "You are a terrible sinner." I answered, "Yes, I am. Go on." He was a Christian missionary. That man would not give me any rest. When I see him, I fly. He said, "I have very good things for you. You are a sinner and you are going to hell." I replied, "Very good, what else?" I asked him, "Where are you going?" "I am going to heaven", he answered. I said, "I will go to hell." That day he gave me up.

Here comes a Christian man and he says, "You are all doomed; but if you believe in this doctrine, Christ will help you out." If this were true — but of course it is nothing but superstition — there would be no wickedness in the Christian countries. Let us believe in it — believing costs nothing — but why is there no result? If I ask, "Why is it that there are so many wicked people?" they say, "We have to work more." Trust in God, but keep your powder dry! Pray to God, and let God come and help you out! But it is I who struggle, pray, and worship; it is I who work out my problems — and God takes the credit. This is not good. I never do it.

Once I was invited to a dinner. The hostess asked me to say grace. I said, "I will say grace to you, madam. My grace and thanks are to you." When I work, I say grace to myself. Praise be unto me that I worked hard and acquired what I have!

All the time you work hard and bless somebody else, because you are superstitious, you are afraid. No more of these superstitions bred through thousands of years! It takes a little hard work to become spiritual. Superstitions are all materialism, because they are all based on the consciousness of body, body, body. No spirit there. Spirit has no superstitions — it is beyond the vain desires of the body.

But here and there these vain desires are being projected even into the realm of the spirit. I have attended several spiritualistic meetings. In one, the leader was a woman. She said to me, "Your mother and grandfather came to me" She said that they greeted her and talked to her. But my mother is living yet! People like to think that even after death their relatives continue to exist in the same bodies, and the spiritualists play on their superstitions. I would be very sorry to know that my dead father is still wearing his filthy body. People get consolation from this, that their fathers are all encased in matter. In another place they brought me Jesus Christ. I said, "Lord, how do you do?" It makes me feel hopeless. If that great saintly man is still wearing the body, what is to become of us poor creatures? The spiritualists did not allow me to touch any of those gentlemen. Even if these were real, I would not want them. I think, "Mother, Mother! atheists — that is what people really are! Just the desire for these five senses! Not satisfied with what they have here, they want more of the same when they die!"

What is the God of Vedanta? He is principle, not person. You and I are all Personal Gods. The Absolute God of the universe, the creator, preserver, and destroyer of the universe, is impersonal principle. You and I, the cat, rat, devil, and ghost, all these are Its persons — all are Personal Gods. You want to worship Personal Gods. It is the worship of your own self. If you take my advice, you will never enter any church. Come out and go and wash off. Wash yourself again and again until you are cleansed of all the superstitions that have clung to you through the ages. Or, perhaps, you do not like to do so, since you do not wash yourself so often in this country — frequent washing is an Indian custom, not a custom of your society.

I have been asked many times, "Why do you laugh so much and make so many jokes?" I become serious sometimes — when I have stomach-ache! The Lord is all blissfulness. He is the reality behind all that exists, He is the goodness, the truth in everything. You are His incarnations. That is what is glorious. The nearer you are to Him, the less you will have occasions to cry or weep. The further we are from Him, the more will long faces come. The more we know of Him, the more misery vanishes. If one who lives in the Lord becomes miserable, what is the use of living in Him? What is the use of such a God? Throw Him overboard into the Pacific Ocean! We do not want Him!

But God is the infinite, impersonal being — ever existent, unchanging, immortal, fearless; and you are all His incarnations, His embodiments. This is the God of Vedanta, and His heaven is everywhere. In this heaven dwell all the Personal Gods there are — you yourselves. Exit praying and laying flowers in the temples! What do you pray for? To go to heaven, to get something, and let somebody else not have it. "Lord, I want more food! Let somebody else starve!" What an idea of God who is the reality, the infinite, ever blessed existence in which there is neither part nor flaw, who is ever free, ever pure, ever perfect! We attribute to Him all our human characteristics, functions, and limitations. He must bring us food and give us clothes. As a matter of fact we have to do all these things ourselves and nobody else ever did them for us. That is the plain truth.

But you rarely think of this. You imagine there is God of whom you are special favourites, who does things for you when you ask Him; and you do not ask of Him favours for all men, all beings, but only for yourself, your own family, your own people. When the Hindu is starving, you do not care; at that time you do not think that the God of the Christians is also the God of the Hindus. Our whole idea of God, our praying, our worshipping, all are vitiated by our ignorance, our foolish idea of ourselves as body. You may not like what I am saying. You may curse me today, but tomorrow you will bless me.

We must become thinkers. Every birth is painful. We must get out of materialism. My Mother would not let us get out of Her clutches; nevertheless we must try. This struggle is all the worship there is; all the rest is mere shadow. You are the Personal God. Just now I am worshipping you. This is the greatest prayer. Worship the whole world in that sense — by serving it. This standing on a high platform, I know, does not appear like worship. But if it is service, it is worship.

The infinite truth is never to be acquired. It is here all the time, undying and unborn. He, the Lord of the universe, is in every one. There is but one temple — the body. It is the only temple that ever existed. In this body, He resides, the Lord of souls and the King of kings. We do not see that, so we make stone images of Him and build temples over them. Vedanta has been in India always, but India is full of these temples — and not only temples, but also caves containing carved images. "The fool, dwelling on the bank of the Ganga, digs a well for water!" Such are we! Living in the midst of God — we must go and make images. We project Him in the form of the image, while all the time He exists in the temple of our body. We are lunatics, and this is the great delusion.

Worship everything as God — every form is His temple. All else is delusion. Always look within, never without. Such is the God that Vedanta preaches, and such is His worship. Naturally there is no sect, no creed, no caste in Vedanta. How can this religion be the national religion of India?

Hundreds of castes! If one man touches another man's food, he cries out, "Lord help me, I am polluted!" When I returned to India after my visit to the West, several orthodox Hindus raised a howl against my association with the Western people and my breaking the rules of orthodoxy. They did not like me to teach the truths of the Vedas to the people of the West.

But how can there be these distinctions and differences? How can the rich man turn up his nose at the poor man, and the learned at the ignorant, if we are all spirit and all the same? Unless society changes, how can such a religion as Vedanta prevail? It will take thousands of years to have large numbers of truly rational human beings. It is very hard to show men new things, to give them great ideas. It is harder still to knock off old superstitions, very hard; they do not die easily. With all his education, even the learned man becomes frightened in the dark — the nursery tales come into his mind, and he see ghosts.

The meaning of the word "Veda", from which the word "Vedanta" comes, is knowledge. All knowledge is Veda, infinite as God is infinite. Nobody ever creates knowledge. Did you ever see knowledge created? It is only discovered — what was covered is uncovered. It is always here, because it is God Himself. Past, present, and future knowledge, all exist in all of us. We discover it, that is all. All this knowledge is God Himself. The Vedas are a great Sanskrit book. In our country we go down on our knees before the man who reads the Vedas, and we do not care for the man who is studying physics. That is superstition; it is not Vedanta at all. It is utter materialism. With God every knowledge is sacred. Knowledge is God. Infinite knowledge abides within every one in the fullest measure. You are not really ignorant, though you may appear to be so. You are incarnations of God, all of you. You are incarnations of the Almighty, Omnipresent, Divine Principle. You may laugh at me now, but the time will come when you will understand. You must. Nobody will be left behind.

What is the goal? This that I have spoken of — vedanta — is not a new religion. So old — as old as God Himself. It is not confined to any time and place, it is everywhere. Everybody knows this truth. We are all working it out. The goal of the whole universe is that. This applies even to external nature — every atom is rushing towards that goal. And do you think that any of the infinite pure souls are left without knowledge of the supreme truth? All have it, all are going to the same goal — the discovery of the innate Divinity. The maniac, the murderer, the superstitious man, the man who is lynched in this country — all are travelling to the same goal. Only that which we do ignorantly we ought to do knowingly, and better.

The unity of all existence — you all have it already within yourselves. None was ever born without it. However you may deny it, it continually asserts itself. What is human love? It is more or less an affirmation of that unity: "I am one with thee, my wife, my child, my friend!" Only you are affirming the unity ignorantly. "None ever loved the husband for the husband's sake, but for the sake of the Self that is in the husband." The wife finds unity there. The husband sees himself in the wife — instinctively he does it, but he cannot do it knowingly, consciously.

The whole universe is one existence. There cannot be anything else. Out of diversities we are all going towards this universal existence. Families into tribes, tribes into races, races into nations, nations into humanity — how many wills going to the One! It is all knowledge, all science — the realisation of this unity. Unity is knowledge, diversity is ignorance. This knowledge is your birthright. I have not to teach it to you. There never were different religions in the world. We are all destined to have salvation, whether we will it or not. You have to attain it in the long run and become free, because it is your nature to be free. We are already free, only we do not know it, and we do not know what we have been doing. Throughout all religious systems and ideals is the same morality; one thing only is preached: "Be unselfish, love others." One says, "Because Jehovah commanded." "Allah," shouted Mohammed. Another cries, "Jesus". If it was only the command of Jehovah, how could it come to those who never knew Jehovah? If it was Jesus alone who gave this command, how could any one who never knew Jesus get it? If only Vishnu, how could the Jews get it, who never were acquainted with that gentleman? There is another source, greater than all of them. Where is it? In the eternal temple of God, in the souls of all beings from the lowest to the highest. It is there — that infinite unselfishness, infinite sacrifice, infinite compulsion to go back to unity.

We have seemingly been divided, limited, because of our ignorance; and we have become as it were the little Mrs. so-and-so and Mr. so-and-so. But all nature is giving this delusion the lie every moment. I am not that little man or little woman cut off from all else; I am the one universal existence. The soul in its own majesty is rising up every moment and declaring its own intrinsic Divinity.

This Vedanta is everywhere, only you must become conscious of it. These masses of foolish beliefs and superstitions hinder us in our progress. If we can, let us throw them off and understand that God is spirit to be worshipped in spirit and in truth. Try to be materialists no more! Throw away all matter! The conception of God must be truly spiritual. All the different ideas of God, which are more or less materialistic, must go. As man becomes more and more spiritual, he has to throw off all these ideas and leave them behind. As a matter of fact, in every country there have always been a few who have been strong enough to throw away all matter and stand out in the shining light, worshipping the spirit by the spirit.

If Vedanta — this conscious knowledge that all is one spirit — spreads, the whole of humanity will become spiritual. But is it possible? I do not know. Not within thousands of years. The old superstitions must run out. You are all interested in how to perpetuate all your superstitions. Then there are the ideas of the family brother, the caste brother, the national brother. All these are barriers to the realisation of Vedanta. Religion has been religion to very few.

Most of those who have worked in the field of religion all over the world have really been political workers. That has been the history of human beings. They have rarely tried to live up uncompromisingly to the truth. They have always worshipped the god called society; they have been mostly concerned with upholding what the masses believe — their superstitions, their weakness. They do not try to conquer nature but to fit into nature, nothing else. God to India and preach a new creed — they will not listen to it. But if you tell them it is from the Vedas —"That is good!" they will say. Here I can preach this doctrine, and you — how many of you take me seriously? But the truth is all here, and I must tell you the truth.

There is another side to the question. Everyone says that the highest, the pure, truth cannot be realised all at once by all, that men have to be led to it gradually through worship, prayer, and other kinds of prevalent religious practices. I am not sure whether that is the right method or not. In India I work both ways.

In Calcutta, I have all these images and temples — in the name of God and the Vedas, of the Bible and Christ and Buddha. Let it be tried. But on the heights of the Himalayas I have a place where I am determined nothing shall enter except pure truth. There I want to work out this idea about which I have spoken to you today. There are an Englishman and an Englishwoman in charge of the place. The purpose is to train seekers of truth and to bring up children without fear and without superstition. They shall not hear about Christs and Buddhas and Shivas and Vishnus — none of these. They shall learn, from the start, to stand upon their own feet. They shall learn from their childhood that God is the spirit and should be worshipped in spirit and in truth. Everyone must be looked upon as spirit. That is the ideal. I do not know what success will come of it. Today I am preaching the thing I like. I wish I had been brought up entirely on that, without all the dualistic superstitions.

Sometimes I agree that there is some good in the dualistic method: it helps many who are weak. If a man wants you to show him the polar star, you first point out to him a bright star near it, then a less bright star, then a dim star, and then the polar star. This process makes it easy for him to see it. All the various practices and trainings, Bibles and Gods, are but the rudiments of religion, the kindergartens of religion.

But then I think of the other side. How long will the

world have to wait to reach the truth if it follows this slow, gradual process? How long? And where is the surety that it will ever succeed to any appreciable degree? It has not so far. After all, gradual or not gradual, easy or not easy to the weak, is not the dualistic method based on falsehood? Are not all the prevalent religious practices often weakening and therefore wrong? They are based on a wrong idea, a wrong view of man. Would two wrong make one right? Would the lie become truth? Would darkness become light?

I am the servant of a man who has passed away. I am only the messenger. I want to make the experiment. The teachings of Vedanta I have told you about were never really experimented with before. Although Vedanta is the oldest philosophy in the world, it has always become mixed up with superstitions and everything else.

Christ said, "I and my father are one", and you repeat it. Yet it has not helped mankind. For nineteen hundred years men have not understood that saying. They make Christ the saviour of men. He is God and we are worms! Similarly in India. In every country, this sort of belief is the backbone of every sect. For thousands of years millions and millions all over the world have been taught to worship the Lord of the world, the Incarnations, the saviours, the prophets. They have been taught to consider themselves helpless, miserable creatures and to depend upon the mercy of some person or persons for salvation. There are no doubt many marvellous things in such beliefs. But even at their best, they are but kindergartens of religion, and they have helped but little. Men are still hypnotised into abject degradation. However, there are some strong souls who get over that illusion. The hour comes when great men shall arise and cast off these kindergartens of religion and shall make vivid and powerful the true religion, the worship of the spirit by the spirit.

WRITINGS: PROSE AND POEMS

THE STRUGGLE FOR EXPANSION[1]

The old dilemma, whether the tree precedes the seed or the seed the tree, runs through all our forms of knowledge. Whether intelligence is first in the order of being or matter; whether the ideal is first or the external manifestation; whether freedom is our true nature or bondage of law; whether thought creates matter or matter thought; whether the incessant change in nature precedes the idea of rest or the idea of rest precedes the idea of change — all these are questions of the same insoluble nature. Like the rise and fall of a series of waves, they follow one another in an invariable succession and men take this side or that according to their tastes or education or peculiarity of temperaments.

For instance, if it be said on the one hand that, seeing the adjustment in nature of different parts, it is clear that it is the effect of intelligent work; on the other hand it may be argued that intelligence itself being created by matter and force in the course of evolution could not have been before this world. If it be said that the production of every form must be preceded by an ideal in the mind, it can be argued, with equal force, that the ideal was itself created by various external experiences. On the one hand, the appeal is to our ever-present idea of freedom; on the other, to the fact that nothing in the universe being causeless, everything, both mental and physical, is rigidly bound by the law of causation. If it be affirmed that, seeing the changes of the body induced by volition, it is evident that thought is the creator of this body, it is equally clear that as change in the body induces a change in the thought, the body must have produced the mind. If it be argued that the universal change must be the outcome of a preceding rest, equally logical argument can be adduced to show that the idea of unchangeability is only an illusory relative notion, brought about by the comparative differences in motion.

Thus in the ultimate analysis all knowledge resolves itself into this vicious circle: the indeterminate interdependence of cause and effect. Judging by the laws of reasoning, such knowledge is incorrect; and the most curious fact is that this knowledge is proved to be incorrect, not by comparison with knowledge which is true, but by the very laws which depend for their basis upon the selfsame vicious circle. It is clear, therefore, that the peculiarity of all our knowledge is that it proves its own insufficiency. Again, we cannot say that it is unreal, for all the reality we know and can think of is within this knowledge. Nor can we deny that it is sufficient for all practical purposes. This state of human knowledge which embraces within its scope both the external and the internal worlds is called Maya. It is unreal because it proves its own incorrectness. It is real in the sense of being sufficient for all the needs of the animal man.

Acting in the external world Maya manifests itself as the two powers of attraction and repulsion. In the internal its manifestations are desire and non-desire (Pravritti and Nivritti). The whole universe is trying to rush outwards. Each atom is trying to fly off from its centre. In the internal world, each thought is trying to go beyond control. Again each particle in the external world is checked by another force, the centripetal, and drawn towards the centre. Similarly in the thought-world the controlling power is checking all these outgoing desires.`

Desires of materialisation, that is, being dragged down more and more to the plane of mechanical action, belong to the animal man. It is only when the desire to prevent all such bondage to the senses arises that religion dawns in the heart of man. Thus we see that the whole scope of religion is to prevent man from falling into the bondage of the senses and to help him to assert his freedom. The first effort of this power of Nivritti towards that end is called morality. The scope of all morality is to prevent this degradation and break this bondage. All morality can be divided into the positive and the negative elements; it says either, "Do this" or "Do not do this". When it says, "Do not", it is evident that it is a check to a certain desire which would make a man a slave. When it says, "Do", its scope is to show

---
1. Written by the Swami during his first visit to America in answer to questions put by a Western disciple.

the way to freedom and to the breaking down of a certain degradation which has already seized the human heart.

Now this morality is only possible if there be a liberty to be attained by man. Apart from the question of the chances of attaining perfect liberty, it is clear that the whole universe is a case of struggle to expand, or in other words, to attain liberty. This infinite space is not sufficient for even one atom. The struggle for expansion must go on eternally until perfect liberty is attained. It cannot be said that this struggle to gain freedom is to avoid pain or to attain pleasure. The lowest grade of beings, who can have no such feeling, are also struggling for expansion; and according to many, man himself is the expansion of these very beings.

THE BIRTH OF RELIGION[1]

The beautiful flowers of the forest with their many-coloured petals, nodding their heads, jumping, leaping, playing with every breeze; the beautiful birds with their gorgeous plumage, their sweet songs echoing through every forest glade — they were there yesterday, my solace, my companions, and today they are gone — where? My playmates, the companions of my joys and sorrows, my pleasures and pastime — they also are gone — where? Those that nursed me when I was a child, who all through their lives had but one thought for me — that of doing everything for me — they also are gone. Everyone, everything is gone, is going, and will go. Where do they go? This was the question that pressed for an answer in the mind of the primitive man. "Why so?" you may ask, "Did he not see everything decomposed, reduced to dust before him? Why should he have troubled his head at all about where they went?"

To the primitive man everything is living in the first place, and to him death in the sense of annihilation has no meaning at all. People come to him,

---

1. Written by the Swami during his first visit to America in answer to questions put by a Western disciple.

go away, and come again. Sometimes they go away and do not come. Therefore in the most ancient language of the world death is always expressed by some sort of going. This is the beginning of religion. Thus the primitive man was searching everywhere for a solution of his difficulty — where do they all go?

There is the morning sun radiant in his glory, bringing light and warmth and joy to a sleeping world. Slowly he travels and, alas, he also disappears, down, down below!

But the next day he appears again — glorious, beautiful! And there is the lotus — that wonderful flower in the Nile, the Indus, and the Tigris, the birth-places of civilisation — opening in the morning as the solar rays strike its closed petals and with the waning sun shutting up again. Some were there then who came and went and got up from their graves revivified. This was the first solution. The sun and the lotus are, therefore, the chief symbols in the most ancient religions. Why these symbols? because abstract thought, whatever that be, when expressed, is bound to come clad in visible, tangible, gross garments. This is the law. The idea of the passing out as not out of existence but in it, had to be expressed only as a change, a momentary transformation; and reflexively, that object which strikes the senses and goes vibrating to the mind and calls up a new idea is bound to be taken up as the support, the nucleus round which the new idea spreads itself for an expression. And so the sun and the lotus were the first symbols.

There are deep holes everywhere — so dark and so dismal; down is all dark and frightful; under water we cannot see, open our eyes though we may; up is light, all light, even at night the beautiful starry hosts shedding their light. Where do they go then, those I love? Not certainly down in the dark, dark place, but up, above in the realm of Everlasting Light. That required a new symbol. Here is fire with its glowing wonderful tongues of flame — eating up a forest in a short time, cooking the food, giving warmth, and driving wild animals away — this life-giving, life-saving fire; and then the flames — they all go upwards, never downwards. Here then was another — this fire that carries them upwards to the places of light — the connecting link between us and those that have passed over to the regions of light. "Thou Ignis", begins the oldest human record, "our messenger to the bright ones." So they put food and drink and whatever they thought would be pleasing to these "bright ones" into the fire. This was the beginning of sacrifice.

So far the first question was solved, at least as far as to satisfy the needs of these primitive men. Then came the other question: Whence has all this come? Why did it not come first? Because we remember a sudden change more. Happiness, joy, addition, enjoyment make not such a deep impression on our mind as unhappiness, sorrow, and subtraction. Our nature is joy, enjoyment, pleasure, and happiness. Anything that violently breaks it makes a deeper impression than the natural course. So the problem of death was the first to be solved as the great disturber. Then with more advancement came the other question: Whence they came? Everything that lives moves: we move; our will moves our limbs; our limbs manufacture forms under the control of our will. Everything then that moved had a will in it as the motor, to the man-child of ancient times as it is to the child-man of the present day. The wind has a will; the cloud, the whole of nature, is full of separate wills, minds, and souls. They are creating all this just as we manufacture many things; they — the "Devas", the "Elohims" are the creators of all this.

Now in the meanwhile society was growing up. In society there was the king — why not among the bright ones, the Elohims? Therefore there was a supreme "Deva", an Elohim-jahveh, God of gods — the one God who by His single will has created all this — even the "bright ones". But as He has appointed different stars and planets, so He has appointed different "Devas" or angels to preside over different functions of nature — some over death, some over birth, etc. One supreme being, supreme by being infinitely more powerful than the rest, is the common conception in the two great sources of all religions, the Aryan and Semitic races. But here the Aryans take a new start, a grand deviation.

Their God was not only a supreme being, but He was the Dyaus Pitar, the Father in heaven. This is the beginning of Love. The Semitic God is only a thunderer, only the terrible one, the mighty Lord of hosts. To all these the Aryan added a new idea, that of a Father. And the divergence becomes more and more obvious all through further progress, which in fact stopped at this place in the Semitic branch of the human race. The God of the Semitic is not to be seen — nay, it is death to see Him; the God of the Aryan cannot only be seen, but He is the goal of being; the one aim of life is to see Him. The Semitic obeys his King of kings for fear of punishment and keeps His commandments. The Aryan loves his father; and further on he adds mother, his friend. And "Love me, love my dog", they say. So each one of His creatures should be loved, because they are His. To the Semitic, this life is an outpost where we are posted to test our fidelity; to the Aryan this life is on the way to our goal. To the Semitic, if we do our duty well, we shall have an ever-joyful home in heaven. To the Aryan, that home is God Himself. To the Semitic, serving God is a means to an end, namely, the pay, which is joy and enjoyment. To the Aryan, enjoyment, misery — everything — is a means, and the end is God. The Semitic worships God to go to heaven. The Aryan rejects heaven to go to God. In short, this is the main difference. The aim and end of the Aryan life is to see God, to see the face of the Beloved, because without Him he cannot live. "Without Thy presence, the sun, the moon, and the stars lose their light."

FOUR PATHS OF YOGA[2]

Our main problem is to be free. It is evident then that until we realise ourselves as the Absolute, we cannot attain to deliverance. Yet there are various ways of attaining to this realisation. These methods have the generic name of Yoga (to join, to join ourselves to our reality). These Yogas, though divided into various groups, can principally be classed into

---

2. Written by the Swami during his first visit to America in answer to questions put by a Western disciple.

four; and as each is only a method leading indirectly to the realisation of the Absolute, they are suited to different temperaments. Now it must be remembered that it is not that the assumed man becomes the real man or Absolute. There is no becoming with the Absolute. It is ever free, ever perfect; but the ignorance that has covered Its nature for a time is to be removed. Therefore the whole scope of all systems of Yoga (and each religion represents one) is to clear up this ignorance and allow the Atman to restore its own nature. The chief helps in this liberation are Abhyasa and Vairagya. Vairagya is non-attachment to life, because it is the will to enjoy that brings all this bondage in its train; and Abhyasa is constant practice of any one of the Yogas.

Karma-yoga . Karma-yoga is purifying the mind by means of work. Now if any work is done, good or bad, it must produce as a result a good or bad effect; no power can stay it, once the cause is present. Therefore good action producing good Karma, and bad action, bad Karma, the soul will go on in eternal bondage without ever hoping for deliverance. Now Karma belongs only to the body or the mind, never to the Atman (Self); only it can cast a veil before the Atman.

The veil cast by bad Karma is ignorance. Good Karma has the power to strengthen the moral powers. And thus it creates non-attachment; it destroys the tendency towards bad Karma and thereby purifies the mind. But if the work is done with the intention of enjoyment, it then produces only that very enjoyment and does not purify the mind or Chitta. Therefore all work should be done without any desire to enjoy the fruits thereof. All fear and all desire to enjoy here or hereafter must be banished for ever by the Karma-yogi. Moreover, this Karma without desire of return will destroy the selfishness, which is the root of all bondage. The watchword of the Karma-yogi is "not I, but Thou", and no amount of self-sacrifice is too much for him. But he does this without any desire to go to heaven, or gain name or fame or any other benefit in this world. Although the explanation and rationale of this unselfish work is only in Jnana-yoga, yet the natural divinity of man makes him love all sacrifice simply for the good of others, without any ulterior motive, whatever his creed or opinion. Again, with many the bondage of wealth is very great; and Karma-yoga is absolutely necessary for them as breaking the crystallisation that has gathered round their love of money.

Next is Bhakti-Yoga . Bhakti or worship or love in some form or other is the easiest, pleasantest, and most natural way of man. The natural state of this universe is attraction; and that is surely followed by an ultimate disunion. Even so, love is the natural impetus of union in the human heart; and though itself a great cause of misery, properly directed towards the proper object, it brings deliverance. The object of Bhakti is God. Love cannot be without a subject and an object. The object of love again must be at first a being who can reciprocate our love. Therefore the God of love must be in some sense a human God. He must be a God of love. Aside from the question whether such a God exists or not, it is a fact that to those who have love in their heart this Absolute appears as a God of love, as personal.

The lower forms of worship, which embody the idea of God as a judge or punisher or someone to be obeyed through fear, do not deserve to be called love, although they are forms of worship gradually expanding into higher forms. We pass on to the consideration of love itself. We will illustrate love by a triangle, of which the first angle at the base is fearlessness. So long as there is fear, it is not love. Love banishes all fear. A mother with her baby will face a tiger to save her child. The second angle is that love never asks, never begs. The third or the apex is that love loves for the sake of love itself. Even the idea of object vanishes. Love is the only form in which love is loved. This is the highest abstraction and the same as the Absolute.

Next is Raja-Yoga . This Yoga fits in with every one of these Yogas. It fits inquirers of all classes with or without any belief, and it is the real instrument of religious inquiry. As each science has its particular method of investigation, so is this Raja-yoga the method of religion. This science also is variously applied according to various constitutions. The chief parts are the Pranayama, concentration, and meditation. For those who believe in God, a symbolical name, such as Om or other sacred words received from a Guru, will be very helpful. Om is the greatest, meaning the Absolute. Meditating on the meaning of these holy names while repeating them is the chief practice.

Next is Jnana-Yoga. This is divided into three parts. First: hearing the truth — that the Atman is the only reality and that everything else is Maya (relativity). Second: reasoning upon this philosophy from all points of view. Third: giving up all further argumentation and realising the truth. This realisation comes from (1) being certain that Brahman is real and everything else is unreal; (2) giving up all desire for enjoyment; (3) controlling the senses and the mind; (4) intense desire to be free. Meditating on this reality always and reminding the soul of its real nature are the only ways in this Yoga. It is the highest, but most difficult. Many persons get an intellectual grasp of it, but very few attain realisation.

CYCLIC REST AND CHANGE[1]

This whole universe is a case of lost balance. All motion is the struggle of the disturbed universe to regain its equilibrium, which, as such, cannot be motion. Thus in regard to the internal world it would be a state which is beyond thought, for thought itself is a motion. Now when all indication is towards perfect equilibrium by expansion and the whole universe is rushing towards it, we have no right to say that that state can never be attained. Again it is impossible that there should be any variety whatsoever in that state of equilibrium. It must be homogeneous; for as long as there are even two atoms, they will attract and repel each other and disturb the balance. Therefore this state of equilibrium is one of unity, of rest, and of homogeneity. In the language of the internal, this state of equilibrium is not thought, nor body, nor anything which we call an attribute. The only thing which we can say it will retain is what is its own nature as existence, self-consciousness, and blissfulness.

This state in the same way cannot be two. It must only be a unit, and all fictitious distinctions of I, thou, etc., all the different variations must vanish, as they belong to the state of change or Maya. It may be said that this state of change has come now upon the Self, showing that, before this, it had the state of rest and liberty; that at present the state of differentiation is the only real state, and the state of homogeneity is the primitive crudeness out of which this changeful state is manufactured; and that it will be only degeneration to go back to the state of undifferentiation. This argument would have had some weight if it could be proved that these two states, viz homogeneity and heterogeneity, are the only two states happening but once through all time. What happens once must happen again and again. Rest is followed by change — the universe. But that rest must have been preceded by other changes, and this change will be succeeded by other rests. It would be ridiculous to think that there was a period of rest and then came this change which will go on for ever. Every particle in nature shows that it is coming again and again to periodic rest and change.

This interval between one period of rest and another is called a Kalpa. But this Kalpic rest cannot be one of perfect homogeneity, for in that case there would be an end to any future manifestation. Now to say that the present state of change is one of great advance in comparison to the preceding state of rest is simply absurd, because in that case the coming period of rest being much more advanced in time must be much more perfect! There is no progression or digression in nature. It is showing again and again the same forms. In fact, the word law means this. But there is a progression with regard to souls. That is to say, the souls get nearer to their own natures, and in each Kalpa large numbers of them get deliverance from being thus whirled around. It may be said, the individual soul being a part of the universe and nature, returning again and again, there cannot be any liberty for the soul, for in that case the universe has to be destroyed. The answer is that

---
1. Written by the Swami during his first visit to America in answer to questions put by a Western disciple.

the individual soul is an assumption through Maya, and it is no more a reality than nature itself. In reality, this individual soul is the unconditioned absolute Brahman (the Supreme).

All that is real in nature is Brahman, only it appears to be this variety, or nature, through the superimposition of Maya. Maya being illusion cannot be said to be real, yet it is producing the phenomena. If it be asked, how can Maya, herself being illusion, produce all this, our answer is that what is produced being also ignorance, the producer must also be that. How can ignorance be produced by knowledge? So this Maya is acting in two ways as nescience and science (relative knowledge); and this science after destroying nescience or ignorance is itself also destroyed. This Maya destroys herself and what remains is the Absolute, the Essence of existence, knowledge, and bliss. Now whatever is reality in nature is this Absolute, and nature comes to us in three forms, God, conscious, and unconscious, i.e. God, personal souls, and unconscious beings. The reality of all these is the Absolute; through Maya it is seen to be diverse. But the vision of God is the nearest to the reality and the highest. The idea of a Personal God is the highest idea which man can have. All the attributes attributed to God are true in the same sense as are the attributes of nature. Yet we must never forget that the Personal God is the very Absolute seen through Maya.

A PREFACE TO THE IMITATION OF CHRIST[1]

The Imitation of Christ is a cherished treasure of the Christian world. This great book was written by a Roman Catholic monk. "Written", perhaps, is not the proper word. It would be more appropriate to say that each letter of the book is marked deep with the heart's blood of the great soul who had renounced all for his love of Christ. That great soul whose words, living and burning, have cast such a spell for the last four hundred years over the hearts of myriads of men and women; whose influence today remains as strong as ever and is destined to endure for all time to come; before whose genius and Sâdhâna (spiritual effort) hundred of crowned have bent down in reverence; and before whose matchless purity the jarring sects of Christendom, whose name is legion, have sunk their differences of centuries in common veneration to a common principle—that great soul, strange to say, has not thought fit to put his name to a book such as this. Yet there is nothing strange here after all, for why should he? Is it possible for one who totally renounced all earthly joys and despised the desire for the bauble fame as so much dirt and filth—is it possible for such a soul to care for that paltry thing, a mere author's name? Posterity, however, has guessed that the author was Thomas à Kempis, a Roman Catholic monk. How far the guess is true is known only to God. But be he who he may, that he deserves the world's adoration is a truth that can be gainsaid by none.

We happen to be the subjects of a Christian government now. Through its favour it has been our lot to meet Christians of so many sects, native as well as foreign. How startling the divergence between their profession and practice! Here stands the Christian missionary preaching: "Sufficient unto the day is the evil thereof. Take no thought for the morrow"—and then busy soon after, making his pile and framing his budget for ten years in advance! There he says that he follows him who "hath not where to lay his head", glibly talking of the glorious sacrifice and burning renunciation of the Master, but in practice going about like a gay bridegroom fully enjoying all the comforts the world can bestow! Look where we may, a true Christian nowhere do we see. The ugly impression left on our mind by the ultra-luxurious, insolent, despotic, barouche-and-brougham-driving Christians of the Protestant sects will be completely removed if we but once read this great book with the attention it deserves.

All wise men think alike. The reader, while reading this book, will hear the echo of the Bhagavad-Gîtâ

---
1. Translated from an original Bengali writing of the Swami in 1889. The passage is the preface to his Bengali translation of *The Imitation of Christ* which he contributed to a Bengali monthly. He translated only six chapters with quotations of parallel passages from the Hindu scriptures.

over and over again. Like the Bhagavad-Gita it says, "Give up all Dharmas and follow Me". The spirit of humility, the panting of the distressed soul, the best expression of Dâsya Bhakti (devotion as a servant) will be found imprinted on every line of this great book and the reader's heart will be profoundly stirred by the author's thoughts of burning renunciation, marvellous surrender, and deep sense of dependence on the will of God. To those of my countrymen, who under the influence of blind bigotry may seek to belittle this book because it is the work of a Christian, I shall quote only one aphorism of Vaisheshika Darshana and say nothing more. The aphorism is this: आप्तोपदेशवाक्यं शब्दः—which means that the teachings of Siddha Purushas (perfected souls) have a probative force and this is technically known as Shabda Pramâna (verbal evidence). Rishi Jaimini, the commentator, says that such Âpta Purushas (authorities) may be born both among the Aryans and the Mlechchhas.

If in ancient times Greek astronomers like Yavanâchârya could have been so highly esteemed by our Aryan ancestors, then it is incredible that this work of the lion of devotees will fail to be appreciated by my countrymen.

Be that as it may, we shall place the Bengali translation of this book before our readers seriatim. We trust that the readers of Bengal will spend over it at least one hundredth part of the time they waste over cart-loads of trashy novels and dramas.

I have tried to make the translation as literal as possible, but I cannot say how far I have succeeded. The allusions to the Bible in several passages are given in the footnotes.

AN INTERESTING CORRESPONDENCE[2]

Now Sister Mary,
You need not be sorry
For the hard raps I gave you,
You know full well,
Though you like me tell,
With my whole heart I love you.
The babies I bet,
The best friends I met,
Will stand by me in weal and woe.
And so will I do,
You know it too.
Life, name, or fame, even heaven forgo
For the sweet sisters four
Sans reproche et sans peur,
The truest, noblest, steadfast, best.
The wounded snake its hood unfurls,
The flame stirred up doth blaze,
The desert air resounds the calls
Of heart-struck lion's rage.
The cloud puts forth its deluge strength
When lightning cleaves its breast,
When the soul is stirred to its inmost depth
Great ones unfold their best.

---

[2]. In order to truly appreciate this correspondence, the reader has to be informed of the occasion which gave rise to it and also to remember the relation that existed between the correspondents. At the outset of the first letter the Swami speaks of "the hard raps" that he gave to his correspondent. These were nothing but a very strong letter which he wrote to her in vindication of his position, on the 1st of February, 1895, which will be found reproduced in the fifth volume of the Complete Works of the Swami. It was a very beautiful letter full of the fire of a Sannyasin's spirit, and we request our readers to go through it before they peruse the following text. Mary Hale, to whom the Swami wrote, was one of the two daughters of Mr. and Mrs. Hale whom the Swami used to address as Father Pope and Mother Church. The Misses Hales and their two cousins were like sisters to him, and they also in their turn held the Swami in great love and reverence. Some of the finest letters of the Swami were written to them. In the present correspondence the Swami is seen in a new light, playful and intensely human, yet keyed to the central theme of his life, Brahmajnana. The first letter was written from New York, 15th February 1895— Ed.

Let eyes grow dim and heart grow faint,
And friendship fail and love betray,
Let Fate its hundred horrors send,
And clotted darkness block the way.
All nature wear one angry frown,
To crush you out — still know, my soul,
You are Divine. March on and on,
Nor right nor left but to the goal.
Nor angel I, nor man, nor brute,
Nor body, mind, nor he or she,
The books do stop in wonder mute
To tell my nature; I am He.
Before the sun, the moon, the earth,
Before the stars or comets free,
Before e'en time has had its birth,
I was, I am, and I will be.
The beauteous earth, the glorious sun,
The calm sweet moon, the spangled sky,
Causation's laws do make them run;
They live in bonds, in bonds they die.
And mind its mantle dreamy net
Cast o'er them all and holds them fast.
In warp and woof of thought are set,
Earth, hells, and heavens, or worst or best.
Know these are but the outer crust —
All space and time, all effect, cause.
I am beyond all sense, all thoughts,
The witness of the universe.
Not two or many, 'tis but one,
And thus in me all me's I have;
I cannot hate, I cannot shun
Myself from me, I can but love.
From dreams awake, from bonds be free,
Be not afraid. This mystery,
My shadow, cannot frighten me,
Know once for all that I am He.

Well, so far my poetry. Hope you are all right. Give my love to mother and Father Pope. I am busy to death and have almost no time to write even a line. So excuse me if later on I am rather late in writing.

Yours eternally,
Vivekananda.

Miss M.B.H. sent Swami the following doggerel in reply:

The monk he would a poet be
And wooed the muse right earnestly;
In thought and word he could well beat her,
What bothered him though was the metre.
His feet were all too short too long,
The form not suited to his song;
He tried the sonnet, lyric, epic,
And worked so hard, he waxed dyspeptic.
While the poetic mania lasted
He e'en from vegetables fasted,
Which Leon[1] had with tender care
Prepared for Swami's dainty fare.
One day he sat and mused alone —
Sudden a light around him shone,
The "still small voice" his thoughts inspire
And his words glow like coals of fire.
And coals of fire they proved to be
Heaped on the head of contrite me —
My scolding letter I deplore
And beg forgiveness o'er and o'er.
The lines you sent to your sisters four
Be sure they'll cherish evermore
For you have made them clearly see
The one main truth that "all is He".
Then Swami:
In days of yore,
On Ganga's shore preaching,

---

1. Leon Landsberg, a disciple of the Swami who lived with him for some time.

A hoary priest was teaching
How Gods they come
As Sita Ram,
And gentle Sita pining, weeping.
The sermons end,
They homeward wend their way —
The hearers musing, thinking.
When from the crowd
A voice aloud
This question asked beseeching, seeking —
"Sir, tell me, pray,
Who were but they
These Sita Ram you were teaching, speaking!"
So Mary Hale,
Allow me tell,
You mar my doctrines wronging, baulking.
I never taught
Such queer thought
That all was God — unmeaning talking!
But this I say,
Remember pray,
That God is true, all else is nothing,
This world's a dream
Though true it seem,
And only truth is He the living!
The real me is none but He,
The real me is none but He,
And never, never matter changing!
With undying love and gratitude to you all. . . .
Vivekananda.
And then Miss M.B.H.:
The difference I clearly see
'Twixt tweedledum and tweedledee —
That is a proposition sane,
But truly 'tis beyond my vein
To make your Eastern logic plain.
If "God is truth, all else is naught,"
This "world a dream", delusion up wrought,

What can exist which God is not?
All those who "many" see have much to fear,
He only lives to whom the "One" is clear.
So again I say
In my poor way,
I cannot see but that all's He,
If I'm in Him and He in me.
Then the Swami replied:
Of temper quick, a girl unique,
A freak of nature she,
A lady fair, no question there,
Rare soul is Miss Mary.
Her feelings deep she cannot keep,
But creep they out at last,
A spirit free, I can foresee,
Must be of fiery cast.
Tho' many a lay her muse can bray,
And play piano too,
Her heart so cool, chills as a rule
The fool who comes to woo.
Though, Sister Mary, I hear they say
The sway your beauty gains,
Be cautious now and do not bow,
However sweet, to chains.
For 'twill be soon, another tune
The moon-struck mate will hear
If his will but clash, your words will hash
And smash his life I fear.
These lines to thee, Sister Mary,
Free will I offer, take
"Tit for tat"— a monkey chat,
For monk alone can make.

THOU BLESSED DREAM[1]

If things go ill or well —
If joy rebounding spreads the face,
Or sea of sorrow swells —
A play — we each have part,
Each one to weep or laugh as may;
Each one his dress to don —
Its scenes, alternative shine and rain.
Thou dream, O blessed dream!
Spread far and near thy veil of haze,
Tone down the lines so sharp,
Make smooth what roughness seems.
No magic but in thee!
Thy touch makes desert bloom to life.
Harsh thunder, sweetest song,
Fell death, the sweet release.

LIGHT[2]

I look behind and after
And find that all is right,
In my deepest sorrows
There is a soul of light.

THE LIVING GOD[3]

He who is in you and outside you,
Who works through all hands,
Who walks on all feet,
Whose body are all ye,
Him worship, and break all other idols!
He who is at once the high and low,
The sinner and the saint,
Both God and worm,
Him worship — visible, knowable, real, omnipresent,
Break all other idols!
In whom is neither past life
Nor future birth nor death,
In whom we always have been
And always shall be one,
Him worship. Break all other idols!
Ye fools! who neglect the living God,
And His infinite reflections with which the world is full.
While ye run after imaginary shadows,
That lead alone to fights and quarrels,
Him worship, the only visible!
Break all other idols!

TO AN EARLY VIOLET[4]

What though thy bed be frozen earth,
Thy cloak the chilling blast;
What though no mate to cheer thy path,
Thy sky with gloom o'ercast;
What though if love itself doth fail,
Thy fragrance strewed in vain;
What though if bad o'er good prevail,
And vice o'er virtue reign:
Change not thy nature, gentle bloom,
Thou violet, sweet and pure,
But ever pour thy sweet perfume
Unasked, unstinted, sure!

---

1. Written to Miss Christine Greenstidel from Paris, 14th August 1900.
2. From a letter to Miss MacLeod, 26th December 1900 (Vide Vol. VI.)
3. Written to an American friend from Almora, 9th July 1897.
4. Written to a Western lady-disciple from New York, 6th January 1896.

TO MY OWN SOUL[5]

Hold yet a while, Strong Heart,
Not part a lifelong yoke
Though blighted looks the present, future gloom.
And age it seems since you and I began our
March up hill or down. Sailing smooth o'er
Seas that are so rare —
Thou nearer unto me, than oft-times I myself —
Proclaiming mental moves before they were!
Reflector true — thy pulse so timed to mine,
Thou perfect note of thoughts, however fine —
Shall we now part, Recorder, say?
In thee is friendship, faith,
For thou didst warn when evil thoughts were brewing —
And though, alas, thy warning thrown away,
Went on the same as ever — good and true.

THE DANCE OF SHIVA[6]

Lo, the God is dancing
— shiva the all-destroyer and Lord of creation,
The Master of Yoga and the wielder of Pinaka[7].
His flaming locks have filled the sky,
Seven worlds play the rhythm
As the trembling earth sways almost to dissolution,
Lo, the Great God Shiva is dancing.

SHIVA IN ECSTASY

Shiva is dancing, lost in the ecstasy of Self, sounding his own cheeks.

His tabor is playing and the garland of skulls is swinging in rhythm.

The waters of the Ganga are roaring among his matted locks.

The great trident is vomiting fire, and the moon on his forehead is fiercely flaming.

TO SHRI KRISHNA

A Song in Hindi

O Krishna, my friend, let me go to the water,
O let me go today.
Why play tricks with one who is already thy slave?
O friend, let me go today, let me go.
I have to fill my pitcher in the waters of the Jumna.
I pray with folded hands, friend, let me go.

A HYMN TO SHRI RAMAKRISHNA

In Sanskrit

1. He who was Shri Rama, whose stream of love flowed with resistless might even to the Chandala (the outcaste); Oh, who ever was engaged in doing good to the world though superhuman by nature, whose renown there is none to equal in the three worlds, Sita's beloved, whose body of Knowledge Supreme was covered by devotion sweet in the form of Sita.

2. He who quelled the noise, terrible like that at the time of destruction, arising from the battle (of Kurukshetra), who destroyed the terrible yet natural night of ignorance (of Arjuna) and who roared out the Gita sweet and appeasing; That renowned soul is born now as Shri Ramakrishna.

---

5. Composed at Ridgely Manor, New York, in 1899.

6. This and the next one are translated from Bengali songs.

7. Trident.

3. Hail, O Lord of Men! Victory unto You! I surrender myself to my Guru, the physician for the malady of Samsara (relative existence) who is, as it were, a wave rising in the ocean of Shakti (Power), who has shown various sports of Love Divine, and who is the weapon to destroy the demon of doubt.

Hail, O Lord of Men! Victory unto You!

4. Hail, O Lord of Men! Victory unto you! I surrender myself to my Guru the Man-god, the physician for the malady of this Samsara (relative existence), whose mind ever dwelt on the non-dualistic Truth, whose personality was covered by the cloth of Supreme Devotion, who was ever active (for the good of humanity) and whose actions were all superhuman.

Hail, O Lord of Men! Victory unto You!

NO ONE TO BLAME[1]

The sun goes down, its crimson rays
Light up the dying day;
A startled glance I throw behind
And count my triumph shame;
No one but me to blame.
Each day my life I make or mar,
Each deed begets its kind,
Good good, bad bad, the tide once set
No one can stop or stem;
No one but me to blame.
I am my own embodied past;
Therein the plan was made;
The will, the thought, to that conform,
To that the outer frame;
No one but me to blame.
Love comes reflected back as love,
Hate breeds more fierce hate,
They mete their measures, lay on me
Through life and death their claim;
No one but me to blame.
I cast off fear and vain remorse,
I feel my Karma's sway
I face the ghosts my deeds have raised —
Joy, sorrow, censure, fame;
No one but me to blame.
Good, bad, love, hate, and pleasure, pain
Forever linked go,
I dream of pleasure without pain,
It never, never came;
No one but me to blame.
I give up hate, I give up love,
My thirst for life is gone;
Eternal death is what I want,
Nirvanam goes life's flame;
No one is left to blame.
One only man, one only God, one ever perfect soul,
One only sage who ever scorned the dark and dubious ways,
One only man who dared think and dared show the goal —
That death is curse, and so is life, and best when stops to be.
Om Nama Bhagavate Sambuddhaya
Om, I salute the Lord, the awakened.

---
1. Written from New York, 16th May, 1895.

NOTES OF CLASS TALKS AND LECTURES

NOTES OF CLASS TALKS

When Will Christ Come Again?

I never take much notice of these things. I have come to deal with principles. I have only to preach that God comes again and again, and that He came in India as Krishna, Rama, and Buddha, and that He will come again. It can almost be demonstrated that after each 500 years the world sinks, and a tremendous spiritual wave comes, and on the top of the wave is a Christ.

There is a great change now coming all over the world, and this is a cycle. Men are finding that they are losing hold of life; which way will they turn, down or up? Up, certainly. How can it be down? Plunge into the breach; fill up the breach with your body, your life. How should you allow the world to go down when you are living?

The Difference Between Man and Christ

There is much difference in manifested beings. As a manifested being you will never be Christ. Out of clay, manufacture a clay elephant, out of the same clay, manufacture a clay mouse. Soak them in water, they become one. As clay, they are eternally one; as fashioned things, they are eternally different. The Absolute is the material of both God and man. As Absolute, Omnipresent Being, we are all one; and as personal beings, God is the eternal master, and we are the eternal servants.

You have three things in you: (1) the body, (2) the mind, (3) the spirit. The spirit is intangible, the mind comes to birth and death, and so does the body. You are that spirit, but often you think you are the body.

When a man says, "I am here", he thinks of the body. Then comes another moment when you are on the highest plane; you do not say, "I am here". But if a man abuses you or curses you and you do not resent it, you are the spirit. "When I think I am the mind, I am one spark of that eternal fire which Thou art; and when I feel that I am the spirit, Thou and I are one"— so says a devotee to the Lord. Is the mind in advance of the spirit?

God does not reason; why should you reason if you knew? It is a sign of weakness that we have to go on crawling like worms to get a few facts and build generalisations, and then the whole thing tumbles down again. The spirit is reflected in the mind and everything. It is the light of the spirit that makes the mind sensate. Everything is an expression of the spirit; the minds are so many mirrors. What you call love and fear, hatred, virtue, and vice are all reflections of the spirit; only when the reflector is base the reflection is bad.

Are Christ and Buddha Identical?

It is my particular fancy that the same Buddha became Christ. Buddha prophesied, "I will come again in five hundred years", and Christ came here in five hundred years. These are the two Lights of the whole human nature. Two men have been produced, Buddha and Christ; these are the two giants, huge gigantic personalities, two Gods. Between them they divide the whole world. Wherever there is the least knowledge in the world, people bow down either to Buddha or Christ. It would be very hard to produce more like them, but I hope there will be. Mohammed came five hundred years after, five hundred years after came Luther with his Protestant wave, and this is five hundred years after that again. It is a great thing in a few thousand years to produce two such men as Jesus and Buddha. Are not two such enough? Christ and Buddha were Gods, the others were prophets. Study the life of these two and see the manifestation of power in them — calm and non-resisting, poor beggars owning nothing, without a cent in their pockets, despised all their lives, called heretic and fool — and think of the immense spiritual power they have wielded over humanity.

Salvation From Sin

We are to be saved from sin by being saved from ignorance. Ignorance is the cause of which sin is the result.

Coming Back to the Divine Mother

When a nurse takes a baby out into the garden and plays with the baby, the Mother may send a word to the baby to come indoors. The baby is absorbed in play, and says, "I won't come; I don't want to eat." After a while the baby becomes tired with his play and says, "I will go to Mother." The nurse says, "Here is a new doll", but the baby says, "I don't care for dolls any more. I will go to Mother", and he weeps until he goes. We are all babies. The Mother is God. We are absorbed in seeking for money, wealth, and all these things; but the time will come when we will awaken; and then this nature will try to give us more dolls, and we will say, "No, I have had enough; I will go to God."

No Individuality Apart From God

If we are inseparable from God, and always one, have we no individuality? Oh yes; that is God. Our individuality is God. This is not real individuality which you have now. You are coming towards that true one. Individuality means what cannot be divided. How can you call this state — we are now — individuality? One hour you are thinking one way, and the next hour another way, and two hours after another way. Individuality is that which changes not. It would be tremendously dangerous for the present state to remain in eternity, then the thief would always remain a thief, and the blackguard, a blackguard. If a baby died, it would have to remain a baby. The real individuality is that which never changes, and will never change; and that is God within us.

MAN THE MAKER OF HIS DESTINY

There was a very powerful dynasty in Southern India. They made it a rule to take the horoscope of all the prominent men living from time to time, calculated from the time of their birth. In this way they got a record of leading facts predicted, and compared them afterwards with events as they happened. This was done for a thousand years, until they found certain agreements; these were generalised and recorded and made into a huge book. The dynasty died out, but the family of astrologers lived and had the book in their possession. It seems possible that this is how astrology came into existence. Excessive attention to the minutiae of astrology is one of the superstitions which has hurt the Hindus very much.

I think the Greeks first took astrology to India and took from the Hindus the science of astronomy and carried it back with them from Europe. Because in India you will find old altars made according to a certain geometrical plan, and certain things had to be done when the stars were in certain positions, therefore I think the Greeks gave the Hindus astrology, and the Hindus gave them astronomy.

I have seen some astrologers who predicted wonderful things; but I have no reason to believe they predicted them only from the stars, or anything of the sort. In many cases it is simply mind-reading. Sometimes wonderful predictions are made, but in many cases it is arrant trash.

In London, a young man used to come to me and ask me, "What will become of me next year?" I asked him why he asked me so. "I have lost all my money and have become very, very poor." Money is the only God of many beings. Weak men, when they lose everything and feel themselves weak, try all sorts of uncanny methods of making money, and come to astrology and all these things. "It is the coward and the fool who says, 'This is fate'" — so says the Sanskrit proverb. But it is the strong man who stands up and says, "I will make my fate." It is people who are getting old who talk of fate. Young men generally do not come to astrology. We may be under planetary influence, but it should not matter much to us. Buddha says, "Those that get a living by calculation of the stars by such art and other lying tricks are to be avoided"; and he ought to know, because he was the greatest Hindu ever born. Let stars come, what harm is there? If a star disturbs my life, it would not be worth a cent. You will find that astrology and all these mystical things are generally signs of a weak mind; therefore as soon as they are becoming prominent in our minds, we should see a physician, take good food and rest.

If you can get an explanation of a phenomenon from within its nature, it is nonsense to look for an explanation from outside. If the world explains itself, it is nonsense to go outside for an explanation. Have you found any phenomena in the life of a man that you have ever seen which cannot be explained by the power of the man himself? So what is the use of going to the stars or anything else in the world? My own Karma is sufficient explanation of my present state. So in the case of Jesus himself. We know that his father was only a carpenter. We need not go to anybody else to find an explanation of his power. He was the outcome of his own past, all of which was a preparation for that Jesus. Buddha goes back and back to animal bodies and tells us how he ultimately became Buddha. So what is the use of going to stars for explanation? They may have a little influence; but it is our duty to ignore them rather than hearken to them and make ourselves nervous. This I lay down as the first essential in all I teach: anything that brings spiritual, mental, or physical weakness, touch it not with the toes of your feet. Religion is the manifestation of the natural strength that is in man. A spring of infinite power is coiled up and is inside this little body, and that spring is spreading itself. And as it goes on spreading, body after body is found insufficient; it throws them off and takes higher bodies. This is the history of man, of religion, civilisation, or progress. That giant Prometheus, who is bound, is getting himself unbound. It is always a manifestation of strength, and all these ideas such as astrology, although there may be a grain of truth in them, should be avoided.

There is an old story of an astrologer who came to a king and said, "You are going to die in six months." The king was frightened out of his wits and was almost about to die then and there from fear. But his minister was a clever man, and this man told the king that these astrologers were fools. The king would not believe him. So the minister saw no other way to make the king see that they were fools but to invite the astrologer to the palace again. There he asked him if his calculations were correct. The astrologer said that there could not be a mistake, but to satisfy him he went through the whole of the calculations again and then said that they were perfectly correct. The king's face became livid. The minister said to the astrologer, "And when do you think that you will die?" "In twelve years", was the reply. The minister quickly drew his sword and separated the astrologer's head from the body and said to the king, "Do you see this liar? He is dead this moment."

If you want your nation to live, keep away from all these things. The only test of good things is that they make us strong. Good is life, evil is death. These superstitious ideas are springing like mushrooms in your country, and women wanting in logical analysis of things are ready to believe them. It is because women are striving for liberation, and women have not yet established themselves intellectually. One gets by heart a few lines of poetry from the top of a novel and says she knows the whole of Browning. Another attends a course of three lectures and then thinks she knows everything in the world. The difficulty is that they are unable to throw off the natural superstition of women. They have a lot of money and some intellectual learning, but when they have passed through this transition stage and get on firm ground, they will be all right. But they are played upon by charlatans. Do not be sorry; I do not mean to hurt anyone, but I have to tell the truth. Do you not see how open you are to these things? Do you not see how sincere these women are, how that divinity latent in all never dies? It is only to know how to appeal to the Divine.

The more I live, the more I become convinced every day that every human being is divine. In no man or woman, however vile, does that divinity die. Only he or she does not know how to reach it and is waiting for the Truth. And wicked people are trying to deceive him or her with all sorts of fooleries. If one man cheats another for money, you say he is a fool and a blackguard. How much greater is the iniquity of one who wants to fool others spiritually! This is too bad. It is the one test, that truth must make you strong and put you above superstition. The duty of the philosopher is to raise you above superstition. Even this world, this body and mind are superstitions; what infinite souls you are! And to be tricked by twinkling stars! It is a shameful condition. You are divinities; the twinkling stars owe their existence to you.

I was once travelling in the Himalayas, and the long road stretched before us. We poor monks cannot get any one to carry us, so we had to make all the way on foot. There was an old man with us. The way goes up and down for hundreds of miles, and when that old monk saw what was before him, he said, "Oh sir, how to cross it; I cannot walk any more; my chest will break." I said to him, "Look down at your feet." He did so, and I said, "The road that is under your feet is the road that you have passed over and is the same road that you see before you; it will soon be under your feet." The highest things are under your feet, because you are Divine Stars; all these things are under your feet. You can swallow the stars by the handful if you want; such is your real nature. Be strong, get beyond all superstitions, and be free.

GOD: PERSONAL AND IMPERSONAL

My idea is that what you call a Personal God is the same as the Impersonal Being, a Personal and Impersonal God at the same time. We are personalised impersonal beings. If you use the word in the absolute sense, we are impersonal; but if you use it in a relative meaning, we are personal. Each one of you is a universal being, each one is omnipresent. It may seem staggering at first, but I am as sure of this as that I stand before you. How can the spirit help being omnipresent? It has neither length, nor breadth, nor thickness, nor any material attribute whatsoever; and if we are all spirits we cannot be limited by space. Space only limits space, matter matter. If we were limited to this body we would be a material something. Body and soul and everything would be material, and such words as "living in the body", "embodying the soul" would be only words used for convenience; beyond that they would have no meaning. Many of you remember the definition I gave of the soul; that each soul is a circle whose centre is in one point and circumference nowhere. The centre is where the body is, and the activity is manifested there. You are omnipresent; only you have the consciousness of being concentrated in one point. That point has taken up particles of matter, and formed them into a machine to express itself. That through which it expresses itself is called the body. So you are everywhere; when one body or machine fails, you, the centre, move on and take up other particles of matter, finer or grosser, and work through that. This is man. And what is God? God is a circle with its circumference nowhere and centre everywhere. Every point in that circle is living, conscious, active, and equally working; with us limited souls, only one point is conscious, and that point moves forward and backward. As the body has a very infinitesimal existence in comparison with that of the universe, so the whole universe, in comparison with God, is nothing. When we talk of God speaking, we say He speaks through His universe; and when we speak of Him beyond all limitations of time and space, we say He is an Impersonal Being. Yet He is the same Being.

To give an illustration: We stand here and see the sun. Suppose you want to go towards the sun. After you get a few thousand miles nearer, you will see another sun, much bigger. Supposing you proceed much closer, you will see a much bigger sun. At last you will see the real sun, millions and millions of miles big. Suppose you divide this journey into so many stages, and take photographs from each stage, and after you have taken the real sun, come back and compare them; they will all appear to be different, because the first view was a little red ball, and the real sun was millions of miles bigger; yet it was the same sun. It is the same with God: the Infinite Being we see from different standpoints, from different planes of mind. The lowest man sees Him as an ancestor; as his vision gets higher, as the Governor of the planet; still higher as the Governor of the universe, and the highest man sees Him as himself. It was the same God, and the different realisations were only degrees and differences of vision.

THE DIVINE INCARNATION OR AVATARA

Jesus Christ was God — the Personal God become man. He has manifested Himself many times in different forms and these alone are what you can worship. God in His absolute nature is not to be worshipped. Worshipping such God would be nonsense. We have to worship Jesus Christ, the human manifestation, as God. You cannot worship anything higher than the manifestation of God. The sooner you give up the worship of God separate from Christ, the better for you. Think of the Jehovah you manufacture and of the beautiful Christ. Any time you attempt to make a God beyond Christ, you murder the whole thing. God alone can worship God. It is not given to man, and any attempt to worship Him beyond His ordinary manifestations will be dangerous to mankind. Keep close to Christ if you want salvation; He is higher than any God you can imagine. If you think that Christ was a man, do not worship Him; but as soon as you can realise that He is God, worship Him. Those who say He was a man and then worship Him commit blasphemy; there is no half-way house for you; you must take the whole strength of it. "He that hath seen the Son hath seen the Father", and without seeing the Son, you cannot see the Father. It would be only tall talk and frothy philosophy and dreams and speculations. But if you want to have a hold on spiritual life, cling close to God as manifest in Christ.

Philosophically speaking, there was no such human being living as Christ or Buddha; we saw God through them. In the Koran, Mohammed again and again repeats that Christ was never crucified, it was a semblance; no one could crucify Christ.

The lowest state of philosophical religion is dualism;

the highest form is the Triune state. Nature and the human soul are interpenetrated by God, and this we see as the Trinity of God, nature, and soul. At the same time you catch a glimpse that all these three are products of the One. Just as this body is the covering of the soul, so this is, as it were, the body of God. As I am the soul of nature, so is God the soul of my soul. You are the centre through which you see all nature in which you are. This nature, soul, and God make one individual being, the universe. Therefore they are a unity; yet at the same time they are separate. Then there is another sort of Trinity which is much like the Christian Trinity. God is absolute. We cannot see God in His absolute nature, we can only speak of that as "not this, not this". Yet we can get certain qualities as the nearest approach to God. First is existence, second is knowledge, third is bliss — very much corresponding to your Father, Son, and Holy Ghost. Father is the existence out of which everything comes; Son is that knowledge. It is in Christ that God will be manifest. God was everywhere, in all beings, before Christ; but in Christ we became conscious of Him. This is God. The third is bliss, the Holy Spirit. As soon as you get this knowledge, you get bliss. As soon as you begin to have Christ within you, you have bliss; and that unifies the three.

PRANAYAMA

First of all we will try to understand a little of the meaning of Pranayama. Prana stands in metaphysics for the sum total of the energy that is in the universe. This universe, according to the theory of the philosophers, proceeds in the form of waves; it rises, and again it subsides, melts away, as it were; then again it proceeds out in all this variety; then again it slowly returns. So it goes on like a pulsation. The whole of this universe is composed of matter and force; and according to Sanskrit philosophers, everything that we call matter, solid and liquid, is the outcome of one primal matter which they call Akasha or ether; and the primordial force, of which all the forces that we see in nature are manifestations, they call Prana. It is this Prana acting upon Akasha, which creates this universe, and after the end of a period, called a cycle, there is a period of rest. One period of activity is followed by a period of rest; this is the nature of everything. When this period of rest comes, all these forms that we see in the earth, the sun, the moon, and the stars, all these manifestations melt down until they become ether again. They become dissipated as ether. All these forces, either in the body or in the mind, as gravitation, attraction, motion, thought, become dissipated, and go off into the primal Prana. We can understand from this the importance of this Pranayama. Just as this ether encompasses us everywhere and we are interpenetrated by it, so everything we see is composed of this ether, and we are floating in the ether like pieces of ice floating in a lake. They are formed of the water of the lake and float in it at the same time. So everything that exists is composed of this Akasha and is floating in this ocean. In the same way we are surrounded by this vast ocean of Prana — force and energy. It is this Prana by which we breathe and by which the circulation of the blood goes on; it is the energy in the nerves and in the muscles, and the thought in the brain. All forces are different manifestations of this same Prana, as all matter is a different manifestation of the same Akasha. We always find the causes of the gross in the subtle. The chemist takes a solid lump of ore and analyses it; he wants to find the subtler things out of which that gross is composed. So with our thought and our knowledge; the explanation of the grosser is in the finer. The effect is the gross and the cause the subtle. This gross universe of ours, which we see, feel, and touch, has its cause and explanation behind in the thought. The cause and explanation of that is also further behind. So in this human body of ours, we first find the gross movements, the movements of the hands and lips; but where are the causes of these? The finer nerves, the movements of which we cannot perceive at all, so fine that we cannot see or touch or trace them in any way with our senses, and yet we know they are the cause of these grosser movements. These nerve movements, again, are caused by still finer movements, which we call thought; and that is caused by something finer still behind, which is the soul of man, the Self, the Atman. In order to understand ourselves we have first to make our perception fine. No microscope or instrument that was ever invented will make it possible for us to see the fine movements that are going on inside; we can never see them by any such means. So the Yogi has a science that manufactures an instrument for the study of his own mind, and that instrument is in the mind. The mind attains to powers of finer perception which no instrument will ever be able to attain.

To attain to this power of superfine perception we have to begin from the gross. And as the power becomes finer and finer, we go deeper and deeper inside our own nature; and all the gross movements will first be tangible to us, and then the finer movements of the thought; we will be able to trace the thought before its beginning, trace it where it goes and where it ends. For instance, in the ordinary mind a thought arises. The mind does not know how it began or whence it comes. The mind is like the ocean in which a wave rises, but although the man sees the wave, he does not know how the wave came there, whence its birth, or whither it melts down again; he cannot trace it any further. But when the perception becomes finer, we can trace this wave long, long before it comes to the surface; and we will be able to trace it for a long distance after it has disappeared, and then we can understand psychology as it truly is. Nowadays men think this or that and write many volumes, which are entirely misleading, because they have not the power to analyse their own minds and are talking of things they have never known, but only theorised about. All science must be based on facts, and these facts must be observed and generalised. Until you have some facts to generalise upon, what are you going to do? So all these attempts at generalising are based upon knowing the things we generalise. A man proposes a theory, and adds theory to theory, until the whole book is patchwork of theories, not one of them with the least meaning. The science of Raja-yoga says, first you must gather facts about your own mind, and that can be done by analysing your mind, developing its finer powers of perception and seeing for yourselves what is happening inside; and when you have got these facts, then generalise; and then alone you will have the real science of psychology.

As I have said, to come to any finer perception we must take the help of the grosser end of it. The current of action which is manifested on the outside is the grosser.

If we can get hold of this and go on further and further, it becomes finer and finer, and at last the finest. So this body and everything we have in this body are not different existences, but, as it were, various links in the same chain proceeding from fine to gross. You are a complete whole; this body is the outside manifestation, the crust, of the inside; the external is grosser and the inside finer; and so finer and finer until you come to the Self. And at last, when we come to the Self, we come to know that it was only the Self that was manifesting all this; that it was the Self which became the mind and became the body; that nothing else exists but the Self, and all these others are manifestations of that Self in various degrees, becoming grosser and grosser. So we will find by analogy that in this whole universe there is the gross manifestation, and behind that is the finer movement, which we can call the will of God. Behind that even, we will find that Universal Self. And then we will come to know that the Universal Self becomes God and becomes this universe; and that it is not that this universe is one and God another and the Supreme Self another, but that they are different states of the manifestation of the same Unity behind.

All this comes of our Pranayama. These finer movements that are going on inside the body are connected with the breathing; and if we can get hold of this breathing and manipulate it and control it, we will slowly get to finer and finer motions, and thus enter, as it were, by getting hold of that breathing, into the realms of the mind.

The first breathing that I taught you in our last lesson was simply an exercise for the time being. Some of these breathing exercises, again, are very difficult, and I will try to avoid all the difficult ones, because the more difficult ones require a great deal of dieting and other restrictions which it is impossible for most of you to keep to. So we will take the slower paths and the simpler ones. This breathing consists of three parts. The first is breathing in, which is called in Sanskrit Puraka, filling; and the second part is called Kumbhaka, retaining, filling the lungs and stopping the air from coming out; the third is called Rechaka, breathing out. The first exercise which I will give you today is simply breathing in and stopping the breath and throwing it out slowly. Then there is one step more in the breathing which I will not give you today, because you cannot remember them all; it would be too intricate. These three parts of breathing make one Pranayama. This breathing should be regulated, because if it is not, there is danger in the way to yourselves. So it is regulated by numbers, and I will give you first the lowest numbers. Breathe in four seconds, then hold the breath for eight seconds, then again throw it out slowly in four seconds[1]. Then begin again, and do this four times in the morning and four times in the evening. There is one thing more. Instead of counting by one, two, three, and all such meaningless things, it is better to repeat any word that is holy to you. In our country we have symbolical words, "Om" for instance, which means God. If that be pronounced instead of one, two, three, four, it will serve your purpose very well. One thing more. This breathing should begin through the left nostril and should turn out through the right nostril, and the next time is should be drawn in through the right and thrown out through the left. Then reverse again, and so on. In the first place you should be able to drive your breathing through either nostril at will, just by the power of the will. After a time you will find it easy; but now I am afraid you have not that power. So we must stop the one nostril while breathing through the other with the finger and during the retention, of course, both nostrils.

The first two lessons should not be forgotten. The first thing is to hold yourselves straight; second to think of the body as sound and perfect, as healthy and strong. Then throw a current of love all around, think of the whole universe being happy. Then if you believe in God, pray. Then breathe.

In many of you certain physical changes will come, twitchings all over the body, nervousness; some of

---

1. This process is more difficult when the ratio is two, eight, and four; for further remarks see later.

you will feel like weeping, sometimes a violent motion will come. Do not be afraid; these things have to come as you go on practicing. The whole body will have to be rearranged as it were. New channels for thought will be made in the brain, nerves which have not acted in your whole life will begin to work, and a whole new series of changes will come in the body itself.

WOMEN OF THE EAST[1]

Report of a lecture in the Chicago Daily Inter-Ocean, September 23, 1893.

Swami Vivekananda, at a special meeting, discussed the present and future of the women of the East. He said, "The best thermometer to the progress of a nation is its treatment of its women. In ancient Greece there was absolutely no difference in the state of man and woman. The idea of perfect equality existed. No Hindu can be a priest until he is married, the idea being that a single man is only half a man, and imperfect. The idea of perfect womanhood is perfect independence. The central idea of the life of a modern Hindu lady is her chastity. The wife is the centre of a circle, the fixity of which depends upon her chastity. It was the extreme of this idea which caused Hindu widows to be burnt. The Hindu women are very spiritual and very religious, perhaps more so than any other women in the world. If we can preserve these beautiful characteristics and at the same time develop the intellects of our women, the Hindu woman of the future will be the ideal woman of the world."

CONGRESS OF RELIGIOUS UNITY

Report of a lecture in the Chicago Sunday Herald, September 24, 1893.

Swami Vivekananda said, "All the words spoken at this parliament come to the common conclusion that the brotherhood of man is the much-to-be-desired end. Much has been said for this brotherhood as being a natural condition, since we are all children of one God. Now, there are sects that do not admit of the existence of God — that is, a Personal God. Unless we wish to leave those sects out in the cold — and in that case our brotherhood will not be universal — we must have our platform broad enough to embrace all mankind. It has been said here that we should do good to our fellow men, because every bad or mean deed reacts on the doer. This appears to me to savour of the shopkeeper — ourselves first, our brothers afterwards. I think we should love our brother whether we believe in the universal fatherhood of God or not, because every religion and every creed recognises man as divine, and you should do him no harm that you might not injure that which is divine in him."

THE LOVE OF GOD — I

Report of a lecture in the Chicago Herald, September 25, 1893.

An audience that filled the auditorium of the

---

1. As many women as could crowd into Hall 7 yesterday afternoon flocked thither to hear something as to the lives of their sisters of the Orient. Mrs. Potter Palmer and Mrs. Charles Henrotin sat upon the platform, surrounded by turbanned representatives of the women of the East. It may interest the reader to know that the published addresses of Swami Vivekananda at the Parliament of Religions in Chicago are not exhaustive and many addresses, specially those delivered at the Scientific Section of the Parliament were not all reported. The Scientific Sessions were conducted simultaneously with the open session at the Hall of Columbus. Swami Vivekananda spoke on the following subjects at the Scientific Section: 1. Orthodox Hinduism and the Vedanta Philosophy. — Friday, September 22, 1893, at 10:30 a.m. 2. The Modern Religions of India. — Friday, September 22, 1893 afternoon session. 3. On the subject of the foregoing addresses. — Saturday, September 23, 1893. 4. The Essence of the Hindu Religion. — Monday, September 25, 1893. The Chicago Daily Inter-ocean of September 23, 1893 published the following note on the first lecture. "In the Scientific Section yesterday morning Swami Vivekananda spoke on 'Orthodox Hinduism'. Hall III was crowded to overflowing and hundreds of questions were asked by auditors and answered by the great Sannyasin with wonderful skill and lucidity. At the close of the session he was thronged with eager questioners who begged him to give a semi-public lecture somewhere on the subject of his religion. He said that he already had the project under consideration."

Third Unitarian Church at Laflin and Monroe streets heard Swami Vivekananda preach yesterday morning. The subject of his sermon was the love of God, and his treatment of the theme was eloquent and unique. He said that God was worshipped in all parts of the world, but by different names and in different ways. It is natural for men, he said, to worship the grand and the beautiful, and that religion was a portion of their nature. The need of God was felt by all, and His love prompted them to deeds of charity, mercy, and justice. All men loved God because He was love itself. The speaker had heard since coming to Chicago a great deal about the brotherhood of man. He believed that a still stronger tie connected them, in that all are the offsprings of the love of God. The brotherhood of man was the logical sequence of God as the Father of all. The speaker said he had travelled in the forests of India and slept in caves, and from his observation of nature he had drawn the belief that there was something above the natural law that kept men from wrong, and that, he concluded, was the love of God. If God had spoken to Christ, Mohammed, and the Rishis of the Vedas, why did He not speak also to him, one of his children? "Indeed, he does speak to me", the Swami continued, "and to all His children. We see Him all around us and are impressed continually by the boundlessness of His love, and from that love we draw the inspiration for our well-being and well-doing."

THE LOVE OF GOD — II

A lecture delivered in the Unitarian Church of Detroit on February 20, 1894 and reported in the Detroit Free Press.

Vivekananda delivered a lecture on "The Love of God" at the Unitarian Church last night before the largest audience that he has yet had. The trend of the lecturer's remarks was to show that we do not accept God because we really want Him, but because we have need of Him for selfish purposes. Love, said the speaker, is something absolutely unselfish, that which has no thought beyond the glorification and adoration of the object upon which our affections are bestowed. It is a quality which bows down and worships and asks nothing in return. Merely to love is the sole request that true love has to ask.

It is said of a Hindu saint that when she was married, she said to her husband, the king, that she was already married. "To whom?" asked the king. "To God", was the reply. She went among the poor and the needy and taught the doctrine of extreme love for God. One of her prayers is significant, showing the manner in which her heart was moved: "I ask not for wealth; I ask not for position; I ask not for salvation; place me in a hundred hells if it be Thy wish, but let me continue to regard Thee as my love." The early language abounds in beautiful prayers of this woman. When her end came, she entered into Samadhi on the banks of a river. She composed a beautiful song, in which she stated that she was going to meet her Beloved.

Men are capable of philosophical analysis of religion. A woman is devotional by nature and loves God from the heart and soul and not from the mind. The songs of Solomon are one of the most beautiful parts of the Bible. The language in them is much of that affectionate kind which is found in the prayers of the Hindu woman saint. And yet I have heard that Christians are going to have these incomparable songs removed. I have heard an explanation of the songs in which it is said that Solomon loved a young girl and desired her to return his royal affection. The girl, however, loved a young man and did not want to have anything to do with Solomon. This explanation is excellent to some people, because they cannot understand such wondrous love for God as is embodied in the songs. Love for God in India is different from love for God elsewhere, because when you get into a country where the thermometer reads 40 degrees below zero, the temperament of the people changes. The aspirations of the people in the climate where the books of the Bible are said to have been written were different from the aspirations of the cold-blooded Western nations, who are more apt to worship the almighty dollar with the warmth expressed in the songs than to worship God. Love for God seems to be based upon a basis of "what can I get out of it?" In their prayers they ask for all kinds of selfish things.

Christians are always wanting God to give them something. They appear as beggars before the throne of the Almighty. A story is told of a beggar who applied to an emperor for alms. While he was waiting, it was time for the emperor to offer up prayers. The emperor prayed, "O God, give me more wealth; give me more power; give me a greater empire." The beggar started to leave. The emperor turned and asked him, "Why are you going?" "I do not beg of beggars", was the reply.

Some people find it really difficult to understand the frenzy of religious fervour which moved the heart of Mohammed.

He would grovel in the dust and writhe in agony. Holy men who have experienced these extreme emotions have been called epileptic. The absence of the thought of self is the essential characteristic of the love for God. Religion nowadays has become a mere hobby and fashion. People go to church like a flock of sheep. They do not embrace God because they need Him. Most persons are unconscious atheists who self-complacently think that they are devout believers.

INDIA

Report of a lecture delivered at Detroit on Thursday, February 15, 1894, with the editorial comments of the Detroit Free Press.

An audience that filled the Unitarian Church heard the renowned monk, Swami Vivekananda, deliver a lecture last night on the manners and customs of his country. His eloquent and graceful manner pleased his listeners, who followed him from beginning to end with the closest attention, showing approval from time to time by outbursts of applause. While his lecture was more popular in character than the celebrated Address before the religious congress in Chicago, it was highly entertaining, especially where the speaker diverted from the instructive portions and was led to an eloquent narration of certain spiritual conditions of his own people. It is upon matters religious and philosophic (and necessarily spiritual) that the Eastern brother is most impressive, and, while outlining the duties that follow the conscientious consideration of the great moral law of nature, his softly modulated tones, a peculiarity of his people, and his thrilling manner are almost prophetic. He speaks with marked deliberation, except when placing before his listeners some moral truth, and then his eloquence is of the highest kind.

It seemed somewhat singular that the Eastern monk, who is so outspoken in his disapproval of missionary labour on the part of the Christian church in India (where, he affirms, the morality is the highest in the world), should have been introduced by Bishop Ninde who in June will depart for China in the interest of foreign Christian missions. The Bishop expects to remain away until

December; but if he should stay longer he will go to India. The Bishop referred to the wonders of India and the intelligence of the educated classes there, introducing Vivekananda in a happy manner. When that dusky gentleman arose, dressed in his turban and bright gown, with handsome face and bright, intelligent eyes, he presented an impressive figure. He returned thanks to the Bishop for his words and proceeded to explain race divisions in his own country, the manners of the people, and the different languages. Principally there are four northern tongues and four southern, but there is one common religion. Four-fifths of the population of 300 million people are Hindus and the Hindu is a peculiar person. He does everything in a religious manner. He eats religiously; he sleeps religiously; he rises in the morning religiously; he does good things religiously; and he also does bad things religiously. At this point the lecturer struck the great moral keynote of his discourse, stating that with his people it was the belief that all non-self is good and all self is bad. This point was emphasised throughout the evening and might be termed the text of the address. To build a home is selfish, argues the Hindu; so he builds it for the worship of God and for the entertainment of guests. To cook food is selfish, so he cooks for the poor; he will serve himself last if any hungry stranger applies, and this feeling extends throughout the length and breadth of the land. Any man can ask for food and shelter, and any house will be opened to him.

The caste system has nothing to do with religion. A man's occupation is hereditary: a carpenter is born a carpenter; a goldsmith, a goldsmith; a workman, a workman; and a priest, a priest. But this is a comparatively modern social evil, since it has existed only about 1,000 years. This period of time does not seem so great in India as in this and other countries. Two gifts are especially appreciated — the gift of learning and the gift of life. But the gift of learning takes precedence. One may save a man's life, and that is excellent; one may impart to another knowledge, and that is better. To instruct for money is an evil, and to do this would bring opprobrium on the head of the man who barters learning for gold, as though it were an article of trade. The government makes gifts from time to time to the instructors, and the moral effect is better than it would be if the conditions were the same as exist in certain alleged civilised countries. The speaker had asked through the length and breadth of the land what was the definition of civilisation, and he had asked the question in many countries. Sometimes the reply had been given: What we are, that is civilisation. He begged to differ in the definition of the word. A nation may control the elements, develop utilitarian problems of life seemingly to the limit, and yet not realise that in the individual the highest type of civilisation is found in him who has learnt to conquer self. This condition is found in India more than in any country on earth, for there the material conditions are subservient to the spiritual, and the individual looks for the soul manifestations in everything that has life, studying nature to this end. Hence that gentle disposition to endure with indomitable patience the flings of what appears unkind fortune, the while there is a full consciousness of a spiritual strength and knowledge greater than those possessed by any other people; hence the existence of a country and a people from which flows an unending stream that attracts the attention of thinkers far and near to approach and throw from their shoulders an oppressive earthly burden. The early king, who in 260 B.C. commanded that there should be no more bloodshed, no more wars, and who sent forth instead of soldiers an army of instructors, acted wisely, although in material things the land has suffered. But though in bondage to brutal nations who conquer by force, the Indian's spirituality endures for ever, and nothing can take it away from him. There is something Christlike in the humility of the people to endure the stings and arrows of outraged fortune, the while the soul is advancing towards the brighter goal. Such a country has no need of Christian missionaries to "preach ideas", for theirs is a religion that makes men gentle, sweet, considerate, and affectionate towards all God's creatures, whether man or beast. Morally, said the speaker, India is head and shoulders above the United States or any other country on the globe. Missionaries would do well to come there and drink of the pure waters, and see what a beautiful influence upon a great community have the lives of the multitude of holy men.

Then marriage condition was described; and the privileges extended to women in ancient times when the system of co-education flourished. In the records of the saints in India there is the unique figure of the prophetess. In the Christian creed they are all prophets, while in India the holy women occupy a conspicuous place in the holy books. The householder has five objects for worship. One of them is learning and teaching. Another is worship of dumb creatures. It is hard for Americans to understand the last worship, and it is difficult for Europeans to appreciate the sentiment. Other nations kill animals by wholesale and kill one another; they exist in a sea of blood. A European said that the reason why in India animals were not killed was because it was supposed that they contained the spirits of ancestors. This reason was worthy of a savage nation who are not many steps from the brute. The fact was that the statement was made by a set of atheists in India who thus carped at the Vedic idea of non-killing and transmigration of souls. It was never a religious doctrine, it was an idea of a materialistic creed. The worship of dumb animals was pictured in a vivid manner. The hospitable spirit — the Indian golden rule, was illustrated by a story. A Brahmin, his wife, his son, and his son's wife had not tasted food for some time on account of a famine. The head of the house went out and after a search found a small quantity of barley. He brought this home and divided it into four portions, and the small family was about to eat, when a knock was heard at the door. It was a guest. The different portions were set before him, and he departed with his hunger satisfied, while the quartette who had entertained him perished. This story is told in India to illustrate what is expected in the sacred name of hospitality.

The speaker concluded in an eloquent manner. Throughout, his speech was simple; but whenever he indulged in imagery, it was delightfully poetic, showing that the Eastern brother has been a close and attentive observer of the beauties of nature. His excessive spirituality is a quality which makes itself felt with his auditors, for it manifests itself in the love for animate and inanimate things and in the keen insight into the mysterious workings of the divine law of harmony and kindly intentions.

HINDUS AND CHRISTIANS

A lecture delivered at Detroit on February 21, 1894, and reported in the Detroit Free Press.

Of the different philosophies, the tendency of the Hindu is not to destroy, but to harmonise everything. If any new idea comes into India, we do not antagonise it, but simply try to take it in, to harmonise it, because this method was taught first by our prophet, God incarnate on earth, Shri Krishna. This Incarnation of God preached himself first: "I am the God Incarnate, I am the inspirer of all books, I am the inspirer of all religions." Thus we do not reject any.

There is one thing which is very dissimilar between us and Christians, something which we never taught. That is the idea of salvation through Jesus' blood, or cleansing by any man's blood. We had our sacrifice as the Jews had. Our sacrifices mean simply this: Here is some food I am going to eat, and until some portion is offered to God, it is bad; so I offer the food. This is the pure and simple idea. But with the Jew the idea is that his sin be upon the lamb, and let the lamb be sacrificed and him go scot-free. We never developed this beautiful idea in India, and I am glad we did not. I, for one, would not come to be saved by such a doctrine. If anybody would come and say, "Be saved by my blood", I would say to him, "My brother, go away; I will go to hell; I am not a coward to take innocent blood to go to heaven; I am ready for hell." So that doctrine never cropped up amongst us, and our prophet says that whenever evil and immortality prevail on earth, He will come down and support His children; and this He is doing from time to time and from place to place. And whenever on earth you see an extraordinary holy man trying to uplift humanity, know that He is in him.

So you see that is the reason why we never fight any religion. We do not say that ours is the only way to salvation. Perfection can be had by everybody, and what is the proof? Because we see the holiest of men in all countries, good men and women everywhere, whether born in our faith or not. Therefore it cannot be held that ours is the only way to salvation. "Like so many rivers flowing from different mountains, all coming and mingling their waters in the sea, all the different religions, taking their births from different standpoints of fact, come unto Thee." This is a part of the child's everyday prayer in India. With such everyday prayers, of course, such ideas as fighting because of differences of religion are simply impossible. So much for the philosophers of India. We have great regard for all these men, especially this prophet, Shri Krishna, on account of his wonderful catholicity in harmonising all the preceding revelations.

Then the man who is bowing down before the idol. It is not in the same sense as you have heard of the Babylonian and the Roman idolatry. It is peculiar to the Hindus. The man is before the idol, and he shuts his eyes and tries to think, "I am He; I have neither life nor death; I have neither father nor mother; I am not bound by time or space; I am Existence infinite, Bliss infinite, and Knowledge infinite; I am He, I am He. I am not bound by books, or holy places, or pilgrimages, or anything whatsoever; I am the Existence Absolute, Bliss Absolute; I am He, I am He." This he repeats and then says, "O Lord, I cannot conceive Thee in myself; I am a poor man." Religion does not depend upon knowledge. It is the soul itself, it is God, not to be attained by simple book-knowledge or powers of speech. You may take the most learned man you have and ask him to think of spirit as spirit; he cannot. You may imagine spirit, he may imagine spirit. It is impossible to think of spirit without training. So no matter how much theology you may learn — you may be a great philosopher and greater theologian — but the Hindu boy would say, "Well, that has nothing to do with religion." Can you think of spirit as spirit? Then alone all doubt ceases, and all crookedness of the heart is made straight. Then only all fears vanish, and all doubtings are for ever silent when man's soul and God come face to face.

A man may be wonderfully learned in the Western sense, yet he may not know the A B C of religion. I would tell him that. I would ask him, "Can you think of spirit as such? Are you advanced in the science of the soul? Have you manifested your own soul above matter?" If he has not, then I say to him, "Religion has not come to you; it is all talk and book and vanity." But this poor Hindu sits before that idol and tries to think that he is That, and then says, "O Lord, I cannot conceive Thee as spirit, so let me conceive of Thee in this form"; and then he opens his eyes and see this form, and prostrating himself he repeats his prayers. And when his prayer is ended, he says, "O Lord, forgive me for this imperfect worship of Thee."

You are always being told that the Hindu worships blocks of stone. Now what do you think of this fervent nature of the souls of these people? I am the first monk to come over to these Western countries — it is the first time in the history of the world that a Hindu monk has crossed the ocean. But we hear such criticism and hear of these talks, and what is the general attitude of my nation towards you? They smile and say, "They are children; they may be great in physical science; they may build huge things; but in religion they are simply children." That is the attitude of my people.

One thing I would tell you, and I do not mean any unkind criticism. You train and educate and clothe and pay men to do what? To come over to my country to curse and abuse all my forefathers, my religion, and everything. They walk near a temple and say, "You idolaters, you will go to hell." But they dare not do that to the Mohammedans of India; the sword would be out. But the Hindu is too mild; he smiles and passes on, and says, "Let the fools talk." That is the attitude. And then you who train men to abuse and criticise, if I just touch you with the least bit of criticism, with the kindest of purpose, you shrink and cry, "Don't touch us; we are Americans. We criticise all the people in the world, curse them and abuse them, say anything; but do not touch us; we are sensitive plants." You may do whatever you please; but at the same time I am going to tell you that we are content to live as we are; and in one thing we are better off — we never teach our children to swallow such horrible stuff: "Where every prospect pleases and man alone is vile." And whenever your ministers criticise us, let them remember this: If all India stands up and takes all the mud that is at the bottom of the Indian Ocean and throws it up against the Western countries, it will not be doing an infinitesimal part of that which you are doing to us. And what for? Did we ever send one missionary to convert anybody in the world? We say to you, "Welcome to your religion, but allow me to have mine." You call yours an aggressive religion. You are aggressive, but how many have you taken? Every sixth man in the world is a Chinese subject, a Buddhist; then there are Japan, Tibet, and Russia, and Siberia, and Burma, and Siam; and it may not be palatable, but this Christian morality, the Catholic Church, is all derived from them. Well, and how was this done? Without the shedding of one drop of blood! With all your brags and boastings, where has your Christianity succeeded without the sword? Show me one place in the whole world. One, I say, throughout the history of the Christian religion — one; I do not want two. I know how your forefathers were converted. They had to be converted or killed; that was all. What can you do better than Mohammedanism, with all your bragging? "We are the only one!" And why? "Because we can kill others." The Arabs said that; they bragged. And where is the Arab now? He is the bedouin. The Romans used to say that, and where are they now? Blessed are the peace-makers; they shall enjoy the earth. Such things tumble down; it is built upon sands; it cannot remain long.

Everything that has selfishness for its basis, competition as its right hand, and enjoyment as its goal, must die sooner or later. Such things must die. Let me tell you, brethren, if you want to live, if you really want your nation to live, go back to Christ. You are not Christians. No, as a nation you are not. Go back to Christ. Go back to him who had nowhere to lay his head. "The birds have their nests and the beasts their lairs, but the Son of Man has nowhere to lay his head." Yours is religion preached in the name of luxury. What an irony of fate! Reverse this if you want to live, reverse this. It is all hypocrisy that I have heard in this country. If this nation is going to live, let it go back to him. You cannot serve God and Mammon at the same time. All this prosperity, all this from Christ! Christ would have denied all such heresies. All prosperity which comes with Mammon is transient, is only for a moment. Real permanence is in Him. If you can join these two, this wonderful prosperity with the ideal of Christ, it is well. But if you cannot, better go back to him and give this up. Better be ready to live in rags with Christ than to live in palaces without him.

CHRISTIANITY IN INDIA

A lecture delivered at Detroit on March 11, 1894 and reported in the Detroit Free Press.

"Vive Kananda spoke to a crowded audience at the Detroit Opera House last night. He was given an extremely cordial reception and delivered his most eloquent address here. He spoke for two hours and a half.

Hon. T. W. Palmer, in introducing the distinguished visitor, referred to the old tale of the shield that was copper on one side and silver on the other and the contest which ensued. If we look on both sides of a question there would be less dispute. It is possible for all men to agree. The matter of foreign missions has been dear to the religious heart. Vive Kananda, from the Christian standpoint, said Mr. Palmer, was a pagan. It would be pleasant to hear from a gentleman who spoke about the copper side of the shield.

Vive Kananda was received with great applause."

. . .

I do not know much about missionaries in Japan and China, but I am well posted about India. The people of this country look upon India as a vast waste, with many jungles and a few civilised Englishmen. India is half as large as the United States, and there are three hundred million people. Many stories are related, and I have become tired of denying these. The first invaders of India, the Aryans, did not try to exterminate the population of India as the Christians did when they went into a new land, but the endeavour was made to elevate persons of brutish habits. The Spaniards came to Ceylon with Christianity. The Spaniards thought that their God commanded them to kill and murder and to tear down heathen temples. The Buddhists had a tooth a foot long, which belonged to their Prophet, and the Spaniards threw it into the sea, killed a few thousand persons, and converted a few scores. The Portuguese came to Western India. The Hindus have a belief in the Trinity and had a temple dedicated to their sacred belief. The invaders looked at the temple and said it was a creation of the devil; and so they brought their cannon to bear upon the wonderful structure and destroyed a portion of it. But the invaders were driven out of the country by the enraged population. The early missionaries tried to get hold of the land, and in their effort to secure a foothold by force, they killed many people and converted a number. Some of them became Christians to save their lives. Ninety-nine percent of the Christians converted by the Portuguese sword were compelled to be so, and they said, "We do not believe in Christianity, but we are forced to call ourselves Christians." But Catholic Christianity soon relapsed.

The East India Company got possession of a part of India with the idea of making hay while the sun shone. They kept the missionaries away. The Hindus were the first to welcome the missionaries, not the Englishmen, who were engaged in trade. I have great admiration for some of the first missionaries of the later period, who were true servants of Jesus and did not vilify the people or spread vile falsehoods about them. They were gentle, kindly men. When Englishmen became masters of India, the missionary enterprise began to become stagnant, a condition which characterises the missionary efforts in India today. Dr. Long, an early missionary, stood by the people. He translated a Hindu drama describing the evils perpetuated in India by indigo-planters, and what was the result? He was placed in jail by the English. Such missionaries were of benefit to the country, but they have passed away. The Suez Canal opened up a number of evils.

Now goes the missionary, a married man, who is hampered because he is married. The missionary knows nothing about the people, he cannot speak the language, so he invariably settles in the little white colony. He is forced to do this because he is married. Were he not married, he could go among the people and sleep on the ground if necessary. So he goes to India to seek company for his wife and children. He stays among the English-speaking people. The great heart of India is today absolutely untouched by missionary effort. Most of the missionaries are incompetent. I have not met a single missionary who understands Sanskrit. How can a man absolutely ignorant of the people and their traditions, get into sympathy with them? I do not mean any offense, but Christians send men as missionaries, who are not persons of ability. It is sad to see money spent to make converts when no real results of a satisfactory nature are reached.

Those who are converted, are the few who make a sort of living by hanging round the missionaries. The converts who are not kept in service in India, cease to be converts. That is about the entire matter in a nutshell. As to the way of converting, it is absolutely absurd. The money the missionaries bring is accepted. The colleges founded by missionaries are all right, so far as the education is concerned. But with religion it is different. The Hindu is acute; he takes the bait but avoids the hook! It is wonderful how tolerant the people are. A missionary once said, "That is the worst of the whole business. People who are self-complacent can never be converted."

As regards the lady missionaries, they go into certain houses, get four shillings a month, teach them something of the Bible, and show them how to knit. The girls of India will never be converted. Atheism and skepticism at home is what is pushing the missionary into other lands.

When I came into this country I was surprised to meet so many liberal men and women. But after the Parliament of Religions a great Presbyterian paper came out and gave me the benefit of a seething article. This the editor called enthusiasm. The missionaries do not and cannot throw off nationality — they are not broad enough — and so they accomplish nothing in the way of converting, although they may have a nice sociable time among themselves. India requires help from Christ, but not from the antichrist; these men are not Christlike. They do not act like Christ; they are married and come over and settle down comfortably and make a fair livelihood. Christ and his disciples would accomplish much good in India, just as many of the Hindu saints do; but these men are not of that sacred character. The Hindus would welcome the Christ of the Christians gladly, because his life was holy and beautiful; but they cannot and will not receive the narrow utterances of the ignorant, hypocritical or self-deceiving men.

Men are different. If they were not, the mentality of the world would be degraded. If there were not different religions, no religion would survive. The

Christian requires his religion; the Hindu needs his own creed. All religions have struggled against one another for years. Those which were founded on a book, still stand. Why could not the Christians convert the Jews? Why could they not make the Persians Christians? Why could they not convert Mohammedans? Why cannot any impression be made upon China or Japan? Buddhism, the first missionary religion, numbers double the number of converts of any other religion, and they did not use the sword. The Mohammedans used the greatest violence. They number the least of the three great missionary religions. The Mohammedans have had their day. Every day you read of Christian nations acquiring land by bloodshed. What missionaries preach against this? Why should the most bloodthirsty nation exalt an alleged religion which is not the religion of Christ? The Jews and the Arabs were the fathers of Christianity, and how they have been persecuted by the Christians! The Christians have been weighed in the balance in India and have been found wanting. I do not mean to be unkind, but I want to show the Christians how they look in others' eyes. The missionaries who preach the burning pit are regarded with horror. The Mohammedans rolled wave after wave over India waving the sword, and today where are they?

The furthest that all religions can see is the existence of a spiritual entity. So no religion can teach beyond that point. In every religion there is the essential truth and the non-essential casket in which this jewel lies. Believing in the Jewish book or in the Hindu book is non-essential. Circumstances change; the receptacle is different; but the central truth remains. The essentials being the same, the educated people of every community retain the essentials. If you ask a Christian what his essentials are, he should reply, "The teachings of Lord Jesus." Much of the rest is nonsense. But the nonsensical part is right; it forms the receptacle. The shell of the oyster is not attractive, but the pearl is within it. The Hindu will never attack the life of Jesus; he reverences the Sermon on the Mount. But how many Christians know or have heard of the teachings of the Hindu holy men? They remain in a fool's paradise. Before a small fraction of the world was converted, Christianity was divided into many creeds. That is the law of nature. Why take a single instrument from the great religious orchestra of the earth? Let the grand symphony go on. Be pure. Give up superstition and see the wonderful harmony of nature. Superstition gets the better of religion. All the religions are good, since the essentials are the same. Each man should have the perfect exercise of his individuality, but these individualities form a perfect whole. This marvelous condition is already in existence. Each creed has something to add to the wonderful structure.

I pity the Hindu who does not see the beauty in Jesus Christ's character. I pity the Christian who does not reverence the Hindu Christ. The more a man sees of himself, the less he sees of his neighbors. Those that go about converting, who are very busy saving the souls of others, in many instances forget their own souls. I was asked by a lady why the women of India were not more elevated. It is in a great degree owing to the barbarous invaders through different ages; it is partly due to the people in India themselves. But our women are any day better than the ladies of this country who devotees of novels and balls. Where is the spirituality one would expect in a country which is so boastful of its civilisation? I have not found it. "Here" and "here-after" are words to frighten children. It is all "here". To live and move in God — even here, even in this body! All self should go out; all superstition should be banished. Such men live in India. Where are such in this country? Your preachers speak against "dreamers". The people of this country would be better off if there were more "dreamers". If a man here followed literally the instruction of his Lord, he would be called a fanatic. There is a good deal of difference between dreaming and the brag of the nineteenth century. The bees look for the flowers. Open the lotus! The whole world is full of God and not of sin. Let us help each other. Let us love each other. A beautiful prayer of the Buddhist is: I bow down to all the saints; I bow down to all the prophets; I bow down to all the holy men and women all over the world!

THE RELIGION OF LOVE

Notes of a lecture delivered in London on November 16, 1895.

Just as it is necessary for a man to go through symbols and ceremonies first in order to arrive at the depth of realisation, so we say in India, "It is good to be born in a church, but bad to die in one". A sapling must be hedged about for protection, but when it becomes a tree, a hedge would be a hindrance. So there is no need to criticise and condemn the old forms. We forget that in religion there must be growth.

At first we think of a Personal God, and call Him Creator, Omnipotent, Omniscient, and so forth. But when loves comes, God is only love. The loving worshipper does not care what God is, because he wants nothing from Him. Says an Indian saint, "I am no beggar!" Neither does he fear. God is loved as a human being.

Here are some of the systems founded on love. (1) Shanta, a common, peaceful love, with such thoughts as those of fatherhood and help; (2) Dasya, the ideal of service; God as master or general or sovereign, giving punishments and rewards; (3) Vatsalya, God as mother or child. In India the mother never punishes. In each of these stages, the worshipper forms an ideal of God and follows it. Then (4) Sakhya, God as friend. There is here no fear. There is also the feeling of equality and familiarity. There are some Hindus who worship God as friend and playmate. Next comes (5) Madhura, sweetest love, the love of husband and wife. Of this St. Teresa and the ecstatic saints have been examples. Amongst the Persians, God has been looked upon as the wife, amongst the Hindus as the husband. We may recall the great queen Mira Bai, who preached that the Divine Spouse was all. Some carry this to such an extreme that to call God "mighty" or "father" seems to them blasphemy. The language of this worship is erotic. Some even use that of illicit passion. To this cycle belongs the story of Krishna and the Gopi-girls. All this probably seems to you to entail great degeneration on the worshipper. And so it does. Yet many great saints have been developed by it. And no human institution is beyond abuse. Would you cook nothing because there are beggars? Would you possess nothing because there are thieves? "O Beloved, one kiss of Thy lips, once tasted, hath made me mad!"

The fruit of this idea is that one can no longer belong to any sect, or endure ceremonial. Religion in India culminates in freedom. But even this comes to be given up, and all is love for love's sake.

Last of all comes love without distinction, the Self. There is a Persian poem that tells how a lover came to the door of his beloved, and knocked. She asked, "Who art thou?" and he replied, "I am so and so, thy beloved!" and she answered only, "Go! I know none such!" But when she had asked for the fourth time, he said, "I am thyself, O my Beloved, therefore open thou to me!" And the door was opened.

A great saint said, using the language of a girl, describing love: "Four eyes met. There were changes in two souls. And now I cannot tell whether he is a man and I am a woman, or he is a woman and I a man. This only I remember, two souls were. Love came, and there was one."

In the highest love, union is only of the spirit. All love of any other kind is quickly evanescent. Only the spiritual lasts, and this grows.

Love sees the Ideal. This is the third angle of the triangle. God has been Cause, Creator, Father. Love is the culmination. The mother regrets that her child is humpbacked, but when she has nursed him for a few days, she loves him and thinks him most beautiful. The lover sees the beauty of Helen in the brow of Ethiopia. We do not commonly realise what happens. The brow of Ethiopia is merely a suggestion: the man sees Helen. His ideal is thrown upon the suggestion and covers it, as the oyster makes sand into a pearl. God is this ideal, through which man may see all.

Hence we come to love love itself. This love cannot be expressed. No words can utter it. We are dumb about it.

The senses become very much heightened in love. Human love, we must remember, is mixed up with attributes. It is dependent, too, on the other's attitude. Indian languages have words to describe this interdependence of love. The lowest love is selfish; it consists in pleasure of being loved. We say in India, "One gives the cheek, the other kisses." Above this is mutual love. But this also ceases mutually. True love is all giving. We do not even want to see the other, or to do anything to express our feeling. It is enough to give. It is almost impossible to love a human being like this, but it is possible to love God.

In India there is no idea of blasphemy if boys fighting in the street use the name of God. We say, "Put your hand into the fire, and whether you feel it or not, you will be burnt. So to utter the name of God can bring nothing but good."

The notion of blasphemy comes from the Jews, who were impressed by the spectacle of Persian loyalty. The ideas that God is judge and punisher are not in themselves bad, but they are low and vulgar. The three angles of the triangle are: Love begs not; Love knows no fear; Love is always the ideal. "Who would be able to live one second,

Who would be able to breathe one moment,

If the Loving one had not filled the universe?"

Most of us will find that we were born for service. We must leave the results to God. The work was done only for love of God. If failure comes, there need be no sorrow. The work was done only for love of God.

In women, the mother-nature is much developed. They worship God as the child. They ask nothing, and will do anything.

The Catholic Church teaches many of these deep things, and though it is narrow, it is religious in the highest sense. In modern society, Protestantism is broad but shallow. To judge truth by what good it does is as bad as to question the value of a scientific discovery to a baby.

Society must be outgrown. We must crush law and become outlaws. We allow nature, only in order to conquer her. Renunciation means that none can serve both God and Mammon.

Deepen your own power of thought and love. Bring your own lotus to blossom: the bees will come of themselves. Believe first in yourself, then in God. A handful of strong men will move the world. We need a heart to feel, a brain to conceive, and a strong arm to do the work. Buddha gave himself for the animals. Make yourself a fit agent to work. But it is God who works, not you. One man contains the whole universe. One particle of matter has all the energy of the universe at its back. In a conflict between the heart and the brain follow your heart.

Yesterday, competition was the law. Today, cooperation is the law. Tomorrow there is no law. Let sages praise thee, or let the world blame. Let fortune itself come, or let poverty and rags stare thee in the face.

Eat the herbs of the forest, one day, for food; and the next, share a banquet of fifty courses. Looking neither to right hand nor to the left, follow thou on!

The Swami began by telling, in answer to questions, the story of how Pavhari Baba snatched up his own vessels and ran after the thief, only to fall at his feet and say: "O Lord, I knew not that Thou wert there! Take them! They are Thine! Pardon me, Thy child!"

Again he told how the same saint was bitten by a cobra, and when, towards nightfall he recovered, he said, "A messenger came to me from the Beloved."

JNANA AND KARMA

Notes of a lecture delivered in London, on November 23, 1895.

The greatest force is derived from the power of thought. The finer the element, the more powerful it is. The silent power of thought influences people even at a distance, because mind is one as well as many. The universe is a cobweb; minds are spiders.

The universe equals the phenomena of one Universal Being. He, seen through our senses, is the universe. This is Maya. So the world is illusion, that is, the imperfect vision of the Real, a semi-revelation, even as the sun in the morning is a red ball.

Thus all evils and wickedness are but weakness, the imperfect vision of goodness.

A straight line projected infinitely becomes a circle. The search for good comes back to Self. I am the whole mystery, God. I am a body, the lower self; and I am the Lord of the universe.

Why should a man be moral and pure? Because this strengthens his will. Everything that strengthens the will by revealing the real nature is moral. Everything that does the reverse is immoral. The standard varies from country to country, from individual to individual. Man must recover from his state of slavery to laws, to words, and so on. We have no freedom of the will now, but we shall have when we are free. Renunciation is this giving up of the world. Through the senses, anger comes, and sorrow comes. As long as renunciation is not there, self and the passion animating it are different. At last they become identified, and the man is an animal at once. Become possessed with the feeling of renunciation.

I once had a body, was born, struggled and died: What awful hallucinations! To think that one was cramped in a body, weeping for salvation!

But does renunciation demand that we all become ascetics? Who then is to help others? Renunciation is not asceticism. Are all beggars Christ? Poverty is not a synonym for holiness; often the reverse. Renunciation is of the mind. How does it come? In a desert, when I was thirsty, I saw a lake. It was in the midst of a beautiful landscape. There were trees surrounding it, and their reflections could be seen in the water, upside down. But the whole thing proved to be a mirage. Then I knew that every day for a month I had seen this; and only that day, being thirsty, I had learnt it to be unreal. Every day for a month I should see it again. But I should never take it to be real. So, when we reach God, the idea of the universe, the body and so on, will vanish. It will return afterwards. But next time we shall know it to be unreal.

The history of the world is the history of persons like Buddha and Jesus. The passionless and unattached do most for the world. Picture Jesus in the slums. He sees beyond the misery, "You, my brethren, are all divine." His work is calm. He removes causes. You will be able to work for the good of the world when you know for a fact that this work is all illusion. The more unconscious this work, the better, because it is then the more superconscious. Our search is not for good or evil; but happiness and good are nearer to truth than their opposites. A man ran a thorn into his finger, and with another thorn took it out. The first thorn is Evil. The second thorn is Good. The Self is that Peace which passeth beyond both evil and good. The universe is melting down: man draws nearer to God. For one moment he is real — god. He is re-differentiated — a prophet. Before him, now, the world trembles. A fool sleeps and wakes a fool — a man unconscious; and superconscious, he returns with infinite power, purity, and love — the God-man. This is the use of the superconscious state.

Wisdom can be practised even on a battlefield. The Gita was preached so. There are three states of mind: the active, the passive, and the serene. The passive state is characterised by slow vibrations; the active by quick vibrations, and the serene by the most intense vibrations of all. Know that the soul is sitting in the chariot. The body is the chariot; the outer senses are the horses; and the mind the reins; and the intellect the charioteer. So man crosses the ocean of Maya. He goes beyond. He reaches God. When a man is under the control of his senses, he is of this world. When he has controlled the senses, he has renounced.

Even forgiveness, if weak and passive, is not true: fight is better. Forgive when you could bring legions of angels to the victory. Krishna, the charioteer of Arjuna, hears him say, "Let us forgive our enemies", and answers, "You speak the words of wise men, but you are not a wise man, but a coward". As a lotus-leaf, living in the water yet untouched by it, so should the soul be in the world. This is a battlefield, fight your way out. Life in this world is an attempt to see God. Make your life a manifestation of will strengthened by renunciation.

We must learn to control all our brain-centres consciously. The first step is the joy of living. Asceticism is fiendish. To laugh is better than to pray.

Sing. Get rid of misery. Do not for heaven's sake infect others with it. Never think God sells a little happiness and a little unhappiness. Surround yourself with flowers and pictures and incense. The saints went to the mountain tops to enjoy nature.

The second step is purity.

The third is full training of the mind. Reason out what is true from what is untrue. See that God alone is true. If for a moment you think you are not God, great terror will seize you. As soon as you think "I am He", great peace and joy will come to you. Control the senses. If a man curses me, I should still see in him God, whom through my weakness I see as a curser. The poor man to whom you do good is extending a privilege to you. He allows you, through His mercy, to worship Him thus.

The history of the world is the history of a few men who had faith in themselves. That faith calls out the divinity within. You can do anything. You fail only when you do not strive sufficiently to manifest infinite power. As soon as a man or a nation loses faith, death comes.

There is a divine within that cannot be overcome either by church dogmas or by blackguardism. A handful of Greeks speak wherever there is civilisation. Some mistakes there must always be. Do not grieve. Have great insight. Do not think, "What is done is done. Oh, that 'twere done better!" If man had not been God, humanity would by this time have become insane, with its litanies and its penitence.

None will be left, none destroyed. All will in the end be made perfect. Say, day and night, "Come up, my brothers! You are the infinite ocean of purity! Be God! Manifest as God!"

What is civilisation? It is the feeling of the divine within. When you find time, repeat these ideas to yourself and desire freedom. That is all. Deny everything that is not God. Assert everything that is God. Mentally assert this, day and night. So the veil grows thinner: "I am neither man nor angel. I have no sex nor limit. I am knowledge itself. I am He. I have neither anger nor hatred. I have neither pain nor pleasure. Death or birth I never had. For I am Knowledge Absolute, and Bliss Absolute. I am He, my soul, I am He!"

Find yourself bodiless. You never had a body. It was all superstition. Give back the divine consciousness to all the poor, the downtrodden, the oppressed, and the sick.

Apparently, every five hundred years or so, a wave of this thought comes over the world. Little waves arise in many directions: but one swallows up all the others and sweeps over society. That wave does this which has most character at its back.

Confucius, Moses, and Pythagoras; Buddha, Christ, Mohammed; Luther, Calvin, and the Sikhs; Theosophy, Spiritualism, and the like; all these mean only the preaching of the Divine-in-man.

Never say man is weak. Wisdom-yoga is no better than the others. Love is the ideal and requires no object. Love is God. So even through devotion we reach the subjective God. I am He! How can one work, unless one loves city, country, animals, the universe? Reason leads to the finding of unity in variety. Let the atheist and the agnostic work for the social good. So God comes.

But this you must guard against: Do not disturb the faith of any. For you must know that religion is not in doctrines. Religion lies in being and becoming, in realisation. All men are born idolaters. The lowest man is an animal. The highest man is perfect. And between these two, all have to think in sound and colour, in doctrine and ritual.

The test of having ceased to be an idolater is: "When you say 'I', does the body come into your thought or not? If it does, then you are still a worshipper of idols." Religion is not intellectual jargon at all, but realisation. If you think about God, you are only a fool. The ignorant man, by prayer and devotion, can reach beyond the philosopher. To know God, no philosophy is necessary. Our duty is not to disturb the faith of others. Religion is experience. Above all and in all, be sincere; identification brings misery, because it brings desire. Thus the poor man sees gold, and identifies himself with the need of gold. Be the witness. Learn never to react.

THE CLAIMS OF VEDANTA ON THE MODERN WORLD

Report of a lecture delivered in Oakland on Sunday, February 25, 1900, with editorial comments of the Oakland Enquirer.

The announcement that Swami Vivekananda, a distinguished savant of the East, would expound the philosophy of Vedanta in the Parliament of Religions at the Unitarian Church last evening, attracted an immense throng. The main auditorium and ante-rooms were packed, the annexed auditorium of Wendte Hall was thrown open, and this was also filled to overflowing, and it is estimated that fully 500 persons, who could not obtain seats or standing room where they could hear conveniently, were turned away.

The Swami created a marked impression. Frequently he received applause during the lecture, and upon concluding, held a levee of enthusiastic admirers. He said in part, under the subject of "The Claims of Vedanta on the Modern World":

Vedanta demands the consideration of the modern world. The largest number of the human race is under its influence. Again and again, millions upon millions have swept down on its adherents in India, crushing them with their great force, and yet the religion lives.

In all the nations of the world, can such a system be found? Others have risen to come under its shadow. Born like mushrooms, today they are alive and flourishing, and tomorrow they are gone. Is this not the survival of the fittest?

It is a system not yet complete. It has been growing for thousands of years and is still growing. So I can give you but an idea of all I would say in one brief hour.

First, to tell you of the history of the rise of Vedanta. When it arose, India had already perfected a religion. Its crystallisation had been going on many years. Already there were elaborate ceremonies; already there had been perfected a system of morals for the different stages of life. But there came a rebellion against the mummeries and mockeries that enter into many religions in time, and great men came forth to proclaim through the Vedas the true religion. Hindus received their religion from the revelation of these Vedas. They were told that the Vedas were without beginning and without end. It may sound ludicrous to this audience — how a book can be without beginning or end; but by the Vedas no books are meant. They mean the accumulated treasury of spiritual laws discovered by different persons in different times.

Before these men came, the popular ideas of a God ruling the universe, and that man was immortal, were in existence. But there they stopped. It was thought that nothing more could be known. Here came the daring of the expounders of Vedanta. They knew that religion meant for children is not good for thinking men; that there is something more to man and God.

The moral agnostic knows only the external dead nature. From that he would form the law of the universe. He might as well cut off my nose and claim to form an idea of my whole body, as argue thus. He must look within. The stars that sweep through the heavens, even the universe is but a drop in the bucket. Your agnostic sees not the greatest, and he is frightened at the universe.

The world of spirit is greater than all — the God of the universe who rules — our Father, our Mother. What is this heathen mummery we call the world? There is misery everywhere. The child is born with a cry upon its lips; it is its first utterance. This child becomes a man, and so well used to misery that the pang of the heart is hidden by a smile on the lips.

Where is the solution of this world? Those who look outside will never find it; they must turn their eyes inward and find truth. Religion lives inside.

One man preaches, if you chop your head off, you get salvation. But does he get any one to follow him? Your own Jesus says, "Give all to the poor and follow me." How many of you have done this? You have not followed out this command, and yet Jesus was the great teacher of your religion. Every one of you is practical in his own life, and you find this would be impracticable.

But Vedanta offers you nothing that is impracticable. Every science must have its own matter to work upon. Everyone needs certain conditions and much of training and learning; but any Jack in the street can tell you all about religion. You may want to follow religion and follow an expert, but you may only care to converse with Jack, for he can talk it.

You must do with religion as with science, come in direct contact with facts, and on that foundation build a marvellous structure. To have a true religion you must have instruments. Belief is not in question; of faith you can make nothing, for you can believe anything.

We know that in science as we increase the velocity, the mass decreases; and as we increase the mass, the velocity decreases. Thus we have matter and force. The matter, we do not know how, disappears into force, and force into matter. Therefore there is something which is neither force nor matter, as these two may not disappear into each other. This is what we call mind — the universal mind.

Your body and my body are separate, you say. I am but a little whirlpool in the universal ocean of mankind. A whirlpool, it is true, but a part of the great ocean. You stand by moving water where every particle is changing, and yet you call it a stream. The water is changing, it is true, but the banks remain the same. The mind is not changing, but the body — how quick its growth! I was a baby, a boy, a man, and soon I will be an old man, stooped and aged. The body is changing, and you say, is the mind not changing also? When I was a child, I was thinking, I have become larger, because my mind is a sea of impressions.

There is behind nature a universal mind. The spirit is simply a unit and it is not matter. For man is a spirit. The question, "Where does the soul go after death?" should be answered like the boy when he asked, "Why does not the earth fall down?" The questions are alike, and their solutions alike; for where could the soul go to?

To you who talk of immortality I would ask when you go home to endeavour to imagine you are dead. Stand by and touch your dead body. You cannot, for you cannot get out of yourself. The question is not concerning immortality, but as to whether Jack will meet his Jenny after death.

The one great secret of religion is to know for yourself that you are a spirit. Do not cry out, "I am a worm, I am nobody!" As the poet says, "I am Existence, Knowledge, and Truth." No man can do any good in the world by crying out, "I am one of its evils." The more perfect, the less imperfections you see.

THE LAWS OF LIFE AND DEATH

Report of a lecture delivered in Oakland on March 7, 1900, with editorial comments of the Oakland Tribune.

Swami Vivekananda delivered a lecture last evening on the subject, "The Laws of Life and Death". The Swami said: "How to get rid of this birth and death — not how to go to heaven, but how one can stop going to heaven — this is the object of the search of the Hindu."

The Swami went on to say that nothing stands isolated — everything is a part of the never-ending procession of cause and effect. If there are higher beings than man, they also must obey the laws. Life can only spring from life, thought from thought, matter from matter. A universe cannot be created out of matter. It has existed for ever. If human beings came into the world fresh from the hands of nature, they would come without impressions; but we do not come in that way, which shows that we are not created afresh. If human souls are created out of nothing, what is to prevent them from going back into nothing? If we are to live all the time in the future, we must have lived all the time in the past.

It is the belief of the Hindu that the soul is neither mind nor body. What is it which remains stable — which can say, "I am I"? Not the body, for it is always changing; and not the mind, which changes more rapidly than the body, which never has the same thoughts for even a few minutes. There must be an identity which does not change — something which is to man what the banks are to the river — the banks which do not change and without whose immobility we would not be conscious of the constantly moving stream. Behind the body, behind the mind, there must be something, viz the soul, which unifies the man. Mind is merely the fine instrument through which the soul — the master — acts on the body. In India we say a man has given up his body, while you say, a man gives up his ghost. The Hindus believe that a man is a soul and has a body, while Western people believe he is a body and possesses a soul.

Death overtakes everything which is complex. The soul is a single element, not composed of anything else, and therefore it cannot die. By its very nature the soul must be immortal. Body, mind, and soul turn upon the wheel of law — none can escape. No more can we transcend the law than can the stars, than can the sun — it is all a universe of law. The law of Karma is that every action must be followed sooner or later by an effect. The Egyptian seed which was taken from the hand of a mummy after 5000 years and sprang into life when planted is the type of the never-ending influence of human acts. Action can never die without producing action. Now, if our acts can only produce their appropriate effects on this plane of existence, it follows that we must all come back to round out the circle of causes and effects. This is the doctrine of reincarnation. We are the slaves of law, the slaves of conduct, the slaves of thirst, the slaves of desire, the slaves of a thousand things. Only by escaping from life can we escape from slavery to freedom. God is the only one who is free. God and freedom are one and the same.

THE REALITY AND THE SHADOW

Report of a lecture delivered in Oakland on March 8, 1900, with editorial comments of the Oakland Tribune.

Swami Vivekananda, the Hindu philosopher, delivered another lecture in Wendte Hall last evening. His subject was: "The Reality and The Shadow". He said: "The soul of man is ever striving after certainty, to find something that does not change. It is never satisfied. Wealth, the gratification of ambition or of appetite are all changeable. Once these are attained, man is not content. Religion is the science which teaches us whence to satisfy this longing after the unchangeable. Behind all the local colours and derivations they teach the same thing — that there is reality only in the soul of man. "The philosophy of Vedanta teaches that there are two worlds, the external or sensory, and the internal or subjective — the thought world. "It posits three fundamental concepts — time, space, and causation. From these is constituted Maya, the essential groundwork of human thought, not the product of thought. This same conclusion was arrived at a later date by the great German philosopher Kant. "My reality, that of nature and of God, is the same, the difference is in form of manifestation. The differentiation is caused by Maya. The contour of the shore may shape the ocean into bay, strait, or inlet; but when this shaping force or Maya is removed, the separate form disappears, the differentiation ceases, all is ocean again."

The Swami then spoke of the roots of the theory of evolution to be found in the Vedanta philosophy. "All modern religions start with the idea," continued the speaker, "that man was once pure, he fell, and will become pure again. I do not see where they get this idea. The seat of knowledge is the soul; external circumstance simply stimulates the soul; knowledge is the power of the soul. Century after century it has been manufacturing bodies. The various forms of incarnation are merely successive chapters of the story of the life of the soul. We are constantly building our bodies. The whole universe is in a state of flux, of expansion and contraction, of change. Vedanta holds that the soul never changes in essence, but it is modified by Maya. Nature is God limited by mind. The evolution of nature is the modification of the soul. The soul in essence is the same in all forms of being. Its expression is modified by the body. This unity of soul, this common substance of humanity, is the basis of ethics and morality. In this sense all are one, and to hurt one's brother is to hurt one's Self. "Love is simply an expression of this infinite unity. Upon what dualistic system can you explain love? One of the European philosophers says that kissing is a survival of cannibalism, a kind of expression of 'how good you taste'. I do not believe it. "What is it we all seek? Freedom. All the effort and struggle of life is for freedom. It is the march universal of races, of worlds, and of systems. "If we are bound, who bound us? No power can bind the Infinite but Itself."

After the discourse an opportunity was afforded for asking questions of the speaker, who devoted half an hour to answering them.

WAY TO SALVATION

Report of a lecture delivered in Oakland on Monday, March 12, 1900, with editorial comments of the Oakland Enquirer.

Wendte Hall of the First Unitarian Church was crowded last evening with a large audience to hear the "Way to Salvation" from the standpoint of the Hindu priest, Swami Vivekananda. This was the last lecture of a series of three which the Swami has delivered. He said in part:

One man says God is in heaven, another that God is in nature and everywhere present. But when the great crisis comes, we find the goal is the same. We all work on different plans, but the end is not different.

The two great watchwords of every great religion are renunciation and self-sacrifice. We all want the truth, and we know that it must come, whether we want it or not. In a way we are all striving for that good. And what prevents our reaching it? It is ourselves. Your ancestors used to call it the devil; but it is our own false self.

We live in slavery, and we would die if we were out of it. We are like the man who lived in total darkness for ninety years and when taken out into the warm sunshine of nature, prayed to be taken back to his dungeon. You would not leave this old life to go into a newer and greater freedom which opens out.

The great difficulty is to go to the heart of things. These little degraded delusions of Jack So-and-so's, who thinks he has an infinite soul, however small he is with his different religions. In one country, all as a matter of religion, a man has many wives; in another one woman has many husbands. So some men have two gods, some one God, and some no God at all.

But salvation is in work and love. You learn something thoroughly; in time you may not be able to call that thing to memory. Yet it has sunk into your inner consciousness and is a part of you. So as you work, whether it be good or bad, you shape your future course of life. If you do good work with the idea of work — work for work's sake — you will go to heaven of your idea and dream of heaven.

The history of the world is not of its great men, of its demi-gods, but it is the little islands of the sea, which build themselves to great continents from fragments of the sea drift. Then the history of the world is in the little acts of sacrifice performed in every household. Man accepts religion because he does not wish to stand on his own judgment. He takes it as the best way of getting out of a bad place.

The salvation of man lies in the great love with which he loves his God. Your wife says, "O John, I could not live without you." Some men when they lose their money have to be sent to the asylum. Do you feel that way about your God? When you can give up money, friends, fathers and mothers, brothers and sisters, all that is in the world and only pray to God that He grant you something of His love, then you have found salvation.

THE PEOPLE OF INDIA

Report of a lecture delivered in Oakland on Monday, March 19, 1900, with editorial comments of the Oakland Enquirer.

The lecture which the Swami Vivekananda gave Monday night in his new course on "The People of India", was interesting, not only for what he had to relate of the people of that country, but for the insight into their mental attitude and prejudices which the speaker gave without really meaning it. It is apparent that the Swami, educated and intellectual man that he is, is no admirer of Western civilisation. He has evidently been a good deal embittered by the talk about child widows, the oppression of women, and other barbarisms alleged against the people of India, and is somewhat inclined to resort to the tu quoque in reply.

In commencing his talk, he gave his hearers an idea of the racial characteristics of the people. He said that the bond of unity in India, as in other countries of Asia, is not language or race, but religion. In Europe the race makes the nation, but in Asia people of diverse origin and different tongues become one nation if they have the same religion. The people of Northern India are divided into four great classes, while in Southern India the languages are so entirely different from those of Northern India that there is no kinship whatever. The people of Northern India belong to the great Aryan race, to which all of the people of Europe, except the Basques in the Pyrennees, and the Finns, are supposed to belong. The Southern India people belong to the same race as the ancient Egyptians and the Semites. To illustrate the difficulties of learning one another's languages in India, the Swami said that when he had occasion to go into Southern India, he always talked with the native people in English, unless they belonged to the select few who could speak Sanskrit.

A good deal of the lecture was taken up in a discussion of the caste system which the Swami characterised by saying that it had its bad side, but that its benefits outweighed its disadvantages. In brief, this caste system had grown by the practice of the son always following the business of the father. In course of time the community came thus to be divided into a series of classes, each held rigidly within its own boundaries. But while this divided the people, it also united them, because all the members of a caste were bound to help their fellows in case of need. And as no man could rise out of his caste, the Hindus have no such struggles for social or personal supremacy as embitter the people of other countries.

The worst feature of the caste is that is suppresses competition, and the checking of competition has really been the cause of the political downfall of India and its conquest by foreign races.

Respecting the much-discussed subject of marriage, the Hindus are socialistic and see nothing good in matches being made by a couple of young people who might be attached to one another, without regard to the welfare of the community, which is more important than that of any two persons. "Because I love Jennie and Jennie loves me", said the Swami, "is no reason why we should be married."

He denied that the condition of the child widows is as bad as has been represented, saying that in India the position of widows in general is one of a great deal of influence, because a large part of the property in the country is held by widows. In fact, so enviable is the position of widows that a woman or a man either might almost pray to be made a widow.

The child widows, or women who have been betrothed to children who died before marriage, might be pitied if a marriage were the only real object in life, but, according to the Hindu way of thinking, marriage is rather a duty than a privilege, and the denial of the right of child widows to marry is no particular hardship.

I AM THAT I AM

Notes of a lecture given in San Francisco on March 20, 1900.

The subject tonight is man, man in contrast with nature. For a long time the word "nature" was used almost exclusively to denote external phenomena. These phenomena were found to behave methodically; and they often repeated themselves: that which had happened in the past happened again — nothing happened only once. Thus it was concluded that nature was uniform. Uniformity is closely associated with the idea of nature; without it natural phenomena cannot be understood. This uniformity is the basis of what we call law.

Gradually the word "nature" and the idea of uniformity came to be applied also to internal phenomena, the phenomena of life and mind. All that is differentiated is nature. Nature is the quality of the plant, the quality of the animal, and the quality of man. Man's life behaves according to definite methods; so does his mind. Thoughts do not just happen, there is a certain method in their rise, existence and fall. In other words, just as external phenomena are bound by law, internal phenomena, that is to say, the life and mind of man, are also bound by law.

When we consider law in relation to man's mind and existence, it is at once obvious that there can be no such thing as free will and free existence. We know how animal nature is wholly regulated by law. The animal does not appear to exercise any free will. The same is true of man; human nature also is bound by law. The law governing functions of the human mind is called the law of Karma.

Nobody has ever seen anything produced out of nothing; if anything arises in the mind, that also must have been produced from something. When we speak of free will, we mean the will is not caused by anything. But that cannot be true, the will is caused; and since it is caused, it cannot be free — it is bound by law. That I am willing to talk to you and you come to listen to me, that is law. Everything that I do or think or feel, every part of my conduct or behaviour, my every movement — all is caused and therefore not free. This regulation of our life and mind — that is the law of Karma.

If such a doctrine had been introduced in olden times into a Western community, it would have produced a tremendous commotion. The Western man does not want to think his mind is governed by law. In India it was accepted as soon as it was propounded by the most ancient Indian system of philosophy. There is no such thing as freedom of the mind; it cannot be. Why did not this teaching create any disturbance in the Indian mind? India received it calmly; that is the speciality of Indian thought, wherein it differs from every other thought in the world.

The external and internal natures are not two different things; they are really one. Nature is the sum total of all phenomena. "Nature" means all that is, all that moves. We make a tremendous distinction between matter and mind; we think that the mind is entirely different from matter. Actually, they are but one nature, half of which is continually acting on the other half. Matter is pressing upon the mind in the form of various sensations. These sensations are nothing but force. The force from the outside evokes the force within. From the will to respond to or get away from the outer force, the inner force becomes what we call thought.

Both matter and mind are really nothing but forces; and if you analyse them far enough, you will find that at root they are one. The very fact that the external force can somehow evoke the internal force shows that somewhere they join each other — they must be continuous and, therefore, basically the same force. When you get to the root of things, they become simple and general. Since the same force appears in one form as matter and in another form as mind, there is no reason to think matter and mind are different. Mind is changed into matter, matter is changed into mind. Thought force becomes nerve force, muscular force; muscular and nerve force become thought force. Nature is all this force, whether expressed as matter or mind.

The difference between the subtlest mind and the

grossest matter is only one of degree. Therefore the whole universe may be called either mind or matter, it does not matter which. You may call the mind refined matter, or the body concretised mind; it makes little difference by which name you call which. All the troubles arising from the conflict between materialism and spirituality are due to wrong thinking. Actually, there is no difference between the two. I and the lowest pig differ only in degree. It is less manifested, I am more. Sometimes I am worse, the pig is better.

Nor is it any use discussing which comes first — mind or matter. Is the mind first, out of which matter has come? Or is matter first, out of which the mind has come? Many of the philosophical arguments proceed from these futile questions. It is like asking whether the egg or the hen is first. Both are first, and both last — mind and matter, matter and mind. If I say matter exists first and matter, growing finer and finer, becomes mind, then I must admit that before matter there must have been mind. Otherwise, where did matter come from? Matter precedes mind, mind precedes matter. It is the hen and the egg question all through.

The whole of nature is bound by the law of causation and is in time and space. We cannot see anything outside of space, yet we do not know space. We cannot perceive anything outside of time, yet we do not know time. We cannot understand anything except in terms of causality, yet we do not know what causation is. These three things — time, space, and causality — are in and through every phenomena, but they are not phenomena. They are as it were the forms or moulds in which everything must be cast before it can be apprehended. Matter is substance plus time, space, and causation. Mind is substance plus time, space and causation.

This fact can be expressed in another way. Everything is substance plus name and form. Name and form come and go, but substance remains ever the same. Substance, form, and name make this pitcher. When it is broken, you do not call it pitcher any more, nor do you see its pitcher form. Its name and form vanish, but its substance remains. All the differentiation in substance is made by name and form. There are not real, because they vanish. What we call nature is not the substance, unchanging and indestructible. Nature is time, space and causation. Nature is name and form. Nature is Maya. Maya means name and form, into which everything is cast. Maya is not real. We could not destroy it or change it if it were real. The substance is the noumenon, Maya is phenomena. There is the real "me" which nothing can destroy, and there is the phenomenal "me" which is continually changing and disappearing.

The fact is, everything existing has two aspects. One is noumenal, unchanging and indestructible; the other is phenomenal, changing and destructible. Man in his true nature is substance, soul, spirit. This soul, this spirit, never changes, is never destroyed; but it appears to be clothed with a form and to have a name associated with it. This form and name are not immutable or indestructible; they continually change and are destroyed.

Yet men foolishly seek immortality in this changeable aspect, in the body and mind — they want to have an eternal body. I do not want that kind of immortality.

What is the relation between me and nature? In so far as nature stands for name and form or for time, space, and causality, I am not part of nature, because I am free, I am immortal, I am unchanging and infinite. The question does not arise whether I have free will or not; I am beyond any will at all. Wherever there is will, it is never free. There is no freedom of will whatever. There is freedom of that which becomes will when name and form get hold of it, making it their slave. That substance — the soul — as it were moulds itself, as it were throws itself into the cast of name and form, and immediately becomes bound, whereas it was free before. And yet its original nature is still there. That is why it says, "I am free; in spite of all this bondage, I am free." And it never forgets this.

But when the soul has become the will, it is no more really free. Nature pulls the strings, and it has to dance as nature wants it to. Thus have you and I danced throughout the years. All the things that we see, do, feel, know, all our thoughts and actions, are nothing but dancing to the dictates of nature. There has been, and there is, no freedom in any of this. From the lowest to the highest, all thoughts and actions are bound by law, and none of these pertain to our real Self.

My true Self is beyond all law. Be in tune with slavery, with nature, and you live under law, you are happy under law. But the more you obey nature and its dictates, the more bound you become; the more in harmony with ignorance you are, the more you are at the beck and call of everything in the universe. Is this harmony with nature, this obedience to law, in accord with the true nature and destiny of man? What mineral ever quarrelled with and disputed any law? What tree or plant ever defied any law? This table is in harmony with nature, with law; but a table it remains always, it does not become any better. Man begins to struggle and fight against nature. He makes many mistakes, he suffers. But eventually he conquers nature and realises his freedom. When he is free, nature becomes his slave.

The awakening of the soul to its bondage and its effort to stand up and assert itself — this is called life. Success in this struggle is called evolution. The eventual triumph, when all the slavery is blown away, is called salvation, Nirvana, freedom. Everything in the universe is struggling for liberty. When I am bound by nature, by name and form, by time, space and causality, I do not know what I truly am. But even in this bondage my real Self is not completely lost. I strain against the bonds; one by one they break, and I become conscious of my innate grandeur. Then comes complete liberation. I attain to the clearest and fullest consciousness of myself — i know that I am the infinite spirit, the master of nature, not its slave. Beyond all differentiation and combination, beyond space, time and causation, I am that I am.

UNITY

Notes of a lecture delivered at the Vedanta Society, New York, in June, 1900.

The different sectarian systems of India all radiate from one central idea of unity or dualism.

They are all under Vedanta, all interpreted by it. Their final essence is the teaching of unity. This, which we see as many, is God. We perceive matter, the world, manifold sensation. Yet there is but one existence.

These various names mark only differences of degree in the expression of that One. The worm of today is the God of tomorrow. These distinctions which we do love are all parts of one infinite fact, and only differ in the degree of expression. That one infinite fact is the attainment of freedom.

However mistaken we may be as to the method, all our struggle is really for freedom. We seek neither misery nor happiness, but freedom. This one aim is the secret of the insatiable thirst of man. Man's thirst, says the Hindu, man's thirst, says the Buddhist, is a burning, unquenchable thirst for more and more. You Americans are always looking for more pleasure, more enjoyment. You cannot be satisfied, true; but at bottom what you seek is freedom.

This vastness of his desire is really the sign of man's own infinitude. It is because he is infinite, that he can only be satisfied when his desire is infinite and its fulfilment infinite.

What then can satisfy man? Not gold. Not enjoyment. Not beauty. One Infinite alone can satisfy him, and that Infinite is Himself. When he realises this, then alone comes freedom. "This flute, with the sense-organs as its keyholes,

With all its sensations, perceptions, and song,

Is singing only one thing. It longs to go back to the wood whence it was cut!"

"Deliver thou thyself by thyself!

Ah, do not let thyself sink!

For thou art thyself thy greatest friend.

And thou thyself thy greatest enemy."

Who can help the Infinite? Even the hand that comes to you through the darkness will have to be your own.

Fear and desire are the two causes of all this, and who creates them? We ourselves. Our lives are but a passing from dream to dream. Man the infinite dreamer, dreaming finite dreams!

Oh, the blessedness of it, that nothing external can be eternal! They little know what they mean, whose hearts quake when they hear that nothing in this relative world can be eternal.

I am the infinite blue sky. Over me pass these clouds of various colours, remain a moment, and vanish. I am the same eternal blue. I am the witness, the same eternal witness of all. I see, therefore nature exists. I do not see, therefore she does not. Not one of us could see or speak if this infinite unity were broken for a moment.

THE WORSHIP OF THE DIVINE MOTHER

Fragmentary notes taken on a Sunday afternoon in New York in June, 1900.

From the tribal or clan-god, man arrives, in every religion, at the sum, the God of gods.

Confucius alone has expressed the one eternal idea of ethics. "Manu Deva" was transformed into Ahriman. In India, the mythological expression was suppressed; but the idea remained. In an old Veda is found the Mantra, "I am the empress of all that lives, the power in everything."

Mother-worship is a distinct philosophy in itself. Power is the first of our ideas. It impinges upon man at every step; power felt within is the soul; without, nature. And the battle between the two makes human life. All that we know or feel is but the resultant of these two forces. Man saw that the sun shines on the good and evil alike. Here was a new idea of God, as the Universal Power behind all — the Mother-idea was born.

Activity, according to Sankhya, belongs to Prakriti, to nature, not to Purusha or soul. Of all feminine types in India, the mother is pre-eminent. The mother stands by her child through everything. Wife and children may desert a man, but his mother never! Mother, again, is the impartial energy of the universe, because of the colourless love that asks not, desires not, cares not for the evil in her child, but loves him the more. And today Mother-worship is the worship of all the highest classes amongst the Hindus.

The goal can only be described as something not yet attained. Here, there is no goal. This world is all alike the play of Mother. But we forget this. Even misery can be enjoyed when there is no selfishness, when we have become the witness of our own lives. The thinker of this philosophy has been struck by the idea that one power is behind all phenomena. In our thought of God, there is human limitation, personality: with Shakti comes the idea of One Universal Power. "I stretch the bow of Rudra when He desires to kill", says Shakti. The Upanisads did not develop this thought; for Vedanta does not care for the God-idea. But in the Gita comes the significant saying to Arjuna, "I am the real, and I am the unreal. I bring good, and I bring evil."

Again the idea slept. Later came the new philosophy. This universe is a composite fact of good and evil; and one Power must be manifesting through both. "A lame one-legged universe makes only a lame one-legged God." And this, in the end, lands us in want of sympathy and makes us brutal. The ethics built upon such a concept is an ethics of brutality. The saint hates the sinner, and the sinner struggles against the saint. Yet even this leads onward. For finally the wicked self-sufficient mind will die, crushed under repeated blows; and then we shall awake and know the Mother.

Eternal, unquestioning self-surrender to Mother alone can give us peace. Love Her for Herself, without fear or favour. Love Her because you are Her child. See Her in all, good and bad alike. Then alone will come "Sameness" and Bliss Eternal that is Mother Herself when we realise Her thus. Until then, misery will pursue us. Only resting in Mother are we safe.

THE ESSENCE OF RELIGION

Report of a lecture delivered in America.

In France the "rights of man" was long a watchword of the race; in America the rights of women still beseech the public ear; in India we have concerned ourselves always with the rights of Gods. The Vedanta includes all sects. We have a peculiar idea in India. Suppose I had a child; I should not teach him any religion, but the practice of concentrating his mind; and just one line of prayer — not prayer in your sense, but this: "I meditate on Him who is the Creator of the universe; may He enlighten my mind." Then, when old enough, he goes about hearing the different philosophies and teachings, till he finds that which seems the truth to him. He then becomes the Shishya or disciple of the Guru (teacher) who is teaching this truth. He may choose to worship Christ or Buddha or Mohammed: we recognise the rights of each of these, and the right of all souls to their own Ishta or chosen way. It is, therefore, quite possible for my son to be a Buddhist, my wife to be a Christian, and myself a Mohammedan at one and the same time with absolute freedom from friction.

We are all glad to remember that all roads lead to God; and that the reformation of the world does not depend upon all seeing God through our eyes. Our fundamental idea is that your doctrine cannot be mine, nor mine yours. I am my own sect. It is true that we have created a system of religion in India which we believe to be the only rational religious system extant; but our belief in its rationality rests upon its all-inclusion of the searchers after God; its absolute charity towards all forms of worship, and its eternal receptivity of those ideas trending towards the evolution of God in the universe. We admit the imperfection of our system, because the reality must be beyond all system; and in this admission lies the portent and promise of an eternal growth. Sects, ceremonies, and books, so far as they are the means of a man's realising his own nature, are all right; when he has realised that, he gives up everything. "I reject the Vedas!" is the last word of the Vedanta philosophy. Ritual, hymns, and scriptures, through which he has travelled to freedom, vanish for him. "So'ham, So'ham"— i am He, I am He — bursts from his lips, and to say "Thou" to God is blasphemy, for he is "one with the Father".

Personally, I take as much of the Vedas as agree with reason. Parts of the Vedas are apparently contradictory. They are not considered as inspired in the Western sense of the word, but as the sum total of the knowledge of God, omniscience, which we possess. But to say that only those books which we call the Vedas contain this knowledge is mere sophistry. We know it is shared in varying degrees by the scriptures of all sects. Manu says, that part only of the Vedas which agrees with reason is Vedas; and many of our philosophers have taken this view. Of all the scriptures of the world, it is the Vedas alone which declare that the study of the Vedas is secondary.

The real study is that "by which we realise the Unchangeable", and that is neither by reading, nor believing, nor reasoning, but by superconscious perception and Samadhi. When a man has reached that perfect state, he is of the same nature as the Personal God: "I and my Father are one." He knows himself one with Brahman, the Absolute, and projects himself as does the Personal God. The Personal God is the Absolute looked at through the haze of Maya — ignorance.

When we approach Him with the five senses, we can only see Him as the Personal God. The idea is that the Self cannot be objectified. How can the knower know himself? But he can cast a shadow, as it were, and the highest form of that shadow, that attempt of objectifying one's Self is the Personal God. The Self is the eternal subject, and we are eternally struggling to objectify that Self, and out of that struggle has come this phenomenon of the universe: that which we call matter. But these are weak attempts, and the highest objectification of the Self, possible to us, is the Personal God. "An honest God's the noblest work of man", said one of your Western thinkers. God is as man is. No man can see God but through these human manifestations. Talk as you may, try as you may, you cannot think of God but as a man; and as you are, He is. An ignorant man was asked to make an image of the God Shiva; and after many days of hard struggle he succeeded only in manufacturing the image of a monkey! So, when we try to think of God as He is in His absolute perfection, we meet with miserable failure, because we are limited and bound by our present constitution to see God as man. If the buffaloes desire to worship God, they, in keeping with their own nature, will see Him as a huge buffalo; if a fish wishes to worship God, its concept of Him would inevitably be a big fish; and man must think of Him as man. Suppose man, the buffalo, and the fish represent so many different vessels; that these vessels all go to the sea of God to be filled, each according to its shape and capacity. In man the water takes the shape of man; in the buffalo the shape of the buffalo; and in the fish the shape of the fish; but in each of these vessels is the same water of the sea of God.

Two kinds of mind do not worship God as man — the human brute who has no religion, and the Paramahamsa who has transcended the limits of his own human nature.

To him all nature has become his own Self; he alone can worship God as He is. The human brute does not worship because of his ignorance, and the Jivanmuktas (free souls) do not worship because they have realised God in themselves. "So'ham, So'ham"— i am He, I am He — they say; and how shall they worship themselves?

I will tell you a little story. There was once a baby lion left by its dying mother among some sheep. The sheep fed it and gave it shelter. The lion grew apace and said "Ba-a-a" when the sheep said "Ba-a-a". One day another lion came by. "What do you do here?" said the second lion in astonishment: for he heard the sheep-lion bleating with the rest. "Ba-a-a," said the other. "I am a little sheep, I am a little sheep, I am frightened." "Nonsense!" roared the first lion, "come with me; I will show you." And he took him to the side of a smooth stream and showed him that which was reflected therein. "You are a lion; look at me, look at the sheep, look at yourself." And the sheep-lion looked, and then he said, "Ba-a-a, I do not look like the sheep — it is true, I am a lion!" and with that he roared a roar that shook the hills to their depths.

That is it. We are lions in sheep's clothing of habit, we are hypnotised into weakness by our surroundings. And the province of Vedanta is the self-dehypnotisation. The goal to be reached is freedom. I disagree with the idea that freedom is obedience to the laws of nature. I do not understand what that means. According to the history of human progress, it is disobedience to nature that has constituted that progress. It may be said that the conquest of lower laws was through the higher, but even there the conquering mind was still seeking freedom; as soon as it found the struggle was through law, it wished to conquer that also. So the ideal is always freedom. The trees never disobey law. I never saw a cow steal. An oyster never told a lie. Yet these are not greater than man.

Obedience to law, in the last issue, would make of us simply matter — either in society, or in politics, or religion. This life is a tremendous assertion of freedom; excess of laws means death. No nation possesses so many laws as the Hindus, and the result is the national death. But the Hindus had one peculiar idea — they never made any doctrines or dogmas in religion; and the latter has had the greatest growth. Therein are we practical — wherein you are impractical — in our religion.

A few men come together in America and say, "We will have a stock company"; in five minutes it is done. In India twenty men may discuss a stock company for as many weeks, and it may not be formed; but if one believes that by holding up his hands in air for forty years he will attain wisdom, it will be done! So we are practical in ours, you in your way.

But the way of all ways to realisation is love. When one loves the Lord, the whole universe becomes dear to one, because it is all His. "Everything is His, and He is my Lover; I love Him", says the Bhakta. In this way everything becomes sacred to the Bhakta, because all things are His. How, then, may we hurt any one? How, then, may we not love another? With the love of God will come, as its effect, the love of every one in the long run. The nearer we approach God, the more do we begin to see that all things abide in Him, our heart will become a perennial fountain of love. Man is transformed in the presence of this Light of Love and realises at last the beautiful and inspiring truth that Love, Lover, and the Beloved are really one.

SAYINGS AND UTTERANCES

SAYINGS AND UTTERANCES

1. "Did Buddha teach that the many was real and the ego unreal, while orthodox Hinduism regards the One as the real, and the many as unreal?" the Swami was asked. "Yes", answered the Swami. "And what Ramakrishna Paramahamsa and I have added to this is, that the Many and the One are the same Reality, perceived by the same mind at different times and in different attitudes."

2. "Remember!" he said once to a disciple, "Remember! the message of India is always "Not the soul for nature, but nature for the soul !"

3. "What the world wants today is twenty men and women who can dare to stand in the street yonder, and say that they possess nothing but God. Who will go? Why should one fear? If this is true, what else could matter? If it is not true, what do our lives matter !"

4. "Oh, how calm would be the work of one who really understood the divinity of man! For such, there is nothing to do, save to open men's eyes. All the rest does itself."

5. "He (Shri Ramakrishna) was contented simply to live that great life and to leave it to others to find the explanation!"

6. "Plans! Plans!" Swami Vivekananda explained in indignation, when one of his disciples had offered him some piece of worldly wisdom. "That is why .. . Western people can never create a religion! If any of you ever did, it was only a few Catholic saints who had no plans. Religion was never preached by planners!"

7. "Social life in the West is like a peal of laughter; but underneath, it is a wail. It ends in a sob. The fun and frivolity are all on the surface: really it is full of tragic intensity. Now here, it is sad and gloomy on the outside, but underneath are carelessness and merriment. "We have a theory that the universe is God's manifestation of Himself just for fun, that the Incarnations came and lived here 'just for fun'. Play, it was all play. Why was Christ crucified? It was mere play. And so of life. Just play with the Lord. Say, "It is all play, it is all play". Do you do anything?"

8. "I am persuaded that a leader is not made in one life. He has to be born for it. For the difficulty is not in organisation and making plans; the test, the real test, of the leader, lies in holding widely different people together along the line of their common sympathies. And this can only be done unconsciously, never by trying."

9. In explanation of Plato's doctrine of Ideas, Swamiji said, "And so you see, all this is but a feeble manifestation of the great ideas, which alone, are real and perfect. Somewhere is an ideal for you, and here is an attempt to manifest it! The attempt falls short still in many ways. Still, go on! You will interpret the ideal some day."

10. Answering the remark of a disciple who felt that it would be better for her to come back to this life again and again and help the causes that were of interest to her instead of striving for personal salvation with a deep longing to get out of life, the Swami retorted quickly: "That's because you cannot overcome the idea of progress. But things do not grow better. They remain as they are; and we grow better by the changes we make in them."

11. It was in Almora that a certain elderly man, with a face full of amiable weakness, came and put him a question about Karma. What were they to do, he asked, whose Karma it was to see the strong oppress the weak? The Swami turned on him in surprised indignation. "Why, thrash the strong, of course!" he said, "You forget your own part in this Karma: Yours is always the right to rebel!"

12. "Ought one to seek an opportunity of death in defense of right, or ought one to take the lesson of the Gita and learn never to react?" the Swami was asked. "I am for no reaction", said the Swami, speaking slowly and with a long pause. Then he added "— for Sannyasins. Self-defense for the householder!"

13. "It is a mistake to hold that with all men pleasure is the motive. Quite as many are born to seek after pain. Let us worship the Terror for Its own sake."

14. "Ramakrishna Paramahamsa was the only man who ever had the courage to say that we must speak to all men in their own language!"

15. "How I used to hate Kali!" he said, referring to his own days of doubts in accepting the Kali ideal, "And all Her ways! That was the ground of my six years' fight — that I would not accept Her. But I had to accept Her at last! Ramakrishna Paramahamsa dedicated me to Her, and now I believe that She guides me in everything I do, and does with me what She will. . . . Yet I fought so long! I loved him, you see, and that was what held me. I saw his marvellous purity. . . . I felt his wonderful love. . . . His greatness had not dawned on me then. All that came afterwards when I had given in. At that time I thought him a brain-sick baby, always seeing visions and the rest. I hated it. And then I, too, had to accept Her! "No, the thing that made me do it is a secret that will die with me. I had great misfortunes at the time. . . . It was an opportunity. . . . She made a slave of me. Those were the very words: 'a slave of you'. And Ramakrishna Paramahamsa made me over to Her. . . . Strange! He lived only two years after doing that, and most of the time he was suffering. Not more than six months did he keep his own health and brightness. "Guru Nanak was like that, you know, looking for the one disciple to whom he would give his power. And he passed over all his own family — his children were as nothing to him — till he came upon the boy to whom he gave it; and then he could die. "The future, you say, will call Ramakrishna Paramahamsa an Incarnation of Kali? Yes, I think there's no doubt that She worked up the body of Ramakrishna for Her own ends. "You see, I cannot but believe that there is somewhere a great Power that thinks of Herself as feminine, and called Kali and Mother. . . . And I believe in Brahman too. . . . But is it not always like that? Is it not the multitude of cells in the body that make up the personality, the many brain-centres, not the one, that produce consciousness? . . . Unity in complexity! Just so! And why should it be different with Brahman? It is Brahman. It is the One. And yet — and yet — it is the gods too!"

16. "The older I grow, the more everything seems to me to lie in manliness. This is my new gospel."

17. Referring to some European reference to cannibalism, as if it were a normal part of life in some societies, the Swami remarked, "That is not true! No nation ever ate human flesh, save as a religious sacrifice, or in war, out of revenge. Don't you see? That's not the way of gregarious animals! It would cut at the root of social life!"

18. "Sex-love and creation! These are at the root of most religions. And these in India are called Vaishnavism, and in the West Christianity. How few have dared to worship Death or Kali! Let us worship Death! Let us embrace the Terrible, because it is terrible, not asking that it be toned down. Let us take misery for misery's own sake!"

19. "The three cycles of Buddhism were five hundred years of the Law, five hundred years of images, and five hundred years of Tantras. You must not imagine that there was ever a religion in India called Buddhism with temples and priests of its own order! Nothing of the sort. It was always within Hinduism. Only at one time the influence of Buddha was paramount, and this made the nation monastic."

20. "The conservative's whole ideal is submission . Your ideal is struggle. Consequently it is we who enjoy the life, and never you! You are always striving to change yours to something better; and before a millionth part of the change is carried out, you die. The Western ideal is to be doing; the Eastern to be suffering. The perfect life would be a wonderful harmony doing and suffering. But that can never be. "In our system it is accepted that a man cannot have all he desires. Life is subjected to many restraints. This is ugly, yet it brings out points of light and strength. Our liberals see only the ugliness and try to throw it off. But they substitute something quite as bad; and the new custom takes as long as the old for us to work to its centres of strength. "Will is not strengthened by change. It is weakened and enslaved by it. But we must be always absorbing. Will grows stronger by absorption. And consciously or unconsciously, will is the one thing in the world that we admire. Suttee is great in the eyes of the whole world, because of the will that it manifests.

"It is selfishness that we must seek to eliminate. I find that whenever I have made a mistake in my life, it has always been because self entered into the calculation. Where self has not been involved, my judgment has gone straight to the mark. "Without self, there would have been no religious system. If man had not wanted anything for himself, do you think he would have had all this praying and worship? Why! he would never have thought of God at all, except perhaps for a little praise now and then, at the sight of a beautiful landscape or something. And that is the only attitude there ought to be. All praise and thanks. If only we were rid of self! "You are quite wrong when you think that fighting is a sign of growth. It is not so at all. Absorption is the sign. Hinduism is a very genius of absorption. We have never cared for fighting. Of course we could strike a blow now and then, in defense of our homes! That was right. But we never cared for fighting for its own sake. Every one had to learn that. So let these races of newcomers whirl on! They'll all be taken into Hinduism in the end!"

21. "The totality of all souls, not the human alone, is the Personal God. The will of the Totality nothing can resist. It is what we know as law. And this is what we mean by Shiva and Kali and so on."

22. "Worship the Terrible! Worship Death! All else is vain. All struggle is vain. That is the last lesson. Yet this is not the coward's love of death, not the love of the weak or the suicide. It is the welcome of the strong man who has sounded everything to its depths and knows that there is no alternative."

23. "I disagree with all those who are giving their superstitions back to my people. Like the Egyptologist's interest in Egypt, it is easy to feel an interest in India that is purely selfish. One may desire to see again the India of one's books, one's studies, one's dreams. My hope is to see again the strong points of that India, reinforced by the strong points of this age, only in a natural way. The new stage of things must be a growth from within. "So I preach only the Upanishads. If you look, you will find that I have never quoted anything but the Upanishads. And of the Upanishads, it is only that One idea, strength. The quintessence of the Vedas and Vedanta and all lies in that one word. Buddha's teaching was non-resistance, or non-injury. But I think this is a better way of teaching the same thing. For behind that non-injury lay a dreadful weakness. It is weakness that conceives the idea of resistance. I do not think of punishing or escaping from a drop of sea-spray. It is nothing to me. Yet to the mosquito it would be serious. Now I would make all injury like that. Strength and fearlessness. My own ideal is that saint whom they killed in the Mutiny and who broke his silence, when stabbed to the heart, to say, "And thou also art He!" "But you may ask, 'What is the place of Ramakrishna in this scheme?' "He is the method, that wonderful unconscious method! He did not understand himself. He knew nothing of England or the English, save that they were queer folk from over the sea. But he lived that great life: and I read the meaning. Never a word of condemnation for any! Once I had been attacking one of our sects of diabolists. I had been raving on for three hours, and he had listened quietly. 'Well, well!' said the old man as I finished, 'perhaps every house may have a backdoor. Who knows?' "Hitherto the great fault of our Indian religion has lain in its knowing only two words: renunciation and Mukti. Only Mukti here! Nothing for the householder! "But these are the very people whom I want to help. For are not all souls of the same quality? Is not the goal of all the same? "And so strength must come to the nation through education."

24. The Puranas, the Swami considered, to be the effort of Hinduism to bring lofty ideas to the door of the masses. There had been only one mind in India that had foreseen this need, that of Krishna, probably the greatest man who ever lived.

The Swami said, "Thus is created a religion that ends in the worship of Vishnu, as the preservation and enjoyment of life, leading to the realisation of God. Our last movement, Chaitanyaism, you remember, was for enjoyment. At the same time Jainism represents the other extreme, the slow destruction of the body by self-torture. Hence Buddhism, you see, is reformed Jainism; and this is the real meaning of Buddha's leaving the company of the five ascetics. In India, in every age, there is a cycle of sects which represents every gradation of physical practice, from the extreme of self-torture to the extreme of excess. And during the same period will always be developed a metaphysical cycle, which represents the realisation of God as taking place by every gradation of means, from that of using the senses as an instrument to that of the annihilation of the senses. Thus Hinduism always consists, as it were, of two counter-spirals, completing each other, round a single axis. "Yes!' Vaishnavism says, 'it is all right — this tremendous love for father, for mother, for brother, husband, or child! It is all right, if only you will think that Krishna is the child, and when you give him food, that you are feeding Krishna!' This was the cry of Chaitanya, 'Worship God through the senses', as against the Vedantic cry, 'Control the senses! suppress the senses!' "I see that India is a young and living organism. Europe is young and living. Neither has arrived at such a stage of development that we can safely criticise its institutions. They are two great experiments, neither of which is yet complete. In India we have social communism, with the light of Advaita — that is, spiritual individualism — playing on and around it; in Europe you are socially individualists, but your thought is dualistic, which is spiritual communism. Thus the one consists of socialist institutions hedged in by individualist thought, while the other is made up of individualist institutions within the hedge of communistic thought. "Now we must help the Indian experiment as it is. Movements which do not attempt to help things as they are, are, from that point of view, no good. In Europe, for instance, I respect marriage as highly as non-marriage. Never forget that a man is made great and perfect as much by his faults as by his virtues. So we must not seek to rob a nation of its character, even if it could be proved that the character was all faults."

25. "You may always say that the image is God. The error you have to avoid is to think God is the image."

26. The Swami was appealed to on one occasion to condemn the fetishism of the Hottentot. "I do not know", he answered, "what fetishism is!" Then a lurid picture was hastily put before him of the object alternately worshipped, beaten, and thanked. "I do that!" he exclaimed. "Don't you see," he went on, a moment later, in hot resentment of injustice done to the lowly and absent, "don't you see that there is no fetishism? Oh, your hearts are steeled, that you cannot see that the child is right! The child sees person everywhere. Knowledge robs us of the child's vision. But at last, through higher knowledge, we win back to it. He connects a living power with rocks, sticks, trees and the rest. And is there not a living Power behind them? It is symbolism, not fetishism! Can you not see?"

27. One day he told the story of Satyabhama's sacrifice and how the word "Krishna", written on a piece of paper and thrown into the balance, made Krishna himself, on the other side, kick the beam. "Orthodox Hinduism", he began, "makes Shruti, the sound, everything. The thing is but a feeble manifestation of the pre-existing and eternal idea. So the name of God is everything: God Himself is merely the objectification of that idea in the eternal mind. Your own name is infinitely more perfect than the person you! The name of God is greater than God. Guard your speech!"

28. "I would not worship even the Greek Gods, for they were separate from humanity! Only those should be worshipped who are like ourselves but greater. The difference between the gods and me must be a difference only of degree."

29. "A stone falls and crushes a worm. Hence we infer that all stones, falling, crush worms. Why do we thus immediately reapply a perception? Experience, says one. But it happens, let us suppose, for the first time. Throw a baby into the air, and it cries. Experience from past lives? But why applied to the future? Because there is a real connection between certain things, a pervasiveness, only it lies with us to see that the quality neither overlaps, nor falls short of, the instance. On this discrimination depends all human knowledge. "With regard to fallacies, it must be remembered that direct perception itself can only be a proof, provided the instrument, the method, and the persistence of the perception are all maintained pure. Disease or emotion will have the effect of disturbing the observation. Therefore

direct perception itself is but a mode of inference. Therefore all human knowledge is uncertain and may be erroneous. Who is a true witness? He is a true witness to whom the thing said is a direct perception. Therefore the Vedas are true, because they consist of the evidence of competent persons. But is this power of perception peculiar to any? No! The Rishi, the Aryan, and the Mlechchha all alike have it. "Modern Bengal holds that evidence is only a special case of direct perception, and that analogy and parity of reasoning are only bad inferences. Therefore, of actual proofs there are only two, direct perception and inference. "One set of persons, you see, gives priority to the external manifestation, the other to the internal idea. Which is prior, the bird to the egg, or the egg to the bird? Does the oil hold the cup or the cup the oil? This is a problem of which there is no solution. Give it up! Escape from Maya!"

30. "Why should I care if the world itself were to disappear? According to my philosophy, that, you know, would be a very good thing! But, in fact, all that is against me must be with me in the end. Am I not Her soldier?"

31. "Yes, my own life is guided by the enthusiasm of a certain great personality, but what of that? Inspiration was never filtered out to the world through one man! "It is true I believe Ramakrishna Paramahamsa to have been inspired. But then I am myself inspired also. And you are inspired. And your disciples will be; and theirs after them; and so on, to the end of time! "Don't you see that the age for esoteric interpretation is over? For good or for ill, that day is vanished, never to return. Truth, in the future, is to be open to the world!"

32. "Buddha made the fatal mistake of thinking that the whole world could be lifted to the height of the Upanishads. And self-interest spoilt all. Krishna was wiser, because He was more politic. But Buddha would have no compromise. The world before now has seen even the Avatara ruined by compromise, tortured to death for want of recognition, and lost. But Buddha would have been worshipped as God in his own lifetime, all over Asia, for a moment's compromise. And his reply was only: 'Buddhahood is an achievement, not a person!' Verily was He the only man is the world who was ever quite sane, the only sane man ever born!"

33. People had told the Swami in the West that the greatness of Buddha would have been more appealing, had he been crucified! This he stigmatised as "Roman brutality", and pointed out, "The lowest and most animal liking is for action. Therefore the world will always love the epic. Fortunately for India, however, she has never produced a Milton, with his 'hurled headlong down the steep abyss'! The whole of that were well exchanged for a couple of lines of Browning!" It had been this epic vigour of the story, in his opinion, that had appealed to the Roman. The crucifixion it was that carried Christianity over the Roman world. "Yes, Yes!" he reiterated. "You Western folk want action ! You cannot yet perceive the poetry of every common little incident in life! What beauty could be greater than that of the story of the young mother coming to Buddha with her dead boy? Or the incident of the goats? You see the Great Renunciation was not new in India! . . . But after Nirvana, look at the poetry! "It is a wet night, and he comes to the cowherd's hut and gathers in to the wall under the dripping eaves. The rain is pouring down and the wind rising. "Within, the cowherd catches a glimpse of a face through the window and thinks, 'Ha, ha! Yellow garb! stay there! It's good enough for you!' And then he begins to sing. '"My cattle are housed, and the fire burns bright. My wife is safe, and my babes sleep sweet! Therefore ye may rain, if ye will, O clouds, tonight!' "And the Buddha answers from without, "My mind is controlled: my senses are all gathered in; my heart firm. Therefore ye may rain, if ye will, O clouds, tonight!' "Again the cowherd: 'The fields are reaped, and the hay is fast in the barn. The stream is full, and the roads are firm. Therefore ye may rain, if ye will, O clouds, tonight.' "And so it goes on, till at last the cowherd rises, in contrition and wonder, and becomes a disciple. "Or what would be more beautiful than the barber's story?

"The Blessed One passed by my house,
my house — the Barber's!

"I ran, but He turned and awaited me,

Awaited me — the Barber!

"I said, 'May I speak, O Lord, with Thee?'

"And He said 'Yes!'

'Yes!' to me — the Barber!

"And I said, 'Is Nirvana for such as I?'

"And He said 'Yes!'

Even for me — the Barber!

"And I said, 'May I follow after Thee?'

"And He said, 'Oh yes!'

Even I — the Barber!

"And I said, 'May I stay, O Lord, near Thee?'

"And He said, 'Thou mayest!'

Even to me — the poor Barber!"

34. "The great point of contrast between Buddhism and Hinduism lies in the fact that Buddhism said, 'Realise all this as illusion', while Hinduism said, 'Realise that within the illusion is the Real.' Of how this was to be done, Hinduism never presumed to enunciate any rigid law. The Buddhist command could only be carried out through monasticism; the Hindu might be fulfilled through any state of life. All alike were roads to the One Real. One of the highest and greatest expressions of the Faith is put into the mouth of a butcher, preaching by the orders of a married woman to a Sannyasin. Thus Buddhism became the religion of a monastic order, but Hinduism, in spite of its exaltation of monasticism, remains ever the religion of faithfulness to duty, whatever it be, as the path by which man may attain God."

35. "Lay down the rules for your group and formulate your ideas," the Swami said, dealing with the monastic ideal for women, "and put in a little universalism, if there is room for it. But remember that not more than half a dozen people in the whole world are ever at any time ready for this! There must be room for sects, as well as for rising above sects. You will have to manufacture your own tools. Frame laws, but frame them in such a fashion that when people are ready to do without them, they can burst them asunder. Our originality lies in combining perfect freedom with perfect authority. This can be done even in monasticism."

36. "Two different races mix and fuse, and out of them rises one strong distinct type. This tries to save itself from admixture, and here you see the beginning of caste. Look at the apple. The best specimens have been produced by crossing; but once crossed, we try to preserve the variety intact."

37. Referring to education of girls in India he said, "In worship of the gods, you must of course use images. But you can change these. Kali need not always be in one position. Encourage your girls to think of new ways of picturing Her. Have a hundred different conceptions of Saraswati. Let them draw and model and paint their own ideas. "In the chapel, the pitcher on the lowest step of the altar must be always full of water, and lights in great Tamil butter-lamps must be always burning. If, in addition, the maintenance of perpetual adoration could be organised, nothing could be more in accord with Hindu feeling. "But the ceremonies employed must themselves be Vedic. There must be a Vedic altar, on which at the hour of worship to light the Vedic fire. And the children must be present to share in the service of oblation. This is a rite which would claim the respect of the whole of India.

"Gather all sorts of animals about you. The cow makes a fine beginning. But you will also have dogs and cats and birds and others. Let the children have a time for going to feed and look after these. "Then there is the sacrifice of learning. That is the most beautiful of all. Do you know that every book is holy in India, not the Vedas alone, but the English and Mohammedan also? All are sacred. "Revive the old arts. Teach your girls fruit-modelling with hardened milk. Give them artistic cooking and sewing. Let them learn painting, photography, the cutting of designs in paper, and gold and silver filigree and embroidery. See that everyone knows something by which she can earn a living in case of need. "And never forget Humanity! The idea of a humanitarian man-worship exists in nucleus in India, but it has never been sufficiently specialised. Let your students develop it. Make poetry, make art, of it. Yes, a daily worship at the feet of beggars, after bathing and before the meal, would be a wonderful practical training of heart and hand together. On some days, again, the worship might be of children, of your own pupils. Or you might borrow babies and nurse and feed them. What was it that Mataji[1] said to me? 'Swamiji! I have no help. But these blessed ones I worship, and they will take me to salvation!' She feels, you see, that she is serving Uma in the Kumari, and that is a wonderful thought, with which to begin a school."

38. "Love is always a manifestation of bliss. The least shadow of pain falling upon it is always a sign of physicality and selfishness."

39. "The West regards marriage as consisting in all that lies beyond the legal tie, while in India it is thought of as a bond thrown by society round two people to unite them together for all eternity. Those two must wed each other, whether they will or not, in life after life. Each acquires half of the merit of the other. And if one seems in this life to have fallen hopelessly behind, it is for the other only to wait and beat time, till he or she catches up again!"

40. "Consciousness is a mere film between two oceans, the subconscious and the superconscious."

41. "I could not believe my own ears when I heard Western people talking so much of consciousness! Consciousness? What does consciousness matter! Why, it is nothing compared with the unfathomable depths of the subconscious and the heights of the superconscious! In this I could never be misled, for had I not seen Ramakrishna Paramahamsa gather in ten minutes, from a man's subconscious mind, the whole of his past, and determine from that his future and his powers?"

42. "All these (visions etc.) are side issues. They are not true Yoga. They may have a certain usefulness in establishing indirectly the truth of our statements. Even a little glimpse gives faith that there is something behind gross matter. Yet those who spend time on such things run into grave dangers. "These (psychic developments) are frontier questions ! There can never be any certainty or stability of knowledge reached by their means. Did I not say they were 'frontier questions'? The boundary line is always shifting!"

43. "Now on the Advaitic side it is held that the soul neither comes nor goes, and that all these spheres or layers of the universe are only so many varying products of Akasha and Prana. That is to say, the lowest or most condensed is the Solar Sphere, consisting of the visible universe, in which Prana appears as physical force, and Akasha as sensible matter. The next is called the Lunar Sphere, which surrounds the Solar Sphere. This is not the moon at all, but the habitation of the gods; that is to say, Prana appears in it as psychic forces, and Akasha as Tanmatras or fine particles. Beyond this is the Electric Sphere; that is to say, a condition inseparable from Akasha, and you can hardly tell whether electricity is force or matter. Next is the Brahmaloka, where there is neither Prana nor Akasha, but both are merged into the mind-stuff, the primal energy. And here — there being neither Prana nor Akasha — the Jiva contemplates the whole universe as Samashti or the sum total of Mahat or mind. This appears as Purusha, an abstract Universal Soul, yet not the Absolute, for still there is multiplicity. From this the Jiva finds at last that Unity which is the end. Advaitism says that these are the visions which arise in succession before the Jiva, who himself neither goes nor comes, and that in the same way this present vision has been projected. The projection (Srishti) and dissolution must take place in the same order, only one means going backward and the other coming out. "Now, as each individual can only see his own universe, that universe is created with his bondage and goes away with his liberation, although it remains for others who are in bondage. Now, name and form constitute the universe. A wave in the ocean is a wave only in so far as it is bound by name and form. If the wave subsides, it is the ocean, but that name-and-form has immediately vanished forever, so that the name and form of a wave could never be without the water that was fashioned into the wave by them. Yet the name and form themselves were not the wave; they die as soon as ever it returns to water, but other names and forms live on in relation to other waves. This name-and-form is called Maya and the water is Brahman.

---

1. Tapaswini Mataji, foundress of the Mahakali Pathashala, Calcutta.

The wave was nothing but water all the time, yet as a wave it had the name and form. Again this name-and-form cannot remain for one moment separated from the wave, although the wave, as water, can remain eternally separate from name and form. But because the name and form can never be separated, they can never be said to exist. Yet they are not zero. This is called Maya."

44. "I am the servant of the servants of the servants of Buddha. Who was there ever like him?— the Lord — who never performed one action for himself — with a heart that embraced the whole world! So full of pity that he — prince and monk — would give his life to save a little goat! So loving that he sacrificed himself to the hunger of a tigress!— to the hospitality of a pariah and blessed him! And he came into my room when I was a boy, and I fell at his feet! For I knew it was the Lord Himself!"

45. "He (Shuka) is the ideal Paramahamsa. To him alone amongst men was it given to drink a handful of the waters of that one undivided Ocean of Sat-chit-ananda — existence, Knowledge, and Bliss Absolute! Most saints die, having heard only the thunder of its waves upon the shore. A few gain the vision, and still fewer, taste of It. But he drank of the Sea of Bliss!"

46. "What is this idea of Bhakti without renunciation? It is most pernicious."

47. "We worship neither pain nor pleasure. We seek through either to come at that which transcends them both."

48. "Shankaracharya had caught the rhythm of the Vedas, the national cadence. Indeed I always imagine that he had some vision such as mine when he was young, and recovered the ancient music that way. Anyway, his whole life's work is nothing but that, the throbbing of the beauty of the Vedas and the Upanishads."

49. "Though the love of a mother is in some ways greater, yet the whole world takes the love of man and woman as the type (of the soul's relation to God). No other has such tremendous idealising power. The beloved actually becomes what he is imagined to be. This love transforms its object."

50. "Is it so easy to be Janaka — to sit on a throne absolutely unattached, caring nothing for wealth or fame, for wife or child? One after another in the West has told me that he has reached this. But I could only say, 'Such great men are not born in India!'".

51. "Never forget to say to yourself and to teach to your children, as the difference between a firefly and the blazing sun, between the infinite ocean and a little pond, between a mustard seed and the mountain Meru, such is the difference between the householder and the Sannyasin! "Everything is fraught with fear: Renunciation alone is fearless. "Blessed be even the fraudulent Sadhus and those who have failed to carry out their vows, inasmuch as they also have witnessed to their ideal and so are in some degree the cause of the success of others!

"Let us never, never, forget our ideal!"

52. "The river is pure that flows, the monk is pure that goes!"

53. "The Sannyasin who thinks of gold, to desire it, commits suicide."

54. "What do I care if Mohammed was a good man, or Buddha? Does that altar my goodness or evil? Let us be good for our own sake on our own responsibility."

55. "You people in this country are so afraid of

losing your in-di-vid-u-al-i-ty! Why, you are not individuals yet. When you realise your whole nature, you will attain your true individuality, not before. There is another thing I am constantly hearing in this country, and that is that we should live in harmony with nature. Don't you know that all the progress ever made in the world was made by conquering nature? We are to resist nature at every point if we are to make any progress."

56. "In India they tell me I ought not to teach Advaita Vedanta to the people at large; but I say, I can make even a child understand it. You cannot begin too early to teach the highest spiritual truths."

57. "The less you read, the better. Read the Gita and other good works on Vedanta. That is all you need. The present system of education is all wrong.

The mind is crammed with facts before it knows how to think. Control of the mind should be taught first. If I had my education to get over again and had any voice in the matter, I would learn to master my mind first, and then gather facts if I wanted them. It takes people a long time to learn things because they can't concentrate their minds at will."

58. "If a bad time comes, what of that? The pendulum must swing back to the other side. But that is no better. The thing to do is to stop it."

EPISTLES - FOURTH SERIES

Before leaving for the USA, Swamiji used to change his name very often. In earlier years he signed as Narendra or Naren; then for some time as Vividishananda or Sachchidananda. But for the convenience of the readers, these volumes use the more familiar name Vivekananda.

I — SIR

Translated from Bengali

BAGHBAZAR,
CALCUTTA,
28th November, 1888.

DEAR SIR, (Shri Pramadadas Mitra)

I have received the book of Pânini which you so kindly sent me. Please accept my gratitude for the same.

I had an attack of fever again — hence I could not reply to you immediately. Please excuse. I am ailing much. I am praying to the Divine Mother to keep you happy physically and mentally.

Your servant,
Vivekananda.

II — SIR

Translated from Bengali

BARANAGORE,
22nd February, 1889.

DEAR SIR, (Shri Pramadadas Mitra)

I had intended to go to Varanasi, and I planned to reach there after visiting the birthplace of my Master. But unluckily on the way to that village I had an attack of high fever followed by vomiting and purging as in cholera. There was again fever after three or four days — and as the body is now so weak that I can barely walk even two steps, I have been compelled now to give up my previous intention. I do not know what is God's will, but my body is quite unfit for treading on this path. Anyway, the body is not everything. Recovering my health after a few days here, I entertain the hope of visiting you there. The will of Vishweshvara, the Lord of the universe, will prevail — whatever that may be. You also kindly bless me. My respects to you and brother Jnanananda.

Your servant,
Vivekananda.

III — SIR

Translated from Bengali

BAGHBAZAR,
CALCUTTA,
21st March, 1889.

RESPECTED SIR, (Shri Pramadadas Mitra)

It is several days since I received your last letter. Please excuse the delay in replying, which was due to some special reasons. I am very ill at present; there is fever now and then, but there is no disorder in the spleen or other organs. I am under homeopathic treatment. Now I have had to give up completely the intention of going to Varanasi. Whatever God dispenses will happen later on, according to the state of the body. If you meet brother Jnanananda, please tell him not to be held up there in expectation of my coming. My going there is very uncertain. My regards to you and Jnanananda.

Yours sincerely,
Vivekananda.

IV — SIR

Translated from Bengali

SIMLA (CALCUTTA),
14th July, 1889.

RESPECTED SIR, (Shri Pramadadas Mitra)

I was very glad to get your letter. In such circumstances many give the advice to incline towards the worldly life. But you are truthful and have an adamantine heart. I have been highly comforted by your encouraging and cheering words. My difficulties here have almost come to a close — only I have engaged the services of a broker for the sale of a piece of land, and I hope the sale will be over soon. In that case, I shall be free from all worry and shall at once go straight off to you to Varanasi.

Your servant,
Vivekananda.

V — SIR

Translated from Bengali

BAGHBAZAR,
CALCUTTA,
4th June, 1890.

RESPECTED SIR, (Shri Pramadadas Mitra)

I got your letter. There is no doubt that your advice is very wise. It is quite true that the Lord's Will will prevail. We also are spreading out here and there in small groups of two or three. I also got two letters from brother Gangadhar. He is at present in the house of Gagan Babu suffering from an attack of influenza. Gagan Babu is taking special care of him. He will come here as soon as he recovers. Our respectful salutations to you.

Your servant,
Vivekananda.

PS. Abhedananda and others are all doing well.

VI — DIWANJI SAHEB

BARODA,
26th April, 1892.

DEAR DIWANJI SAHEB, (Shri Haridas Viharidas Desai)

Very happy to receive your kind letter even here. I had not the least difficulty in reaching your house from the station of Nadiad. And your brothers, they are what they should be, your brothers. May the Lord shower his choicest blessings on your family. I have never found such a glorious one in all my travels. Your friend Mr. Manibhai has provided every comfort for me; but, as to his company, I have only seen him twice; once for a minute, the other for ten minutes at the most when he talked about the system of education here. Of course, I have seen the Library and the pictures of Ravi Varma, and that is about all worth seeing here. So I am going off this evening to Bombay. My thanks to the Diwanji here (or to you) for his kind behaviour. More from Bombay.

Yours in affection,
Vivekananda.

PS. At Nadiad I met Mr. Manilal Nabhubhai. He is a very learned and pious gentleman, and I enjoyed his company much.

VII — DIWANJI SAHEB

ELLAPA BALARAM'S HOUSE,
C/O. THAKORE OF LIMDI,
NEUTRAL LINE, POONA,
15th June, 1892.

DEAR DIWANJI SAHEB, (Shri Haridas Viharidas Desai)

It is a long time since I heard from you. I hope I have not offended you anyway. I came down with the Thakore Saheb of Mahabaleshwar, and I am living here with him. I would remain here a week or more and then proceed to Rameshwaram via Hyderabad.

Perhaps by this time every hitch has been removed from your way in Junagad; at least I hope so. I am very anxious to learn about your health, especially that sprain, you know.

I saw your friend the Surti tutor to the Prince of Bhavnagar. He is a perfect gentleman. It was quite a privilege to make his acquaintance; he is so good and noble-natured a man.

My sincerest greetings to your noble-minded brothers and to our friends there. Kindly send to Mr. Nabhubhai my earnest good wishes in your letter home. I hope you would gratify me by a speedy reply.

With my sincerest respects and gratitude and prayers for you and yours, I remain,

Yours faithfully,
Vivekananda.

VIII — DIWANJI SAHEB

BOMBAY,
1892

DEAR DIWANJI SAHEB, (Shri Haridas Viharidas Desai)

The bearer of this letter, Babu Akshaya Kumar Ghose, is a particular friend of mine. He comes of a respectable family of Calcutta. I found him at Khandwa where I made his acquaintance, although I knew his family long before in Calcutta.

He is a very honest and intelligent boy and is an undergraduate of the Calcutta University. You know how hard the struggle is in Bengal nowadays, and the poor boy has been out in search of some job. Knowing your native kindness of heart, I think I am not disturbing you by asking and entreating you to do something for this young man. I need not write more. You will find him an honest and hard-working lad. If a single act of kindness done to a fellow creature renders his whole life happy, I need not remind you that this boy is a Pâtra (a person quite deserving of help), noble and kind as you are.

I hope you are not disturbed and troubled by this request of mine. This is the first and the last of its kind and made only under very peculiar circumstances. Hoping and relying on your kind nature, I remain,

Yours faithfully,
Vivekananda.

IX — DIWANJI SAHEB

BOMBAY,
22nd August, 1892.

DEAR DIWANJI SAHEB, (Shri Haridas Viharidas Desai)

I am very much gratified on receiving your letter, especially as that is the proof that you have the same kindness towards me.

About the kindness and gentlemanliness of your friend Mr. Bederkar of Indore and of the Dakshinis in general, the less said the better; but of course there are Dakshinis and Dakshinis, and I would only quote to you what Shankar Pandurang wrote me at Mahabaleshwar on my informing him that I had found shelter with the Limdi Thakore:

"I am so glad to learn that you have found Limdi Thakore there, else you would have been in serious troubles, our Maratha people not being so kind as the Gujaratis." So kind? heaven and hell!

I am very glad that your joint has now been nearly perfectly cured. Kindly tell your noble brother to excuse my promise-breaking as I have got here some Sanskrit books and help, too, to read, which I do not hope to get elsewhere, and am anxious to finish them. Yesterday I saw your friend Mr. Manahsukharam who has lodged a Sannyâsin friend with him. He is very kind to me and so is his son.

After remaining here for 15 to 20 days I would proceed toward Rameshwaram, and on my return would surely come to you.

The world really is enriched by men, high-souled, noble-minded, and kind, like you; the rest are "only as axes which cut at the tree of youth of their mothers', as the Sanskrit poet puts it.

It is impossible that I should ever forget your fatherly kindness and care of me, and what else can a poor fakir like me do in return to a mighty minister but pray that the Giver of all gifts may give you all that is desirable on earth and in the end — which may He postpone to a day long, long ahead — may take you in His shelter of bliss and happiness and purity infinite.

Yours,
Vivekananda.

PS. One thing that I am very sorry to notice in these parts is the thorough want of Sanskrit and other learning. The people of this part of the country have for their religion a certain bundle of local superstitions about eating, drinking, and bathing, and that is about the whole of their religion.

Poor fellows! Whatever the rascally and wily priests teach them — all sorts of mummery and tomfoolery as the very gist of the Vedas and Hinduism (mind you, neither these rascals of priests nor their forefathers have so much as seen a volume of the Vedas for the last 400 generations) — they follow and degrade themselves. Lord help them from the Râkshasas in the shape of the Brahmins of the Kaliyuga.

I have sent a Bengali boy to you. Hope he would be treated kindly.

X — HARIPADA

Translated from Bengali

To Shri Haripada Mitra

MARGAON,
1893.

DEAR HARIPADA,

I just now received a letter from you. I reached here safe. I went to visit Panjim and a few other villages and temples near by. I returned just today. I have not given up the intention of visiting Gokarna, Mahabaleshwar, and other places. I start for Dharwar by the morning train tomorrow. I have taken the walking-stick with me. Doctor Yagdekar's friend was very hospitable to me. Please give my compliments to Mr. Bhate and all others there. May the Lord shower His blessings on you and your wife. The town of Panjim is very neat and clean. Most of the Christians here are literate. The Hindus are mostly uneducated.

Yours affectionately,
Sachchidananda.

(Swamiji used to call himself such in those days.)

XI — ALASINGA

To Shri Alasinga Perumal

C/o Babu Madhusudan Chattopadhyaya Superintending Engineer

KHARTABAD, HYDERABAD,
11th February, 1893.

DEAR ALASINGA,

Your friend, the young graduate, came to receive me at the station, so also a Bengali gentleman. At present I am living with the Bengali gentleman; tomorrow I go to live with your young friend for a few days, and then I see the different sights here, and in a few days you may expect me at Madras. For I am very sorry to tell you that I cannot go back at present to Rajputana. It is so very dreadfully hot here already. I do not know how hot it would be at Rajputana, and I cannot bear heat at all. So the next thing, I would do, would be to go back to Bangalore and then to Ootacamund to pass the summer there. My brain boils in heat.

So all my plans have been dashed to the ground. That is why I wanted to hurry off from Madras early. In that case I would have months left in my hands to seek out for somebody amongst our northern princes to send me over to America. But alas, it is now too late. First, I cannot wander about in this heat — I would die. Secondly, my fast friends in Rajputana would keep me bound down to their sides if they get hold of me and would not let me go over to Europe. So my plan was to get hold of some new person without my friends' knowledge. But this delay at Madras has dashed all my hopes to the ground, and with a deep sigh I give it up, and the Lord's will be done! However, you may be almost sure that I shall see you in a few days for a day or two in Madras and then go to Bangalore and thence to Ootacamund to see "if" the M—Maharaja sends me up. "If" — because you see I cannot be sure of any promise of a Dakshini (southern) Raja. They are not Rajputs. A Rajput would rather die than break his promise. However, man learns as he lives, and experience is the greatest teacher in the world.

"Thy will be done on earth as it is in heaven, for Thine is the glory and the kingdom for ever and ever." My compliments to you all.

Yours affectionately,
Sachchidananda.

(Swamiji used to call himself such in those days.)

XII — DIWANJI SAHEB

To Shri Haridas Viharidas Desai
KHETRI
28th April, 1893.

DEAR DIWANJI SAHEB,

On my way here, I wanted to go to your place at Nadiad and redeem my pledge, but certain circumstances prevented me, and the greatest of them was that you were not there; and to play Hamlet leaving Hamlet's part out is a ridiculous affair; and as I know for certain that you are to return in a few days to Nadiad, and as I am shortly going back to Bombay, say in 20 days, I thought it better to postpone my visit for that time.

Here the Khetri Rajaji was very, very anxious to see me and had sent his Private Secretary to Madras; and so I was bound to leave for Khetri. But the heat is quite intolerable, and so I am flying off very soon.

By and by, I have made the acquaintances of nearly all the Dakshini Rajas and have seen most queer sights in many places of which I would tell you in extenso when we meet next. I know your love for me and am sure that you would excuse my not going down to your place. However, I am coming to you in a few days.

One thing more. Have you got lion's cubs now in Junagad? Can you lend me one for my Raja? He can give you some Rajputana animals in exchange, if you like.

I saw Ratilalbhai in the train. He is the same nice and kind gentleman; and what more shall I wish for you, my dear Diwanji Saheb, but that the Lord would be your all in all in your well-merited, well-applauded and universally respected latter end of a life which was ever holy, good, and devoted to the service of so many of the sons and daughters of the great Father of Mercies. Amen!

Yours affectionately,
Vivekananda.

XIII — DIWANJI SAHEB

To Shri Haridas Viharidas Desai

KHETRI
May, 1893.

DEAR DIWANJI SAHEB,

Surely my letter had not reached you before you wrote to me. The perusal of your letter gave me both pleasure and pain simultaneously: pleasure, to see that I have the good fortune to be loved by a man of your heart, power, and position; and pain, to see that my motive has been misinterpreted throughout. Believe me, that I love you and respect you like a father and that my gratitude towards you and your family is surely unbounded. The fact is this. You may remember that I had from before a desire to go to Chicago. When at Madras, the people there, of their own accord, in conjunction with H.H. of Mysore and Ramnad made every arrangement to send me up. And you may also remember that between H.H. of Khetri and myself there are the closest ties of love. Well, I, as a matter of course, wrote to him that I was going to America. Now the Raja of Khetri thought in his love that I was bound to see him once before I departed, especially as the Lord has given him an heir to the throne and great rejoicings were going on here; and to make sure of my coming he sent his Private Secretary all the way to Madras to fetch me, and of course I was bound to come. In the meanwhile I telegraphed to your brother at Nadiad to know whether you were there, and, unfortunately, the answer I could not get; therefore, the Secretary who, poor fellow, had suffered terribly for his master in going to and from Madras and with his eye wholly on the fact that his master would be unhappy if we could not reach Khetri within the Jalsa (festival), bought tickets at once for Jaipur. On our way we met Mr. Ratilal who informed me that my wire was received and duly answered and that Mr. Viharidas was expecting me. Now it is for you to judge, whose duty it has been so long to deal even justice. What would or could I do in this connection? If I would have got down, I could not have reached in time for the Khetri rejoicings; on the other hand, my motives might be misinterpreted. But I know you and your brother's love for me, and I knew also that I would have to go back to Bombay in a few days on my way to Chicago. I thought that the best solution was to postpone my visit till my return. As for my feeling affronted at not being attended by your brothers, it is a new discovery of yours which I never even dreamt of; or, God knows, perhaps, you have become a thought-reader. Jokes apart, my dear Diwanji Saheb, I am the same frolicsome, mischievous but, I assure you, innocent boy you found me at Junagad, and my love for your noble self is the same or increased a hundredfold, because I have had a mental comparison between yourself and the Diwans of nearly all the states in Dakshin, and the Lord be my witness how my tongue was fluent in your praise (although I know that my powers are quite inadequate to estimate your noble qualities) in every Southern court. If this be not a sufficient explanation, I implore you to pardon me as a father pardons a son, and let me not be haunted with the impression that I was ever ungrateful to one who was so good to me.

Yours,
Vivekananda.

P.S. I depend on you to remove any misconception in the mind of your brother about my not getting down and that, even had I been the very devil, I could not forget their kindness and good offices for me.

As to the other two Swamis, they were my Gurubhais, who went to you last at Junagad; of them one is our leader. I met them after three years, and we came together as far as Abu and then I left them. If you wish, I can take them back to Nadiad on my way to Bombay. May the Lord shower His blessings on you and yours.

XIV — DIWANJI SAHEB

To Shri Haridas Viharidas Desai

BOMBAY,
22nd May, 1893.

DEAR DIWANJI SAHEB,

Reached Bombay a few days ago and would start off in a few days. Your friend, the Banya gentleman to whom you wrote for the house accommodation, writes to say that his house is already full of guests and some of them are ill and that he is very sorry he cannot accommodate me. After all we have got a nice, airy place.

... The Private Secretary of H. H. of Khetri and I are now residing together. I cannot express my gratitude to him for his love and kindness to me. He is what they call a Tazimi Sardar in Rajputana, i.e.

one of those whom the Rajas receive by rising from their seats. Still he is so simple, and sometimes his service for me makes me almost ashamed.

. . . Often and often, we see that the very best of men even are troubled and visited with tribulations in this world; it may be inexplicable; but it is also the experience of my life that the heart and core of everything here is good, that whatever may be the surface waves, deep down and underlying everything, there is an infinite basis of goodness and love; and so long as we do not reach that basis, we are troubled; but having once reached that zone of calmness, let winds howl and tempests rage. The house which is built on a rock of ages cannot shake. I thoroughly believe that a good, unselfish and holy man like you, whose whole life has been devoted to doing good to others, has already reached this basis of firmness which the Lord Himself has styled as "rest upon Brahman" in the Gita.

May the blows you have received draw you closer to that Being who is the only one to be loved here and hereafter, so that you may realise Him in everything past, present, and future, and find everything present or lost in Him and Him alone. Amen!

Yours affectionately,
Vivekananda.

XV — DIWANJI SAHEB

To Shri Haridas Viharidas Desai

CHICAGO,
29th January, 1894.

DEAR DIWANJI SAHEB,

Your last letter reached me a few days ago. You had been to see my poor mother and brothers. I am glad you did. But you have touched the only soft place in my heart. You ought to know, Diwanji, that I am no hard-hearted brute. If there is any being I love in the whole world, it is my mother. Yet I believed and still believe that without my giving up the world, the great mission which Ramakrishna Paramahamsa, my great Master came to preach would not see the light, and where would those young men be who have stood as bulwarks against the surging waves of materialism and luxury of the day? These have done a great amount of good to India, especially to Bengal, and this is only the beginning. With the Lord's help they will do things for which the whole world will bless them for ages. So on the one hand, my vision of the future of Indian religion and that of the whole world, my love for the millions of beings sinking down and down for ages with nobody to help them, nay, nobody with even a thought for them; on the other hand, making those who are nearest and dearest to me miserable; I choose the former. "Lord will do the rest." He is with me, I am sure of that if of anything. So long as I am sincere, nothing can resist me, because He will be my help. Many and many in India could not understand me; and how could they, poor men? Their thoughts never strayed beyond the everyday routine business of eating and drinking. I know only a few noble souls like yourself appreciate me. Lord bless your noble self. But appreciation or no appreciation, I am born to organise these young men; nay, hundreds more in every city are ready to join me; and I want to send them rolling like irresistible waves over India, bringing comfort, morality, religion, education to the doors of the meanest and the most downtrodden. And this I will do or die.

Our people have no idea, no appreciation. On the other hand, that horrible jealousy and suspicious nature which is the natural outcome of a thousand years of slavery make them stand as enemies to every new idea. Still the Lord is great.

About the Ârati as well as other things you speak of, it is the form in every one of the monasteries in all parts of India, and the worshipping of Guru is the first duty inculcated in the Vedas. It has its bad and good sides. But you must remember we are a unique company, nobody amongst us has a right to force his faith upon the others. Many of us do not believe in any form of idolatry; but they have no right to object when others do it, because that would break the first principle of our religion. Again, God can only be known in and through man. Vibrations of light are everywhere, even in the darkest corners; but it is only in the lamp that it becomes visible to man. Similarly God, though everywhere, we can only conceive Him as a big man. All ideas of God such as merciful preserver, helper, protector — all these are human ideas, anthropomorphic; and again these must cling to a man, call him a Guru or a Prophet or an Incarnation. Man cannot go beyond his nature, no more than you can jump out of your body. What harm is there in some people worshipping their Guru when that Guru was a hundred times more holy than even your historical prophets all taken together? If there is no harm in worshipping Christ, Krishna, or Buddha, why should there be any in worshipping this man who never did or thought anything unholy, whose intellect only through intuition stands head and shoulders above all the other prophets, because they were all one-sided? It was he that brought first to the world this idea of truth, not in but of every religion, which is gaining ground all over the world, and that without the help of science or philosophy or any other acquirement.

But even this is not compulsory, none of the brethren has told you that all must worship his Guru. No, no, no. But again none of us has a right to object when another worships. Why? Because that would overthrow this most unique society the world has ever seen, ten men of ten different notions and ideas living in perfect harmony. Wait, Diwanji, the Lord is great and merciful, you will see more.

We do not only tolerate but accept every religion, and with the Lord's help I am trying to preach it to the whole world.

Three things are necessary to make every man great, every nation great:

1. Conviction of the powers of goodness.
2. Absence of jealousy and suspicion.
3. Helping all who are trying to be and do good.

Why should the Hindu nation with all its wonderful intelligence and other things have gone to pieces? I would answer you, jealousy. Never were there people more wretchedly jealous of one another, more envious of one another's fame and name than this wretched Hindu race. And if you ever come out in the West, the absence of this is the first feeling which you will see in the Western nations.

Three men cannot act in concert together in India for five minutes. Each one struggles for power, and in the long run the whole organisation comes to grief. Lord! Lord! When will we learn not to be jealous! In such a nation, and especially in Bengal, to create a band of men who are tied and bound together with a most undying love in spite of difference — is it not wonderful? This band will increase. This idea of wonderful liberality joined with eternal energy and progress must spread over India. It must electrify the whole nation and must enter the very pores of society in spite of the horrible ignorance, spite, caste-feeling, old boobyism, and jealousy which are the heritage of this nation of slaves.

You are one of the few noble natures who stand as rocks out of water in this sea of universal stagnation. Lord bless you for ever and ever!

Yours ever faithfully,
Vivekananda.

XVI — SISTERS

To the Hale Sisters

DETROIT,
12th March, 1894.

DEAR SISTERS,

I am now living with Mr. Palmer. He is a very nice gentleman. He gave a dinner the night before last to a group of his old friends, each more than 60 years of age, which he calls his "old boys' club". I spoke at an opera house for two hours and a half. People were very much pleased. I am going to Boston and New York. I will get here sufficient to cover my expenses there. I have forgotten the addresses of both Flagg and Prof. Wright. I am not going to lecture in Michigan, Mr. Holden tried to persuade me this morning to lecture in Michigan but I am quite bent upon seeing a little of Boston and New York. To tell you the truth, the more I am getting popularity and facility in speaking, the more I am getting fed up. My last address was the best I ever delivered. Mr. Palmer was in ecstasies and the audience remained almost spellbound, so much so that it was after the lecture that I found I had spoken so long. A speaker always feels the uneasiness or inattention of the audience. Lord save me from such nonsense, I am fed up. I would take rest in Boston or New York if the Lord permits. My love to you all. May you ever be happy!

Your affectionate brother,
Vivekananda.

XVII — BABIES

To the Hale Sisters

DETROIT,
15th March, 1894.

DEAR BABIES,

I am pulling on well with old Palmer. He is a very jolly, good old man. I got only 127 dollars by my last lecture. I am going to speak again in Detroit on Monday. Your mother asked me to write to a lady in Lynn. I have never seen her. Is it etiquette to write without any introduction? Please post me a little letter about this lady. Where is Lynn? The funniest thing said about me here was in one of the papers which said, "The cyclonic Hindu has come and is a guest with Mr. Palmer. Mr. Palmer has become a Hindu and is going to India; only he insists that two reforms should be carried out: firstly that the Car of Jagannath should be drawn by Percherons raised in Mr. Palmer's Loghouse Farm, and secondly that the Jersey cow be admitted into the pantheon of Hindu sacred cows." Mr. Palmer is passionately fond of both Percheron horse and Jersey cow and has a great stock of both in his Loghouse Farm.

The first lecture was not properly managed, the cost of the hall being 150 dollars. I have given up Holden. Here is another fellow cropped up; let me see if he does better. Mr. Palmer makes me laugh the whole day. Tomorrow there is going to be another dinner party. So far all is well; but I do not know — I have become very sad in my heart since I am here — do not know why.

I am wearied of lecturing and all that nonsense. This mixing with hundreds of varieties of the human animal has disturbed me. I will tell you what is to my taste; I cannot write, and I cannot speak, but I can think deeply, and when I am heated, can speak fire. It should be, however, to a select, a very select — few. Let them, if they will, carry and scatter my ideas broadcast — not I. This is only a just division of labour. The same man never succeeded both in thinking and in scattering his thoughts. A man should be free to think, especially spiritual thoughts.

Just because this assertion of independence, this proving that man is not a machine, is the essence of all religious thought, it is impossible to think it in the routine mechanical way. It is this tendency to bring everything down to the level of a machine that has given the West its wonderful prosperity. And it is this which has driven away all religion from its doors. Even the little that is left, the West has reduced to a systematic drill.

I am really not "cyclonic" at all. Far from it. What I want is not here, nor can I longer bear this "cyclonic" atmosphere. This is the way to perfection, to strive to be perfect, and to strive to make perfect a few men and women. My idea of doing good is this: to evolve out a few giants, and not to strew pearls before swine, and so lose time, health, and energy.

Just now I got a letter from Flagg. He cannot help me in lecturing. He says, "First go to Boston." Well, I do not care for lecturing any more. It is too disgusting, this attempt to bring me to suit anybody's or any audience's fads. However, I shall come back to Chicago for a day or two at least before I go out of this country. Lord bless you all.

Ever gratefully your brother,
Vivekananda.

XVIII — SISTER MARY

To Miss Mary Hale

DETROIT,
18th March, 1894.

DEAR SISTER MARY,

My heartfelt thanks for your kindly sending me the letter from Calcutta. It was from my brethren at Calcutta, and it is written on the occasion of a private invitation to celebrate the birthday of my Master about whom you have heard so much from me — so I send it over to you. The letter says that Mazoomdar has gone back to Calcutta and is preaching that Vivekananda is committing every sin under the sun in America. . . . This is your America's wonderful spiritual man! It is not their fault; until one is really spiritual, that is, until one has got a real insight into the nature of one's own soul and has got a glimpse of the world of the soul, one cannot distinguish chaff from seed, tall talk from depth, and so on. I am sorry for poor Mazoomdar that he should stoop so low! Lord bless the old boy!

The address inside the letter is in English and is my old, old name as written by a companion of my childhood who has also taken orders. It is a very poetic name. That written in the letter is an abbreviation, the full name being Narendra meaning the "Chief of men" ("nara" means "man", and "indra" stands for "ruler", "chief") — very ludicrous, isn't it? But such are the names in our country; we cannot help, but I am glad I have given that up.

I am all right. Hoping it is same with you.

I remain your brother,
Vivekananda.

XIX — SISTER

To Miss Mary Hale

DETROIT,
30th March, 1894.

DEAR SISTER,

Your and Mother Church's letters came together just now, acknowledging the receipt of the money. I am very glad to receive the Khetri letter, which I send back for your perusal. You would find from it that he wants some newspaper clippings. I do not think I have any except the Detroit one, which I will send to him. If you can get hold of some others, kindly send some over to him if it be possible and convenient. You know his address — H. H. the Maharajah of Khetri, Rajputana, India. Of course, this letter is for the perusal of the holy family alone. Mrs. Breed wrote to me a stiff burning letter first, and then today I got a telegram from her inviting me to be her guest for a week. Before this I got a letter from Mrs. Smith of New York writing on her behalf and another lady Miss Helen Gould and another Dr.__ to come over to New York. As the Lynn Club wants me on the 17th of next month, I am going to New York first and come in time for their meeting at Lynn.

Next summer, if I do not go away, which Mrs. Bagley insists I should not, I may go to Annisquam where Mrs. Bagley has engaged a nice house. Mrs. Bagley is a very spiritual lady, and Mr. Palmer a spirituous gentleman but very good. What shall I write more? I am all right in nice health of body and mind. May you all be blessed, ever blessed, my dear, dear sisters. By the by, Mrs. Sherman has presented me with a lot of things amongst which is a nail set and letter holder and a little satchel etc., etc. Although I objected, especially to the nail set, as very dudish with mother-of-pearl handles, she insisted and I had to take them, although I do not know what to do with that brushing instrument. Lord bless them all. She gave me one advice — never to wear this Afrikee dress in society. Now I am a society man! Lord! What comes next? Long life brings queer experiences! My inexpressible love for you all, my holy family.

Your brother,
Vivekananda.

XX — DIWANJI SAHEB

To Shri Haridas Viharidas Desai

CHICAGO,
20th June, 1894.

DEAR DIWANJI SAHEB,

Your very kind note came today. I am so sorry that I could have caused pain to such a noble heart as yours with my rash and strong words. I bow down to your mild corrections. "Thy son am I, teach me thus bowing" — Gita. But you well know, Diwanji Saheb, it was my love that prompted me to say so. The backbiters, I must tell you, have not indirectly benefited me; on the other hand, they have injured me immensely in view of the fact that our Hindu people did not move a finger to tell the Americans that I represented them. Had our people sent some words thanking the American people for their kindness to me and stating that I was representing them! ... have been telling the American people that I have donned the Sannyasin's garb only in America and that I was a cheat, bare and simple. So far as reception goes, it has no effect on the American nation; but so far as helping me with funds goes, it has a terrible effect in making them take off their helping hands from me. And it is one year since I have been here, and not one man of note from India has thought it fit to make the Americans know that I am no cheat. There again the missionaries are always seeking for something against me, and they are busy picking up anything said against me by the Christian papers of India and publishing it here. Now you must know that the people here know very little of the distinction in India between the Christian and the Hindu.

Primarily my coming has been to raise funds for an enterprise of my own. Let me tell it all to you again.

The whole difference between the West and the East is in this: They are nations, we are not, i.e., civilisation, education here is general, it penetrates into the masses. The higher classes in India and America are the same, but the distance is infinite between the lower classes of the two countries. Why was it so easy for the English to conquer India? It was because they are a nation, we are not. When one of our great men dies, we must sit for centuries to have another; they can produce them as fast as they die. When our Diwanji Saheb will pass away (which the Lord may delay long for the good of my country), the nation will see the difficulty at once of filling his place, which is seen even now in the fact that they cannot dispense with your services. It is the dearth of great ones. Why so? Because they have such a bigger field of recruiting their great ones, we have so small. A nation of 300 millions has the smallest field of recruiting its great ones compared with nations of thirty, forty, or sixty millions, because the number of educated men and women in those nations is so great. Now do not mistake me, my kind friend, this is the great defect in our nation and must be removed.

Educate and raise the masses, and thus alone a nation is possible. Our reformers do not see where the wound is, they want to save the nation by marrying the widows; do you think that a nation is saved by the number of husbands its widows get? Nor is our religion to blame, for an idol more or less makes no difference. The whole defect is here: The real nation who live in cottage have forgotten their manhood, their individuality. Trodden under the foot of the Hindu, Mussulman, or Christian, they have come to think that they are born to be trodden under the foot of everybody who has money enough in his pocket. They are to be given back their lost individuality. They are to be educated. Whether idols will remain or not, whether widows will have husbands enough or not, whether caste is good or bad, I do not bother myself with such questions. Everyone must work out his own salvation. Our duty is to put the chemicals together, the crystallisation will come through God's laws. Let us put ideas into their heads, and they will do the rest. Now this means educating the masses. Here are these difficulties. A pauper government cannot, will not, do anything; so no help from that quarter.

Even supposing we are in a position to open schools in each village free, still the poor boys would rather go to the plough to earn their living than come to your school. Neither have we the money, nor can we make them come to education. The problem seems hopeless. I have found a way out. It is this. If the mountain does not come to Mohammed, Mohammed must go to the mountain. If the poor cannot come to education, education must reach them at the plough, in the factory, everywhere. How? You have seen my brethren. Now I can get hundreds of such, all over India, unselfish, good, and educated. Let these men go from village to village bringing not only religion to the door of everyone but also education. So I have a nucleus of organising the widows also as instructors to our women.

Now suppose the villagers after their day's work have come to their village and sitting under a tree or somewhere are smoking and talking the time away. Suppose two of these educated Sannyasins get hold of them there and with a camera throw astronomical or other pictures, scenes from different nations, histories, etc. Thus with globes, maps, etc. — and all this orally — how much can be done that way, Diwanji? It is not that the eye is the only door of knowledge, the ear can do all the same. So they would have ideas and morality, and hope for better. Here our work ends. Let them do the rest. What would make the Sannyasins do this sacrifice, undertake such a task? — religious enthusiasm. Every new religious wave requires a new centre. The old religion can only be revivified by a new centre. Hang your dogmas or doctrines, they never pay. It is a character, a life, a centre, a God-man that must lead the way, that must be the centre round which all other elements will gather themselves and then fall like a tidal wave upon the society, carrying all before it, washing away all impurities. Again, a piece of wood can only easily be cut along the grain. So the old Hinduism can only be reformed through Hinduism, and not through the new-fangled reform movements. At the same time the reformers must be able to unite in themselves the culture of both the East and the West. Now do you not think that you have already seen the nucleus of such a great movement, that you have heard the low rumblings of the coming tidal wave? That centre, that God-man to lead was born in India. He was the great Ramakrishna Paramahamsa, and round him this band is slowly gathering. They will do the work. Now, Diwanji Maharaj, this requires an organisation, money — a little at least to set the wheel in motion. Who would have given us money in India? — So, Diwanji Maharaj, I crossed over to America. You may remember I begged all the money from the poor, and the offers of the rich I would not accept because they could not understand my ideas. Now lecturing for a year in this country, I could not succeed at all (of course, I have no wants for myself) in my plan for raising some funds for setting up my work. First, this year is a very bad year in America; thousands of their poor are without work. Secondly, the missionaries and the Brahmo Samajists try to thwart all my views. Thirdly, a year has rolled by, and our countrymen could not even do so much for me as to say to the American people that I was a real Sannyasin and no cheat, and that I represented the Hindu religion. Even this much, the expenditure of a few words, they could not do! Bravo, my countrymen! I love them, Diwanji Saheb. Human help I spurn with my foot. He who has been with me through hills and dales, through deserts or forests, will be with me, I hope; if not, some heroic soul would arise some time or other in India, far abler than myself, and carry it out. So I have told you all about it. Diwanji, excuse my long letter, my noble friend, one of the few who really feel for me, have real kindness for me. You are at liberty, my friend, to think that I am a dreamer, a visionary; but believe at least that I am sincere to the backbone, and my greatest fault is that I love my country only too, too well. May you and yours be blessed ever and ever, my noble, noble friend. May the shadow of the Almighty ever rest on all those you love. I offer my eternal gratitude to you. My debt to you is immense, not only because you are my friend, but also because you have all your life served the Lord and your motherland so well.

Ever yours in gratitude,
Vivekananda.

XXI — DEAR__

To a Madras disciple

541 DEARBORN AVE.,
CHICAGO,
28 June, 1894.

DEAR__,

The other day I received a letter from G. G., Mysore. G. G. unfortunately thinks that I am all-knowing, else he would have written his Canarese address on the top of the letter more legibly. Then again it is a great mistake to address me letters to any other place but Chicago. It was my mistake of course at first, because I ought to have thought of the fine Buddhi (intellect) of our friends who are throwing letters at me anywhere they find an address at the top. But tell our Madras Brihaspatis (i.e. wise fellows) that they already knew full well that before their letters reach, I may be 1000 miles away from that particular place, for I am continuously travelling. In Chicago there is a friend whose house is my headquarters.

Now as to my prospects here — it is well-nigh zero. Why, because although I had the best purpose, it has been made null and void by these causes. All that I get about India is from Madras letters. Your letters say again and again how I am being praised in India. But that is between you and me, for I never saw a single Indian paper writing about me, except the three square inches sent to me by Alasinga. On the other hand, everything that is said by Christians in India is sedulously gathered by the missionaries and regularly published, and they go from door to door to make my friends give me up. They have succeeded only too well, for there is not one word for me from India. Indian Hindu papers may laud me to the skies, but not a word of that ever came to America, so that many people in this country think me a fraud. In the face of the missionaries and with the jealousy of the Hindus here to back them, I have not a word to say.

I now think it was foolish of me to go to the Parliament on the strength of the urging of the Madras boys. They are boys after all. Of course, I am eternally obliged to them, but they are after all enthusiastic young men without any executive abilities. I came here without credentials. How else to show that I am not a fraud in the face of the missionaries and the Brahmo Samaj? Now I thought nothing so easy as to spend a few words; I thought nothing would be so easy as to hold a meeting of some respectable persons in Madras and Calcutta and pass a resolution thanking me and the American people for being kind to me and sending it over officially, i.e. through the Secretary of the function, to America, for instance, sending one to Dr. Barrows and asking him to publish it in the papers and so on, to different papers of Boston, New York, and Chicago. Now after all, I found that it is too terrible a task for India to undertake. There has not been one voice for me in one year and every one against me, for whatever you may say of me in your homes, who knows anything of it here? More than two months ago I wrote to Alasinga about this. He did not even answer my letter. I am afraid his heart has grown lukewarm. So you must first think of that and then show this letter to the Madras people. On the other hand, my brethren foolishly talk nonsense about Keshab Sen; and the Madrasis, telling the Theosophists anything I write about them, are creating only enemies.... Oh! If only I had one man of some true abilities and brains to back me in India! But His will be done. I stand a fraud in this country. It was my foolishness to go to the Parliament without any credentials, hoping that there would be many for me. I have got to work it out slowly.

On the whole, the Americans are a million times nobler than the Hindus, and I can work more good here than in the country of the ingrate and the heartless. After all, I must work my Karma out. So far as pecuniary circumstances go I am all right and will be all right. The number of Theosophists in all America is only 625 by the last census. Mixing up with them will smash me in a minute rather than help me in any way. What nonsense does Alasinga mean by my going to London to see Mr. Old etc. Fool! the boys there don't know what they are talking. And this pack of Madras babies cannot even keep a counsel in their blessed noodles! Talk nonsense all day, and when it comes to the least business, they are nowhere! Boobies, who cannot get up a few meetings of 50 men each and send up a few empty words only to help me, talk big about influencing the world. I have written to you about the phonograph. Now there is here an electric fan costing $20 and working beautifully. The battery works 100 hours and then can be replenished at any electric plant. Good-bye, I have had enough of the Hindus. Now His will be done, I obey and bow down to my Karma. However, do not think me ungrateful. . . . The Madras people have done for me more than I deserved and more than was in their power. It was my foolishness — the forgetting for a moment that we Hindus have not yet become human beings and giving up for a moment my self-reliance and relying upon the Hindus — that I came to grief. Every moment I expected something from India. No, it never came. Last two months especially I was in torture at every moment. No, not even a newspaper from India! My friends waited — waited month after month; nothing came, not a voice. Many consequently grew cold and at last gave me up. But it is the punishment for relying upon man and upon brutes, for our countrymen are not men as yet. They are ready to be praised, but when their turn comes even to say a word, they are nowhere.

My thanks eternal to the Madras young men. May the Lord bless them for ever. America is the best field in the world to carry on my idea; so I do not think of leaving America soon. And why? Here I have food and drink and clothes, and everybody so kind, and all this for a few good words! Why should I give up such a noble nation to go to the land of brutes and ingrates and the brainless boobies held in eternal thraldom of superstitious, merciless, pitiless wretches? So good-bye again. You may show this letter to the people with discretion, even Alasinga upon whom I built so much. By the by, will you kindly send up a few copies of the sketch of Ramakrishna Paramahamsa's life written by Mazumdar to Chicago? They have lots in Calcutta. Don't forget the address 541 Dearborn Avenue (not Street), Chicago, or c/o Thomas Cook, Chicago. Any other address would cause much delay and confusion, as I am continually travelling, and Chicago is my headquarters, although even this much did not come to the brains of our Madras friends. Kindly give G. G., Alasinga, Secretary, and all others my eternal blessings. I am always praying for their welfare, and I am not in the least displeased with them, but I am not pleased with myself. I committed a terrible error — of calculating upon others' help — once in my life — and I have paid for it. It was my fault and not theirs. Lord bless all the Madras people. They are at least far superior to the Bengalis, who are simply fools and have no souls, no stamina at all. Good-bye, good-bye. I have launched my boat in the waves, come what may. Regarding my brutal criticisms, I have really no right to make them. You have done for me infinitely more than I deserve. I must bear my own Karma, and that without a murmur. Lord bless you all.

Yours truly,
Vivekananda.

PS. I am afraid Alasinga's college has closed, but I have no intimation of it, and he never gave me his home address. Kidi has dropped out, I am afraid.

XXII — MOTHER

To Mrs. George W. Hale

C/O Dr. E. Guernsey,
FISHKILL LANDING, N.Y.,
July, 1894.

DEAR MOTHER,

I came yesterday to this place, and shall remain here a few days. I received in New York a letter from you but did not receive any Interior, for which I am glad, because I am not perfect yet, and knowing the "unselfish love" the Presbyterian priests, especially the Interior has for "me", I want to keep aloof from rousing bad feelings towards these "sweet Christian gentlemen" in my heart.

Our religion teaches that anger is a great sin,

even if it is "righteous". Each must follow his own religion. I could not for my soul distinguish ever the distinction between "religious anger" and "commonplace anger", "religious killing" and "commonplace killing", "religious slandering and irreligious", and so forth. Nor may that "fine" ethical distinction ever enter into the ethics of our nation! Jesting apart, Mother Church, I do not care the least for the gambols these men play, seeing as I do through and through the insincerity, the hypocrisy, and love of self and name that is the only motive power in these men.

As to the photographs, the first time the Babies got a few copies, and the second time you brought a few copies; you know they are to give 50 copies in all. Sister Isabelle knows better than I.

With my sincerest love and respects for you and Father Pope.

I remain,

Yours,
Vivekananda.

PS. How are you enjoying the heat? I am bearing the heat very well here. I had an invitation to Swampscott on the sea from a very rich lady whose acquaintance I made last winter in New York, but I declined with thanks. I am very careful not to take the hospitality of anybody here, especially the rich. I had a few other invitations from some very rich people here. I refused; I have by this time seen the whole business through. Lord bless you and yours, Mother Church, for your sincerity. Oh! it is so rare in this world.

XXIII — SISTERS

To the Hale Sisters (about the Calcutta meeting of 5th Sept., 1894)

NEW YORK
9th July (Sept.?), 1894.

O MY SISTERS,

Glory unto Jagadambâ (Mother of the Universe)! I have gained beyond expectations. The prophet has been honoured and with a vengeance. I am weeping like a child at His mercy — He never leaves His servant, sisters. The letter I send you will explain all, and the printed things are coming to the American people. The names there are the very flower of our country. The President was the chief nobleman of Calcutta, and the other man Mahesh Chandra Nyâyaratna is the principal of the Sanskrit College and the chief Brahmin in all India and recognised by the Government as such. The letter will tell you all. O sisters! What a rogue am I that in the face of such mercies sometimes the faith totters — seeing every moment that I am in His hands. Still the mind sometimes gets despondent. Sister, there is a God — a Father — a Mother who never leaves His Children, never, never, never. Put uncanny theories aside and becoming children take refuge in Him. I cannot write more — I am weeping like a woman.

Blessed, blessed art Thou, Lord God of my soul!

Yours affectionately,
Vivekananda.

XXIV — BABIES

To the Hale Sisters

SWAMPSCOTT,
26th July, 1894.

DEAR BABIES,

Now don't let my letters stray beyond the circle, please. I had a beautiful letter from sister Mary. See how I am getting the dash, sister Jeany teaches me all that. She can jump and run and play and swear like a devil and talk slang at the rate of 500 a minute; only she does not much care for religion, only a little. She is gone today home, and I am going to Greenacre. I had been to see Mrs. Breed. Mrs. Stone was there, with whom is residing Mrs. Pullman and all the golden bugs, my old friends hereabouts. They are kind as usual. On my way back from Greenacre I am going to Annisquam to see Mrs. Bagley for a few days.

Darn it, forget everything. I had duckings in the sea like a fish. I am enjoying every bit of it. What nonsense was the song Harriet taught me "dans la plaine" the deuce take it. I told it to a French scholar and he laughed and laughed till the fellow was well-nigh burst at my wonderful translation. That is the way you would have taught me French! You are a pack of fools and heathens, I tell you. Now are you gasping for breath like a huge fish stranded? I am glad that you are sizzling. Oh! how nice and cool it is here, and it is increased a hundred-fold when I think about the gasping, sizzling, boiling, frying four old maids, and how cool and nice I am here. Whooooo!

Miss Phillips has a beautiful place somewhere in N.Y. State — mountain, lake, river, forest altogether — what more? I am going to make a Himalayas there and start a monastery as sure as I am living — I am not going to leave this country without throwing one more apple of discord into this already roaring, fighting, kicking, mad whirlpool of American religion. Well, dear old maids, you sometimes have a glimpse of the lake and on every hot noon, think of going down to the bottom of the lake, down, down, down, until it is cool and nice, and then to lie down on the bottom, with that coolness above and around, and lie there still, silent, and just doze — not sleep, but dreamy dozing half unconscious sort of bliss — very much like that which opium brings; that is delicious; and drinking lots of iced water. Lord bless my soul — I had such cramps several times as would have killed an elephant. So I hope to keep myself away from the cold water.

May you be all happy, dear fin de siècle young ladies, is the constant prayer of.

Vivekananda.

XXV — SISTERS

To the Hale Sisters

GREENACRE,
11th August, 1894.

DEAR SISTERS,

I have been all this time in Greenacre. I enjoyed this place very much. They have been all very kind to me. One Chicago lady, Mrs. Pratt of Kenilworth, wanted to give me $500; she became so much interested in me; but I refused. She has made me promise that I would send word to her whenever I need money, which I hope the Lord will never put me in. His help alone is sufficient for me. I have not heard anything from you nor from Mother. Neither have I any news from India as to the arrival of the phonograph.

If there was anything in my letter to you which was offensive, I hope you all know that I meant everything in love. It is useless to express my gratitude to you for your kindness. Lord bless you and shower His choicest blessings on you and those you love. To your family I am ever, ever beholden. You know it. You feel it. I cannot express it. On Sunday I am going to lecture at Plymouth at the "Sympathy of Religions" meetings of Col. Higginson. Herewith I send a photograph Cora Stockham took of the group under the tree. It is only a proof and will fade away under exposure, but I cannot get anything better at present. Kindly tender my heartfelt love and gratitude to Miss Howe. She has been so, so kind to me. I do not need anything at present. I shall be very glad to let you know if I need anything. I think I am going to Fishkill from Plymouth, where I will be only a couple of days. I will write you again from Fishkill. Hope you are all happy, or rather I know you are. Pure and good souls can never be unhappy. I shall have a very nice time the few weeks I am here. I will be in New York next fall. New York is a grand and good place. The New York people have a tenacity of purpose unknown in any other city. I had a letter from Mrs. Potter Palmer asking me to see her in August. She is a very gracious and kind lady, etc. I have not much to say. There is my friend Dr. Janes of New York, President of the Ethical Culture Society, who has begun his lectures. I must go to hear him. He and I agree so much. May you be always happy!

Ever your well-wishing brother,
Vivekananda.

XXVI — SISTER

To Miss Mary Hale

C/O. MRS. BAGLEY,
ANNISQUAM,
31st August, 1894.

DEAR SISTER,

The letter from the Madras people was published in yesterday's Boston Transcript. I hope to send you a copy. You may have seen it in some Chicago paper. I am sure there is some mail for me at Cook & Sons — I shall be here till Tuesday next at least, on which day I am going to lecture here in Annisquam.

Kindly inquire at Cook's for my mail and send it over at Annisquam.

I had no news of you for some time. I sent two pictures to Mother Church yesterday and hope you will like them. I am very anxious about the Indian mail. With love for all,

I am your ever affectionate brother,
Vivekananda.

PS. As I do not know where you are I could not send something else which I have to send over to you.

XXVII — LEON

To Mr. Leon Landsberg

HOTEL BELLEVUE,
BOSTON,
13th September, 1894.

DEAR LEON,

Forgive me, but I have the right, as your Guru, to advise you, and I insist that you buy some clothes for yourself, as the want of them stands in the way of your doing anything in this country. Once you have a start, you may dress in whatever way you like. People do not object.

You need not thank me, for this is only a duty. According to Hindu law, if a Guru dies, his disciple is his heir, and not even his son — supposing him to have had one before becoming a Sannyasin. This is, you see, an actual spiritual relationship, and none of your Yankee "tutor" business!

With all blessings and prayers for your success,

Yours,
Vivekananda.

XXVIII — SISTER

To Miss Mary Hale

HOTEL BELLEVUE,
BEACON ST., BOSTON,
13th September, 1894.

DEAR SISTER,

Your kind note reached me this morning. I have been in this hotel for about a week. I will remain in Boston some time yet. I have plenty of gowns already, in fact, more than I can carry with ease. When I had that drenching in Annisquam, I had on that beautiful black suit you appreciate so much, and I do not think it can be damaged any way; it also has been penetrated with my deep meditations on the Absolute. I am very glad that you enjoyed the summer so well. As for me, I am vagabondising. I was very much amused the other day at reading Abe Hue's description of the vagabond lamas of Tibet — a true picture of our fraternity. He says they are queer people. They come when they will, sit at everybody's table, invitation or no invitation, live where they will, and go where they will. There is not a mountain they have not climbed, not a river they have not crossed, not a nation they do not know, not a language they do not talk. He thinks that God must have put into them a part of that energy which makes the planets go round and round eternally. Today this vagabond lama was seized with a desire of going right along scribbling, and so I walked down and entering a store bought all sorts of writing material and a beautiful portfolio which shuts with a clasp and has even a little wooden inkstand. So far it promises well. Hope it will continue. Last month I had mail enough from India and am greatly delighted with my countrymen at their generous appreciation of my work. Good enough for them. I cannot find anything more to write. Prof. Wright, his wife, and children were as good as ever. Words cannot express my gratitude to them.

Everything so far is not going bad with me except that I had a bad cold. Now I think the fellow is gone. This time I tried Christian Science for insomnia and really found it worked very well. Wishing you all happiness,

I remain, ever your affectionate brother,
Vivekananda.

PS. Kindly tell Mother that I do not want any coat now.

XXIX — DIWANJI SAHEB

CHICAGO,
September, 1894.

DEAR DIWANJI SAHEB (Shri Haridas Viharidas Desai),

Your kind letter reached long ago, but as I had not anything to write I was late in answering.

Your kind note to G. W. Hale has been very gratifying, as I owed them that much. I have been travelling all over this country all this time and seeing everything. I have come to this conclusion that there is only one country in the world which understands religion — it is India; that with all their faults the Hindus are head and shoulders above all other nations in morality and spirituality; and that with proper care and attempt and struggle of all her disinterested sons, by combining some of the active and heroic elements of the West with the calm virtues of the Hindus, there will come a type of men far superior to any that have ever been in this world.

I do not know when I come back; but I have seen enough of this country, I think, and so soon will go over to Europe and then to India.

With my best love, gratitude to you and all your brothers,

I remain, yours faithfully,
Vivekananda.

XXX — DIWANJI SAHEB

CHICAGO(?),
September, 1894(3?),

DEAR DIWANJI SAHEB (Shri Haridas Viharidas Desai),

Very kind of you to send up a man inquiring about my health and comfort. But that's quite of a piece with your fatherly character. I am all right here. Your kindness has left nothing more to be desired here. I hope soon to see you in a few days. I don't require any conveyance while going down. Descent is very bad, and the ascent is the worst part of the job, that's the same in everything in the world. My heartful gratitude to you.

Yours faithfully,
Vivekananda.

XXXI — MOTHER

To Mrs. George W. Hale

1125 ST. PAUL ST.,
BALTIMORE,
October, 1894.

DEAR MOTHER,

You see where I am now. Did you see a telegram from India in the Chicago Tribune? Did they print the address from Calcutta? From here I go to Washington, thence to Philadelphia and then to New York; send me the address of Miss Mary in Philadelphia so that I may look in on my way to New York. Hope your worry is over.

> Yours affectionately,
> Vivekananda.

from heretofore. These newspapers of India will be my death, I am sure. They will now talk what I ate on such and such a date and how I sneezed. Lord bless them, it was all my foolery. I really came here to raise a little money secretly and go over but was caught in the trap and now no more of a reserved life.

Wishing you all enjoyments,

> I remain, yours affectionately,
> Vivekananda.

XXXII — SISTER

To Miss Mary Hale

> C/O MRS. E. TOTTEN,
> 1703, 1ST STREET,
> WASHINGTON,
> [November 1(?), 1894]

DEAR SISTER,

I have received two letters which you were very kind to take the trouble to write. I am going to talk here today, tomorrow at Baltimore, then again Monday at Baltimore, and Tuesday at Washington again. So I will be in Philadelphia a few days after that. I shall write to you the day I start from Washington. I shall be in Philadelphia a few days only to see Prof. Wright, and then I go to New York and run for a little while between New York and Boston, and then go to Chicago via Detroit; and then "whist"..., as Senator Palmer says, to England.

The word "Dharma" means religion. I am very sorry they treated Petro very badly in Calcutta. I have been very well treated here and am doing very well. Nothing extraordinary in the meantime except I got vexed at getting loads of newspapers from India; so after sending a cart-load to Mother Church and another to Mrs. Guernsey, I had to write them to stop sending their newspapers. I have had "boom" enough in India. Alasinga writes that every village all over the country now has heard of me. Well, the old peace is gone for ever and no rest anywhere

XXXIII — DIWANJI SAHEB

> CHICAGO,
> 15th November, 1894(3?).

DEAR DIWANJI SAHEB (Shri Haridas Viharidas Desai),

I here received your kind note. So very kind of you to remember me even here, I have not seen your Narayan Hemchandra. He is not in America, I believe. I have seen many strange sights and grand things. I am glad that there is a good chance of your coming over to Europe. Avail yourself of it by any means. The fact of our isolation from all the other nations of the world is the cause of our degeneration and its only remedy is getting back into the current of the rest of the world. Motion is the sign of life. America is a grand country. It is a paradise of the poor and women. There is almost no poor in the country, and nowhere else in the world women are so free, so educated, so cultured. They are everything in society.

This is a great lesson. The Sannyasin has not lost a bit of his Sannyasinship, even his mode of living. And in this most hospitable country, every home is open to me. The Lord who guides me in India, would He not guide me here? And He has.

You may not understand why a Sannyasin should be in America, but it was necessary. Because the only claim you have to be recognised by the world is your religion, and good specimens of our religious men are required to be sent abroad to give other nations an idea that India is not dead.

Some representative men must come out of India and go to all the nations of the earth to show at least that you are not savages. You may not feel the necessity of it from your Indian home, but, believe me, much depends upon that for your nation. And a Sannyasin who has no idea of doing good to his fellows is a brute, not a Sannyasin.

I am neither a sightseer nor an idle traveller; but you will see, if you live to see, and bless me all your life.

Mr. Dvivedi's papers were too big for the Parliament, and they had to be cut short.

I spoke at the Parliament of Religions, and with what effect I may quote to you from a few newspapers and magazines ready at hand. I need not be self-conceited, but to you in confidence I am bound to say, because of your love, that no Hindu made such an impression in America, and if my coming has done nothing, it has done this that the Americans have come to know that India even today produces men at whose feet even the most civilised nations may learn lessons of religion and morality. Don't you think that is enough to say for the Hindu nation sending over here their Sannyasin? You would hear the details from Virchand Gandhi.

These I quote from the journals: "But eloquent as were many of the brief speeches, no one expressed as well the spirit of the Parliament (of religions) and its limitations as the Hindu monk. I copy his address in full, but I can only suggest its effect upon the audience; for he is an orator by Divine right, and his strong intelligent face in its picturesque setting of yellow and orange was hardly less interesting than these earnest words and the rich rhythmical utterance he gave them." (Here the speech is quoted in extenso.) New York Critique.

"He has preached in clubs and churches until his faith has become familiar to us. . . . His culture, his eloquence, and his fascinating personality have given us a new idea of Hindu civilisation . . . . His fine, intelligent face and his deep musical voice, prepossessing one at once in his favour. . . . He speaks without notes, presenting his facts and his conclusions with the greatest art and the most convincing sincerity, and rising often to rich inspiring eloquence." (ibid.)

"Vivekananda is undoubtedly the greatest figure in the Parliament of Religions. After hearing him we feel how foolish it is to send missionaries to this learned nation." Herald (the greatest paper here).

I cease from quoting more lest you think me conceited; but this was necessary to you who have become nearly frogs in the well and would not see how the world is going on elsewhere. I do not mean you personally, my noble friend, but our nation in general.

I am the same here as in India, only here in this highly cultural land there is an appreciation, a sympathy which our ignorant fools never dream of. There our people grudge us monks a crumb of bread, here they are ready to pay one thousand rupees a lecture and remain grateful for the instructions for ever.

I am appreciated by these strangers more than I was ever in India. I can, if I will, live here all my life in the greatest luxury; but I am a Sannyasin, and "India, with all thy faults I love thee still". So I am coming back after some months, and go on sowing the seeds of religion and progress from city to city as I was doing so long, although amongst a people who know not what appreciation and gratefulness are.

I am ashamed of my own nation when I compare their beggarly, selfish, unappreciative, ignorant ungratefulness with the help, hospitality, sympathy, and respect which the Americans have shown to me, a representative of a foreign religion. Therefore come out of the country, see others, and compare.

Now after these quotations, do you think it was worth while to send a Sannyasin to America?

Please do not publish it. I hate notoriety in the same manner as I did in India.

I am doing the Lord's work, and wherever He leads I follow. lame cross a mountain, He will help me. I do not care for human help. He is ready to help me in India, in America, on the North Pole, if

He thinks fit. If He does not, none else can help me. Glory unto the Lord for ever and ever.

Yours with blessings,
Vivekananda.

XXXIV — DIWANJI

541 DEARBORN AVENUE,
CHICAGO,
November(?), 1894.

DEAR DIWANJI (Shri Haridas Viharidas Desai),

Your letter pleased me extremely. I, of course, understand the joke, but I am not the baby to be put off with a joke; now take more.

The secret of success of the Westerners is the power of organisation and combination. That is only possible with mutual trust and co-operation and help. Now here is Virchand Gandhi, the Jain, whom you well knew in Bombay. This man never takes anything but pure vegetables even in this terribly cold climate, and tooth and nail tries to defend his countrymen and religion. The people of this country like him very well, but what are they doing who sent him over? They are trying to outcast him. Jealousy is a vice necessarily generated in slaves. Again it is jealousy that holds them down.

Here were . . .; they were all trying to lecture and get money thereby. They did something, but I succeeded better than they — why, I did not put myself as a bar to their success. It was the will of the Lord. But all these . . . except . . . have fabricated and circulated the most horrible lies about me in this country, and behind my back. Americans will never stoop to such meanness.

. . . If any man tries to move forward here, everybody is ready to help him. In India you may try tomorrow by writing a single line of praise for me in any of our papers (Hindu), and the next day they would be all against me. Why? It is the nature of slaves. They cannot suffer to see any one of their brethren putting his head the least above their rank. . . . Do you mean to compare such stuff with these children of liberty, self-help, and brotherly love? The nearest approach to our people are the freed slaves of the U.S.A., the Negroes. Why, in the South they are about twenty millions and are now free. The whites are a handful, still the whites hold them down all the same. Why, even when they have every right by law, a bloody war between the brothers has been fought to free these slaves? The same defect — jealousy. Not one of these Negroes would bear to see his brother-Negro praised or pushing on. Immediately they would join the whites to crush him down. You can have no idea about it until you come out of India. It is all right for those who have plenty of money and position to let the world roll on such, but I call him a traitor who, having been educated, nursed in luxury by the heart's blood of the downtrodden millions of toiling poor, never even takes a thought for them. Where, in what period of history your rich men, noblemen, your priests and potentates took any thought for the poor — the grinding of whose faces is the very life-blood of their power?

But the Lord is great, the vengeance came sooner or later, and they who sucked the life-blood of the poor, whose very education was at their expense, whose very power was built on their poverty, were in their turn sold as slaves by hundreds and thousands, their wives and daughters dishonoured, their property robbed for the last 1,000 years, and do you think it was for no cause?

Why amongst the poor of India so many are Mohammedans? It is nonsense to say, they were converted by the sword. It was to gain their liberty from the . . . zemindars and from the . . . priest, and as a consequence you find in Bengal there are more Mohammedans than Hindus amongst the cultivators, because there were so many zemindars there. Who thinks of raising these sunken downtrodden millions? A few thousand graduates do not make a nation, a few rich men do not make a nation. True, our opportunities are less, but still there is enough to feed and clothe and made 300 millions more comfortable, nay, luxurious. Ninety per cent of our people are without education — who thinks of that? — these Babus, the so-called patriots?

Now, let me tell you — still there is a God, no joke. He is ordering our lives, and although I know a nation of slaves cannot but try to bite at the hand that wants to give them medicine, yet, pray with me, you — one of the few that have real sympathy for everything good, for everything great, one at least whom I know to be a man of true ring, nobility of nature, and a thorough sincerity of head and heart — pray with me:

"Lead, kindly Light,
amid th' encircling gloom."

I do not care what they say. I love my God, my religion, my country, and above all, myself, a poor beggar. I love the poor, the ignorant, the downtrodden, I feel for them — the Lord knows how much. He will show me the way. I do not care a fig for human approbation or criticism. I think of most of them as ignorant, noisy children — they have not penetrated into the inner nature of sympathy, into the spirit which is all love.

I have that insight through the blessing of Ramakrishna. I am trying to work with my little band, all of these poor beggars like me, you have seen them. But the Lord's works have been always done by the lowly, by the poor. You bless me that I may have faith in my Guru, in my God, and in myself.

The only way is love and sympathy. The only worship is love.

May He help you and yours ever and ever!

With prayers and blessings,
Vivekananda.

XXXV — SISTER

To Miss Mary Hale

168, BRATTLE STREET,
CAMBRIDGE,
8th December, 1894.

DEAR SISTER,

I have been here three days. We had a nice lecture from Lady Henry Somerset. I have a class every morning here on Vedanta and other topics. Perhaps you have got the copy of Vedantism by this time which I left with Mother Temple to be sent over. I went to dine with the Spaldings another day. That day they urged me, against my repeated protests, to criticise the Americans. I am afraid they did not relish it. It is of course always impossible to do it. What about Mother Church and the family at Chicago? I had no letters from them a long time. I would have run into town to see you before this, had I time. I am kept pretty busy the whole day. Then there is the fear of not meeting you.

If you have time, you may write, and I shall snatch the first opportunity to see you. My time of course is always in the afternoon, so long I shall be here, that is until the 27th or 28th of this month; I will have to be very busy in the morning till 12 or 1.

With my love to you all,

Ever your affectionate brother,
Vivekananda.

XXXVI — SISTER

To Miss Mary Hale

CAMBRIDGE,
December, 1894.

DEAR SISTER,

I received your letter just now. If it is not against the rules of your society, why do you not come to see Mrs. Ole Bull, Miss Farmer, and Mrs. Adams the physical culturist from Chicago?

Any day you will find them there.

Yours ever affectionately,
Vivekananda.

XXXVII — SISTER

To Miss Mary Hale

CAMBRIDGE,
21st December, 1894.

DEAR SISTER,

I had not anything from you since your last. I am going away next Tuesday to New York. You must have received Mrs. Bull's letter in the meanwhile. If you cannot accept it, I shall be very glad to come over any day — I have time now as the lectures are at an end, except Sunday next.

Yours ever affectionately,
Vivekananda.

XXXVIII — MISS BELL

To Miss Isabelle McKindley

528, 5TH AVE., NEW YORK,
24th Jan., 1895.

DEAR MISS BELL,

I hope you are well....

My last lecture was not very much appreciated by the men but awfully so by vemen. You know this Brooklyn is the centre of anti-women's rights movements; and when I told them that women deserve and are fit for everything, they did not like it of course. Never mind, the women were in ecstasies.

I have got again a little cold. I am going to the Guernseys. I have got a room downtown also where I will go several hours to hold my classes etc. Mother Church must be all right by this time, and you are all enjoying this nice weather. Give Mrs. Adams mountain high love and regard from me when you see her next.

Send my letters as usual to the Guernseys.

With love for all,

Ever your affectionate brother,
Vivekananda.

XXXIX — FRIEND

To Mr. Francis Leggett

NEW YORK,
10th April, 1895.

DEAR FRIEND,

It is impossible to express my gratitude for your kindly inviting me to your country seat [Ridgely]. I am involved in a mistake now and find it impossible for me to come tomorrow. Tomorrow I have a class at Miss Andrews' of 40 W. 9th Street. As I was given to understand by Miss MacLeod that that class could be postponed, I was only too glad at the prospect of joining the company tomorrow. But I find that Miss MacLeod was mistaken and Miss Andrews came to tell me that she could not by any means stop the class tomorrow or even give notice to the members, who are about 50 or 60 in number.

In view of this I sincerely regret my inability and hope that Miss MacLeod and Mrs. Sturges will understand that it is an unavoidable circumstance, and not the will, that stands in the way of my taking advantage of your kind invitation.

I shall only be too glad to come day after tomorrow, or any other day this week, as it suits you.

Ever sincerely yours,
Vivekananda.

XL — FRIEND

To Mr. E. T. Sturdy

54 W. 33RD STREET,
NEW YORK,
24th April, 1895.

DEAR FRIEND,

I am perfectly aware that although some truth underlies the mass of mystical thought which has burst upon the Western world of late, it is for the most part full of motives, unworthy, or insane. For this reason, I have never had anything to do with these phases of religion, either in India or elsewhere, and mystics as a class are not very favourable to me....

I quite agree with you that only the Advaita philosophy can save mankind, whether in East or West, from "devil worship" and kindred superstitions, giving tone and strength to the very nature of man. India herself requires this, quite as much or even more than the West. Yet it is hard uphill work, for we have first to create a taste, then teach, and lastly proceed to build up the whole fabric.

Perfect sincerity, holiness, gigantic intellect, and an all-conquering will. Let only a handful of men work with these, and the whole world will be revolutionised. I did a good deal of platform work in this country last year, and received plenty of applause, but found that I was only working for myself. It is the patient upbuilding of character, the intense struggle to realise the truth, which alone will tell in the future of humanity. So this year I am hoping to work along this line — training up to practical Advaita realisation a small band of men and women. I do not know how far I shall succeed. The West is the field for work if a man wants to benefit humanity, rather than his own particular sect or country. I agree perfectly as to your idea of a magazine. But I have no business capacity at all to do these things. I can teach and preach, and sometimes write. But I have intense faith in Truth. The Lord will send help and hands to work with me. Only let me be perfectly pure, perfectly sincere, and perfectly unselfish.

"Truth alone triumphs, not untruth; through truth alone stretches the way to the Lord" (Atharva-Veda). He who gives up the little self for the world will find the whole universe his.... I am very uncertain about coming to England. I know no one there, and here I am doing some work. The Lord will guide, in His own time.

Yours etc.,
Vivekananda.

XLI — FRIEND

To Mr. E. T. Sturdy

19 W. 38TH ST.,
NEW YORK

DEAR FRIEND,

I received your last duly, and as I had a previous arrangement to come to Europe by the end of this August, I take your invitation as a Divine Call.

"Truth alone triumphs, not untruth. Through truth alone lies the way to Devayâna (the way to the gods)." Those who think that a little sugar-coating of untruth helps the spread of truth are mistaken and will find in the long run that a single drop of poison poisons the whole mass.... The man who is pure, and who dares, does all things. May the Lord ever protect you from illusion and delusion! I am ever ready to work with you, and the Lord will send us friends by the hundred, if only we be our own friends first. "The Atman alone is the friend of the Atman."

Europe has always been the source of social, and Asia of spiritual power; and the whole history of the world is the tale of the varying combinations of those two powers. Slowly a new leaf is being turned in the story of humanity. The signs of this are everywhere. Hundreds of new plans will be created and destroyed. Only the fit will survive. And what but the true and the good is the fit?

Yours etc.,
Vivekananda.

XLII — BABIES

To the Hale Sisters

NEW YORK,
5th May, 1895.

DEAR BABIES,

What I expected has come. I always thought that although Prof. Max Muller in all his writings on the

Hindu religion adds in the last a derogatory remark, he must see the whole truth in the long run. As soon as you can, get a copy of his last book Vedantism; there you will find him swallowing the whole of it — reincarnation and all.

Of course, you will not find it difficult at all to understand, as it is only a part of what I have been telling you all this time.

Many points you will find smack of my paper in Chicago.

I am glad now the old man has seen the truth, because that is the only way to have religion in the face of modern research and science.

Hope you are enjoying Todd's Rajasthan.

With all love, your brother,
Vivekananda.

PS. When is Miss Mary coming to Boston?

XLIII — ALASINGA

C/O MISS PHILIPS,
19 WEST 38TH STREET,
NEW YORK
28th May, 1895.

DEAR ALASINGA,

Herewith I send a hundred dollars or £20-8-7 in English money. Hope this will go just a little in starting your paper. Hoping to do more by and by.

I remain, ever yours, with blessings,
Vivekananda.

PS. Reply immediately to it C/o the above address. New York will be my headquarters henceforth.

I have succeeded in doing something in this country at last.

XLIV — JOE

To Miss Josephine MacLeod

21 W. 34TH ST.,
NEW YORK,
June, 1895.

DEAR JOE,

Experiences are gathering a bit thick round you. I am sure they will lift many a veil more.

Mr. Leggett told me of your phonograph. I told him to get a few cylinders — I talk in them through somebody's phonograph and send them to Joe — to which he replied that he could buy one, because "I always do what Joe asks me to do." I am glad there is so much of hidden poetry in his nature.

I am going today to live with the Guernseys as the doctor wants to watch me and cure me.... Doctor Guernsey, after examining other things, was feeling my pulse, when suddenly Landsberg (whom they had forbidden the house) got in and retreated immediately after seeing me. Dr. Guernsey burst out laughing and declared he would have paid that man for coming just then, for he was then sure of his diagnosis of my case. The pulse before was so regular, but just at the sight of Landsberg it almost stopped from emotion. It is sure only a case of nervousness. He also advises me strongly to go on with Doctor Helmer's treatment. He thinks Helmer will do me a world of good, and that is what I need now. Is not he broad?

I expect to see "the sacred cow" today in town. I will be in New York a few days more. Helmer wants me to take three treatments a week for four weeks, then two a week for four more, and I will be all right. In case I go to Boston, he recommends me to a very good ostad (expert) there whom he would advise on the matter.

I said a few kind words to Landsberg and went upstairs to Mother Guernsey to save poor Landsberg from embarrassment.

Ever yours in the Lord,
Vivekananda.

XLV — SISTER

To Miss Mary Hale

(Written on birch bark)
PERCY N. H.,
17 June, 1895.

DEAR SISTER,

Going tomorrow to the Thousand Islands care Miss Dutcher's, Thousand Island Park, N.Y. Where are you now? Where will you all be in summer? I have a chance of going to Europe in August, I will come to see you before I go. So write to me. Also I expect books and letters from India. Kindly send them care Miss Phillips, 19 W. 38th Street, N.Y. This is the bark in which all holy writings are written in India. So I write Sanskrit: May the husband of Uma (Shiva) protect you always.

May you all be blessed ever and ever,
Vivekananda.

XLVI — SISTER

To Miss Mary Hale

54 W. 33RD STREET,
NEW YORK,
22nd June, 1895.

DEAR SISTER,

The letters from India and the parcel of books reached me safe. I am so happy to know of Mr. Sam's arrival. I am sure he is "bewaring of the vidders" nicely. I met a friend of Mr. Sam's one day on the street. He is an Englishman with a name ending in "ni". He was very nice. He said he was living in the same house with Sam somewhere in Ohio.

I am going on pretty nearly in the same old fashion. Talking when I can and silent when forced to be. I do not know whether I will go to Greenacre this summer. I saw Miss Farmer the other day. She was in a hurry to go away, so I had but very little talk with her. She is a noble, noble lady.

How are you going on with your Christian Science lessons? I hope you will go to Greenacre. There you will find quite a number of them and also the Spiritualists, table turnings, palmists, astrologers, etc., etc. You will get all the "cures" and all the "isms" presided over by Miss Farmer.

Landsberg has gone away to live in some other place, so I am left alone. I am living mostly on nuts and fruits and milk, and find it very nice and healthy too. I hope to lose about 30 to 40 lbs. this summer. That will be all right for my size. I am afraid I have forgotten all about Mrs. Adam's lessons in walking. I will have to renew them when she comes again to N.Y. Gandhi has gone to England en route to India from Boston, I suppose.

I would like to know about his "chaperon" Mrs. Howard and her present bereaved state. I am very glad to hear that the rugs did not go down to the bottom of the Atlantic and are at last coming.

This year I could hardly keep my head up, and I did not go about lecturing. The three great commentaries on the Vedanta philosophy belonging to the three great sects of dualists, qualified dualists, and monists are being sent to me from India. Hope they will arrive safe. Then I will have an intellectual feast indeed. I intend to write a book this summer on the Vedanta philosophy. This world will always be a mixture of good and evil, of happiness and misery; this wheel will ever go up and come down; dissolution and resolution is the inevitable law. Blessed are those who struggle to go beyond. Well, I am glad all the babies are doing well but sorry there was no "catch" even this winter, and every winter the chances are dwindling down. Here near my lodgings is the Waldorf-Hotel, the rendezvous of lots of titled but penniless Europeans on show for "Yankee" heiresses to buy. You may have any selection here, the stock is so full and varied. There is the man who talks no English; there are others who lisp a few words which no one can understand; and others are there who talk nice English, but their chance is not so great as that of the dumb ones — the girls do not think them enough foreign who talk plain English fluently.

I read somewhere in a funny book that an American vessel was being foundered in the sea; the men were desperate and as a last solace wanted some religious service being done. There was "Uncle Josh" on board who was an elder in the Presbyterian Church. They all began to entreat, "Do something religious, Uncle Josh! We are all going to die." Uncle Joseph took his hat in his hand and took up a collection on the spot!

That is all of religion he knew. And that is more or less characteristic of the majority of such people. Collections are about all the religion they know or will ever know. Lord bless them. Good-bye for present. I am going to eat something; I feel very hungry.

Yours affectionately,
Vivekananda.

XLVII — SISTER

To Miss Mary Hale

C/O MISS DUTCHER,
THOUSAND ISLAND PARK, N.Y.
26th June, 1895.

DEAR SISTER,

Many thanks for the Indian mail. It brought a good deal of good news. You are enjoying by this time, I hope, the articles by Prof. Max Müller on the "Immortality of the Soul" which I sent to Mother Church. The old man has taken in Vedanta, bones and all, and has boldly come out. I am so glad to know the arrival of the rugs. Was there any duty to pay? If so I will pay that, I insist on it. There will come another big packet from the Raja of Khetri containing some shawls and brocades and nick-nacks. I want to present them to different friends. But they are not going to arrive before some months, I am sure.

I am asked again and again, as you will find in the letters from India, to go over. They are getting desperate. Now if I go to Europe, I will go as the guest of Mr. Francis Leggett of N.Y. He will travel all over Germany, England, France, and Switzerland for six weeks. From there I shall go to India, or I may return to America. I have a seed planted here and wish it to grow. This winter's work in N.Y. was splendid, and it may die if I suddenly go over to India, so I am not sure about going to India soon.

Nothing noticeable has happened during this visit to the Thousand Islands. The scenery is very beautiful and I have some of my friends here with me to talk about God and soul ad libitum. I am eating fruits and drinking milk and so forth, and studying huge Sanskrit books on Vedanta which they have kindly sent me from India.

If I come to Chicago I cannot come at least within six weeks or more. Baby needn't alter any of her plans for me. I will see you all somehow or other before I go.

You fussed so much over my reply to Madras, but it has produced a tremendous effect there. A late speech by the President of the Madras Christian College, Mr. Miller, embodies a large amount of my ideas and declares that the West is in need of Hindu ideas of God and man and calls upon the young men to go and preach to the West. This has created quite a furore of course amongst the Missions. What you allude to as being published in the Arena I did not see a bit of it. The women did not make any fuss over me at all in New York. Your friend must have drawn on his imagination. They were not of the "bossing" type at all. I hope Father Pope will go to Europe and Mother Church too. Travelling is the best thing in life. I am afraid I shall die if made to stick to one place for a long time. Nothing like a nomadic life!

The more the shades around deepen, the more the ends approach and the more one understands the true meaning of life, that it is a dream; and we begin to understand the failure of everyone to grasp it, for they only attempted to get meaning out of the meaningless. To get reality out of a dream is boyish enthusiasm. "Everything is evanescent, everything is changeful" — knowing this, the sage gives up both pleasure and pain and becomes a witness of this panorama (the universe) without attaching himself to anything.

"They indeed have conquered Heaven even in this life whose mind has become fixed in sameness. God is pure and same to all, therefore they are said to be in God" (Gita, V.19). Desire, ignorance, and inequality — this is the trinity of bondage.

Denial of the will to live, knowledge, and same-sightedness is the trinity of liberation.

Freedom is the goal of the universe.

"Nor love nor hate nor pleasure nor pain nor death nor life nor religion nor irreligion: not this, not this, not this."

Yours ever,
Vivekananda.

XLVIII — SISTER

To Miss Mary Hale

C/O MISS DUTCHER,
THOUSAND ISLAND PARK, N.Y.
26th June, 1895.

DEAR SISTER,

Many thanks for the Indian mail. I cannot express in words my gratitude to you. As you have already read in Max Müller's article on Immortality I sent Mother Church, that he thinks that those we love in this life we must have loved in the past, so it seems I must have belonged to the Holy Family in some past life. I am expecting some books from India. I hope they have arrived. If so, will you kindly send them over here? If any postage is due I shall send it as soon as I get intimation. You did not write about the duty on the rugs; there will be another big packet from Khetri containing carpets and shawls and some brocades and other nick-nacks. I have written them to get the duty paid there if it is possible through the American Consul in Bombay. If not I shall have to pay it here. I do not think they will arrive for some months yet. I am anxious about the books. Kindly send them as soon as they arrive.

My love to Mother and Father Pope and all the sisters. I am enjoying this place immensely. Very little eating and good deal of thinking and talking and study. A wonderful calmness is coming over my soul. Every day I feel I have no duty to do; I am always in eternal rest and peace. It is He that works. We are only the instruments. Blessed be His name! The threefold bondage of lust and gold and fame is, as it were, fallen from me for the time being, and once more, even here, I feel what sometimes I felt in India, "From me all difference has fallen, all right or wrong, all delusion and ignorance has vanished, I am walking in the path beyond the qualities." What law I obey, what disobey? From that height the universe looks like a mud-puddle. Hari Om Tat Sat. He exists; nothing else does. I in Thee and Thou in me. Be Thou Lord my eternal refuge! Peace, Peace, Peace! Ever with love and blessings,

Your brother,
Vivekananda.

IL — FRIEND

To Mr. E. T. Sturdy

19 WEST 38TH ST., NEW YORK,
2nd August, 1895.

DEAR FRIEND,

Your kind note received today. I am going to Paris first with a friend and start for Europe on the 17th of August. I will however remain in Paris only a week to see my friend married, and then I go over to London.

Your advice about an organisation was very good indeed. And I am trying to act on that line.

I have many strong friends here, but unfortunately they are most of them poor. So the work here must be slow. Moreover it requires a few months more of work in New York to carry it to some visible shape: as such I will have to return to New York early this winter, and in summer I will return to London again. So far as I see now I can stay only a few weeks in London. But if the Lord wills, that small time may prove to be the beginning of great things. From Paris I will inform you by wire when I arrive in England.

Some Theosophists came to my classes in New York, but as soon as human beings perceive the glory of the Vedanta, all abracadabras fall off of themselves. This has been my uniform experience. Whenever mankind attains a higher vision, the lower vision disappears of itself. Multitude counts for nothing. A few heart-whole, sincere, and energetic men can do more in a year than a mob in a century. If there is heat in one body, then those others that come near it must catch it. This is the law. So success is ours, so long as we keep up the heat, the spirit of truth, sincerity, and love. My own life has been a very chequered one, but I have always found the eternal words verified: "Truth alone triumphs, not untruth. Through truth alone lies the way to God."

May the Sat in you be always your infallible guide! May He speedily attain to freedom and help others to attain it!

Ever yours in the Sat,
Vivekananda.

L — FRIEND

To Mr. E. T. Sturdy

19, WEST 38TH STREET,
NEW YORK,
9th August, 1895.

DEAR FRIEND,

... It is only just that I should try to give you a little of my views. I fully believe that there are periodic ferments of religion in human society, and that such a period is now sweeping over the educated world. While each ferment, moreover, appears broken into various little bubbles, these are all eventually similar, showing the cause or causes behind them to be the same. That religious ferment which at present is every day gaining a greater hold over thinking men, has this characteristic that all the little thought-whirlpools into which it has broken itself declare one single aim — a vision and a search after the Unity of Being. On planes physical, ethical, and spiritual, an ever-broadening generalisation — leading up to a concept of Unity Eternal — is in the air; and this being so, all the movements of the time may be taken to represent, knowingly or unknowingly, the noblest philosophy of the unity man ever had — the Advaita Vedanta.

Again, it has always been observed that as a result of the struggles of the various fragments of thought in a given epoch, one bubble survives. The rest only arise to melt into it and form a single great wave, which sweeps over society with irresistible force.

In India, America, and England (the countries I happen to know about) hundreds of these are struggling at the present moment. In India, dualistic formulae are already on the wane, the Advaita alone holds the field in force. In America, many movements are struggling for the mastery. All these represent Advaita thought more or less, and that series, which is spreading most rapidly, approaches nearer to it than any of the others. Now if anything was ever clear to me, it is that one of these must survive, swallowing up all the rest, to be the power of the future. Which is it to be?

Referring to history, we see that only that fragment which is fit will survive, and what makes fit to survive but character? Advaita will be the future religion of thinking humanity. No doubt of that. And of all the sects, they alone shall gain the day who are able to show most character in their lives, no matter how far they may be.

Let me tell you a little personal experience. When my Master left the body, we were a dozen penniless and unknown young men. Against us were a hundred powerful organisations, struggling hard to nip us in the bud. But Ramakrishna had given us one great gift, the desire, and the lifelong struggle not to talk alone, but to live the life. And today all India knows and reverences the Master, and the truths he taught are spreading like wild fire. Ten years ago I could not get a hundred persons together to celebrate his birthday anniversary. Last year there were fifty thousand.

Neither numbers nor powers nor wealth nor learning nor eloquence nor anything else will prevail, but purity, living the life, in one word, anubhuti, realisation. Let there be a dozen such lion-souls in each country, lions who have broken their own bonds, who have touched the Infinite, whose whole soul is gone to Brahman, who care neither for wealth nor power nor fame, and these will be enough to shake the world.

Here lies the secret. Says Patanjali, the father of Yoga, "When a man rejects all the superhuman powers, then he attains to the cloud of virtue." He sees God. He becomes God and helps others to become the same. This is all I have to preach. Doctrines have been expounded enough. There are books by the million. Oh, for an ounce of practice!

As to societies and organisations, these will come of themselves. Can there be jealousy where there is nothing to be jealous of? The names of those who will wish to injure us will be legion. But is not that the surest sign of our having the truth? The more I have been opposed, the more my energy has always found expression. I have been driven and worshipped by princes. I have been slandered by priests and laymen alike. But what of it? Bless them all! They are my very Self, and have they not helped me by acting as a spring-board from which my energy could take higher and higher flights?

. . . I have discovered one great secret — I have nothing to fear from talkers of religion. And the great ones who realise — they become enemies to none! Let talkers talk! They know no better! Let them have their fill of name and fame and money and woman. Hold we on to realisation, to being Brahman, to becoming Brahman. Let us hold on to truth unto death, and from life to life. Let us not pay the least attention to what others say, and if, after a lifetime's effort, one soul, only one, can break the fetters of the world and be free, we have done our work. Hari Om!

. . . One word more. Doubtless I do love India. But every day my sight grows clearer. What is India, or England, or America to us? We are the servants of that God who by the ignorant is called MAN. He who pours water at the root, does he not water the whole tree?

There is but one basis of well-being, social, political or spiritual — to know that I and my brother are one. This is true for all countries and all people. And Westerners, let me say, will realise it more quickly than Orientals, who have almost exhausted themselves in formulating the idea and producing a few cases of individual realisation.

Let us work without desire for name or fame or rule over others. Let us be free from the triple bonds of lust, greed of gain, and anger. And this truth is with us!

Ever yours in the Lord,
Vivekananda.

LI — FRIEND

To Mr. E. T. Sturdy

C/O MISS MACLEOD,
HOTEL HOLLANDE,
RUE DE LA PAIX,
PARIS,
5th September, 1895.

DEAR AND BLESSED FRIEND,

It is useless to express my gratitude for your kindness; it is too great for expression. . . .

I have a cordial invitation from Miss Müller, and as her place is very near to yours, I think it will be nice to come to her place first for a day or two and then to come over to you.

My body was very ill for a few days, which caused this delay in writing you.

Hoping soon for the privilege of mingling hearts and heads together.

I remain, ever yours in love, and fellowship in the Lord,
Vivekananda.

LII — JOE JOE

To Miss Josephine MacLeod

C/O E. T. STURDY, ESQ.,
HIGH VIEW, CAVERSHAM,
READING, ENGLAND,
September, 1895.

DEAR JOE JOE,

A thousand pardons for not promptly writing to you. I arrived safe in London, found my friend, and am all right in his home. It is beautiful. His wife is surely an angel, and his life is full of India. He has been years there — mixing with the Sannyasins, eating their food, etc., etc.; so you see I am very happy. I found already several retired Generals from India; they were very civil and polite to me. That wonderful knowledge of the Americans that identify every black man with the negro is entirely absent here, and nobody even stares at me in the street.

I am very much more at home here than anywhere out of India. The English people know us, we know them. The standard of education and civilisation is very high here — that makes a great change, so does the education of many generations.

Have the Turtle-doves returned? The Lord bless them and theirs for ever and ever. How are the babies — Alberta and Holister? Give them my oceans of love and know it yourself.

My friend being a Sanskrit scholar, we are busy working on the great commentaries of Shankara etc. Nothing but philosophy and religion here, Joe Joe. I am going to try to get up classes in October in London.

Ever affectionately with love and blessings,
Vivekananda.

LIII — KALI

Translated from Bengali

To Swami Abhedananda

C/O E. T. STURDY, ESQ.,
HIGH VIEW, CAVERSHAM,
READING, ENGLAND,
October, 1895.

DEAR KALI,

You may have got my earlier letter. At present send all letters to me at the above address. Mr. Sturdy is known to Târakdâ. He has brought me to his place, and we are both trying to create a stir in England. I shall this year leave again in November for America. So I require a man well-up in Sanskrit and English, particularly the latter language — either Shashi or you or Sâradâ. Now, if you have completely recovered, very well, you come; otherwise send Sharat. The work is to teach the devotees I shall be leaving here, to make them study the Vedanta, to do a little translation work into English, and to deliver occasional lectures. "Work is apt to cloud spiritual vision." X__ is very eager to come, but unless the foundation is strongly laid, there is every likelihood of everything toppling down. I am sending you a cheque along with this letter. Buy clothes and other necessary things — whoever comes. I am sending the cheque in the name of Master Mahashay Mahendra Babu. Gangâdhar's Tibetan choga is in the Math; get the tailor to make a similar choga of gerua colour. See that the collar is a little high, that is, the throat and neck should be covered. . . . Above all, you must have a woolen overcoat, for it is very cold. If you do not put on an overcoat on the ship, you will suffer much. . . . I am sending a second class ticket, as there is not much difference between a first class and a second class berth. . . . If it is decided to send Shashi then inform the purser of the ship beforehand to provide him with vegetarian diet.

Go to Bombay and see Messrs. King, King & Co., Fort, Bombay, and tell them that you are Mr. Sturdy's man. They will then give you a ticket to

England. A letter is being sent from here to the Company with instructions. I am writing to the Maharaja of Khetri to instruct his Bombay agent to look after the booking of your passage. If this sum of Rs. 150/- is not sufficient for your outfit, get the remainder from Rakhal. I shall send him the amount afterwards. Keep another Rs. 50/- for pocket expenses — take it from Rakhal; I shall pay back later. I have not up to now got any acknowledgement of the amount I sent to Chuni Babu. Start as quickly as possible. Inform Mahendra Babu that he is my Calcutta agent. Tell him to send a letter to Mr. Sturdy by next mail informing him that he is ready to look after all business transactions in Calcutta on your behalf. In effect, Mr. Sturdy is my secretary in England, Mahendra Babu in Calcutta, and Alasinga in Madras. Send this information to Madras also. Can any work be done unless all of us gird up our loins? And be up and doing! "Fortune favours the brave and energetic." Don't look back — forward, infinite energy, infinite enthusiasm, infinite daring, and infinite patience — then alone can great deeds be accomplished. We must set the whole world afire.

Now on the day the steamer is due to start, write a letter to Mr. Sturdy informing him by which steamer you are leaving for England. Otherwise there is some likelihood of your having difficulties when you reach London. Take the ship that comes directly to London, for even if it takes a few days longer on the voyage, the fares are less. At the moment our purse is lean. In time we shall send preachers in large numbers to all the quarters of the globe.

Yours affectionately,
Vivekananda.

PS. Write at once to the Maharaja of Khetri, that you are going to Bombay and that you will be glad if his agent attends to the booking of your passage and sees you off the board.

Keep my address with you written in a pocket-book, lest there should be difficulties afterwards.

LIV — JOE JOE

To Miss Josephine MacLeod

HIGH VIEW, CAVERSHAM,
READING, ENGLAND,
October, 1895.

DEAR JOE JOE,

I was so glad to hear from you. I was afraid you had forgotten me.

I am going to have a few lectures in and about London. One of them, a public one, will be at Princes' Hall on the 22nd at 8-30.

Come over and try to form a class. I have as yet done almost nothing here. Of course, breaking the ice is slow always. It took me two years in America to work up that little which we had in New York.

With love for all,

Yours ever,
Vivekananda.

LV — JOE JOE

To Miss Josephine MacLeod

HIGH VIEW, CAVERSHAM,
READING, ENGLAND,
20th October, 1895.

DEAR JOE JOE,

This note is to welcome the Leggetts to London. This being in a sense my native country, I send you my welcome first, I shall receive your welcome next Tuesday the 22nd at Princes' Hall half past eight p.m.

I am so busy till Tuesday, I am afraid, I shall not be able to run in to see you. I, however, shall come to see you any day after that. Possibly I may come on Tuesday.

With everlasting love and blessings,

Yours,
Vivekananda.

LVI — JOE JOE

To Miss Josephine MacLeod

> 80 OAKLEY STREET,
> CHELSEA,
> 31st October, 1895.

DEAR JOE JOE,

I shall be only too glad to come to lunch on Friday and see Mr. Coit at the Albemarle.

Two American ladies, mother and daughter, living in London came in to the class last night — Mrs. and Miss Netter. They were very sympathetic of course. The class there at Mr. Chamier's is finished. I shall begin at my lodgings from Saturday night next. I expect to have a pretty good-sized room or two for my classes. I have been also invited to Moncure Conways's Ethical Society where I speak on the 10th. I shall have a lecture in the Balboa Society next Tuesday. The Lord will help. I am not sure whether I can go up with you on Saturday. You will have great fun in the country anyway, and Mr. and Mrs. Sturdy are such nice people.

> With love and blessings,
> Vivekananda.

PS. Kindly order some vegetables for me. I don't care much for rice — bread will do as well. I have become an awful vegetarian now.

LVII — FRIEND

> 80 OAKLEY ST., CHELSEA,
> 31st October, 1895 (5 p.m.).

DEAR FRIEND (Mr. E. T. Sturdy),

Just now two young gentlemen, Mr. Silverlock and his friend, left. Miss Müller also came this afternoon and left just when these gentlemen came in.

One is an Engineer and the other is in the grain trade. They have read a good deal of modern philosophy and science and have been much struck by the similarity with the latest conclusions of both with the ancient Hindu thought. They are very fine, intelligent, and educated men. One has given up the Church, the other asked me whether he should or not. Now, two things struck me after this interview. First, we must hurry the book through. We will touch a class thereby who are philosophically religious without the least mystery-mongering. Second, both of them want to know the rituals of my creed! This opened my eyes. The world in general must have some form. In fact, in the ordinary sense religion is philosophy concretised through rituals and symbols.

It is absolutely necessary to form some ritual and have a Church. That is to say, we must fix on some ritual as fast as we can. If you can come Saturday morning or sooner, we shall go to the Asiatic Society library or you can procure for me a book which is called Hemâdri Kosha, from which we can get what we want, and kindly bring the Upanishads. We will fix something grand, from birth to death of a man. A mere loose system of philosophy gets no hold on mankind.

If we can get it through, before we have finished the classes, and publish it by publicly holding a service or two under it, it will go on. They want to form a congregation, and they want ritual; that is one of the causes why — will never have a hold on Western people.

The Ethical Society has sent me another letter thanking me for the acceptance of this offer. Also a copy of their forms. They want me to bring with me a book from which to read for ten minutes. Will you bring the Gita (translation) and the Buddhist Jâtaka (translation) with you?

I would not do anything in this matter without seeing you first.

> With love and blessings,
> Vivekananda.

LVIII — FRIEND

80 OAKLEY STREET,
CHELSEA,
1st November, 1895.

DEAR FRIEND (Mr. E. T. Sturdy),

The tickets of the Balleren (?) Society are 35 in number.

The subject is "Indian Philosophy and Western Society". Chairman blank.

As you did not ask me to send them over, I do not. I got your letters properly.

Yours in the Sat,
Vivekananda.

LIX — FRIEND

2nd November, 1895.

DEAR FRIEND (Mr. E. T. Sturdy),

I think you are right; we shall work on our own lines and let things grow.

I send you the note of the lecture.

I shall come on Sunday if nothing extraordinary prevents me.

Yours with love,
Vivekananda.

LX — BLESSED AND BELOVED

R.M.S. "BRITANNIC"

BLESSED AND BELOVED (Mr. E. T. Sturdy),

So far the journey has been very beautiful. The purser has been very kind to me and gave me a cabin to myself. The only difficulty is the food — meat, meat, meat. Today they have promised to give me some vegetables.

We are standing at anchor now. The fog is too thick to allow the ship to proceed. So I take this opportunity to write a few letters.

It is a queer fog almost impenetrable though the sun is shining bright and cheerful. Kiss baby for me; and with love and blessings for you and Mrs. Sturdy,

I remain, Yours,
Vivekananda.

PS. Kindly convey my love to Miss Müller. I left the night shirt at Avenue Road. So I shall have to do without any until the trunk is brought out of the hold.

LXI — FRIEND

228 WEST 39TH STREET,
NEW YORK,
8th December, 1895.

DEAR FRIEND (Mr. E. T. Sturdy),

After ten days of a most tedious and rough voyage I safely arrived in New York. My friends had already engaged some rooms at the above where I am living now and intend to hold classes ere long. In the meanwhile the Theosophists have been alarmed very much and are trying their best to hurt me; but they and their followers are of no consequence whatever.

I went to see Mrs. Leggett and other friends, and they are as kind and enthusiastic as ever.

Did you hear anything from India about the coming Sannyasin?

I will write later fuller particulars of the work here.

Kindly convey my best love to Miss Müller and to Mrs. Sturdy and all the other friends and kiss baby for me.

Yours ever in the Sat,
Vivekananda.

LXII — JOE JOE

To Miss Josephine MacLeod

228 WEST 39TH STREET,
NEW YORK,
8th December, 1895.

DEAR JOE JOE,

After 10 days of the most disastrous voyage I ever had I arrived in New York. I was so so sick for days together.

After the clean and beautiful cities of Europe, New York appears very dirty and miserable. I am going to begin work next Monday. Your bundles have been safely delivered to the heavenly pair, as Alberta calls them. They are as usual very kind. Saw Mrs. and Mr. Salomon and other friends. By chance met Mrs. Peak at Mrs. Guernsey's but yet have no news of Mrs. Rothinburger. Going with the birds of paradise to Ridgely this Christmas. Wish ever so much you were there.

Had you a nice visit with Lady Isabelle? Kindly give my love to all our friends and know oceans yourself.

Excuse this short letter. I shall write bigger ones by the next.

Yours ever in the Lord,
Vivekananda.

LXIII — STURDY

To Mr. E. T. Sturdy

NEW YORK,
1895.

The work here is going on splendidly. I have been working incessantly at two classes a day since my arrival. Tomorrow I go out of town with Mr. Leggett for a week's holiday. Did you know Madame Antoinette Sterling, one of your greatest singers? She is very much interested in the work.

I have made over all the secular part of the work to a committee and am free from all that botheration. I have no aptitude for organising. It nearly breaks me to pieces.

. . . What about the Nârada-Sutra? There will be a good sale of the book here, I am sure. I have now taken up the Yoga-Sutras and take them up one by one and go through all the commentators along with them. These talks are all taken down, and when completed will form the fullest annotated translation of Patanjali in English. Of course it will be rather a big work.

At Trübner's I think there is an edition of Kurma Purâna. The commentator, Vijnâna Bhikshu, is continually quoting from that book. I have never seen the book myself. Will you kindly find time to go and see if in it there are some chapters on Yoga? If so, will you kindly send me a copy? Also of the Hatha-Yoga-Pradipikâ, Shiva-Samhitâ, and any other book on Yoga? The originals of course. I shall send you the money for them as soon as they arrive. Also a copy of Sânkhya-Kârikâ of Ishwara Krishna by John Davies. Just now your letter reached along with Indian letters. The one man who is ready is ill. The others say that they cannot come over on the spur of the moment. So far it seems unlucky. I am sorry they could not come. What can be done? Things go slow in India!

Ramanuja's theory is that the bound soul or Jiva has its perfections involved, entered, into itself. When this perfection again evolves, it becomes free. The Advaitin declares both these to take place only in show; there was neither involution nor evolution. Both processes were Maya, or apparent only.

In the first place, the soul is not essentially a knowing being. Sachchidânanda is only an approximate definition, and Neti Neti is the essential definition. Schopenhauer caught this idea of willing from the Buddhists. We have it also in Vâsanâ or Trishnâ, Pali tanhâ. We also admit that it is the cause of all manifestation which are, in their turn, its effects. But, being a cause, it must be a combination of the Absolute and Maya. Even knowledge, being a compound, cannot be the Absolute itself, but it is the nearest approach to it, and higher than Vasana, conscious or unconscious. The Absolute first becomes the mixture of knowledge, then, in the second degree, that of will. If it be said that plants have no consciousness, that they are at best only unconscious wills, the answer is that even the unconscious plant-will is a manifestation of the consciousness, not of the plant, but of the cosmos, the Mahat of the Sankhya Philosophy. The Buddhist analysis of everything into will is imperfect, firstly, because will is itself a compound, and secondly, because consciousness or knowledge which is a compound of the first degree, precedes it. Knowledge is action. First action, then reaction. When the mind perceives, then, as the reaction, it wills. The will is in the mind. So it is absurd to say that will is the last analysis. Deussen is playing into the hands of the Darwinists.

But evolution must be brought in accordance with the more exact science of Physics, which can demonstrate that every evolution must be preceded by an involution. This being so, the evolution of the Vasana or will must be preceded by the involution of the Mahat or cosmic consciousness. (See also Vol VIII [6]Sayings and Utterances & Vol V [7]Letter to Mr. Sturdy.) There is no willing without knowing. How can we desire unless we know the object of desire?

The apparent difficulty vanishes as soon as you divide knowledge also into subconscious and conscious. And why not? If will can be so treated, why not its father?

Vivekananda.

LXIV — BLESSED AND BELOVED

To Mr. E. T. Sturdy

228 WEST 39TH STREET,
NEW YORK,
16th December, 1895.

BLESSED AND BELOVED,

All your letters reached by one mail today. Miss Müller also writes me one. She has read in the Indian Mirror that Swami Krishnananda is coming over to England. If that is so, he is the strongest man that I can get.

The classes I had here were six in the week, besides a question class. The general attendance varies between 70 to 120. Besides every Sunday I have a public lecture. The last month my lectures were in a small hall holding about 600. But 900 will come as a rule, 300 standing, and about 300 going off, not finding room. This week therefore I have a bigger hall, with a capacity of holding 1200 people.

There is no admission charged in these lectures, but a collection covers the rent. The newspapers have taken me up this week, and altogether I have stirred up New York considerably this year. If I could have remained here this summer and organised a summer place, the work would be going on sure foundations here. But as I intended to come over in May to England, I shall have to leave it unfinished. If, however, Krishnananda comes to England, and you find him strong and able, and if you find the work in London will not be hurt by my absence this summer, I would rather be here this summer.

Again, I am afraid my health is breaking down under constant work. I want some rest. We are so unused to these Western methods, especially the keeping to time. I will leave you to decide all these. The Brahmavâdin is going on here very satisfactorily. I have begun to write articles on Bhakti; also send them a monthly account of the work. Miss Müller wants to come to America. I do not know whether she will or not. Some friends here are publishing my Sunday lectures. I have sent you a few copies of the first one. I shall send you next mail a few of the next two lectures, and if you like them I shall ask them to send you a number. Can you manage to get a few hundred copies sold in England? That will encourage them in publishing the subsequent ones.

Next month I go to Detroit, then to Boston, and Harvard University. Then I shall have a rest, and then I come to England, unless you think that things go on without me and with Krishnananda.

Ever yours with love and blessings,
Vivekananda.

LXV — SHARAT

To Swami Saradananda

228 WEST 39TH STREET,
NEW YORK,
23rd December, 1895.

DEAR SHARAT,

Your letter only made me sad. I see you have lost all enthusiasm. I know all of you, your powers and your limitations. I would not have called you to any task which you are incompetent to do. The only task I would have given you was to teach elementary Sanskrit, and with the help of dictionaries and other things assist S. in his translations and teachings. I would have moulded you to it. Anyone could have done as well — only a little smattering of Sanskrit was absolutely necessary. Well, everything is for the best. If it is the Lord's work the right man for the right place will be forthcoming in the right time. None of you need feel disturbed. As for Sanyal, I don't care who takes money or not, but I have a strong hatred for child-marriage. I have suffered terribly from it, and it is the great sin for which our nation has to suffer. As such, I would hate myself if I help such a diabolical custom directly or indirectly. I wrote to you pretty plain about it, and Sanyal had no right to play a hoax upon me about his "lawsuit" and his attempts to become free. I am sorry for his playing tricks on me who have never done him any harm. This is the world. What good you do goes for nothing, but if you stop doing it, then, Lord help you, you are counted as a rogue. Isn't it? Emotional natures like mine are always preyed upon by relatives and friends. This world is merciless. This world is our friend when we are its slaves and no more. This world is broad enough for me. There will always be a corner found for me somewhere. If the people of India do not like me, there will be others who do. I must set my foot to the best of my ability upon this devilish custom of child-marriage. No blame will entail on you. You keep at a safe distance if you are afraid. I am sorry, very sorry, I cannot have any partnership with such doings as getting husbands for babies. Lord help me, I never had and never will have. Think of the case of M__ Babu! Did you ever meet a more cowardly or brutal one than that? I can kill the man who gets a husband for a baby. The upshot of the whole thing is — I want bold, daring, adventurous spirits to help me. Else I will work alone. I have a mission to fulfil. I will work it out alone. I do not care who comes or who goes. Sanyal is already done for by Samsâra. Beware, boy! That was all the advice I thought it my duty to give you. Of course, you are great folks now — my words will have no value with you. But I hope the time will come when you will see clearer, know better, and think other thoughts than you are now doing.

Good-bye! I would not bother you any more, and all blessings go with you all. I am very glad I have been of some service to you sometimes if you think so. At least I am pleased with myself for having tried my best to discharge the duties laid on me by my Guru, and well done or ill, I am glad that I tried. So good-bye. Tell Sanyal that I am not at all angry with him, but I am sorry, very sorry. It is not the money — that counts nothing — but the violation of a principle that pained me, and the trick he played on me. Good-bye to him also, and to you all. One chapter of my life is closed. Let others come in their due order. They will find me ready. You need not disturb yourselves at all about me. I want no help from any human being in any country. So good-bye! May the Lord bless you all for ever and ever!

Vivekananda.

LXVI — FRIEND

To Mr. E. T. Sturdy

RIDGELY MANOR,
29th December, 1895.

DEAR FRIEND,

By this time the copies of the lectures must have reached you. Hope they may be of some use.

I think, in the first place, there are so many difficulties to overcome; in the second place, they think that they are fit for nothing — that is the national disease; thirdly, they are afraid to face the winter at once; the Tibet man they don't think is a very strong man to work in England. Some one will come sooner or later.

Yours in the Sat,
Vivekananda.

PS. My Christmas greetings to all our friends — to Mrs. and Mr. Johnson, to Lady Margesson, Mrs. Clark, Miss Hawes, Miss Müller, Miss Steel, and all the rest.

Kiss baby for me and bless him. My greetings to Mrs. Sturdy. We will work. "Wah guru ki fateh."

LXVII — SISTER

To Miss Mary Hale

NEW YORK,
6th January, 1896.

DEAR SISTER,

Many thanks for your kind New Year's greetings. I am glad to learn you enjoyed your six weeks with the Esq. although they be only golf playing. I have been in the midst of the genuine article in England. The English people received me with open arms, and I have very much toned down my ideas about the English race. First of all, I found that those fellows as Lund etc. who came over from England to attack me were nowhere. Their existence is simply ignored by the English people. None but a person belonging to the English Church is thought to be genteel. Again, some of the best men of England belonging to the English Church and some of the highest in position and fame became my truest friends. This was quite another sort of experience from what I met in America, was it not?

The English people laughed and laughed when I told them about my experience with the Presbyterians and other fanatics here and my reception in hotels etc. I also found at once the difference in culture and breeding between the two countries and came to understand why American girls go in shoals to be married to Europeans. Everyone was kind to me there, and I have left many noble friends of both sexes anxiously waiting my return in the spring.

As to my work there, the Vedantic thought has already permeated the higher classes of England. Many people of education and rank, and amongst them not a few clergymen, told me that the conquest of Rome by Greece was being re-enacted in England.

There are two sorts of Englishmen who have lived in India. One consisting of those who hate everything Indian, but they are uneducated. The other, to whom India is the holy land, its very air is holy. And they try to out-Herod Herod in their Hinduism. They are awful vegetarians, and they want to form a caste in England. Of course, the majority of the English people are firm believers in caste. I had eight classes a week apart from public lectures, and they were so crowded that a good many people, even ladies of high rank, sat on the floor and did not think anything of it. In England I find strong-minded men and women to take up the work and carry it forward with the peculiar English grip and energy. This year my work in New York is going on splendidly. Mr. Leggett is a very rich man of New York and very much interested in me. The New Yorker has more steadiness than any other people in this country, so I have determined to make my centre here. In this country my teachings are thought to be queer by the "Methodist" and "Presbyterian" aristocracy. In England it is the highest philosophy to the English Church aristocracy.

Moreover those talks and gossips, so characteristic of the American woman, are almost unknown in England. The English woman is slow; but when she works up to an idea, she will have a hold on it sure; and they are regularly carrying on my work there and sending every week a report — think of that! Here is I go away for a week, everything falls to pieces. My love to all — to Sam and to yourself. May the Lord bless you ever and ever!

Your affectionate brother,
Vivekananda.

LXVIII — BLESSED AND BELOVED

To Mr. E. T. Sturdy

228 WEST 39TH STREET,
NEW YORK,
16th January, 1896.

BLESSED AND BELOVED,

Many many thanks for the books. The Sankhya Karika is a very good book, and the Kurma Purana, though I do not find in it all expected, has a few verses on Yoga. The words dropped in my last letter were Yoga-Sutra, which I am translating with notes from various authorities. I want to incorporate the chapter in Kurma Purana in my notes. I have very enthusiastic accounts of your classes from Miss MacLeod. Mr. Galsworthy seems to be very much interested now.

I have begun my Sunday lectures here and also the classes. Both are very enthusiastically received. I make them all free and take up a collection to pay the hall etc. Last Sunday's lecture was very much appreciated and is in the press. I shall send you a few copies next week. It was the outline of our work.

As my friends have engaged a stenographer (Goodwin), all these class lessons and public lectures are taken down. I intend to send you a copy of each. They may suggest you some ideas.

My great want here is a strong man like you, possessing intellect, and ability, and love. In this nation of universal education, all seem to melt down into a mediocrity, and the few able are weighed down by the eternal money-making.

I have a chance of getting a piece of land in the country, and some buildings on it, plenty of trees and a river, to serve as a summer meditation resort. That, of course, requires a committee to look after it in my absence, as also the handling of money and printing and other matters.

I have separated myself entirely from money questions, yet without it the movement cannot go on. So necessarily I have to make over everything executive to a committee, which will look after these things in my absence. Steady work is not in the line of the Americans. The only way they work, is in a herd. So let them have it. As to the teaching part, my friends will go over this country from place to place, each one independent, and let them form independent circles. That is the easiest way to spread. Then, when there will be sufficient strength, we shall have yearly gatherings to concentrate our energies.

The committee is entirely executive and it is confined to New York alone. . . .

Ever yours with love and blessings,
Vivekananda.

LXIX — ALASINGA

23rd January, 1896.

DEAR ALASINGA,

By this time you must have got enough of matter on Bhakti from me. The last copy, dated 21st December, of Brahmavadin is in. I have been smelling something since the last few issues of the Brahmavadin. Are you going to join the Theosophists? This time you simply gave yourselves up. Why, you get in a notice of the Theosophists' lectures in the body of your notes! Any suspicion of my connection with the Theosophists will spoil my work both in America and England, and well it may. They are thought by all people of sound mind to be wrong, and true it is that they are held so, and you know it full well. I am afraid you want to overreach me. You think you can get more subscribers in England by advertising Annie Besant? Fool that you are.

I do not want to quarrel with the Theosophists, but my position is entirely ignoring them. Had they paid for the advertisement? Why should you go forward to advertise them? I shall get more than enough subscribers in England when I go next.

Now, I would have no traitors, I tell you plainly, I would not be played upon by any rogue. No hypocrisy with me. Hoist your flag and give public notice in your paper that you have given up all connections with me, and join the . . . camp of the Theosophists or cease to have anything whatsoever to do with them. I give you very plain words indeed. I shall have one man only to follow me, but he must be true and faithful unto death. I do not care for success or no success. I am tired of this nonsense of preaching all over the world. Did any of Annie Besant's people come to my help when I was in England? Fudge! I must keep my movement pure or I will have none.

Yours,
Vivekananda.

PS. Reply sharp your decision. I am very decided on this point. You ought to have told me so before, had your intentions been such from the very beginning. The Brahmavadin is for preaching Vedanta and not Theosophy. I almost lose my patience when I see these underhand dealings. This is the world — those whom you love best and help most try to cheat you.

LXX — BLESSED AND BELOVED

To Mr. E. T. Sturdy

228 WEST 39TH STREET,
NEW YORK,
29th February, 1896.

BLESSED AND BELOVED,

I am coming before May if possible. You need not worry about that. The pamphlet was beautiful. The newspaper cuttings from here will be forwarded if we can get them.

The books and pamphlets here have been got up this way. A committee was formed in New York. They paid all the expenses of stenographing and printing on condition the books will belong to them. So these pamphlets and books are theirs. One book, the Karma-Yoga has been already published; the Raja-Yoga, a much bigger one, is in the course of publication; the Jnana-Yoga may be published later on. These will be popular books, the language being that of talk, as you have seen already. I have purged everything that is objectionable, and they help me in getting up the books.

The books are the property of this Committee, of which Mrs. Ole Bull is the principal backer, also Mrs. Leggett.

It is only just that they should have the books as they paid all the expenses. There is no fear of the publishers meddling with them, as they are the publishers themselves.

If any books come from India please keep them.

The stenographer, who is an Englishman named Goodwin, has become so interested in the work that I have now made him a Brahmachârin, and he is going round with me, and we shall come over together to England. He will be very helpful as he has been always.

Yours with all blessings,
Vivekananda.

LXXI — BLESSED AND BELOVED

To Mr. E. T. Sturdy

NEW YORK,
17th March, 1896.

BLESSED AND BELOVED,

I received your last just now and it frightened me

LXXI — BLESSED AND BELOVED

To Mr. E. T. Sturdy

NEW YORK,
17th March, 1896.

BLESSED AND BELOVED,

I received your last just now and it frightened me immensely.

The lectures were delivered under the auspices of certain friends who paid for the stenography and all other expenses on condition they alone will have the right to publish them. As such, they have already published the Sunday lectures as well as three books on "Karma-Yoga", "Raja-Yoga", and "Jnana-Yoga". The Raja-Yoga especially has been much altered and re-arranged along with the translation of "Yoga-Sutras of Patanjali". The Raja-Yoga is in the hands of Longmans. The friends here are furious at the idea of these books being published in England; and as they have been made over to them by me legally, I am at a loss what to do. The publication of the pamphlets was not so serious, but the books have been so much re-arranged and changed that the American edition will not recognise the English one. Now pray don't publish these books, as they will place me in a very false position and create endless quarrel and destroy my American work.

By last mail from India I learn that a Sannyasin has started from India. I had a beautiful letter from Miss Müller, also one from Miss MacLeod; the Leggett family has become very attached to me.

I do not know anything about Mr. Chatterji. I hear from other sources that his trouble is money, which the Theosophists cannot supply him with. Moreover the help he will be able to give me is very rudimentary and useless in the face of the fact of a much stronger man coming from India. So far with him. We need not be in a hurry.

I pray you again to think about this publishing business and write some letters to Mrs. Ole Bull and through her ask the opinion of the American friends of the Vedanta, remembering "ours is the Gospel of oneness of all beings", and all national feelings are but wicked superstitions. Moreover I am sure that the person who is always ready to give way to other's opinions finds at last that his opinion has triumphed. Yielding always conquers at last. With love to all our friends,

Yours with love and blessings,
Vivekananda.

PS. I am coming sure in March as early as possible.

friends of the Vedanta, remembering "ours is the Gospel of oneness of all beings", and all national feelings are but wicked superstitions. Moreover I am sure that the person who is always ready to give way to other's opinions finds at last that his opinion has triumphed. Yielding always conquers at last. With love to all our friends,

Yours with love and blessings,
Vivekananda.

PS. I am coming sure in March as early as possible.

LXXII — SISTER

To Miss Mary Hale

DEAR SISTER,

I am afraid you are offended and did not answer any of my letters. Now I beg a hundred thousand pardons. By very good luck, I have found the orange cloth and am going to have a coat made as soon as I can. I am glad to hear you met Mrs. Bull. She is such a noble lady and kind friend. Now, sister, there are two very thin Sanskrit pamphlets in the house. Kindly send them over if it does not bother you. The books from India have arrived safe, and I had not to pay any duty on them. I am surprised that the rugs do not arrive yet. I have not been to see Mother Temple any more. I could not find time. Every little bit of time I get I spend in the library.

With everlasting love and gratitude to you all,

Ever your loving brother,
Vivekananda.

PS. Mr. Howe has been a very constant student except the last few days. Kindly give my love to Miss Howe.

LXXIII — SISTERS

To the Hale Sisters

6 WEST 43RD STREET,
NEW YORK,
14th April, 1896.

DEAR SISTERS,

I arrived safe on Sunday and on account of illness could not write earlier. I sail on board the White Star Line Germanic tomorrow at 12 noon. With everlasting memory of love, gratitude and blessings,

I am, your ever loving brother,
Vivekananda.

LXXIV — STURDY

WAVENEY MANSIONS,
FAIRHAZEL GARDENS,
LONDON N.W.
April, 1896 Thursday Afternoon.

DEAR STURDY,

I forgot to tell you in the morning that Prof. Max Müller also offered in his letter to me to do everything he could if I went to lecture at Oxford.

Yours affectionately,
Vivekananda.

PS. Have you written for the Artharva-Veda Samhita edited by Shankara Pandurang?

LXXV — SISTERS

To the Hale sisters

HIGH VIEW, READING,
20th April, 1896.

DEAR SISTERS,

Greetings to you from the other shore. The voyage

has been pleasant and no sickness this time. I gave myself treatment to avoid it. I made quite a little run through Ireland and some of the Old English towns and now am once more in Reading amidst Brahma and Maya and Jiva, the individual and the universal soul, etc. The other monk is here; he is one of the nicest of men I see, and is quite a learned monk too. We are busy editing books now. Nothing of importance happened on the way. It was dull, monotonous, and prosaic as my life. I love America more when I am out of it. And, after all, those years there have been some of the best I have yet seen.

Are you trying to get some subscribers for the Brahmavadin? Give my best love and kindest remembrance to Mrs. Adams and Mrs. Conger. Write me as soon as is convenient all about yourselves, and what you are doing, what breaks the monotony of eating, drinking, and cycling. I am in a hurry just now, shall write a bigger letter later; so good-bye and may you be always happy.

Your ever affectionate brother,
Vivekananda.

PS. I will write to Mother Church as soon as I get time. Give my love to Sam and sister Locke.

LXXVI — MARY

To Miss Mary Hale

63 ST. GEORGE'S ROAD,
LONDON, S.W.,
30th May, 1896.

DEAR MARY,

Your letter reached just now. Of course, you were not jealous but all of a sudden were inspired with sympathy for poor India. Well, you need not be frightened. Wrote a letter to Mother Church weeks ago, but have not been able to get a line from her yet. I am afraid the whole party have taken orders and entered a Catholic convent — four old maids are enough to drive any mother to a convent. I had a beautiful visit with Prof. Max Müller. He is a saint — a Vedantist through and through. What think you? He has been a devoted admirer of my old Master for years. He has written an article on my Master in The Nineteenth Century, which will soon come out. We had long talk on Indian things. I wish I had half his love for India. We are going to start another little magazine here. What about The Brahmavadin? Are you pushing it? If four pushful old maids cannot push a journal, I am blowed. You will hear from me now and then. I am not a pin to be lost under a bushel. I am having classes here just now. I begin Sunday lectures from next week. The classes are very big and are in the house. We have rented it for the season. Last night I made a dish. It was such a delicious mixture of saffron, lavender, mace, nutmeg, cubebs, cinnamon, cloves, cardamom, cream, limejuice, onions, raisins, almonds, pepper, and rice, that I myself could not eat it. There was no asafoetida, though that would have made it smoother to swallow.

Yesterday I went to a marriage à la mode. Miss Müller, a rich lady, a friend who has adopted a Hindu boy and to help my work has taken rooms in this house, took us to see it. One of her nieces was married to somebody's nephew I suppose. What tiring nonsense! I am glad you do not marry. Good-bye, love to all. No more time as I am going to lunch with Miss MacLeod.

Yours ever affectionately,
Vivekananda.

LXXVII — BABIES

To the Hale sisters

LONDON,
7th July, 1896.

DEAR BABIES,

The work here progressed wonderfully. I had one monk here from India. I have sent him to the U.S.A. and sent for another from India. The season is closed; the classes, therefore, and the Sunday lectures are to be closed on the 16th next. And on the 19th I go for a month or so for quiet and rest in the Swiss Mountains to return next autumn to London and begin again. The work here has been very satisfactory. By rousing interest here I really do more for India than in India. Mother wrote to me that if you could rent your flat, she would be glad to take you with her to see Egypt. I am going with three English friends to the Swiss Hills. Later on, towards the end of winter, I expect to go to India with some English friends who are going to live in my monastery there, which, by the by, is in the air yet. It is struggling to materialise somewhere in the Himalayas.

Where are You? Now the summer is in full swing, even London is getting very hot. Kindly give my best love to Mrs. Adams, Mrs. Conger, and all the rest of my friends in Chicago.

Your affectionate brother,
Vivekananda.

LXXVIII — BLESSED AND BELOVED

To Mr. E. T. Sturdy

GRAND HOTEL,
VALAIS,
SWITZERLAND.

BLESSED AND BELOVED,

. . . I am reading a little, starving a good deal, and practising a good deal more. The strolls in the woods are simply delicious. We are now situated under three huge glaciers, and the scenery is very beautiful.

By the by, whatever scruples I may have had as to the Swiss-lake origin of the Aryans have been taken clean off my mind. The Swiss is a Tartar minus a pigtail. . . .

Yours ever affectionately,
Vivekananda.

LXXIX — BLESSED AND BELOVED

To Mr. E. T. Sturdy

SWITZERLAND,
5th August, 1896.

BLESSED AND BELOVED,

A letter came this morning from Prof. Max Müller telling me that the article of Shri Ramakrishna Paramahamsa has been published in The XIX Century August number. Have you read it? He asked my opinion about it. Not having seen it yet, I can't write anything to him. If you have it, kindly send it to me. Also The Brahmavadin, if any have arrived. Max Müller wants to know about our plans . . . and again about the magazine. He promises a good deal of help and is ready to write a book on Shri Ramakrishna Paramahamsa.

I think it is better that you should directly correspond with him about the magazine etc. You will see from his letter which I shall send you as soon as I have replied (after reading The XIX Century) that he is very much pleased with our movement and is ready to help it as much as he can. . . .

Yours with blessings and love,
Vivekananda.

PS. I hope you will consider well the plan for the big magazine. Some money can be raised in America, and we can keep the magazine all to ourselves at the same time. I intend to write to America on hearing about the plan you and Prof. Max Muller decide upon. "A great tree is to be taken refuge in, when it has both fruits and shade. If, however, we do not get the fruit, who prevents our enjoyment of the shade?" So ought great attempts to be made, is the moral.

LXXX — DEAR__

To Kripananda

SWITZERLAND,
August, 1896.

DEAR__,

Be you holy and, above all, sincere; and do not for a moment give up your trust in the Lord, and you will see the light. Whatever is truth will remain for ever; whatever is not, none can preserve. We are helped in being born in a time when everything is quickly searched out. Whatever others think or do, lower not your standard of purity, morality, and love of God; above all, beware of all secret organisations. No one who loves God need fear any jugglery. Holiness is the highest and divinest power in earth and in heaven. "Truth alone triumphs, not untruth. Through truth alone is opened the way to God" (Mundaka, III. i. 6). Do not care for a moment who joins hands with you or not, be sure that you touch the hand of the Lord. That is enough. . . .

I went to the glacier of Monte Rosa yesterday and gathered a few hardy flowers growing almost in the midst of eternal snow. I send you one in this letter hoping that you will attain to a similar spiritual hardihood amidst all the snow and ice of this earthly life. . . .

Your dream was very, very beautiful. In dream our souls read a layer of our mind which we do not read in our waking hours, and however unsubstantial imagination may be, it is behind the imagination that all unknown psychic truths lie. Take heart. We will try to do what we can for the good of humanity — the rest depends upon the Lord. . . .

Well, do not be anxious, do not be in a hurry. Slow, persistent and silent work does everything. The Lord is great. We will succeed, my boy. We must. Blessed be His name! . . .

Here in America are no Ashramas. Would there was one! How would I like it and what an amount of good it would do to this country!

LXXXI — GOODWIN

To Mr. J. J. Goodwin

SWITZERLAND,
8th August, 1896.

DEAR GOODWIN,

I am now taking rest. I read from different letters a lot about Kripananda. I am sorry for him. There must be something wrong in his head. Let him alone. None of you need bother about him.

As for hurting me, that is not in the power of gods or devils. So be at rest. It is unswerving love and perfect unselfishness that conquer everything. We Vedantists in every difficulty ought to ask the subjective question, "Why do I see that?" "Why can I not conquer this with love?"

I am very glad at the reception the Swami has met with, also at the good work he is doing. Great work requires great and persistent effort for a long time. Neither need we trouble ourselves if a few fail. It is in the nature of things that many should fall, that troubles should come, that tremendous difficulties should arise, that selfishness and all the other devils in the human heart should struggle hard when they are about to be driven out by the fire of spirituality. The road to the Good is the roughest and steepest in the universe. It is a wonder that so many succeed, no wonder that so many fall. Character has to be established through a thousand stumbles.

I am much refreshed now. I look out of the window and see the huge glaciers just before me and feel that I am in the Himalayas. I am quite calm. My nerves have regained their accustomed strength; and little vexations, like those you write of, do not touch me at all. How shall I be disturbed by this child's play? The whole world is a mere child's play — preaching, teaching, and all included. "Know him to be the Sannyasin who neither hates not desires" (Gita, V.3). And what is there to be desired in this little mud-puddle of a world, with its ever-recurring misery, disease, and death? "He who has given up all desires, he alone is happy."

This rest, eternal, peaceful rest, I am catching a

glimpse of now in this beautiful spot. "Having once known that the Atman alone, and nothing else, exists, desiring what, or for whose desire, shall you suffer misery about the body?" (Brihadâranyaka, IV. iv. 12.)

I feel as if I had my share of experience in what they call "work". I am finished, I am longing now to get out. "Out of thousands, but one strives to attain the Goal. And even of those who struggle hard, but few attain" (Gita, VII. 3); for the senses are powerful, they drag men down.

"A good world", "a happy world", and "social progress", are all terms equally intelligible with "hot ice" or "dark light". If it were good, it would not be the world. The soul foolishly thinks of manifesting the Infinite in finite matter, Intelligence through gross particles; but at last it finds out its error and tries to escape. This going-back is the beginning of religion, and its method, destruction of self, that is, love. Not love for wife or child or anybody else, but love for everything else except this little self. Never be deluded by the tall talk, of which you will hear so much in America, about "human progress" and such stuff. There is no progress without corresponding digression. In one society there is one set of evils; in another, another. So with periods of history. In the Middle Ages, there were more robbers, now more cheats. At one period there is less idea of married life; at another, more prostitution. In one, more physical agony; in another, a thousandfold more mental. So with knowledge. Did not gravitation already exist in nature before it was observed and named? Then what difference does it make to know that it exists? Are you happier than the Red Indians?

The only knowledge that is of any value is to know that all this is humbug. But few, very few, will ever know this. "Know the Atman alone, and give up all other vain words." This is the only knowledge we gain from all this knocking about the universe. This is the only work, to call upon mankind to "Awake, arise, and stop not till the goal is reached". It is renunciation, Tyâga, that is meant by religion, and nothing else.

Ishwara is the sum total of individuals; yet He Himself also is an individual in the same way as the human body is a unit, of which each cell is an individual. Samashti or the Collective is God. Vyashti or the component is the soul of Jiva. The existence of Ishwara, therefore, depends on that of Jiva, as the body on the cell, and vice versa. Jiva, and Ishwara are co-existent beings. As long as the one exists, the other also must. Again, since in all the higher spheres, except on our earth, the amount of good is vastly in excess of the amount of bad, the sum total or Ishwara may be said to be All-good, Almighty, and Omniscient. These are obvious qualities, and need no argument to prove, from the very fact of totality.

Brahman is beyond both of these, and is not a state. It is the only unit not composed of many units. It is the principle which runs through all, from a cell to God, and without which nothing can exist. Whatever is real is that principle or Brahman. When I think "I am Brahman", then I alone exist. It is so also when you so think, and so on. Each one is the whole of that principle. . . .

A few days ago, I felt a sudden irresistible desire to write to Kripananda. Perhaps he was unhappy and thinking of me. So I wrote him a warm letter. Today from the American news, I see why it was so. I sent him flowers gathered near the glaciers. Ask Miss Waldo to send him some money and plenty of love. Love never dies. The love of the father never dies, whatever the children may do or be. He is my child. He has the same or more share in my love and help, now that he is in misery.

Yours with blessings,
Vivekananda.

LXXXII — BLESSESD AND BELOVED

To Mr. E. T. Sturdy

GRAND HOTEL, SAAS FEE,
VALAIS, SWITZERLAND,
8th August, 1896

BLESSED AND BELOVED,

A large packet of letters came along with yours. Herewith I send you the letter written to me by Max Müller. It is very kind and good of him.

Miss Müller thinks that she will go away very soon to England. In that case I will not be able to go to Berne for that Purity Congress I have promised. Only if the Seviers consent to take me along, I will go to Kiel and write to you before. The Seviers are good and kind, but I have no right to take advantage of their generosity. Nor can I take the same of Miss Müller, as the expenses there are frightful. As such, I think it best to give up the Berne Congress, as it will come in the middle of September, a long way off.

I am thinking, therefore, of going towards Germany, ending in Kiel, and thence back to England.

Bala Gangadhara Tilak (Mr. Tilak) is the name and Orion that of the book.

Yours,
Vivekananda.

PS. There is also one by Jacobi — perhaps translated on the same lines and with the same conclusions.

PS. I hope you will ask Miss Müller's opinion about the lodgings and the Hall, as I am afraid she will be very displeased if she and others are not consulted.

Miss Müller telegraphed to Prof. Deussen last night; the reply came this morning, 9th August, welcoming me; I am to be in Kiel at Deussen's on the 10th September. So where will you meet me? At Kiel? Miss Müller goes to England from Switzerland. I am going with the Seviers to Kiel. I will be there on the 10th September.

PS. I have not fixed yet anything about the lecture. I have no time to read. The Salem Society most probably is a Hindu community and no faddists.

LXXXIII — BLESSED AND BELOVED

To Mr. E. T. Sturdy

SWITZERLAND,
12th August, 1896.

BLESSED AND BELOVED,

Today I received a letter from America, which I send to you. I have written them that my idea of course is concentration, at least for the present beginning. I have also suggested them that instead of having too many papers, they may start by putting in a few sheets in The Brahmavadin — written in America — and raise the subscription a little which will cover the American expenses. Do not know what they will do.

We will start from here towards Germany next week. Miss Müller goes to England as soon as we have crossed over to Germany.

Capt. and Mrs. Sevier and myself will expect you at Kiel.

I haven't yet written anything nor read anything. I am indeed taking a good rest. Do not be anxious, you will have the article ready. I had a letter from the Math stating that the other Swami is ready to start. He will, I am sure, be just the man you want. He is one of the best Sanskrit scholars we have … and as I hear, he has improved his English much. I had a number of newspaper cuttings from America about Saradananda — I hear from them that he has done very well there. America is a good training ground to bring out all that is in a man. There is such a sympathy in the air. I had letters from Goodwin and Saradananda. S. sends his love to you and Mrs. Sturdy and the baby.

With everlasting love and blessings,
Vivekananda.

LXXXIV — FRIEND

To Mr. E. T. Sturdy

KIEL,
10th September, 1896.

DEAR FRIEND,

I have at last seen Prof. Deussen.... The whole of yesterday was spent very nicely with the Professor, sight-seeing and discussing about the Vedanta.

He is what I should call "a warring Advaitist". No compromise with anything else. "Ishwara" is his bug-bear. He would have none of it if he could. He is very much delighted with the idea of your magazine and wants to confer with you on these subjects in London, where he is shortly going....

LXXXV — SISTER

To Miss Mary Hale

AIRLIE LODGE, RIDGEWAY GARDENS,
WIMBLEDON, ENGLAND,
17th September, 1896.

DEAR SISTER,

Today I reached London, after my two months of climbing and walking and glacier seeing in Switzerland. One good it has done me — a few pounds of unnecessary adipose tissue have returned back to the gaseous state. Well, there is no safety even in that, for the solid body of this birth has taken a fancy to outstrip the mind towards infinite expansion. If it goes on this way, I would have soon to lose all personal identity even in the flesh — at least to all the rest of the world.

It is impossible to express my joy in words at the good news contained in Harriet's letter. I have written to her today. I am sorry I cannot come over to see her married, but I will be present in "fine body" with all good wishes and blessings. Well, I am expecting such news from you and other sisters to make my joy complete. Now, my dear Mary, I will tell you a great lesson I have learnt in this life. It is this: "The higher is your ideal, the more miserable you are"; for such a thing as an ideal cannot be attained in the world, or in this life even. He who wants perfection in the world is a madman, for it cannot be.

How can you find the Infinite in the finite? Therefore I tell you, Harriet will have a most blessed and happy life, because she is not so imaginative and sentimental as to make a fool of herself. She has enough of sentiment as to make life sweet, and enough of common sense and gentleness as to soften the hard points in life which must come to everyone. So has Harriet McKindley in a still higher degree. She is just the girl to make the best of wives, only this world is so full of idiots that very few can penetrate beyond the flesh! As for you and Isabelle, I will tell you the truth, and my "language is plain".

You, Mary, are like a mettlesome Arab — grand, splendid. You will make a splendid queen — physically, mentally. You will shine alongside of a dashing, bold, adventurous, heroic husband; but, my dear sister, you will make one of the worst of wives. You will take the life out of our easy-going, practical, plodding husbands of the everyday world. Mind, my sister, although it is true that there is more romance in actual life than in any novel, yet it is few and far between. Therefore my advice to you is that until you bring down your ideals to a more practical level, you ought not to marry. If you do, the result will be misery for both of you. In a few months you will lose all regard for a commonplace, good, nice, young man, and then life will become insipid. As to sister Isabelle, she has the same temperament as you; only this kindergarten has taught her a good lesson of patience and forbearance. Perhaps she will make a good wife.

There are two sorts of persons in the world. The one — strong-nerved, quiet, yielding to nature, not given to much imagination, yet good, kind, sweet, etc. For such is this world; they alone are born to be happy. There are others again with high-strung nerves, tremendously imaginative, with intense feeling, always going high one moment and coming down the next. For them there is no happiness. The first class will have almost an even tenor of happiness; the last will have to run between ecstasy and misery. But of these alone what we call geniuses are made. There is some truth in the recent theory that "genius is a sort madness".

Now, persons of this class if they want to be great, they must fight to finish — clear out the deck for battle. No encumbrance — no marriage, no children, no undue attachment to anything except the one idea, and live and die for that. I am a person of this sort. I have taken up the one idea of "Vedanta" and I have "cleared the deck for action". You and Isabelle are made of this metal; but let me tell you, though it is hard, you are spoiling your lives in vain. Either take up one idea, clear the deck, and to it dedicate the life; or be contented and practical; lower the ideal, marry, and have a happy life. Either "Bhoga" or "Yoga" — either enjoy this life, or give up and be a Yogi; none can have both in one. Now or never, select quick. "He who is very particular gets nothing", says the proverb. Now sincerely and really and for ever determine to "clear the deck for fight", take up anything, philosophy or science or religion or literature, and let that be your God for the rest of your life. Achieve happiness or achieve greatness. I have no sympathy with you and Isabelle; you are neither for this nor for that. I wish to see you happy, as Harriet has well chosen, or great. Eating, drinking, dressing, and society nonsense are not things to throw a life upon — especially you, Mary. You are rusting away a splendid brain and abilities, for which there is not the least excuse. You must have ambition to be great. I know you will take these rather harsh remarks from me in the right spirit knowing I like you really as much or more than what I call you, my sisters. I had long had a mind to tell you this, and as experience is gathering I feel like telling you. The joyful news from Harriet urged me to tell you this. I will be overjoyed to hear that you are married also and happy, so far as happiness can be had here, or would like to hear of you as doing great deeds.

I had a pleasant visit with Prof. Deussen in Germany. I am sure you have heard of him as the greatest living German philosopher. He and I travelled together to England and today came together to see my friend here with whom I am to stop for the rest of my stay in England. He (Deussen) is very fond of talking Sanskrit and is the only Sanskrit scholar in the West who can talk in it. As he wants to get a practice, he never talks to me in any other language but Sanskrit.

I have come over here amongst my friends, shall work for a few weeks, and then go back to India in the winter.

Ever your loving brother,
Vivekananda.

LXXXVI — JOE

To Miss Josephine MacLeod

GREY COAT GARDENS,
WESTMINSTER, S.W.,
LONDON,
3rd December, 1896.

DEAR JOE,

Many, many thanks, dear Joe Joe, for your kind invitation; but the Dear God has disposed it this way, viz I am to start for India on the 16th with Captain and Mrs. Sevier and Mr. Goodwin. The Seviers and myself take steamer at Naples. And as there will be four days at Rome, I will look in to say good-bye to Alberta.

Things are in a "hum" here just now; the big hall for the class, 39 Victoria, is full and yet more are coming.

Well, the good old country now calls me; I must go. So good-bye to all projects of visiting Russia this April.

I just set things a-going a little in India and am off again for the ever beautiful U.S. and England etc.

So very kind of you to send Mabel's letter — good news indeed. Only I am a little sorry for poor Fox. However, Mabel escaped him; that is better.

You did not write anything about how things are going on in New York. I hope it is all well there. Poor Cola! is he able now to make a living?

The coming of Goodwin was very opportune, as it captured the lectures here which are being published in a periodical form. Already there have been subscribers enough to cover the expenses.

Three lectures next week, and my London work is finished for this season. Of course, everybody here thinks it foolish to give it up just now the "boom" is on, but the Dear Lord says, "Start for Old India". I obey.

To Frankincense, to Mother, to Holister and everyone else my eternal love and blessings, and with the same for you,

Yours ever sincerely,
Vivekananda.

because such printing as he does is only cheating the public.

If there are oranges in Calcutta, send a hundred to Madras care of Alasinga, so that I may have them when I reach Madras.

Mazoomdar writes that the Sayings of Shri Ramakrishna published in The Brahmavadin are not genuine and are lies! In that case ask Suresh Dutt and Ram Babu to give him the lie in The Indian Mirror. As I did not do anything about the collection of the Uktis (Sayings), I cannot say anything.

Yours affectionately,
Vivekananda.

PS. Don't mind these fools; "No fool like an old fool" is the proverb. Let them bark a little. Their occupation is gone. Poor souls! Let them have a little satisfaction in barking.

LXXXVII — RAKHAL

To Swami Brahmananda

HOTEL MINERVA, FLORENCE,
20th December, 1896.

DEAR RAKHAL,

As you see, by this time I am on my way. Before leaving London, I got your letter and the pamphlet. Take no heed of Mazoomdar's madness. He surely has gone crazy with jealousy. Such foul language as he has used would only make people laugh at him in a civilised country. He has defeated his purpose by the use of such vulgar words.

All the same, we ought not to allow Hara Mohan or any one else to go and fight Brahmos and others in our name. The public must know that we have no quarrel with any sect, and if anybody provokes a quarrel, he is doing it on his own responsibility. Quarrelling and abusing each other are our national traits. Lazy, useless, vulgar, jealous, cowardly, and quarrelsome, that is what we are, Bengalis. Anyone who wants to be my friend must give up these. Neither do you allow Hara Mohan to print any book,

LXXXVIII — MARY

To Miss Mary Hale

DAMPFER, "PRINZ-REGENT LEOPOLD"
3rd January, 1897.

DEAR MARY,

I received your letter forwarded from London in Rome. It was very very kind of you to write such a beautiful letter, and I enjoyed every bit of it. I do not know anything about the evolution of the orchestra in Europe. We are nearing Port Said after four days of frightfully bad sailing from Naples. The ship is rolling as hard as she can, and you must pardon my scrawls under such circumstances.

From Suez begins Asia. Once more Asia. What am I? Asiatic, European, or American? I feel a curious medley of personalities in me. You didn't write anything about Dharmapala, his goings and doings. I am much more interested in him than in Gandhi.

I land in a few days at Colombo and mean to "do" Ceylon a bit. There was a time when Ceylon had more than 20 million inhabitants and a huge capital of which the ruins cover nearly a hundred square miles!

The Ceylonese are not Dravidians but pure Aryans. It was colonised from Bengal about 800 B.C., and they have kept a very clear history of their country from that time. It was the greatest trade centre of the ancient world, and Anuradhapuram was the London of the ancients.

I enjoyed Rome more than anything in the West, and after seeing Pompeii I have lost all regard for the so-called "Modern Civilisation". With the exception of steam and electricity they had everything else and infinitely more art conceptions and executions than the Moderns.

Please tell Miss Locke that I was mistaken when I told her that sculpturing of the human figure was not developed in India as among the Greeks. I am reading in Fergusson and other authorities that in Orissa or Jagannath, which I did not visit, there are among the ruins human figures which for beauty and anatomical skill would compare with any production of the Greeks. There is a colossal figure of Death, a huge female skeleton covered with a shrivelled skin — the awful fidelity to anatomical details are frightening and disgusting. Says my author, one of the female figures in the niche is exactly like the Venus de Medici and so on. But you must remember that everything almost has been destroyed by the iconoclastic Mohammedan, yet the remnants are more than all European debris put together! I have travelled eight years and not seen many of the masterpieces.

Tell sister Locke also that there is a ruined temple in a forest in India which and the Parthenon of Greece Fergusson considers as the climax of architectural art — each of its type — the one of conception, the other of conception and detail. The later Mogul buildings etc., the Indo-Saracenic architecture, does not compare a bit with the best types of the ancients....

With all my love,
Vivekananda.

PS. Just by chance saw Mother Church and Father Pope at Florence. You know of it already.

LXXXIX — RAKHAL

To Swami Brahmananda

MADRAS,
12th February, 1897.

DEAR RAKHAL,

I am to start by S.S. Mombasa next Sunday. I had to give up invitations from Poona and other places on account of bad health. I am very much pulled down by hard work and heat.

The Theosophists and others wanted to intimidate me. Therefore I had to give them a bit of my mind. You know they persecuted me all the time in America, because I did not join them. They wanted to begin it here. So I had to clear my position. If that displeases any of my Calcutta friends, "God help them". You need not be afraid, I do not work alone, but He is always with me. What could I do otherwise?

Yours,
Vivekananda.

PS. Take the house if furnished.

XC — SHASHI

Translated from Bengali

To Swami Ramakrishnananda

DARJEELING,
20th April, 1897.

DEAR SHASHI,

All of you have doubtless reached Madras by this time. I should think Biligiri is certainly taking great care of you, and that Sadananda serves you as your attendant. In Madras the worship should be done in a completely Sattvic manner, without a trace of Rajas in it. I hope Alasinga has by now returned to Madras. Don't enter into wrangles with anybody — always maintain a calm attitude. For the present let the worship of Shri Ramakrishna be established and continued in the house of Biligiri. But see that the worship does not become very elaborate and long. Time thus saved should be utilised in holding classes and doing some preaching. It is good to initiate as many as you can. Supervise the work of the two papers, and help in whatever way you can. Biligiri has two widowed daughters. Kindly educate them and make special efforts that through them more such widowed women get a thorough grounding in their own religion and learn a little English and Sanskrit. But all this work should be done from a distance. One has to be exceedingly careful before young women. Once you fall, there is no way out, and the sin is unpardonable.

I am very sorry to hear that Gupta was bitten by a dog; but I hear that the dog was not a mad one, so there is no cause for alarm. In any case, see that he takes the medicine sent by Gangadhar.

Early morning, finish daily your worship and other duties briefly, and calling together Biligiri with his family, read before them the Gita and other sacred books. There is not the least necessity for teaching the divine Love of Râdhâ and Krishna. Teach them pure devotion to Sitâ-Râm and Hara-Pârvati. See that no mistake is made in this respect. Remember that the episodes of the divine relationship between Radha and Krishna are quite unsuitable for young minds. Specially Biligiri and other followers of Râmânujâchârya are worshippers of Rama; so see to it that their innate attitude of pure devotion is never disturbed.

In the evenings give some spiritual teaching like that to the general public. Thus gradually "even the mountain is crossed". See that an atmosphere of perfect purity is always maintained, and that there enters not the slightest trace of Vâmâchâra. For the rest, the Lord Himself will guide you, there is no fear. Give to Biligiri my respectful salutations and loving greetings, and convey my salutations to similar devotees.

My illness is now much less — it may even be cured completely, if the Lord wills. My love, blessings, and greetings to you.

Yours affectionately,
Vivekananda.

PS. Please tender my specially affectionate greetings and blessings to Dr. Nanjunda Rao and help him as much as you can. Try your best to particularly encourage the study of Sanskrit among the non-Brahmins.

XCI — MISS NOBLE

To Sister Nivedita

ALAMBAZAR MATH,
CALCUTTA,
5th May, 1897.

MY DEAR MISS NOBLE,

Your very very kind, loving, and encouraging letter gave me more strength than you think of.

There are moments when one feels entirely despondent, no doubt — especially when one has worked towards an ideal during a whole life's time and just when there is a bit of hope of seeing it partially accomplished, there comes a tremendous thwarting blow. I do not care for the disease, but what depresses me is that my ideals have not had yet the least opportunity of being worked out. And you know, the difficulty is money.

The Hindus are making processions and all that, but they cannot give money. The only help I got in the world was in England, from Miss Müller, and Mr. Sevier. I thought there that a thousand pounds was sufficient to start at least the principal centre in Calcutta, but my calculation was from the experience of Calcutta ten or twelve years ago. Since then the prices have gone up three or four times.

The work has been started anyhow. A rickety old little house has been rented for six or seven shillings, where about twenty-four young men are being trained. I had to go to Darjeeling for a month to recover my health, and I am glad to tell you I am very much better, and would you believe it, without taking any medicine, only by the exercise of mental healing! I am going again to another hill station tomorrow, as it is very hot in the plains. Your society is still living, I am sure. I will send you a report, as least every month, of the work done here. The London work is not doing well at all, I hear, and that was the main reason why I would not come to England just now — although some of our Rajas going for the Jubilee tried their best to get me with them — as I would have to work hard again to revive the interest in Vedanta. And that would mean a good deal more trouble physically.

I may come over for a month or so very soon however. Only if I could see my work started here, how gladly and freely would I travel about!

So far about work. Now about you personally. Such love and faith and devotion and appreciation like yours, dear Miss Noble, repays a hundred times over any amount of labour one undergoes in this life. May all blessings be yours. My whole life is at your service, as we may say in our mother tongue.

It never was and never will be anything but very very welcome, any letters from you and other friends in England. Mr. and Mrs. Hammond wrote two very kind and nice letters and Mr. Hammond a beautiful poem in The Brahmavadin, although I did not deserve it a bit. I will write to you again from the Himalayas, where thought will be clear in sight of the snows and the nerves more settled than in this burning plains. Miss Müller is already in Almora. Mr. and Mrs. Sevier go to Simla. They have been in Darjeeling so long. So things come and go, dear friend. Only the Lord is unchangeable and He is Love. May He make our heart His eternal habitation is the constant prayer of,

Vivekananda.

XCII — RAKHAL

To Swami Brahmananda

ALMORA,
20th May, 1897.

MY DEAR RAKHAL,

From your letter I got all the important news. I got a letter from Sudhir also and also one from Master Mahashay. I have also got two letters from Nityananda (Yogen Chatterjee) from the famine areas.

Even now money is floating on the waters, as it were, . . . but it will surely come. When it comes, buildings, land, and a permanent fund — everything will come all right. But one can never rest assured until the chickens are hatched; and I am not now going down to the hot plains within two or three months. After that I shall make a tour and shall certainly secure some money. This being so, if you think that the [land with a] frontage of eight Kâthâs cannot be acquired . . ., there is no harm in paying the earnest money to the middle-man vendor as though you were losing it for nothing. In all these matters use your own discretion; I cannot give any further advice. There is particularly a chance of making mistake through hurry. . . . Tell Master Mahashay that I quite approve of what he had said.

Write to Gangadhar that if he finds it difficult to get alms etc. there, he should feed himself by spending from his own pocket, and that he should publish a weekly letter in Upen's paper (The Basumati). In that case others also may help.

I understand from a letter of Shashi . . . he wants Nirbhayananda. If you think this course to be the best, then send Nirbhayananda and bring back Gupta. . . . Send Sashi a copy of the Bengali Rules and Regulations of the Math or an English version of it, and write to him to see that the work there is done in accordance with the Rules and Regulations.

I am glad to learn that the Association in Calcutta is going on nicely. It does not matter if one or two keep out. Gradually everyone will come. Be friendly and sympathetic with everybody. Sweet words are heard afar; it is particularly necessary to try and make new people come. We want more and more new members.

Yogen is doing well. On account of the great heat in Almora, I am now in an excellent garden twenty miles from there. This place is comparatively cool, but still warm. The heat does not seem to be particularly less than that of Calcutta. ...

The feverishness is all gone. I am trying to go to a still cooler place. Heat or the fatigue of walking, I find, at once produces trouble of the liver. The air here is so dry that there is a burning sensation in the nose all the time, and the tongue becomes, as it were, a chip of wood. You have stopped criticising; otherwise I would have gone to a colder place by this time just for the fun of it. "He constantly neglects diet restrictions" — what rot do you talk? Do you really listen to the words of these fools? It is just like your not allowing me to take Kalâi-dâl (black pulses), because it contains starch! And what is more — there will be no starch if rice and Roti (bread) are eaten after frying them! What wonderful knowledge, my dear. The fact of the matter is my old nature is coming back — this I am seeing clearly. In this part of the country now, an illness takes on the colour and fashion of this locality; and in that part of the country, it takes on the colour and fashion of the illnesses in that locality. I am thinking of making my meals at night very light; I shall eat to the full in the morning and at noon; at night milk, fruits, etc. That is why I am staying in this orchard, "in expectation of fruits"! Don't you see?

Now don't be alarmed. Does a companion of Shiva die so quickly? Just now the evening lamp has been lighted, and singing has to be done throughout the whole night. Nowadays my temper also is not very irritable, and feverishness is all due to the liver — I see this clearly. Well, I shall make that also come under control — what fear? ... Bravely brace yourself up and do work; let us create a mighty commotion.

Tender my love to all at the Math. At the next meeting of the Association give my greetings to everybody and tell them that though I am not physically present there, yet my spirit is where the name of our Lord is sung — " goes the round on the earth" — because, you see, the Atman is omnipresent.

Yours affectionately,
Vivekananda.

XCIII — SUDHIR

ALMORA,
20th May, 1897.

DEAR SUDHIR,

Your letter gave me much pleasure. One thing, perhaps, I forget to tell you — to keep a copy of the letter you sent me. Also all important communications to the Math from different persons and to different persons should be copied and preserved.

I am very glad to learn that things are going on well, that the work there is steadily progressing as well as that of Calcutta.

I am all right now except for the fatigue of the travel which I am sure will go off in a few days.

My love and blessings to you all.

Yours,
Vivekananda.

XCIV — MARIE

To Marie Halboister

ALMORA,
2nd June, 1897.

DEAR MARIE,

I begin here my promised big chatty letter with the best intention as to its growth, and if it fails, it will be owing to your own Karma. I am sure you are enjoying splendid health. I have been very, very bad indeed; now recovering a bit — hope to recover very soon.

What about the work in London? I am afraid it is going to pieces. Do you now and then visit London? Hasn't Sturdy got a new baby?

The plains of India are blazing now. I cannot bear it. So I am here in this hill station — a bit cooler than the plains.

I am living in a beautiful garden belonging to a merchant of Almora — a garden abutting several miles of mountains and forests. Night before last a leopard came here and took away a goat from the flock kept in this garden. It was a frightful din the servants made and the barking of the big Tibet watchdogs. These dogs are kept chained at a distance all night since I am here, so that they may not disturb my sleep with their deep barks. The leopard thus found his opportunity and got a decent meal, perhaps, after weeks. May it do much good to him!

Do you remember Miss Müller? She has come here for a few days and was rather frightened when she heard of the leopard incident. The demand for tanned skins in London seems very great, and that is playing havoc with our leopards and tigers more than anything else.

As I am writing to you, before me, reflecting the afternoon's glow, stand long, long lines of huge snow peaks. They are about twenty miles as the crow flies from here, and forty through the circuitous mountain roads.

I hope your translations have been well received in the Countess's paper. I had a great mind and very good opportunity of coming over to England this Jubilee season with some of our Princes, but my physicians would not allow me to venture into work so soon. For going to Europe means work, isn't it? No work, no bread.

Here the yellow cloth is sufficient, and I would have food enough. Anyhow I am taking a much desired rest, hope it will do me good.

How are you going on with your work? With joy or sorrow? Don't you like to have a good rest, say for some years, and no work? Sleep, eat, and exercise; exercise, eat, and sleep — that is what I am going to do some months yet. Mr. Goodwin is with me. You ought to have seen him in his Indian clothes. I am very soon going to shave his head and make a full-blown monk of him.

Are you still practising some of the Yogas? Do you find any benefit from them? I learn that Mr. Martin is dead. How is Mrs. Martin — do you see her now and then?

Do you know Miss Noble? Do you ever see her? Here my letter comes to an end, as a huge dust storm is blowing over me, and it is impossible to write. It is all your Karma, dear Marie, for I intended to write so many wonderful things and tell you such fine stories; but I will have to keep them for the future, and you will have to wait.

Ever yours in the Lord,
Vivekananda.

XCV — MISS NOBLE

To Sister Nivedita

ALMORA,
20th June, 1897.

MY DEAR MISS NOBLE,

... Let me tell you plainly. Every word you write I value, and every letter is welcome a hundred times. Write whenever you have a mind and opportunity, and whatever you like, knowing that nothing will be misinterpreted, nothing unappreciated. I have not had any news of the work for so long. Can you tell me anything? I do not expect any help from India, in spite of all the jubilating over me. They are so poor!

But I have started work in the fashion in which I myself was trained — that is to say, under the trees, and keeping body and soul together anyhow. The plan has also changed a little. I have sent some of my boys to work in the famine districts. It has acted like a miracle. I find, as I always thought, that it is through the heart, and that alone, that the world can be reached. The present plan is, therefore, to train up numbers of young men (from the highest classes, not the lowest. For the latter I shall have to wait a little), and the first attack will be made by sending a number of them over a district. When these sappers and miners of religion have cleared the way, there will then be time enough to put in theory and philosophy.

A number of boys are already in training, but the recent earthquake has destroyed the poor shelter we had to work in, which was only rented, anyway.

Never mind. The work must be done without shelter and under difficulties. . . . As yet it is shaven heads, rags, and casual meals. This must change, however, and will, for are we not working for it, head and heart? . . .

It is true in one way that the people here have so little to give up — yet renunciation is in our blood. One of my boys in training has been an executive engineer, in charge of a district. That means a very big position here. He gave it up like straw! . . .

With all love,

Yours in the Truth,
Vivekananda.

XCVI — MISS NOBLE

To Sister Nivedita

ALMORA,
4th July, 1897.

MY DEAR MISS NOBLE,

I am being played upon curiously by both good and evil influences from London these times here. . . . On the other hand, your letters are full of life and sunshine, and bring strength and hope to my spirits, and they sadly want these now. God knows.

Although I am still in the Himalayas, and shall be here for at least a month more, I started the work in Calcutta before I came, and they write progress every week.

Just now I am very busy with the famine, and except for training a number of young men for future work, have not been able to put more energy into the teaching work. The "feeding work" is absorbing all my energy and means. Although we can work only on a very small scale as yet, the effect is marvellous. For the first time since the days of Buddha, Brahmin boys are found nursing by the bed-side of cholera-stricken pariahs.

In India, lectures and teaching cannot do any good. What we want is Dynamic Religion. And that, "God willing", as the Mohammedans say, I am determined to show. . . . I entirely agree with the prospectus of your Society, and you may take for granted my agreement with everything you will do in the future. I have entire faith in your ability and sympathy. I already owe you an immense debt, and you are laying me every day under infinite obligations. My only consolation is that it is for the good of others. Else I do not deserve in the least the wonderful kindness shown to me by the Wimbledon friends. You good, steady, genuine English people, may the Lord always bless you. I appreciate you every day more and more from a distance. Kindly convey my love everlasting to __ and all the rest of our friends there.

With all love, yours ever in the Truth,
Vivekananda.

XCVII — JOE JOE

To Miss Josephine MacLeod

ALMORA,
10th July, 1897.

MY DEAR JOE JOE,

I am glad to learn that you have at last found out that I have time to read your letters.

I have taken to the Himalayas, tired of lecturing and orating. I am so sorry the doctors would not allow my going over with the Raja of Khetri to England, and that has made Sturdy mad.

The Seviers are at Simla and Miss Müller here in Almora.

The plague has subsided, but the famine is still here, and as it looks (on account of no rain as yet), it may wear yet a terrible aspect.

I am very busy from here directing work by my boys in some of the famine districts.

Do come by all means; only you must remember this. The Europeans and the Hindus (called "Natives" by the Europeans) live as oil and water. Mixing with Natives is damning to the Europeans.

There are no good hotels to speak of even at the capitals. You will have to travel with a number of servants about you (cost cheaper than hotels). You will have to bear with people who wear only a loin cloth; you will see me with only a loin cloth about me. Dirt and filth everywhere, and brown people. But you will have plenty of men to talk to you philosophy. If you mix with the English much here, you will have more comforts but see nothing of the Hindus as they are. Possibly I will not be able to eat with you, but I promise that I will travel to good many places with you and do everything in my power to make your journey pleasant. These are what you expect; if anything good comes, so much the better. Perhaps Mary Hale may come over with you. There is a young lady, Miss Campbell, Orchard Lake, Orchard Island, Michigan, who is a great worshipper of Krishna and lives alone in that Island, fasting and praying. She will give anything to be able to see India once, but she is awfully poor. If you bring her with you, I will anyhow manage to pay her expenses. If Mrs. Bull brings old Landsberg with her, that will be saving that fool's life as it were.

Most probably I may accompany you back to America. Kiss Holister for me and the baby. My love to Alberta, to the Leggetts, and to Mabel. What is Fox doing? Give him my love when you see him. To Mrs. Bull and S. Saradananda my love. I am as strong as ever, but it all depends upon leading a quiet life ever afterwards. No hurly-burly any more.

I had a great mind to go to Tibet this year; but they would not allow me, as the road is dreadfully fatiguing. However, I content myself with galloping hard over precipices on mountain ponies. (This is more exciting than your bicycle even, although I had an experience of that at Wimbledon.) Miles and miles of uphill and miles and miles of downhill, the road a few feet broad hanging over sheer precipices several thousand feet deep below.

Ever yours in the Lord,
Vivekananda.

PS. The best time to come is to arrive in India by October or beginning of November. December, January, and February you see things all over and then start by the end of February. From March it begins to get hot. Southern India is always hot.

Goodwin has gone to work in Madras on a paper to be started there soon.

XCVIII — RAKHAL

Translated from Bengali

To Swami Brahmananda

DEULDHAR, ALMORA,
13th July, 1897.

MY DEAR RAKHAL,

Going to Almora from here I made special efforts for Yogen. But he left for the plains as soon as he had recovered a little. From Subhala valley he will write to me of his safe arrival there. As it is impossible to procure a Dandi (a carrying chair) or any other conveyance, Latu could not go. Achyut and myself have again come back to this place. Today my health is a little bad owing to this riding on horseback at breakneck speed in the sun. I took Shashi Babu's medicine for two weeks — I find no special benefit.... The pain in the liver is gone, and owing to plenty of exercise my hands and legs have become muscular, but the abdomen is distending very much. I feel suffocated while getting up or sitting down. Perhaps this is due to the taking of milk. Ask Shashi if I can give up milk. Previously I suffered from two attacks of sunstroke. From that time, my eyes become red if I expose myself to the sun, and the health continues to be bad for two or three days at a stretch.

I was very pleased to get all the news from the Math, and I also heard that the famine relief work is going on well. Please let me know if any money has been received from the office of the Brahmavadin for famine relief. Some money will be sent soon from here also. There is famine in many other places as well, so it is not necessary to stay so long in one place. Tell them to move to other localities and write to each man to go to a separate place. All such work is real work. If the field is made ready in this way, the seeds of spiritual knowledge can be sown. Remember this always — that the only answer to those conservative fanatics who abuse us is such work. I have no objection to getting the thing printed as Shashi and Sarada have suggested.

You yourselves come to a decision as to what the name of the Math should be. . . . The money will come within seven weeks; but I have no further news about the land. In this matter it seems to me that it will be good if we can get the garden of Kristo Gopal in Cossipore. (Where Shri Ramakrishna passed his last days.) What do you say? In future great works will be accomplished. If you agree with me, don't let this matter out to anybody either within the Math or outside, but quietly make inquiries. The work is spoiled if plans are not kept secret. If it can be bought with fifteen or sixteen thousand, then buy at once — of course, only if you think it good. If something more is demanded, make some advance payment and wait for those seven weeks. My view is that for the present it is better to buy it. Everything else will come by and by. All our associations centre round that garden. In reality that is our first Math. Let the thing be done very privately.

A work can be judged by its results only, just as one can infer the nature of previous mental tendencies by their resultant in present behaviour. . . .

Undoubtedly the price of the land of the garden at Cossipore has increased; but our purse has, on the other hand, dwindled. Do something or other, but do it quickly. All work is spoilt by dilatoriness. This garden also has to be acquired — if not today, tomorrow — however big the Math on the banks of the Ganga may be. It will be still better if you can broach the subject through a proxy. If they hear that we are willing to buy, they will bid high. Do the work very confidentially. Be fearless; Shri Ramakrishna is our helper, what fear? Give my love to all.

Yours affectionately,
Vivekananda.

PS. (on the cover): . . . Make special efforts for Cossipore. . . . Give up the land at Belur. Should the poor (The famine-stricken people for whom the Mahabodhi Society agreed to pay, on condition that the work would be done in its name.) die of starvation while you people at the top are indulging in controversy regarding to whom the credit should go? If "Mahabodhi" takes all the credit, let it. Let the poor be benefited. That the work is going on well is good news. Work on with greater energy. I am beginning to send articles. The saccharine and lime have reached.

IC — MARIE

To Marie Halboister

ALMORA,
25th July, 1897.

MY DEAR MARIE,

I have time, will, and opportunity now to clear my promise. So my letter begins. I have been very weak for some time, and with that and other things my visit to England this Jubilee season had to be postponed.

I was very sorry at first not to be able to meet my nice and very dear friends once more, but Karma cannot be avoided, and I had to rest contented with my Himalayas. It is a sorry exchange, after all; for the beauty of the living spirit shining through the human face is far more pleasurable than any amount of material beauty.

Is not the soul the Light of the world?

The work in London had to go slow — for various reasons, and last though not the least was l'argent, mon amie! When I am there l'argent comes in somehow, to keep the mare going. Now everybody shrugs his shoulder. I must come again and try my best to revive the work.

I am having a good deal of riding and exercise, but I had to drink a lot of skimmed milk per prescription of the doctors, with the result that I am more to the front than back! I am always a forward man though — but do not want to be too prominent just now, and I have given up drinking milk.

I am glad to learn that you are eating your meals with good appetite.

Do you know Miss Margaret Noble of Wimbledon? She is working hard for me. Do correspond with her if you can, and you help me a good deal there. Her address is, Brantwood, Worple Road, Wimbledon.

So you saw my little friend Miss Orchard and you liked her too — good. I have great hopes for her. And how I should like to be retired from life's activities entirely when I am very old, and hear the world ringing with the names of my dear, dear young friends like yourself and Miss Orchard etc.!

By and by, I am glad to find that I am aging fast, my hair is turning grey. "Silver threads among the gold" — I mean black — are coming in fast.

It is bad for a preacher to be young, don't you think so? I do, as I did all my life. People have more confidence in an old man, and it looks more venerable. Yet the old rogues are the worst rogues in the world, isn't it?

The world has its code of judgment which, alas, is very different from that of truth's.

So your "Universal Religion" has been rejected by the Revue de deux Mondes. Never mind, try again some other paper. Once the ice is broken, you get in at a quick rate, I am sure. And I am so glad that you love the work: it will make its way, I have no doubt of it. Our ideas have a future, ma chere Marie — and it will be realised soon.

I think this letter will meet you in Paris — your beautiful Paris — and I hope you will write me lots about French journalism and the coming "World's Fair" there.

I am so glad that you have been helped by Vedanta and Yoga. I am unfortunately sometimes like the circus clown who makes others laugh, himself miserable!

You are naturally of a buoyant temperament. Nothing seems to touch you. And you are moreover a very prudent girl, inasmuch as you have scrupulously kept yourself away from "love" and all its nonsense. So you see you have made your good Karma and planted the seed of your lifelong well-being. Our difficulty in life is that we are guided by the present and not by the future. What gives us a little pleasure now drags us on to follow it, with the result that we always buy a mass of pain in the future for a little pleasure in the present.

I wish I had nobody to love, and I were an orphan in my childhood. The greatest misery in my life has been my own people — my brothers and sisters and mother etc. Relatives are like deadly clogs to one's progress, and is it not a wonder that people will still go on to find new ones by marriage!!!

He who is alone is happy. Do good to all, like everyone, but do not love anyone. It is a bondage, and bondage brings only misery. Live alone in your mind — that is happiness. To have nobody to care for and never minding who cares for one is the way to be free.

I envy so much your frame of mind — quiet, gentle, light, yet deep and free. You are already free, Marie, free already — you are Jivanmukta. I am more of a woman than a man, you are more of a man than woman. I am always dragging other's pain into me — for nothing, without being able to do any good to anybody — just as women, if they have no children, bestow all their love upon a cat!!!

Do you think this has any spirituality in it? Nonsense, it is all material nervous bondage — that is what it is. O! to get rid of the thraldom of the flesh!

Your friend Mrs. Martin very kindly sends me copies of her magazine every month — but Sturdy's thermometer is now below zero, it seems. He seems to be greatly disappointed with my non-arrival in England this summer. What could I do?

We have started two Maths (monasteries) here, one in Calcutta, the other in Madras. The Calcutta Math (a wretched rented house) was awfully shaken in the late earthquake.

We have got in a number of boys, and they are in training; also we have opened famine relief in several places and the work is going on apace. We will try to start similar centres in different places in India.

In a few days I am going down to the plains and

from thence go to the Western parts of the mountains. When it is cooler in the plains, I will make a lecture tour all over and see what work can be done.

Here I cannot find any more time to write — so many people are waiting — so here I stop, dear Marie, wishing you all joy and happiness.

May you never be lured by flesh is the constant prayer of —

Ever yours in the Lord,
Vivekananda.

C — SHASHI

Translated from Bengali

To Swami Ramakrishnananda

ALMORA,
29th July, 1897.

DEAR SHASHI,

I got information that your work there is going on very well. Get a thorough mastery of the three Bhâshyas (commentaries), and also study well European philosophy and allied subjects — see to it without fail. To fight with others one requires sword and shield — this fact should never be forgotten. I hope Sukul has now reached there and is attending on you all right. If Sadananda does not like to stay there, send him to Calcutta. Don't forget to send to the Math every week a report of the work including income and expenditure and other information.

Alasinga's sister's husband borrowed four hundred rupees from Badridas here, promising to send it back as soon as he reached Madras; inquire from Alasinga and tell him to send it quickly. For I am leaving this place the day after tomorrow — whether for Mussoorie Hills or somewhere else I shall decide later.

Yesterday I delivered a lecture in the circle of the local English people, and all were highly pleased with it. But I was very much pleased with the lecture in Hindi that I delivered the previous day — I did not know before that I could be oratorical in Hindi.

Are there any new boys joining the Math? If so, then carry on the work in the same manner as it is being done in Calcutta. At present don't use up your wisdom too much, lest it should become completely exhausted — you can do that later on.

Pay particular attention to your health, but too much coddling of the body will, on the contrary, also spoil the health. If there is not the strength of knowledge, nobody would care twopence for your ringing of the bell — this is certain; and knowing this for certain equip yourself accordingly. My heart's love and blessings to you and to Goodwin and others.

Yours affectionately,
Vivekananda.

CI — SHASHI

Translated from Bengali

To Swami Ramakrishnananda

AMBALA,
19th August, 1897.

DEAR SHASHI,

I am very much pained to hear that the work in Madras is not prospering for want of funds. I am glad to learn that the amount borrowed by Alasinga's brother-in-law (sister's husband) has been received back in Almora. Goodwin has written to me to inform the Reception Committee to take some money for expenses from the amount that is left as a result of the lecture. It is a very mean thing to spend the money received on the occasion of that lecture for the purpose of the Reception — and I do not like to tell anybody anything about this matter. I have understood quite well what the people of our country are when it comes to money-matters. . . . On my behalf, you personally talk with the friends there and politely make them understand that it is all right if they can find ways and means to bear the expenses; but if they cannot do so, all of you come back to the Math at Calcutta or go to Ramnad and establish the Math there.

I am now going to the hills at Dharamsala. Niranjan, Dinu, Krishnalal, Latu, and Achyut will stay at Amritsar. Why did you not, all these days, send Sadananda to the Math? If he is still there, then send him to the Punjab on receipt of a letter from Niranjan from Amritsar. I intend to start work in the Punjab after a few days' more rest in the Punjab hills. The Punjab and Rajputana are indeed fields for work. I shall write to you again soon after starting work....

My health was very bad recently. Now I am very slowly recovering. It will be all right, if I stay in the hills for some more days. My love to you and to Alasinga, G. G., R. A., Goodwin, Gupta, Sukul, and all others.

Yours affectionately,
Vivekananda.

CII — RAKHAL

Translated from Bengali

To Swami Brahmananda

AMRITSAR,
2nd September, 1897.

MY DEAR RAKHAL,

Yogen tells me in a letter to buy the house at Baghbazar for Rs. 20,000. Even if we buy that house, there are still a lot of difficulties; for example, we shall have to break it down in part and make the drawing room into a big hall, and similar alterations and repairs. Moreover the house is very old and ramshackle. However, consult Girish Babu and Atul and do what you decide to be best. Today I am leaving by the two o'clock train with all my party for Kashmir. The recent stay at Dharamsala Hills has improved my health much, and the tonsillitis, fever, etc. have completely disappeared. From a letter of yours I got all the news. Niranjan, Latu, Krishnalal, Dinanath, Gupta, and Achyut are all going to Kashmir with me.

The gentleman from Madras who donated Rs. 1,500 for famine relief wants an account of how exactly the money was expended. Send him such an account. We are doing more or less well.

Yours affectionately,
Vivekananda.

PS. Give my love to all at the Math.

CIII — RAKHAL

Translated from Bengali

To Swami Brahmananda

C/O RISHIBAR MUKHOPADHYAYA,
CHIEF JUSTICE,
SRINAGAR, KASHMIR,
13th September, 1897.

MY DEAR RAKHAL,

Now Kashmir. The excellent accounts you heard of this place are all true. There is no place so beautiful as this; and the people also are fair and good-looking, though their eyes are not beautiful. But I have also never seen elsewhere villages and towns so horribly dirty. In Srinagar I am now putting up at the house of Rishibar Babu. He is very hospitable and kind. Send all my letters to his address. In a few days I shall go out somewhere else on excursions; but while returning, I shall come by way of Srinagar, and so shall get the letters also. I have read the letter that you sent regarding Gangadhar. Write to him that there are many orphans in Central India and in Gorakhpur. From there the Punjabis are getting many children. You must persuade Mahendra Babu and get up an agitation about this matter, so that the people of Calcutta are induced to take up the charge of these orphans — such a movement is very desirable. Especially a memorial should be sent to the Government requesting it to see that orphans taken over by the missionaries are returned to the Hindus. Tell Gangadhar to come over; and on behalf of the Ramakrishna Society a tearing campaign should be made. Gird up your loins, and go to every house to carry on the campaign. Hold mass meetings etc. Whether you succeed or not, start a furious agitation. Get all the facts from the important Bengali friends at Gorakhpur by writing to them, and let there be a countrywide agitation over this. Let the Ramakrishna Society be fully established. The secret of the whole thing is to agitate and agitate without respite. I am much pleased to see the orderliness of Sarada's work. Gangadhar and Sarada should not rest satisfied until they have succeeded in creating a centre in every place they visit.

Just now I received a letter from Gangadhar. It is good news that he is determined to start a centre in that district. Write to him saying that his friend, the Magistrate, has sent an excellent reply to my letter. As soon as we come down to the plains from Kashmir, I shall send back Latu, Niranjan, Dinu, and Khoka. For there is no suitable work for them here any more; also within three to four weeks send Shuddhananda, Sushil, and one other to me. Send them to the house of Mr. Shyamacharan Mukhopadhyaya, Medical Hall, Cantonment, Ambala. From there I shall go to Lahore. They should have each two thick gerua-coloured jerseys, and two blankets for bedding. I shall buy them woollen chaddars, and other woollen necessities in Lahore. If the translation of Râja-Yoga has been completed, get it published bearing all the cost.... Where the language is obscure, make it very simple and clear, and let Tulsi make a Hindi translation of it if he can. If these books are published, they will help the Math very greatly.

I hope your health is now quite all right. Since reaching Dharamsala I have been all right. I like the cold places; there the body keeps well. I have a desire either to visit a few places in Kashmir and then choose an excellent site and live a quiet life there, or to go on floating on the water. I shall do what the doctor advises. The Raja is not here now. His brother, the one just next to him in age, is the Commander-in-Chief. Efforts are being made to arrange a lecture under his chairmanship. I shall write all about this afterwards. If the meeting for the lecture is held in a day or two, I shall stay back, otherwise I go out again on my travels. Sevier is still at Murree. His health is very bad — going about in the jolting tongas and jutkas. The Bengali gentlemen of Murree are very good and courteous. Give my respects to G. C. Ghosh, Atul, Master Mahashay, and others, and keep up the spirits of everybody. What is the news about the house which Yogen suggested we should buy? In October I shall go down from here and shall deliver a few lectures in the Punjab. After that I may go via Sind to Cutch, Bhuj, and Kathiawar — even down to Poona if circumstances are favourable; otherwise I go to Rajputana via Baroda. From Rajputana I go to the North-Western Province, (In those days this was made up of Uttar Pradesh and part of the Punjab.) then Nepal, and finally Calcutta — this is my present programme. Everything, however, is in God's hands. My love and greetings to all.

Yours affectionately,
Vivekananda.

CIV — SHUDDHANANDA

To Swami Shuddhananda
C/O RISHIBAR MUKHOPADHYAYA,
CHIEF JUSTICE,
SRINAGAR, KASHMIR,
15th September, 1897.

MY DEAR SHUDDHANANDA,

We are in Kashmir at last. I need not tell you of all the beauties of the place. It is the one land fit for Yogis, to my mind. But the land is now inhabited by a race who though possessing great physical beauty are extremely dirty. I am going to travel by water for a month seeing the sights and getting strong. But the city is very malarious just now, and Sadananda and Kristolal have got fever. Sadananda is all right today, but Kristolal has fever yet. The doctor came today and gave him a purgative. He will be all right by tomorrow, we hope; and we start also tomorrow. The State has lent me one of its barges, and it is fine and quite comfortable. They have also sent orders to the Tahsildars of different districts. The people here are crowding in banks to see us and are doing everything they can to make us comfortable.

A clipping from The Indian Mirror, quoting passages from an article written by Dr. Barrows in an American paper, has been sent over to me by somebody without a name and asking me what reply to give. I send back the cutting to Brahmananda with my answer to the passages which are damned lies!

I am glad to learn you are doing well there and going on with your usual work. I also had a letter from Shivananda giving the details of work there.

After a month I go back to the Punjab, and I will expect three of you at Ambala. In case a centre is founded, one of you will be left in charge. Niranjan, Latu, and Kristolal will be sent back.

I intend to make a rapid march through the Punjab and Sind via Kathiawar and Baroda, back to Rajputana, and thence to Nepal and last Calcutta.

Write to me C/o Rishibar Babu at Srinagar. I will get the letter on my way back.

With love to all and blessings,

Yours,
Vivekananda.

CV — HARIPADA

Translated from Bengali

To Sri Haripada Mitra

SRINAGAR, KASHMIR,
1897.

DEAR HARIPADA,

My health has been very bad for the last nine months, and the heat made it still worse. So I have been wandering over the hills from place to place. Now I am in Kashmir. I have travelled far and wide, but I have never seen such a country. I shall soon leave for the Punjab and again go to work. From Sadananda I have heard all the news about you and continue to get it. I am sure to go to Karachi after visiting the Punjab. So we shall meet in person there.

With blessings,
Vivekananda.

CVI — MISS MACLEOD

To Miss Josephine MacLeod

SRINAGAR, KASHMIR,
30th September, 1897.

MY DEAR MISS MACLEOD,

Come soon if you intend to come really. From November to the middle of February India is cool; after that it is hot. You will be able to see all you want within that time, but to see all takes years.

I am in a hurry; therefore excuse this hasty card. Kindly tender my love to Mrs. Bull and my good wishes and earnest thoughts for Goodwin's speedy recovery. My love to Mother, to Alberta, to the baby, to Holister, and last, not the least, to Franky.

Yours in the Lord,
Vivekananda.

CVII — RAKHAL

To Swami Brahmananda

SRINAGAR, KASHMIR,
30th September, 1897

DEAR RAKHAL,

I received your affectionate letter and also the letter from the Math. I am leaving for the Punjab in two or three days. I have received the foreign mail. The following are my answers to Miss Noble's questions in her letter:

1. Nearly all the branches have been started, but the movement is only just beginning.

2. Most of the monks are educated. Those that are not are also having secular education. But above all, to do good, perfect unselfishness is absolutely necessary. To ensure that, more attention is given to spiritual exercises than to anything else.

3. Secular educators: We get mostly those who have already educated themselves. What is needed is training them into our method and building up of character. The training is to make them obedient and fearless; and the method is to help the poor physically first and then work up to higher regions of mentality.

Arts and Industries: This part of the programme alone cannot be begun for want of funds. The simplest method to be worked upon at present is to induce Indians to use their own produce and get markets for Indian artware etc. in other countries. This should be done by persons who are not only not middlemen themselves, but will devote the entire proceeds of this branch to the benefit of the workmen.

4. Wandering from place to place will be necessary till "people come to education". The religious character of the wandering monks will carry with it a much greater weight than otherwise.

5. All castes are open to our influence. So long the highest only have been worked upon. But since the work department is in full operation in different famine-centres, we are influencing the lower classes more and more.

6. Nearly all the Hindus approve our work, only they are not used to practical co-operation in such works.

7. Yes, from the very start we are making no distinction in our charities or other good works between the different religions of India.

Reply to Miss N. according to these hints.

See that there is no remissness whatever in the medical treatment of Yogen — if necessary spend money by drawing on the capital. Did you go and meet Bhavanath's wife?

If Brahmachari Hariprasanna can come, it will be very helpful. Mr. Sevier has become very impatient about acquiring a house somewhere; it will be good if something is done quickly about it! Hariprasanna is an engineer; so he will be able to do something quickly about it. Also he understands better about the suitability of places. They (the Seviers) like to have a place somewhere near about Dehra Dun or Mussoorie; that is to say, the place must not be too cold and must be habitable throughout the year. So send Hariprasanna at once straight to Sj. Shyamapada Mukherjee, Medical Hall, Ambala Cantonment. As soon as I go down to the Punjab, I shall send Mr. Sevier along with him. I am returning (to the Math) in a trice after a tour of the Punjab, Karachi, and then via Rajputana, not via Kathiawar and Gujarat — to Nepal. Tulsi has gone to Madhya Bharat — is it for the famine-relief work? . . .

My blessings and love to all. I have got the news that Kali has reached New York; but he has not written any letter. Sturdy writes that his work had increased so much that people were amazed — and a few persons have also written me praising him highly. However, there is not so much difficulty in America; the work will go on somehow or other. Send Shuddhananda and his brother along with Hariprasanna. Of the party only Gupta and Achyut will accompany me.

Yours affectionately,
Vivekananda.

CVIII — SHASHI

Translated from Bengali

To Swami Ramakrishnananda

SRINAGAR, KASHMIR,
30th September, 1897

MY DEAR SHASHI,

Now I am returning from a visit to places in Kashmir. In a day or two I shall leave for the Punjab. As my health is now much better, I have decided to tour again in the same way as before. Not too much lecturing — one or two lectures, perhaps, in the Punjab, otherwise none. The people of our country have not yet offered me even as much as a pice for my travelling expenses — and to cap it all, to take with you a whole party, well, you can easily understand how troublesome it all is. It is also a matter of shame to have to draw upon only the English disciples. So, as before, I start out "with only a blanket". In this place there is no need for any person like Goodwin, as you can see.

A monk from Ceylon, P. C. Jinawar Vamar by name, has written to me among other things that he wants to visit India. Perhaps he is the same monk who comes of the Siamese royal family. His address is Wellawatta, Ceylon. If convenient, invite him to Madras. He believes in the Vedanta. It will not be so difficult to send him to other places from Madras. It is also good to have such a person in the Order. My love and blessings to you and all others.

Yours affectionately,
Vivekananda.

PS. The Maharaja of Khetri is reaching Bombay on the 10th October. Don't forget to present him an address of welcome.

CIX — RAKHAL

To Swami Brahmananda
SRINAGAR, KASHMIR,
30th September, 1897

DEAR RAKHAL,

I understand from a letter of Gopal Dada that you have seen that piece of land at Konnagar. It seems that that site is rent-free and measures 16 bighas (about 5 acres), and that the price is below eight or ten thousand rupees. Do what you think best after considering the healthiness and other factors. In a day or two I shall leave for the Punjab. So don't write any more letters to me at this address. I shall telegraph to you my next address. Don't forget to send Hariprasanna. Tell Gopal Dada thus: "Your health will soon be all right — winter is coming, what fear? Eat well and be merry." Write a letter to Mrs. C. Sevier at Spring Dale, Murree, as to Yogen's present state of health, marking on the cover "to await arrival". Give my love and blessings to all.

Yours affectionately,
Vivekananda.

PS. The Maharaja of Khetri reaches Bombay on the 10th October. Don't forget to give him an address of welcome.

CX — MARGO

To Sister Nivedita
SRINAGAR, KASHMIR,
1st October, 1897.

DEAR MARGO,

Some people do the best work when led. Not every one is born to lead. The best leader, however, is one who "leads like the baby". The baby, though apparently depending on everyone, is the king of the household. At least, to my thinking, that is the secret. . . . Many feel, but only a few can express. It is the power of expressing one's love and appreciation and sympathy for others, that enables one person to succeed better in spreading the idea than others. . . .

I shall not try to describe Kashmir to you. Suffice it to say, I never felt sorry to leave any country except this Paradise on earth; and I am trying my best, if I can, to influence the Raja in starting a centre. So much to do here, and the material so hopeful! . . .

The great difficulty is this: I see persons giving me almost the whole of their love. But I must not give anyone the whole of mine in return, for that day the work would be ruined. Yet there are some who will look for such a return, not having the breadth of the impersonal view. It is absolutely necessary to the work that I should have the enthusiastic love of as many as possible, while I myself remain entirely impersonal. Otherwise jealousy and quarrels would break up everything. A leader must be impersonal. I am sure you understand this. I do not mean that one should be a brute, making use of the devotion of others for his own ends, and laughing in his sleeve meanwhile. What I mean is what I am, intensely personal in my love, but having the power to pluck out my own heart with my own hand, if it becomes necessary, "for the good of many, for the welfare of many", as Buddha said. Madness of love, and yet in it no bondage. Matter changed into spirit by the force of love. Nay, that is the gist of our Vedanta. There is but One, seen by the ignorant as matter, by the wise as God. And the history of civilisation is the progressive reading of spirit into matter. The ignorant see the person in the non-person. The sage sees the non-person in the person. Through pain and pleasure, joy and sorrow, this is the one lesson we are learning. . . .

Yours ever with love and truth,
Vivekananda.

CXI — RAKHAL

Translated from Bengali

To Swami Brahmananda

MURREE,
11th October, 1897.

MY DEAR RAKHAL,

I feel I have been working as if under an irresistible impulse for the last ten days, beginning from Kashmir. It may be either a physical or a mental disease. Now I have come to the conclusion that I am unfit for further work. . . . I now understand that I have been very harsh to all of you. But I knew, however, that you would bear with all my shortcomings; in the Math there is no one else who will do so. I have been increasingly harsh to you. Whatever has happened is now past — it is all the result of past Karma. What is the good of my repentance? I do not believe in it. It is all Karma. Whatever of Mother's work was to be accomplished through me, She made me do, and has now flung me aside breaking down my body and mind. Her will be done!

Now I retire from all this work. In a day or two I shall give up everything and wander out alone; I shall spend the rest of my life quietly in some place or other. Forgive me if you all will, or do what you like.

Mrs. Bull has given much of the money. She has implicit confidence in Sharat. Do the work of the Math with Sharat's advice; or do as you will.

But I have all along been like a hero — I want my work to be quick like lightning, and firm as adamant. Likewise shall I die also. Therefore kindly do my work for me — no question of success or defeat enters here at all. I have never retreated in a fight — shall I now . . . ? There is success and failure in every work. But I am inclined to believe that one who is a coward will be born after death as an insect or a worm, that there is no salvation for a coward even after millions of years of penance. Well, shall I after all be born as a worm? . . . In my eyes this world is mere play — and it will always remain as such. Should one spend six long months brooding over the questions of honour and disgrace, gain and loss pertaining to this? . . . I am a man of action. Simply advice upon advice is being given — this one says this, that one says that; again that man threatens, and this one frightens! This life is not, in my view, such a sweet thing that I would long to live through so much care and caution and fear. Money, life, friends, and relatives, and the love of men and myself — if one wants to enter into work fully assured beforehand of all these — if one has to be so much ridden with fear, then one will get just what Gurudeva used to say, "The crow thinks itself very clever but . . ." (The crow thinks itself very clever, but it cannot help eating filth.) — well, he will get that. After all, what is the purpose behind all these — money and wealth, Maths and institutions, preaching and lecturing? There is only one purpose in the whole of life — education. Otherwise what is the use of men and women, land and wealth?

So loss of money, or loss of anything else — I cannot bother about, and I will not. When I fight, I fight with girded loins — that much I fully understand; and I also understand that man, that hero, that god, who says, "Don't care, be fearless. O brave one, here I am by your side!" To such a man-god I offer a million salutations. Their presence purifies the world, they are the saviours of the world. And the others who always wail, "Oh, don't go forward, there is this danger, there is that danger" — those dyspeptics — they always tremble with fear. But through the grace of the Divine Mother my mind is so strong that even the most terrible dyspepsia shall not make me a coward. To cowards what advice shall I offer? — nothing whatsoever have I to say. But this I desire, that I should find shelter at the feet of those brave souls who dared to do great deeds even though they failed to succeed, of those heroes who never quailed nor shirked, of those fighters who never disobeyed orders through fear or pride. I am the child of the Divine Mother, the source of all power and strength. To me, cringing, fawning, whining, degrading inertia and hell are one and the same thing. O Mother of the Universe, O my Gurudeva, who would constantly say, "This is a hero!" — I pray that I may not have to die a coward. This is my prayer, O brother. " [111_rakhal_01.jpg] — certainly there is, or there will be born one equal to me"; some one or other will certainly arise from these thousands of devotees of Shri Ramakrishna who will be like me, and who will be able to understand me.

O hero, awake, and dream no more. Death has caught you by the forelock . . . still fear not. What I have never done — fleeing from the battle — well, will that happen today? For fear of defeat shall I retreat from the fight? Defeat is the ornament the hero adorns himself with. What, to acknowledge defeat without fighting! O Mother, Mother! . . . Not one capable of even playing second fiddle and yet the mind filled with petty self-importance, "We understand everything". . . . Now I retire; . . . everything I leave in your control. If Mother sends me men again in whose heart there is courage, in whose hands strength, in whose eyes there is fire, real children of the Mother — if She gives me even one such, then I shall work again, then I shall return. Otherwise, I shall take it that, by Mother's will, this is the end. I am in a tremendous hurry, I want to work at hurricane speed, and I want fearless hearts.

I have rebuked poor Sarada severely. What to do? . . . I do scold; but I also have much to complain. . . . Almost suffocated by short breathing, standing and standing, I have written an article for him. . . . It is all good, otherwise how will renunciation come? . . . Will Mother in the end kill me with attachment? I have offended all of you — do what you want.

I bless you all with a full heart. May Mother enshrine Herself in your hearts as strength: [111_rakhal_02.jpg] — the support that is fearlessness — may She make you all fearless. This I have seen in life — he who is over-cautious about himself falls into dangers at every step; he who is afraid of losing honour and respect, gets only disgrace; he who is always afraid of loss always loses. . . . May all good attend you all.

Yours affectionately,
Vivekananda.

CXII — RAKHAL

Translated from Bengali

To Swami Brahmananda

MURREE,
12th October, 1897.

MY DEAR RAKHAL,

I wrote at length in yesterday's letter. I think it desirable to give you special directions about certain matters. . . . (1) To all those who collect money and send it to the Math . . . the acknowledgment of the amounts will be issued from the Math. (2) The acknowledgment must be in duplicate, one for the sender, and one for filing in the Math. (3) There must be a big register in which all the names and addresses of the donors will be entered. (4) Accounts, accurate to the last pie, must be kept of the amounts that are donated to the Math Fund, and fully accurate accounts should be obtained from Sarada and others to whom money is given. For lack of accurate account-keeping . . . see that I am not accused as a cheat. These accounts should afterwards be published. (5) Immediately go and register a will under lawyer's advice to the effect that in case you and I die then Hari and Sharat will succeed to all that there is in our Math.

I have not yet got any news from Ambala, whether Hariprasanna and others have reached there or not. Give the other half-sheet of this letter to Master Mahashay.

Yours affectionately,
Vivekananda.

CXIII — MISS NOBLE

To Sister Nivedita

JAMMU,
3rd November, 1897.

MY DEAR MISS NOBLE, (This was the last letter received in England by Sister Nivedita.)

. . . Too much sentiment hurts work. "Hard as steel and soft as a flower" is the motto.

I shall soon write to Sturdy. He is right to tell you that in case of trouble I will stand by you. You will have the whole of it if I find a piece of bread in India — you may rest assured of that. I am going to write to Sturdy from Lahore, for which I start tomorrow. I have been here for 15 days to get some land in Kashmir from the Maharaja. I intend to go to Kashmir again next summer, if I am here, and start some work there.

With everlasting love,

Yours,
Vivekananda.

CXIV — RAKHAL

Translated from Bengali

To Swami Brahmananda

LAHORE,
11th November, 1897.

MY DEAR RAKHAL,

The lecture at Lahore is over somehow. I shall start for Dehra Dun in a day or two. I have now postponed my tour to Sind, as none of you are agreeable to it, and also because of various other obstacles. Somebody has opened my two letters from England on the way. So don't send me letters any further for the present. Send them after I have written for them from Khetri. If you go to Orissa, then make arrangements that some one will do all the work as your representative — say Hari, especially now, when I am daily expecting letters from America.

Perhaps the will that I asked you to make in favour of Hari and Sharat has now been made.

Probably I shall leave Sadananda and Sudhir here after establishing a Society. Now no more lecturing — I go in a hurry straight to Rajputana.

The establishment of the Math must have precedence over everything.

Without regular exercise the body does not keep fit; talking, talking all the time brings illness — know this for certain. My love to all.

Yours affectionately,
Vivekananda.

CXV — RAKHAL

Translated from Bengali

To Swami Brahmananda

LAHORE,
15th November, 1897.

MY DEAR RAKHAL,

I hope you and Hari are now in good health. The work in Lahore went off with great éclat. Now I go to Dehra Dun. The Sind tour is postponed. I have yet no news whether Dinu, Latu, and Krishnalal have reached Jaipur. Babu Nagendranath Gupta will collect subscriptions and donations from here and send them to the Math to meet expenses. Send him regular receipts. Let me know if you have received anything from Murree, Rawalpindi, and Sialkot.

Reply to me C/o Post Master, Dehra Dun. Other letters you may send me after hearing from me from Dehra Dun. My health is good; only I have to get up at night once or twice. I am having sound sleep; sleep is not spoiled even after exhausting lectures; and I am doing exercise every day.... There is no trouble at all. Now, come on, work with redoubled energy. Keep an eye on that big piece of land — in all secrecy. We are making regular efforts so that big Utsava (Celebration — of Shri Ramakrishna's birthday.)can be held there. My love to all.

Yours affectionately,
Vivekananda.

PS. It will be a very good thing if Master Mahashay will write now and then about us in The Tribune, so that Lahore will not become cold again — now it is quite warmed up. Spend money a little economically; pilgrimage expenses should be borne by you personally; preaching and propaganda expenses should be charged to the Math.

CXVI — BABURAM

Translated from Bengali

To Swami Premananda

DEHRA DUN,
24th November, 1897.

MY DEAR BABURAM,

I got all news about you from Hariprasanna. I am especially pleased to hear that Rakhal and Hari are now quite well.

Now Babu Raghunath Bhattacharya of Tehri is suffering very much from some pain in the neck; I also have been suffering for a long time from some pain at the back of my neck. If you can get hold of some very old ghee, then send some of it to him at Dehra Dun and some of it to me also at my Khetri address. You are sure to get it from Habu or Sharat (lawyer). Address it to Babu Raghunath Bhattacharya, Dehra Dun, N.W.P.... and it will reach him.

The day after tomorrow I am leaving for Saharanpur; from there to Rajputana.

Yours affectionately,
Vivekananda.

PS. My love to all.

CXVII — RAKHAL

Translated from Bengali

To Swami Brahmananda

DELHI,
30th November, 1897.

MY DEAR RAKHAL,

Part of the money that Miss Müller promised has reached Calcutta. The balance will come afterwards in a short while. We have also some amount. Miss Müller will deposit the money in your name as well as mine with Messrs. Grindlay & Co. As you have got the power of attorney, you alone can draw all the money. As soon as the money is deposited, you yourself with Hari go to Patna and meet that gentleman and by some means or other influence him; and if the price of the land is reasonable, buy it. If it cannot be had, try for some other plot of ground. I am trying to get some money in these parts too. We must hold the big festival on our own plot of ground — remember this must be your first and foremost work, come what may.

You have shown great pluck; the work you have done these last eight or nine months does you great credit. Now you must see to it that a Math and a centre in Calcutta are steadily established before everything else. Work hard to this end but quietly and in secret. Get information about the Cossipore house also. Tomorrow I am going to Khetri via Alwar. My health is good, even though I have caught a cold. Send all letters to Khetri. My love to all.

Yours affectionately,
Vivekananda.

PS. What about the will I asked you to make in favour of Sharat and Hari? Or will you buy the land and other things in my name, and I shall make a will?

CXVIII — RAKHAL

Translated from Bengali

To Swami Brahmananda

DELHI,
8th December, 1897.

MYDEAR RAKHAL,

We shall start for Khetri tomorrow. Gradually the luggage has greatly increased. After Khetri I intend to send everybody to the Math. I could get done through them none of the work which I had hoped. That is to say, it is quite certain that none of them can do anything if he always remains with me. Unless each goes about independently, he will not be able to do anything. The fact is, who will care for them if they are in my company? Only waste of time. So I am sending them to the Math.

Keep as a fund for some permanent work the balance of the money left after the famine relief. Do not spend that money for any other purpose, and after giving the full accounts of the famine work, note down thus, "So much balance is left for some other good work"....

Work I want — I don't want any humbug. To those who have no desire to work I say, "My dear fellow, now go and follow your own way." As soon as I reach Khetri, I will send you the power of attorney with my signature if the document has reached there meanwhile. Open only those letters from America which bear the Boston postmark, not the others. Send all my letters to Khetri. I shall get money in Rajputana itself; no cause for anxiety on that score. Try energetically for the piece of land; we must have the celebration on our own ground this time.

Is the money in the Bengal Bank, or have you kept it elsewhere? Be very careful about money matters; keep detailed accounts, and regarding money know for certain that one cannot rely even on one's own father.

Give my love to all. Write to me how Hari is doing. Recently I met at Dehra Dun the Udâsi Sâdhu, Kalyân Dev, and a few others. I hear the people at Hrishikesh are very eager to see me and are asking again and again about me.

Yours affectionately,
Vivekananda.

CXIX — RAKHAL

Translated from Bengali

To Swami Brahmananda

KHETRI,
14th December, 1897.

MY DEAR RAKHAL,

I have today sent your power of attorney with my signature.... Draw the money as early as you can, and wire to me as soon as you have done so. A Raja of a place in Bundelkhand named Chatrapur has invited me. I shall visit the place on my way to the Math. The Raja of Limbdi, too, is writing earnestly. I cannot avoid going there also. I shall make a lightning tour of Kathiawar — that is what it will come to. I shall feel great relief as soon as I reach Calcutta.... There is no news from Boston as yet; perhaps Sharat is coming; anyway, whenever any news comes from anywhere, write to me immediately.

Yours affectionately,
Vivekananda.

PS. How is Kanai? I hear that his health is not good. Pay special attention to him and see that nobody is unduly bossed over. Write to me about your health as well as Hari's.

CXX — SHIVANANDA

Translated from Bengali

To Swami Shivananda

JAIPUR,
27th December, 1897.

MY DEAR SHIVANANDA,

Mr. Setlur of Girgaon, Bombay, whom you know very well from Madras writes to me to send somebody to Africa to look after the religious needs of the Indian emigrants in Africa. He will of course send the man and bear all expenses.

The work will not be congenial at present, I am afraid, but it is really the work for a perfect man. You know the emigrants are not liked at all by the white people there. To look after the Indians, and at the same time maintain cool — headedness so as not to create more strife — is the work there. No immediate result can be expected, but in the long run it will prove a more beneficial work for India than any yet attempted. I wish you to try your luck in this. If you agree, please write to Setlur, about your willingness and ask for more information, mentioning this letter. And godspeed to you! I am not very well, but am going to Calcutta in a few days and will be all right.

Yours in the Lord,
Vivekananda.

CXXI — RAJAJI

To Raja Pyari Mohan Mukherjee

THE MATH, BELUR,
25th February, 1898.

MY DEAR RAJAJI,

My gratitude for your very kind invitation to speak. I had a talk with Mr. Bhattacharya on the subject a few days back, and I am trying my best as a result to find time for your Society. I also promised to let them know the result on Sunday.

A friend to whom I owe much is here, presumably, to take me to his place in Darjeeling.

There are some American friends come, and every spare moment is occupied in working for the new Math and several organisations therein, and I expect to leave India next month for America.

Believe me, I am trying my best to be able to take advantage of this invitation of yours and shall communicate the result to you on Sunday through Mr. Bhattacharya.

Yours with love and blessings,
Vivekananda.

CXXII — SHASHI

To Swami Ramakrishnananda

MATH, BELUR,
HOWRAH P.O.,
25th February, 1898.

MY DEAR SHASHI,

Our congratulations for the successful carrying out of the Mahotsava (Big celebration of Shri Ramakrishna's birthday.) in Madras. Hope you had a good gathering and plenty of spiritual food. We are all so glad that you have girded yourself to teach more of spirituality to the Madras people than those finger twistings and kling phat (Cryptic Mantras or sound formulae.) you are so fond of. Really your lecture on Shriji (Shri Ramakrishna.) was splendid. I could only catch a report in the Madras Mail in Khandwa, and the Math people have not had any. Why don't you send us over a copy?

I learn that you complain about my silence, is it? I have written you more letters, however, than you ever wrote me, from Europe and America even. You ought to give me all the news you can from Madras every week. Simplest way is to put down a few lines and a few items of news every day on a sheet.

My health has not been all right of late; at present it is much better. Calcutta is unusually cool just now, and the American friends who are here are enjoying it ever so much. Today we take possession of the land we have bought, and though it is not practicable to have the Mahotsava on it just now, I must have something on it on Sunday. Anyhow, Shriji's relics must be taken to our place for the day and worshipped. Gangadhar is here and asks me to write to you that though he has succeeded in getting some subscriptions for the Brahmavadin, the delivery being very irregular, he is afraid of losing them also soon. I received your letter of recommendation for the young man with the old story of "having nothing to eat, Your Honour"; only added in the Madras edition: "got a number of children too", for generating whom no recommendation was needed! I would be very glad to help him, but the fact is, I have no money; every cent I had I have made over to Raja, (Rakhal or Swami Brahmananda.) as they all say I am a spendthrift and are afraid of keeping money with me. I have, however, sent the letter to Rakhal if he can find the way to help your friend, the young man, in having some more children. He writes that the Christians will help him out if he becomes a convert, but he won't. Perhaps he is afraid that his conversion will make Hindu India lose one of her brightest jewels and Hindu society the benefit of his propagating power to eternal misery!

The boys here are rather seedy owing to the unusual amount of pure and cool air they are made to breathe in and live on the bank of the Ganga in the new Math. Sarada has his malaria brought over from Dinajpur. I made him eat a dose of opium the other day without much benefit to him except his brain which progressed for some hours towards its natural direction, namely, idiocy. Hari also has a touch; I hope it will take off a good bit of their avoirdupois. By the by, we have once more started the dancing business here, and it would make your heart glad to see Hari and Sarada and my own good self in a waltz. How we keep balance at all is a wonder to me.

Sharat has come and is hard at work as usual. We have got some good furniture now, and a big jump from the old Châtâi (mat) in the old Math to nice tables and chairs and three Khâts (cots), mind you. We have curtailed the Pujâ (worship) work a good deal, and the amount of pruning your klings and phats and svâhâs have undergone would make you faint. The puja occupied only the day, and they slept soundly all night. How are Tulsi and Khoka? Are they more tractable with you than under Rakhal? You may run in to Calcutta for a few days giving charge to Tulsi, but it is so expensive, and then you must go back, as Madras has to be thoroughly worked up. I am going to America again with Mrs. Bull in a few months.

Give my love to Goodwin and tell him that we are going to see him at any rate on our way to Japan. Shivananda is here, and I have toned down a bit his great desire to go to the Himalayas for food! Is Tulsi contemplating the same? The bandicoot-hole will be a sufficient cave for him, I suppose.

So the Math here is a fait accompli, and I am going over to get more help.... Work on with energy. India is a rotten corpse inside and outside. We shall revive it by the blessings of Shri Maharaj. With all love,

Ever yours in the Lord,
Vivekananda.

CXXIII — MARY

To Miss Mary Hale

>MATH, BELUR,
>HOWRAH DISTRICT,
>BENGAL, INDIA,
>2nd March, 1898.

MY DEAR MARY,

You have news of me already, I hope, through the letter I wrote to Mother Church. You are all so kind, the whole family, to me, I must have belonged to you in the past, as we Hindus say. My only regret is that the millionaires do not materialise: and I want them so badly just now that I am growing decrepit and old and hot in the midst of building and organising. Though Harriet has got one of a million virtues, a few millions of cash virtue would have made it more shining, I am sure; so you do not commit the same mistake.

A certain young couple had everything favourable to make them man and wife except that the bride's father was determined not to give his daughter to anyone who had not a million. The young people were in despair when a clever matchmaker came to the rescue. He asked the bridegroom whether he was willing to part with his nose on payment of a million — which he refused. The matchmaker then swore before the bride's father that the bridegroom had in store goods worth several millions, and the match was completed. Don't you take like millions.

Well, well, you could not get the millionaire, so I could not get the money; so I had to worry a good deal and work hard to no purpose; so I got the disease. It requires brains like mine to find out the true cause — I am charmed with myself!

Well, it was in Southern India, when I came from London and when the people were feting and feasting and pumping all the work out of me, that an old hereditary disease made its appearance. The tendency was always there, and excess of mental work made it "express" itself. Total collapse and extreme prostration followed, and I had to leave Madras immediately for the cooler North; a day's delay meant waiting for a week in that awful heat for another steamer. By the by, I learnt afterwards that Mr. Barrows arrived in Madras next day and was very much chagrined at not finding me as he expected, though I helped getting up an address for him and arranged for his reception. Poor man, he little knew I was at death's door then.

I have been travelling in the Himalayas all through last summer; and a cold climate, I found immediately, brought me round; but as soon as I come into the heat of the plains I am down again. From today the heat in Calcutta is becoming intense, and I will soon have to fly. This time to cool America as Mrs. Bull and Miss MacLeod are here. I have bought a piece of land for the institution on the river Ganga near Calcutta, on which is a little house where they are living now; within a stone's throw is the house where the Math is situated at present in which we live.

So I see them every day and they are enjoying it immensely à L'Inde. They intend making a trip to Kashmir in a month, and I am going with them as a guide and friend and philosopher perhaps, if they are willing. After that we all sail for the land of freedom and scandal.

You need not be alarmed with me as the disease will take two or three years at worst to carry me off. At best it may remain a harmless companion. I am content. Only I am working hard to set things all right and always so that the machine moves forward when I am off the stage. Death I have conquered long ago when I gave up life. My only anxiety is the work, and even that to the Lord I dedicate, and He knows best.

>Ever yours in the Lord,
>Vivekananda.

CXXIV — SHASHI

To Swami Ramakrishnananda

MATH, BELUR,
(Howrah), March, 1898.

MY DEAR SHASHI,

I forgot to write you about two things. 1. That Tulsi ought to learn shorthand from Goodwin, at least the beginning. 2. I had to write a letter almost every mail to Madras while I was out of India. I have in vain written for a copy of those letters. Send me all those letters. I want to write out my travels. Do not fail, and I shall send them back as soon as they have been used up. The Dawn can manage with 200 subscribers to come out regularly on Rs. 40/- an issue expenditure. This is a great fact to know. The P.B. (Prabuddha Bhârata) seems to be very disorganised; try best to organise it. Poor Alasinga, I am sorry for him. Only thing I can do is to make him entirely free for a year so that he may devote all his energy to the Brahmavadin work. Tell him not to worry; I have him always in mind, poor child; his devotion I can never repay.

I am thinking of going to Kashmir again with Mrs. Bull and Miss MacLeod. (I) return to Calcutta and start for America from here.

Miss Noble is really an acquisition. She will soon surpass Mrs. Besant as a speaker, I am sure.

Do look after Alasinga. I have an idea that he is breaking himself with work. Tell him, the best work is only done by alternate repose and work. Give him all my love. We had two public lectures in Calcutta, one from Miss Noble and the other from our Sharat. Both of them did very well indeed; there was great enthusiasm, which shows that the Calcutta public has not forgotten us. Some of the members of the Math had a touch of influenza. They are all right now. The thing is working nicely. Shri (Holy) Mother is here, and the European and American ladies went the other day to see her, and what do you think, Mother ate with them even there! Is not that grand? The Lord is watching over us; there is no fear; do not lose your nerves, keep your health and take things easy. It is always good to give a few strong strokes and rest on your oars. Rakhal is living with the new land and buildings. I was not satisfied with the Mahotsava this year. What it should be is a grand mixture of all the different phases here. We shall try it next year — I shall send instructions. With love to all of you there and blessings.

Vivekananda.

CXXV — JOE JOE

To Miss Josephine MacLeod

DARJEELING,
18th April, 1898.

MY DEAR JOE JOE,

I was down with fever brought upon, perhaps, by excessive mountain climbing and the bad health in the station.

I am better today and intend leaving this in a day or two. In spite of the great heat there, I used to sleep well in Calcutta and had some appetite. Here both have vanished — this is all the gain.

I could not see Miss Müller yet on the subject of Marguerite; but I intend to write her today. She is making all arrangements to receive her here. Mr. Gupta is also invited to teach them Bengali. She may now do something about her. I shall, however, write.

It will be easy for Marguerite to see Kashmir any time during her stay; but if Miss M. is not willing, there will be a big row again to injure both her and Marguerite.

I am not sure whether I go to Almora again. Much riding it seems is sure to bring on a relapse. I will wait for you at Simla — whilst you pay your visit to the Seviers. We will think on it when I am in. I am so glad to learn that Miss Noble delivered an address at the R.K. Mission. With all love to the Trinity,

Ever yours in the Lord,
Vivekananda.

CXXVI — RAKHAL

Translated from Bengali

To Swami Brahmananda

DARJEELING,
23rd April, 1898.

MY DEAR RAKHAL,

My health was excellent on my return from Sandukphu (11,924 ft.) and other places; but after returning to Darjeeling, I had first an attack of fever, and after recovering from that, I am now suffering from cough and cold. I try to escape from this place every day; but they have been constantly putting it off for a long time. However, tomorrow, Sunday, I am leaving; after halting at Kharsana for a day I start again for Calcutta on Monday. I shall send you a wire after starting. We should hold an annual meeting of the Ramakrishna Mission, and also one for the Math. In both the meetings the accounts of famine relief must be submitted, and the report of the famine relief must be published. Keep all this ready.

Nityagopal says, managing an English magazine will not cost much. So let us first get this one out, and we shall see to the Bengali magazine afterwards. All these points will have to be discussed. Is Yogen willing to shoulder the responsibility of running the paper? Shashi writes that if Sharat goes some time to Madras, they may make a lecture tour jointly. Oh, how hot it is now! Ask Sharat if G. G., Sarada, Shashi Babu, and others have got their articles ready. Give my love and blessing to Mrs. Bull, Miss MacLeod, and Nivedita.

Yours affectionately,
Vivekananda.

CXXVII — JOE JOE

To Miss Josephine MacLeod

DARJEELING,
29th April, 1898.

MY DEAR JOE JOE,

I have had several attacks of fever, the last being influenza.

It has left me now, only I am very weak yet. As soon as I gather strength enough to undertake the journey, I come down to Calcutta.

On Sunday I leave Darjeeling, probably stopping for a day or two at Kurseong, then direct to Calcutta. Calcutta must be very hot just now. Never mind, it is all the better for influenza. In case the plague breaks out in Calcutta, I must not go anywhere; and you start for Kashmir with Sadananda. How did you like the old gentleman, Devendra Nath Tagore? Not as stylish as "Hans Baba" with Moon God and Sun God of course. What enlightens your insides on a dark night when the Fire God, Sun God, Moon God, and Star Goddesses have gone to sleep? It is hunger that keeps my consciousness up, I have discovered. Oh, the great doctrine of correspondence of light! Think how dark the world has been all these ages without it! And all this knowledge and love and work and all the Buddhas and Krishnas and Christs — vain, vain have been their lives and work, for they did not discover that "which keeps the inner light when the Sun and Moon were gone to the limbo" for the night! Delicious, isn't it?

If the plague comes to my native city, I am determined to make myself a sacrifice; and that I am sure is a "Darn sight, better way to Nirvâna" than pouring oblations to all that ever twinkled.

I have had a good deal of correspondence with Madras with the result that I need not send them any help just now. On the other hand I am going to start a paper in Calcutta. I will be ever so much obliged if you help me starting that. As always with undying love,

Ever yours in the Lord,
Vivekananda.

CXXVIII — RAKHAL

Translated from Bengali

To Swami Brahmananda

ALMORA,
20th May, 1898.

MY DEAR RAKHAL,

I have got all the news from your letter and have replied to your wire already. Niranjan and Govindalal Shah will wait at Kathgodam for Yogen-Ma. After I reached Naini Tal, Baburam went from here to Naini Tal on horseback against everybody's advice, and while returning, he also accompanied us on horseback. I was far behind as I was in a Dandi. When I reached the dak bungalow at night, I heard that Baburam had again fallen from the horse and had hurt one of his arms — though he had no fractures. Lest I should rebuke him, he stayed in a private lodging house. Because of his fall, Miss MacLeod gave him her Dandi and herself came on the horse. He did not meet me that night. Next day I was making arrangements for a Dandi for him, when I heard that he had already left on foot. Since then I have not heard of him. I have wired to one or two places, but no news. Perhaps he is putting up at some village. Very well! They are experts in increasing one's worries.

There will be a Dandi for Yogen-Ma; but all the rest will have to go on foot.

My health is much better, but the dyspepsia has not gone, and again insomnia has set in. It will be very helpful if you can soon send some good Ayurvedic medicine for dyspepsia.

Since only one or two sporadic cases of plague have occurred there, there is plenty of accommodation in the Government plague hospital, and there is a talk of having hospitals in every Ward. Taking all this into consideration, do what the situation demands. But remember that something said by somebody in Baghbazar does not constitute public opinion.... Take care that funds do not run short in times of need and that there is no waste of money. For the present buy a plot of ground for Ramlal in the name of Raghuvir (The family deity of Shri Ramakrishna's birthpalce, Kamarpukur, Ramlal being his nephew.) after careful consideration.... Holy Mother will be the Sebâit (worshipper-in-charge); after her will come Ramlal, and Shibu will succeed them as Sebait; or make any other arrangement that seems best. You can, if you think it right, begin the construction of the building even now. For it is not good to live in a new house for the first one or two months, as it will be damp.... The anti-erosion wall can be completed afterwards. I am trying to raise money for the magazine. See that the sum of Rs. 1,200 which I gave for the magazine is kept only for that account.

All the others are well here. Sadananda sprained his foot yesterday. He says he will be all right by the evening. The climate at Almora is excellent at this time. Moreover the bungalow rented by Sevier is the best in Almora. On the opposite side Annie Besant is staying in a small bungalow with Chakravarty. Chakravarty is now the son-in-law of Gagan (of Ghazipur). One day I went to see him. Annie Besant told me entreatingly that there should be friendship between her organisation and mine all over the world, etc., etc. Today Besant will come here for tea. Our ladies are in a small bungalow near by and are quite happy. Only Miss MacLeod is a little unwell today. Harry Sevier is becoming more and more a Sadhu as the days pass by.... Brother Hari sends you his greetings and Sadananda, Ajoy, and Suren send you their respectful salutations. My love to you and all the others.

Yours affectionately,
Vivekananda.

PS. Give my love to Sushil and Kanai and all the others.

CXXIX — STURDY

To Mr. E. T. Sturdy

KASHMIR,
3rd July, 1898.

DEAR STURDY,

Both the editions had my assent, as it was arranged between us that we would not object to anybody's publishing my books. Mrs. Bull knows about it all and is writing to you.

I had a beautiful letter from Miss Souter the other day. She is as friendly as ever.

With love to the children, Mrs. Sturdy, and yourself

Ever yours in the Lord,
Vivekananda.

CXXX — RAKHAL

Translated from Bengali

To Swami Brahmananda

SRINAGAR,
17th July, 1898.

MY DEAR RAKHAL,

I got all the news from your letter. . . . My opinion regarding what you have written about Sarada is only that it is difficult to make a magazine in Bengali paying; but if all of you together canvass subscribers from door to door, it may be possible. In this matter do as you all decide. Poor Sarada has already been disappointed once. What harm is there if we lose a thousand rupees by supporting such an unselfish and very hardworking person? What about the printing of Raja-Yoga? As a last resort, you may give it to Upen on certain terms of sharing the profit in the sales. . . . About money matters, the advice given previously is final. Henceforward do what you consider best regarding expenditure and other things. I see very well that my policy is wrong, and yours is correct, regarding helping others; that is to say, if you help with money too much at a time, people instead of feeling grateful remark on the contrary that hey have got a simpleton to bank upon. I always lost sight of the demoralising influence of charity on the receiver. Secondly, we have no right to deviate even slightly from the purposes for which we collect the donations. Mrs. Bull will get her rosary all right if you send it care of Chief Justice Rishibar Mukhopadhyaya, Kashmir. Mr. Mitra and the Chief Justice are taking every care of them. We could not get a plot of ground in Kashmir yet, but there is a chance that we shall do so soon. If you can spend a winter here, you are sure to recoup your health. If the house is a good one and if you have enough fuel and warm clothing, then life in a land of snow is nothing but enjoyable. Also for stomach troubles a cold climate is an unfailing remedy. Bring Yogen with you; for the earth here is not stony, it is clay like that of Bengal.

If the paper is brought out in Almora, the work will progress much; for poor Sevier will have something to do, and the local people also will get some work. Skilful management lies in giving every man work after his own heart. By all the means in our power the Nivedita Girls' School in Calcutta should be put on a firm footing. To bring Master Mahashay to Kashmir is still a far cry, for it will be long before a college is established here. But he has written that it is possible to start a college in Calcutta, with him as the principal, at an initial expense of a thousand rupees. I hear that you all also favour this proposal. In this matter do what you all consider best. My health is all right. I have to get up seldom at night, even though I take twice a day rice and potatoes, sugar, or whatever I get. Medicine is useless — it has no action on the system of a Knower of Brahman! Everything will be digested — don't be afraid.

The ladies are doing well, and they send you their greetings. Two letters from Shivananda have come. I have also received a letter from his Australian disciple. I hear that the outbreak of plague in Calcutta has completely subsided.

Yours affectionately,
Vivekananda.

CXXXI — RAKHAL

Translated from Bengali

To Swami Brahmananda

SRINAGAR,
1st August, 1898.

MY DEAR RAKHAL,

You are always under a delusion, and it does not leave you because of the strong influence, good or bad, of other brains. It is this: whenever I write to you about accounts, you feel that I have no confidence in you.... My great anxiety is this: the work has somehow been started, but it should go on and progress even when we are not here; such thoughts worry me day and night. Any amount of theoretical knowledge one may have; but unless one does the thing actually, nothing is learnt. I refer repeatedly to election, accounts, and discussion so that everybody may be prepared to shoulder the work. If one man dies, another — why another only, ten if necessary — should be ready to take it up. Secondly, if a man's interest in a thing is not roused, he will not work whole-heartedly; all should be made to understand that everyone has a share in the work and property, and a voice in the management. This should be done while there is yet time. Give a responsible position to everyone alternately, but keep a watchful eye so that you can control when necessary; thus only can men be trained for the work. Set up such a machine as will go on automatically, no matter who dies or lives. We Indians suffer from a great defect, viz we cannot make a permanent organisation — and the reason is that we never like to share power with others and never think of what will come after we are gone.

I have already written everything regarding the plague. Mrs. Bull and Miss Müller and others are of opinion that it is not desirable to spend money uselessly when hospitals have been started in every Ward. We lend our services as nurses and the like. Those that pay the piper must command the tune.

The Maharaja of Kashmir has agreed to give us a plot of land. I have also visited the site. Now the matter will be finalised in a few days, if the Lord wills. Right now, before leaving, I hope to build a small house here. I shall leave it in the charge of Justice Mukherjee when departing. Why not come here with somebody else and spend the winter? Your health will improve, and a need, too, will be fulfilled. The money I have set apart for the press will be sufficient for the purpose, but all will be as you decide. This time I shall surely get some money from N.W.P., Rajputana, and other places. Well, give as directed . . . money to a few persons. I am borrowing this amount from the Math and will pay it back to you with interest.

My health is all right in a way. It is good news that the building work has begun. My love to all.

Yours affectionately,
Vivekananda.

CXXXII — MARY

To Miss Mary Hale

SRINAGAR, KASHMIR,
28th August, 1898.

MY DEAR MARY,

I could not make an earlier opportunity of writing you, and knowing that you were in no hurry for a letter, I will not make apologies. You are learning all about Kashmir and ourselves from Miss MacLeod's letter to Mrs. Leggett, I hear — therefore needless going into long rigmaroles about it.

The search for Heinsholdt's Mahatmas in Kashmir will be entirely fruitless; and as the whole thing has first to be established as coming from a creditable source, the attempt will also be a little too early. How are Mother Church and Father Pope and where? How are you ladies, young and old? Going on with the old game with more zest now that one has fallen off the ranks? How is the lady that looks like a certain statue in Florence? (I have forgotten the name) I always bless her arms when I think of the comparison.

I have been away a few days. Now I am going to join the ladies. The party then goes to a nice quiet spot behind a hill, in a forest, through which a murmuring stream flows, to have meditation deep and long under the deodars (trees of God) cross-legged à la Buddha.

This will be for a month or so, when by that time our good work will have spent its powers and we shall fall from this Paradise to earth again; then work out our Karma a few months and then will have to go to hell for bad Karma in China, and our evil deeds will make us sink in bad odours with the world in Canton and other cities. Thence Purgatory in Japan? And regain Paradise once more in the U.S. of America. This is what Pumpkin Swami, brother of the Coomra Swami, foretells (in Bengali Coomra means squash). He is very clever with his hands. In fact his cleverness with his hands has several times brought him into great dangers.

I wished to send you so many nice things, but alas! the thought of the tariff makes my desires vanish "like youth in women and beggars' dreams".

By the by, I am glad now that I am growing grey every day. My head will be a full-blown white lotus by the time you see me next.

Ah! Mary, if you could see Kashmir — only Kashmir; the marvellous lakes full of lotuses and swans (there are no swans but geese — poetic licence) and the big black bee trying to settle on the wind-shaken lotus (I mean the lotus nods him off refusing a kiss — poetry), then you could have a good conscience on your death-bed. As this is earthly paradise and as logic says one bird in the hand is equal to two in the bush, a glimpse of this is wiser, but economically the other better; no trouble, no labour, no expense, a little namby-pamby dolly life and later, that is all.

My letter is becoming a bore . . . so I stop. (It is sheer idleness). Good night.

Ever yours in the Lord,
Vivekananda.

My address always is:
Math, Belur,
Howrah Dist., Bengal, India.

CXXXIII — HARIPADA

Translated from Bengali

To Shri Haripada Mitra

SRINAGAR, KASHMIR,
17th September, 1898.

DEAR HARIPADA,

I got all news from your letter and wire. That you may easily pass your examination in Sindhi is my prayer to the Lord.

Recently my health was very bad, and so I have been delayed, otherwise I had intended to leave for the Punjab this week. The doctor had advised me not to go to the plains at the present time, as it is very hot there. Perhaps I may reach Karachi by about the last week of October. Now I am doing somewhat well. There is nobody else with me now excepting two American friends — ladies. Probably I shall part from them at Lahore. They will wait for me in Calcutta or in Rajputana. I shall probably visit Cutch, Bhuj, Junagad, Bhavnagar, Limbdi, and Baroda and then proceed to Calcutta. My present plan is to go to America via China and Japan in November or December, but it is all in the hands of the Lord. The above-mentioned American friends bear all my expenses, and I shall take from them all my expenses including railway fare up to Karachi. But if it is convenient to you, send me Rs. 50/- by wire C/o Rishibar Mukhopadhyaya, Chief Justice, Kashmir State, Srinagar. It will be a great help to me, for I have incurred much extra expense of late owing to illness, and I feel a little ashamed to have to depend always on my foreign devotees. With best wishes,

Yours affectionately,
Vivekananda.

CXXXIV — HARIPADA

Translated from Bengali

To Shri Haripada Mitra

LAHORE,
16th October, 1898.

MY DEAR HARIPADA,

In Kashmir my health has completely broken down, and I have not witnessed the Durga-Puja for the last nine years; so I am starting for Calcutta. I have for the present given up the plan of going to America. I think I shall have plenty of time to go to Karachi during the winter.

My brother-disciple Saradananda will send Rs. 50/- from Lahore to Karachi. Don't yield to sorrow — everything is in God's hands. Certainly I won't go anywhere this year without meeting all of you. My blessings to all.

Yours affectionately,
Vivekananda.

CXXXV — JOE

To Miss Josephine MacLeod

57 RAM KANTA BOSE STREET,
CALCUTTA,
12th November, 1898.

MY DEAR JOE,

I have invited a few friends to dinner tomorrow, Sunday. . . .

We expect you at tea. Everything will be ready then.

Shri Mother is going this morning to see the new Math. I am also going there. Today at 6 p.m. Nivedita is going to preside. If you feel like it, and Mrs. Bull strong, do come.

Ever yours in the Lord,
Vivekananda.

CXXXVI — MARY

To Miss Mary Hale

MATH, BELUR,
HOWRAH DISTRICT,
16th March, 1899.

MY DEAR MARY,

Thanks to Mrs. Adams; she roused you naughty girls to a letter at last. "Out of sight out of mind" — as true in India as in America. And the other young lady, who just left her love as she flitted by, deserves a ducking I suppose.

Well, I have been in a sort of merry-go-round with my body which has been trying to convince me for months that it too much exists.

However, no fear, with four mental-healing sisters as I have, no sinking just now. Give me a strong pull and a long pull, will you, all together, and then I am up!

Why do you talk so much about me in your one-letter-a-year and so little about the four witches mumbling Mantras over the boiling pot in a corner of Chicago?

Did you come across Max Müller's new book, Ramakrishna: His Life and Sayings?

If you have not, do, and let Mother see it. How is Mother? Growing grey? And Father Pope? Who have been our last visitors from America do you suppose? "Brother, love is a drawing card" and "Misses Meel"; they have been doing splendid in Australia and elsewhere; the same old "fellies", little changed if any. I wish you could come to visit India — that will be some day in the future. By the by, Mary, I heard a few months ago, when I was rather worrying over your long silence, that you were just hooking a "Willy", and so busy with your dances and parties; that explained of course your inability to write. But "Willy" or no "Willy", I must have my money, don't forget. Harriet is discreetly silent since she got her boy; but where is my money, please? Remind her and her husband of it. If she is Woolley, I am greasy Bengali, as the English call us here — Lord, where is my money?

I have got a monastery on the Ganga now, after all, thanks to American and English friends. Tell Mother to look sharp. I am going to deluge your Yankee land with idolatrous missionaries.

Tell Mr. Woolley he got the sister but has not paid the brother yet. Moreover, it was the fat black queerly dressed apparition smoking in the parlour that frightened many a temptation away, and that was one of the causes which secured Harriet to Mr. Woolley; therefore, I want to be paid for my great share in the work etc., etc. Plead strong, will you?

I do so wish I could come over to America with Joe for this summer; but man proposes and who disposes? Not God surely always. Well, let things slide as they will. Here is Abhayananda, Marie Louse you know, and she has been very well received in Bombay and Madras. She will be in Calcutta tomorrow, and we are going to give her a good reception too.

My love to Miss Howe, Mrs. Adams, to Mother Church, and Father Pope and all the rest of my friends across the seven oceans. We believe in seven oceans — one of milk, one of honey, one of curd, one wine, one sugar-cane juice, one salt, one I forget what. To you four sisters I waft my love across the ocean of honey. . . .

Ever sincerely, your brother,
Vivekananda.

PS. Write when you find time between dances.

CXXXVII — STURDY

To Mr. E. T. Sturdy

PORT SAID,
14th July, 1899.

MY DEAR STURDY,

I got your letter all right just now. I have one from M. Nobel of Paris too. Miss Noble has several from America.

M. Nobel writes to me to defer my visit to him at Paris to some other date, from London, as he will have to be away for a long time. As you know sure, I shall not have many friends staying now in London, and Miss MacLeod is so desirous I should come. A stay in England under these circumstances is not advisable. Moreover, I do not have much life left. At least I must go on with that supposition. I mean, if anything has to be done in America, it is high time we bring our scattered influence in America to a head — if not organise regularly. Then I shall be free to return to England in a few months and work with a will till I return to India.

I think you are absolutely wanted to gather up, as it were, the American work. If you can, therefore, you ought to come over with me. Turiyananda is with me. Saradananda's brother is going to Boston. . . . In case you cannot come to America, I ought to go, ought I not?

Yours,
Vivekananda.

CXXXVIII — JOE

To Miss Josephine MacLeod

THE LYMES,
WOODSIDES, WIMBLEDON,
3rd August, 1899.

MY DEAR JOE,

We are in at last. Turiyananda and I have beautiful lodgings here. Saradananda's brother is with Miss Noble and starts Monday next.

I have recovered quite a bit by the voyage. It was brought about by the exercise on the dumb-bells and monsoon storms tumbling the steamer about the waves. Queer, isn't it? Hope it will remain. Where is our Mother, the Worshipful Brahmini cow of India? She is with you in New York, I think.

Sturdy is away, Mrs. Johnson and everybody. Margo is rather worried at that. She cannot come to U.S. till next month. Already I have come to love the sea. The fish Avatâra is on me, I am afraid — good deal of him in me, I am sure, a Bengali.

How is Alberta, . . . the old folks and the rest of them? I had a beautiful letter from dear Mrs. Brer Rabbit; she could not meet us in London; she started before we arrived.

It is nice and warm here; rather too much they say. I have become for the present a Shunyavâdi, a believer in nothingness, or void. No plans, no afterthought, no attempt, for anything, laissez faire to the fullest. Well, Joe, Margo would always take your side on board the steamer, whenever I criticised you or the Divine cow. Poor child, she knows so little! The upshot of the whole is, Joe, that there cannot be any work in London, because you are not here. You seem to be my fate! Grind on, old lady; it is Karma and none can avoid. Say, I look several years younger by this voyage. Only when the heart gives a lurch, I feel my age. What is this osteopathy, anyway? Will they cut off a rib or two to cure me? Not I, no manufacturing of . . . from my ribs, sure. Whatever it be, it will be hard work for him to find my bones. My bones are destined to make corals in the Ganga. Now I am going to study French if you give me a lesson every day; but no grammar business — only I will read and you explain in English. Kindly give my love to Abhedananda, and ask him to get ready for Turiyananda. I will leave with him. Write soon.

With all love etc.,
Vivekananda.

CXXXIX — MARIE

To Miss Marie Halboister

C/O MISS NOBLE,
21A HIGH STREET, WIMBLEDON.
August, 1899.

MY DEAR MARIE,

I am in London again. This time not busy, not hustling about but quietly settled down in a corner — waiting to start for the U.S. America on the first opportunity. My friends are nearly all out of London in the country and elsewhere, and my health not sufficiently strong.

So you are happy in the midst of your lakes and gardens and seclusion in Canada. I am glad, so glad to know that you are up again on top of the tide. May you remain there for ever!

You could not finish the Raja-Yoga translation yet — all right, there is no hurry. Time and opportunity must come if it is to be done you know, otherwise we vainly strive.

Canada must be beautiful now, with its short but vigorous summer, and very healthy.

I expect to be in New York in a few weeks, and don't know what next. I hope to come back to England next spring.

I fervently wish no misery ever came near anyone; yet it is that alone that gives us an insight into the depths of our lives, does it not?

In our moments of anguish, gates barred for ever seem to open and let in many a flood of light.

We learn as we grow. Alas! we cannot use our knowledge here. The moment we seem to learn, we are hurried off the stage. And this is Mâyâ!

This toy world would not be here, this play could not go on, if we were knowing players. We must play blindfolded. Some of us have taken the part of the rogue of the play, some heroic — never mind, it is all play. This is the only consolation. There are demons and lions and tigers and what not on the stage, but they are all muzzled. They snap but cannot bite. The world cannot touch our souls. If you want, even if the body be torn and bleeding, you may enjoy the greatest peace in your mind.

And the way to that is to attain hopelessness. Do you know that? Not the imbecile attitude of despair, but the contempt of the conqueror for things he has attained, for things he struggled for and then throws aside as beneath his worth.

This hopelessness, desirelessness, aimlessness, is just the harmony with nature. In nature there is no harmony, no reason, no sequence; it was chaos before, it is so still.

The lowest man is in consonance with nature in his earthy-headedness; the highest the same in the fullness of knowledge. All three aimless, drifting, hopeless — all three happy.

You want a chatty letter, don't you? I have not much to chat about. Mr. Sturdy came last two days. He goes home in Wales tomorrow.

I have to book my passage for N.Y. in a day or two.

None of my old friends have I seen yet except Miss Souter and Max Gysic, who are in London. They have been very kind, as they always were.

I have no news to give you, as I know nothing of London yet. I don't know where Gertrude Orchard is, else would have written to her. Miss Kate Steel is also away. She is coming on Thursday or Saturday.

I had an invitation to stay in Paris with a friend, a very well-educated Frenchman, but I could not go this time. I hope another time to live with him some days.

I expect to see some of our old friends and say good day to them.

I hope to see you in America sure. Either I may unexpectedly turn up in Ottawa in my peregrinations or you come to N.Y.

Good-bye, all luck be yours.

Ever yours in the Lord,
Vivekananda.

CXL — RAKHAL

Translated from Bengali

To Swami Brahmananda

LONDON,
10th August, 1899.

MY DEAR RAKHAL,

I got a lot of news from your letter. My health was much better on the ship, but, after landing, owing to flatulence it is rather bad now. . . . There is a lot of difficulty here — all friends have gone out of town for the summer. In addition my health is not so good, and there is a lot of inconvenience regarding food etc. So in a few days I leave for America. Send an account to Mrs. Bull as to how much was spent on purchase of land, how much on buildings, how much on maintenance etc.

Sarada writes that the magazine is not going well. . . . Let him publish the account of my travels, and thoroughly advertise it beforehand — he will have subscribers rushing in. Do people like a magazine if three-fourths of it are filled with pious stuff? Anyway pay special attention to the magazine. Mentally take it as though I were not. Act independently on this basis. "We depend on the elder brother for money, learning, everything" — such an attitude is the road to ruin. If all the money even for the magazine is to be collected by me and all the articles too are from my pen — what will you all do? What are our Sahibs then doing? I have finished my part. You do what remains to be done. Nobody is there to collect a single penny, nobody to do any preaching, none has brains enough to take proper care of his own affairs, none has the capacity to write one line, and all are saints for nothing! . . . If this be your condition, then for six months give everything into the hands of the boys — magazine, money, preaching work, etc. If they are also not able to do anything, then sell off everything, and returning the proceeds to the donors go about as mendicants. I get no news at all from the Math. What is Sharat doing? I want to see work done. Before dying, I want to see that what I have established as a result of my lifelong struggle is put in a more or less running condition. Consult the Committee in every detail regarding money matters. Get the signatures of the Committee for every item of expenditure. Otherwise you also will be in for a bad name. This much is customary that people want some time or other an account of their donations. It is very wrong not to have it ready at every turn. . . . By such lethargy in the beginning, people finally become cheats. Make a committee of all those who are in the Math, and no expenditure will be made which is not countersigned by them — none at all! I want work, I want vigour — no matter who lives or dies. What are death and life to a Sannyasin?

If Sharat cannot rouse up Calcutta, . . . if you are not able to construct the embankment this year, then you will see the fun! I want work — no humbug about it. My respectful salutations to Holy Mother.

Yours affectionately,
Vivekananda.

CXLI — MOTHER

To Mrs. Ole Bull

RIDGELY MANOR,
4th September, 1899.

MY DEAR MOTHER,

It is an awful spell of the bad turn of fortune with me last six months. Misfortune follows me ever wherever I go. In England, Sturdy seems to have got disgusted with the work; he does not see any asceticism in us from India. Here no sooner I reach than Olea gets a bad attack.

Shall I run up to you? I know I cannot be of much help, but I will try my best in being useful.

I hope everything will soon come right with you, and Olea will be restored to perfect health even before this reaches you. Mother knows best; that is all about me.

Ever yours affectionately,
Vivekananda.

CXLII — STURDY

To Mr. E. T. Sturdy

RIDGELY MANOR,
14th September, 1899.

MY DEAR STURDY,

I have simply been taking rest at the Leggetts' and doing nothing. Abhedananda is here. He has been working hard.

He goes in a day or two to resume his work in different places for a month. After that he comes to New York to work.

I am trying to do something in the line you suggested, but don't know how far an account of the Hindus will be appreciated by the Western public when it comes from a Hindu. . . .

Mrs. Johnson is of opinion that no spiritual person ought to be ill. It also seems to her now that my smoking is sinful etc., etc. That was Miss Müller's reason for leaving me, my illness. They may be perfectly right, for aught I know — and you too — but I am what I am. In India, the same defects plus eating with Europeans have been taken exception to by many. I was driven out of a private temple by the owners for eating with Europeans. I wish I were malleable enough to be moulded into whatever one desired, but unfortunately I never saw a man who could satisfy everyone. Nor can anyone who has to go to different places possibly satisfy all.

When I first came to America, they ill-treated me if I had not trousers on. Next I was forced to wear cuffs and collars, else they would not touch me etc., etc. They thought me awfully funny if I did not eat what they offered etc., etc. . . .

In India the moment I landed they made me shave my head and wear "Kaupin" (loin cloth), with the result that I got diabetes etc. Saradananda never gave up his underwear — this saved his life, with just a touch of rheumatism and much comment from our people.

Of course, it is my Karma, and I am glad that it is so. For, though it smarts for the time, it is another great experience of life, which will be useful, either in this or in the next. . . .

As for me, I am always in the midst of ebbs and flows. I knew it always and preached always that every bit of pleasure will bring its quota of pain, if not with compound interest. I have a good deal of love given to me by the world; I deserve a good deal of hatred therefore. I am glad it is so — as it proves my theory of "every wave having its corresponding dip" on my own person.

As for me, I stick to my nature and principle —

once a friend, always a friend — also the true Indian principle of looking subjectively for the cause of the objective.

I am sure that the fault is mine, and mine only, for every wave of dislike and hatred that I get. It could not be otherwise. Thanking you and Mrs. Johnson for thus calling me once more to the internal,

> I remain as ever with love and blessings,
> Vivekananda.

CXLIII — MARY

To Miss Mary Hale

RIDGELY MANOR,
September 1899.

MY DEAR MARY,

Yes, I have arrived. I had a letter from Isabelle from Greenacre. I hope to see her soon and Harriet. Harriet Woolley has been uniformly silent. Never mind, I will bide my time, and as soon as Mr. Woolley becomes a millionaire, demand my money. You did not write any particulars about Mother Church and Father Pope, only the news of something about me in some newspapers. I have long ceased to take any interest in papers; only they keep me before the public and get a sale of my books "anyway" as you say. Do you know what I am trying to do now? Writing a book on India and her people — a short chatty simple something. Again I am going to learn French. If I fail to do it this year, I cannot "do" the Paris Exposition next year properly. Well, I expect to learn much French here where even the servants talk it.

You never saw Mrs. Leggett, did you? She is simply grand. I am going to Paris next year as their guest, as I did the first time.

I have now got a monastery on the Ganga for the teaching of philosophy and comparative religion and a centre of work.

What have you been doing all this time? Reading? Writing? You did not do anything. You could have written lots by this time. Even if you had taught me French, I would be quite a Froggy now, and you did not, only made me talk nonsense. You never went to Greenacre. I hope it is getting strength every year.

Say, you 24 feet and 600 lbs. of Christian Science, you could not pull me up with your treatments. I am losing much faith in your healing powers. Where is Sam? "Bewaring" all this time as he could; bless his heart, such a noble boy!

I was growing grey fast, but somehow it got checked. I am sorry, only a few grey hairs now; a research will unearth many though. I like it and am going to cultivate a long white goaty. Mother Church and Father Pope were having a fine time on the continent. I saw a bit on my way home. And you have been Cinderella-ing in Chicago — good for you. Persuade the old folks to go to Paris next year and take you along. There must be wonderful sights to see; the French are making a last great struggle, they say, before closing business.

Well, you did not write me long, long. You do not deserve this letter, but — I am so good you know, especially as death is drawing near — I do not want to quarrel with anyone. I am dying to see Isabelle and Harriet. I hope they have got a great supply of healing power at Greenacre Inn and will help me out of my present fall. In my days the Inn was well stored with spiritual food, and less of material stuff. Do you know anything of osteopathy? Here is one in New York working wonders really.

I am going to have my bones searched by him in a week. Where is Miss Howe? She is such a noble soul, such a friend. By the by, Mary, it is curious your family, Mother Church and her clergy, both monastic and secular, have made more impression on me than any family I know of. Lord bless you ever and ever.

I am taking rest now, and the Leggetts are so kind. I feel perfectly at home. I intend to go to New York to see the Dewy procession. I have not seen my friends there.

Write me all about yourselves. I so long to hear. You know Joe Joe of course. I marred their visit to India with my constant break-downs, and they were so good, so forgiving. For years Mrs. Bull and she have been my guardian angels. Mrs. Bull is expected here next week.

She would have been here before this, but her daughter (Olea) had a spell of illness. She suffered much, but is now out of danger. Mrs. Bull has taken one of Leggett's cottages here, and if the cold weather does not set in faster than usual, we are going to have a delightful month here even now. The place is so beautiful — well wooded and perfect lawns.

I tried to play golf the other day; I do not think it difficult at all — only it requires good practice. You never went to Philadelphia to visit your golfing friends? What are your plans? What do you intend to do the rest of your life? Have you thought out any work? Write me a long letter, will you? I saw a lady in the streets of Naples as I was passing, going along with three others, must be Americans, so like you that I was almost going to speak to her; when I came near I saw my mistake. Good-bye for the present. Write sharp. . . .

Ever your affectionate brother,
Vivekananda.

CXLIV — MARY

To Miss Mary Hale
RIDGELY MANOR,
3rd October, 1899.

MY DEAR MARY,

Thanks for your very kind words. I am much better now and growing so every day. Mrs. Bull and her daughter are expected today or tomorrow. We hope thus to have another spell of good time — you are having yours all the time, of course. I am glad you are going to Philadelphia, but not so much now as then — when the millionaire was on the horizon. With all love,

Ever your affectionate brother,
Vivekananda.

CXLV — OPTIMIST

To Miss Mary Hale
RIDGELY MANOR,
30th October, 1899.

MY DEAR OPTIMIST,

I received your letter and am thankful that something has come to force optimistic laissez faire into action. Your questions have tapped the very source of pessimism, however. British rule in modern India has only one redeeming feature, though unconscious; it has brought India out once more on the stage of the world; it has forced upon it the contact of the outside world. If it had been done with an eye to the good of the people concerned, as circumstances favoured Japan with, the results could have been more wonderful for India. No good can be done when the main idea is blood-sucking. On the whole the old regime was better for the people, as it did not take away everything they had, and there was some justice, some liberty.

A few hundred, modernised, half-educated, and denationalised men are all the show of modern English India — nothing else. The Hindus were 600 million in number according to Ferishta, the Mohammedan historian, in the 12th century — now less than 200 million.

In spite of the centuries of anarchy that reigned during the struggles of the English to conquer, the terrible massacre the English perpetrated in 1857 and 1858, and the still more terrible famines that have become the inevitable consequence of British rule (there never is a famine in a native state) and that take off millions, there has been a good increase of population, but not yet what it was when the country was entirely independent — that is, before the Mohammedan rule. Indian labour and produce can support five times as many people as there are now in India with comfort, if the whole thing is not taken off from them.

This is the state of things — even education will no more be permitted to spread; freedom of the press stopped already, (of course we have been disarmed long ago), the bit of self-government granted to them for some years is being quickly taken off. We are watching what next! For writing a few words of innocent criticism, men are being hurried to transportation for life, others imprisoned without any trial; and nobody knows when his head will be off.

There has been a reign of terror in India for some years. English soldiers are killing our men and outraging our women — only to be sent home with passage and pension at our expense. We are in a terrible gloom — where is the Lord? Mary, you can afford to be optimistic, can I? Suppose you simply publish this letter — the law just passed in India will allow the English Government in India to drag me from here to India and kill me without trial. And I know all your Christian governments will only rejoice, because we are heathens. Shall I also go to sleep and become optimistic? Nero was the greatest optimistic person! They don't think it worth while to write these terrible things as news items even! If necessary, the news agent of Reuter gives the exactly opposite news fabricated to order! Heathen-murdering is only a legitimate pastime for the Christians! Your missionaries go to preach God and dare not speak a word of truth for fear of the English, who will kick them out the next day.

All property and lands granted by the previous governments for supporting education have been swallowed up, and the present Government spends even less than Russia in education. And what education?

The least show of originality is throttled. Mary, it is hopeless with us, unless there really is a God who is the father of all, who is not afraid of the strong to protect the weak, and who is not bribed by wealth. Is there such a God? Time will show.

Well, I think I am coming to Chicago in a few weeks and talk of things fully! Don't quote your authority.

With all love, ever your brother,
Vivekananda.

PS. As for religious sects — the Brahmo Samaj, the Arya Samaj, and other sects have been useless mixtures; they were only voices of apology to our English masters to allow us to live! We have started a new India — a growth — waiting to see what comes. We believe in new ideas only when the nation wants them, and what will be true for us. The test of truth for this Brahmo Samaj is "what our masters approve"; with us, what the Indian reasoning and experience approves. The struggle has begun — not between the Brahmo Samaj and us, for they are gone already, but a harder, deeper, and more terrible one.

CXLVI — STURDY

To Mr. E. T. Sturdy

C/O F. LEGGETT ESQ.,
RIDGELY MANOR,
ULSTER COUNTY, N.Y.

MY DEAR STURDY,

Your last letter reached me after knocking about a little through insufficient address.

It is quite probable that very much of your criticism is just and correct. It is also possible that some day you may find that all this springs from your dislike of certain persons, and I was the scapegoat.

There need be no bitterness, however, on that account, as I don't think I ever posed for anything but what I am. Nor is it ever possible for me to do so, as an hour's contact is enough to make everybody see through my smoking, bad temper, etc. "Every meeting must have a separation" — this is the nature of things. I carry no feeling of disappointment even. I hope you will have no bitterness. It is Karma that brings us together, and Karma separates.

I know how shy you are, and how loath to wound others' feelings. I perfectly understand months of torture in your mind when you have been struggling to work with people who were so different from your ideal. I could not guess it before at all, else I could have saved you a good deal of unnecessary mental trouble. It is Karma again.

The accounts were not submitted before, as the

work is not yet finished; and I thought of submitting to my donor a complete account when the whole thing was finished. The work was begun only last year, as we had to wait for funds a long time, and my method is never to ask but wait for voluntary help.

I follow the same idea in all my work, as I am so conscious of my nature being positively displeasing to many, and wait till somebody wants me. I hold myself ready also to depart at a moment's notice. In the matter of departure thus, I never feel bad about it or think much of it, as, in the constant roving life I lead, I am constantly doing it. Only so sorry, I trouble others without wishing it. Will you kindly send over if there is any mail for me at your address?

May all blessings attend you and yours for ever and ever will be the constant prayer of

Vivekananda.

CXLVII — MRS. BULL

To Mrs. Ole Bull

C/O E. GUERNSEY, M.D.,
THE MADRID, 180 W. 59,
15th November, 1899.

MY DEAR MRS. BULL,

After all I decide to come to Cambridge just now. I must finish the stories I began. The first one I don't think was given back to me by Margo.

My clothes will be ready the day after tomorrow, and then I shall be ready to start; only my fear is, it will be for the whole winter a place for becoming nervous and not for quieting of nerves, with constant parties and lectures. Well, perhaps you can give me a room somewhere, where I can hide myself from all the goings on in the place. Again I am so nervous of going to a place where indirectly the Indian Math will be. The very name of these Math people is enough to frighten me. And they are determined to kill with these letters etc.

Anyhow, I come as soon as I have my clothes —

this week. You need not come to New York for my sake. If you have business of your own, that is another matter. I had a very kind invitation from Mrs. Wheeler of Montclair. Before I start for Boston, I will have a turn-in in Montclair for a few hours at least.

I am much better and am all right; nothing the matter with me except my worry, and now I am sure to throw that all overboard.

Only one thing I want — and I am afraid I cannot get it of you — there should be no communication about me in your letters to India even indirect. I want to hide for a time or for all time. How I curse the day that brought me celebrity!

With all love,
Vivekananda.

CXLVIII — RAKHAL

Translated from Bengali

To Swami Brahmananda

U.S.A.,
20th November, 1899.

MY DEAR RAKHAL,

Got some news from Sharat's letter. . . . Get experience while still there is a chance; I am not concerned whether you win or lose. . . . I have no disease now. Again. . . . I am going to tour from place to place. There is no reason for anxiety, be fearless. Everything will fly away before you; only don't be disobedient, and all success will be yours. . . . Victory to Kâli! Victory to the Mother! Victory to Kali! Wâh Guru, Wah Guru ki Fateh (Victory unto the Guru)!

. . . Really, there is no greater sin than cowardice; cowards are never saved — that is sure. I can stand everything else but not that. Can I have any dealings with one who will not give that up? . . . If one gets one blow, on must return ten with redoubled fury. . . . Then only one is a man. . . . The coward is an object to be pitied.

I bless you all; today, on this day sacred to the Divine Mother, on this night, may the Mother dance in your hearts, and bring infinite strength to your arms. Victory to Kali! Victory to Kali! Mother will certainly come down — and with great strength will bring all victory, world victory. Mother is coming, what dear? Whom to fear? Victory to Kali! At the tread of each one of you the earth will tremble. . . . Victory to Kali! Again onward, forward! Wah Guru! Victory to the Mother! Kali! Kali! Kali! Disease, sorrow, danger, weakness — all these have departed from you all. All victory, all good fortune, all prosperity yours. Fear not! Fear not! The threat of calamity is vanishing, fear not! Victory to Kali! Victory to Kali!

Vivekananda.

PS. I am the servant of the Mother, you are all servants of the Mother — what destruction, what fear is there for us? Don't allow egoism to enter your minds, and let love never depart from your hearts. What destruction can touch you? Fear not. Victory to Kali! Victory to Kali!

CXLIX — MARY

To Miss Mary Hale

1 EAST 39 ST., NEW YORK,
20th November, 1899.

MY DEAR MARY,

I start tomorrow most probably for California. On my way I would stop for a day or two in Chicago. I send a wire to you when I start. Send somebody to the station, as I never was so bad as now in finding my way in and out.

Ever your brother,
Vivekananda.

CL — BRAHMANANDA

To Swami Brahmananda

21 WEST 34 ST.,
NEW YORK,
21st November, 1899.

MY DEAR BRAHMANANDA,

The accounts are all right. I have handed them over to Mrs. Bull who has taken charge of reporting the different parts of the accounts to different donors. Never mind what I have said in previous harsh letters. They would do you good. Firstly, they will make you business-like in the future to keep regular and clear accounts and get the brethren into it. Secondly, if these scolding don't make you brave, I shall have no more hopes of you. I want to see you die even, but you must make a fight. Die in obeying commands like a soldier, and go to Nirvana, but no cowardice.

It is necessary that I must disappear for some time. Let not anyone write me or seek me during that time, it is absolutely necessary for my health. I am only nervous, that is all, nothing more.

All blessings follow you. Never mind my harshness. You know the heart always, whatever the lips say. All blessings on you. For the last year or so I have not been in my senses at all. I do not know why. I had to pass through this hell — and I have. I am much better — well, in fact. Lord help you all. I am going to the Himalayas soon to retire for ever. My work is done.

Ever yours in the Lord,
Vivekananda.

PS. Mrs. Bull sends her love.

CLI — DHIRA MATA

To Mrs. Ole Bull

22nd December, 1899.

MY DEAR DHIRA MATA,

I have a letter from Calcutta today, from which I learn your cheques have arrived; a great many thanks and grateful words also came.

Miss Souter of London sends me a printed New Year's greetings. I think she must have got the accounts you sent her by this time.

Kindly send Saradananda's letters that have come to your care.

As for me, I had a slight relapse of late, for which the healer has rubbed several inches of my skin off.

Just now I am feeling it, the smart. I had a very hopeful note from Margo. I am grinding on in Pasadena; hope some result will come out of my work here. Some people here are very enthusiastic; the Raja-Yoga book did indeed great services on this coast. I am mentally very well; indeed I never really was so calm as of late. The lectures for one thing do not disturb my sleep, that is some gain. I am doing some writing too. The lectures here were taken down by a stenographer, the people here want to print them.

I learn they are well and doing good work at the Math — from Swami Saradananda's letter to Joe. Slowly as usual plans are working; but Mother knows, as I say. May She give me release and find other workers for Her plans. By the by, I have made a discovery as to the mental method of really practising what the Gita teaches, of working without an eye to results. I have seen much light on concentration and attention and control of concentration, which if practised will take us out of all anxiety and worry. It is really the science of bottling up our minds whenever we like. Now what about yourself, poor Dhira Mata! This is the result of motherhood and its penalties; we all think of ourselves, and never of the Mother. How are you? How are things going on with you? What about your daughter? about Mrs. Briggs?

I hope Turiyananda is completely recovered now and working. Poor man, suffering is the lot! Never mind; there is a pleasure in suffering even, when it is for others, is there not? Mrs. Leggett is doing well; so is Joe; I — they say — I too am. May be they are right. I work anyway and want to die in harness; if that be what Mother wants, I am quite content.

Ever your son,
Vivekananda.

CLII — DHIRA MATA

To Mrs. Ole Bull

921 W. 21ST STREET,
LOS ANGELES,
27th December, 1899.

BELOVED DHIRA MATA,

An eventful and happy New Year to you and many such returns!

I am much better in health — able enough to work once more. I have started work already and have sent to Saradananda some money — Rs. 1,300 already — as expenses for the law suit. I shall send more, if they need it. I had a very bad dream this morning and had not any news of Saradananda for three weeks. Poor boys! How hard I am on them at times. Well, they know, in spite of all that, I am their best friend.

Mr. Leggett has got a little over £500 I had with Sturdy on account of Raja-Yoga and the Maharaja of Khetri. I have now about a thousand dollars with Mr. Leggett. If I die, kindly send that money to my mother. I wired to the boys three weeks ago that I was perfectly cured. If I don't get any worse, this much health as I have now will do well enough. Do not worry at all on my account; I am up and working with a will.

I am sorry I could not write any more of the stories. I have written some other things and mean to write something almost every day.

I am very much more peaceful and find that the

only way to keep my peace is to teach others. Work is my only safety valve.

I only want some clear business head to take care of the details as I push onwards and work on. I am afraid it will be a long time to find such in India, and if there are any, they ought to be educated by somebody from the West.

Again, I can only work when thrown completely on my own feet. I am at my best when I am alone. Mother seems to arrange so. Joe believes great things are brewing — in Mother's cup; hope it is so.

Joe and Margot have developed into actual prophets, it seems. I can only say, every blow I had in this life, every pang, will only become joyful sacrifice if Mother becomes propitious to India once more.

Miss Greenstidel writes a beautiful letter to me, about you most of it. She thinks a lot about Turiyananda too. Give Turiyananda my love. I am sure he will work well. He has the pluck and stamina.

I am going soon to work in California; when I leave I shall send for Turiyananda and make him work on the Pacific coast. I am sure here is a great field. The Raja-Yoga book seems to be very well known here. Miss Greenstidel had found great peace under your roof and is very happy. I am so glad it is so. May things go a little better with her every day. She has a good business head and practical sense.

Joe has unearthed a magnetic healing woman. We are both under her treatment. Joe thinks she is pulling me up splendidly. On her has been worked a miracle, she claims. Whether it is magnetic healing, California ozone, or the end of the present spell of bad Karma, I am improving. It is a great thing to be able to walk three miles, even after a heavy dinner.

All love and blessings to Olea. My love to Dr. Janes and other Boston friends.

Ever your son,
Vivekananda.

CLIII — MARY

To Miss Mary Hale

C/O MRS. BLODGETT,
921, WEST 21ST ST.,
LOS ANGELES,
27th December, 1899.

MY DEAR MARY,

Merry Christmas and Happy New Year and many, many glorious returns of such for your birthday. All these wishes, prayers, greetings in one breath. I am cured, you will be glad to know. It was only indigestion and no heart or kidney affection, quoth the healers; nothing more. And I am walking three miles a day — after a heavy dinner.

Say — the person healing me insisted on my smoking! So I am having my pipe nicely and am all the better for it. In plain English the nervousness etc. was all due to dyspepsia and nothing more.

. . . I am at work too; working, working, not hard; but I don't care, and I want to make money this time. Tell this to Margot, especially the pipe business. You know who is healing me? No physician, no Christian Science healer, but a magnetic healing woman who skins me every time she treats me. Wonders — she performs operations by rubbing — internal operations too, her patients tell me.

It is getting late in the night. I have to give up writing separate letters to Margot, Harriet, Isabelle, and Mother Church. Wish is half the work. They all know how I love them dearly, passionately; so you become the medium for my spirit for the time, and carry them my New Year's messages.

It is exactly like Northern Indian winter here, only some days a little warmer; the roses are here and the beautiful palms. Barley is in the fields, roses and many other flowers round about the cottage where I live. Mrs. Blodgett, my host, is a Chicago lady — fat, old, and extremely witty. She heard me in Chicago and is very motherly.

I am so sorry, the English have caught a Tartar in South Africa. A soldier on duty outside a camp bawled out that he had caught a Tartar. "Bring him in", was the order from inside the tent. "He will not come", replied the sentry. "Then you come yourself", rang the order again. "He will not let me come either". Hence the phrase "to catch a Tartar". Don't you catch any.

I am happy just now and hope to remain so for all the rest of my life. Just now I am Christian Science — no evil, and "love is a drawing card".

I shall be very happy if I can make a lot of money. I am making some. Tell Margot, I am going to make a lot of money and go home by way of Japan, Honolulu, China, and Java. This is a nice place to make money quick in; and San Francisco is better, I hear. Has she made any?

You could not get the millionaire. Why don't you start for half or one-fourth million? Something is better than nothing. We want money; he may go into Lake Michigan, we have not the least objection. We had a bit of an earthquake here the other day. I hope it has gone to Chicago and raised Isabelle's mud-puddle up. It is getting late. I am yawning, so here I quit.

Good-bye; all blessings, all love,
Vivekananda.

CLIV — DHIRA MATA

To Mrs. Ole Bull

17th January, 1900.

MY DEAR DHIRA MATA,

I received yours with the enclosures for Saradananda; and there was some good news. I hope to get some more news this week. You did not write anything about your plans. I had a letter from Miss Greenstidel expressing her deep gratitude for your kindness — and who does not? Turiyananda is getting well by this time, I hope.

I have been able to remit Rs. 2,000 to Saradananda, with the help of Miss MacLeod and Mrs. Leggett. Of course they contributed the best part. The rest was got by lectures. I do not expect anything much here or anywhere by lecturing. I can scarcely make expenses. No, not even that; whenever it comes to paying, the people are nowhere. The field of lecturing in this country has been overworked; the people have outgrown that.

I am decidedly better in health. The healer thinks I am now at liberty to go anywhere I choose, the process will go on, and I shall completely recover in a few months. She insists on this, that I am cured already; only nature will have to work out the rest.

Well, I came here principally for health. I have got it; in addition I got Rs. 2,000, to defray the law expenses. Good.

Now it occurs to me that my mission from the platform is finished, and I need not break my health again by that sort of work.

It is becoming clearer to me that I lay down all the concerns of the Math and for a time go back to my mother. She has suffered much through me. I must try to smooth her last days. Do you know, this was just exactly what the great Shankarâchârya himself had to do! He had to go back to his mother in the last few days of her life! I accept it, I am resigned. I am calmer than ever. The only difficulty is the financial part. Well, the Indian people owe something. I will try Madras and a few other friends in India. Anyhow, I must try, as I have forebodings that my mother has not very many years to live. Then again, this is coming to me as the greatest of all sacrifices to make, the sacrifice of ambition, of leadership, of fame. I am resigned and must do the penance. The one thousand dollars with Mr. Leggett and if a little more is collected, will be enough to fall back upon in case of need. Will you send me back to India? I am ready any time. Don't go to France without seeing me. I have become practical at least compared to the visionary dreams of Joe and Margot. Let them work their dreams out for me — they are not more than dreams. I want to make out a trust-deed of the Math in the names of Saradananda, Brahmananda, and yourself. I will do it as soon as I get the papers from Saradananda. Then I am quits. I want rest, a meal, a few books, and I want to do some scholarly work. Mother shows this light vividly now. Of course you were the one to whom She showed it first. I would not believe it then. But then, it is now shown that — leaving my mother was a great renunciation in 1884 — it is a greater renunciation to go back to my mother now. Probably Mother wants me to undergo the same that She made the great Âchârya undergo in old days. Is it? I am surer of your guidance than of my own. Joe and Margot are great souls, but to you Mother is now sending the light for my guidance. Do you see light? What do you advise? At least do not go out of this country without sending me home.

I am but a child; what work have I to do? My powers I passed over to you. I see it. I cannot any more tell from the platform. Don't tell it to anyone — not even to Joe. I am glad. I want rest; not that I am tired, but the next phase will be the miraculous touch and not the tongue — like Ramakrishna's. The word has gone to you and the voice to Margo. No more it is in me. I am glad. I am resigned. Only get me out to India, won't you? Mother will make you do it. I am sure.

Ever your son,
Vivekananda.

CLV — DHIRA MATA

To Mrs. Ole Bull

LOS ANGELES,
15th February, 1900.

DEAR DHIRA MATA,

Before this reaches you, I am off to San Francisco. You already know all about the work. I have not done much work, but my heart is growing stronger every day, physically and mentally. Some days I feel I can bear everything and suffer everything. There was nothing of note inside the bundle of papers sent by Miss Müller. I did not write her, not knowing her address. Then again, I am afraid.

I can always work better alone, and am physically and mentally best when entirely alone! I scarcely had a day's illness during my eight years of lone life away from my brethren. Now I am again getting up, being alone. Strange, but that is what Mother wants me to be. "Wandering alone like the rhinoceros", as Joe likes it. I think the conferences are ended. Poor Turiyananda suffered so much and never let me know; he is so strong and good. Poor Niranjan, I learn from Mrs. Sevier, is so seriously ill in Calcutta that I don't know whether he has passed away or not. Well, good and evil both love company; queer, they come in strings. I had a letter from my cousin telling me her daughter (the adopted little child) was dead. Suffering seems to be the lot of India! Good. I am getting rather callous, rather stilted, of late. Good. Mother knows. I am so ashamed of myself — of this display of weakness for the last two years! Glad it is ended.

Ever your loving son,
Vivekananda.

CLVI — MARY

To Miss Mary Hale

PASADENA,
20th February, 1900.

MY DEAR MARY,

Your letter bearing the sad news of Mr. Hale's passing away reached me yesterday. I am sorry, because in spite of monastic training, the heart lives on; and then Mr. Hale was one of the best souls I met in life. Of course you are sorry, miserable, and so are Mother Church and Harriet and the rest, especially as this is the first grief of its kind you have met, is it not? I have lost many, suffered much, and the most curious cause of suffering when somebody goes off is the feeling that I was not good enough to that person. When my father died, it was a pang for months, and I had been so disobedient. You have been very dutiful; if you feel anything like that, it is only a form of sorrow.

Just now I am afraid life begins for you, Mary,

in earnest. We may read books, hear lectures, and talk miles, but experience is the one teacher, the one eye-opener. It is best as it is. We learn, through smiles and tears we learn. We don't know why, but we see it is so; and that is enough. Of course Mother Church has the solace of her religion. I wish we could all dream undisturbed good dreams.

You have had shelter all your life. I was in the glare, burning and panting all the time. Now for a moment you have caught a glimpse of the other side. My life is made up of continuous blows like that, and hundred times worse, because of poverty, treachery, and my own foolishness! Pessimism! You will understand it, how it comes. Well, well, what shall I say to you, Mary? You know all the talks; only I say this and it is true — if it were possible to exchange grief, and had I a cheerful mind, I would exchange mine for your grief ever and always. Mother knows best.

Your ever faithful brother,
Vivekananda.

CLVII — MARY

To Miss Mary Hale

1251 PINE STREET,
SAN FRANCISCO,
2nd March, 1900.

DEAR MARY,

Very kind of you to write to invite me to Chicago. I wish I could be there this minute. But I am busy making money; only I do not make much. Well, I have to make enough to pay my passage home at any rate. Here is a new field, where I find ready listeners by hundreds, prepared beforehand by my books.

Of course money making is slow and tedious. If I could make a few hundreds, I would be only too glad. By this time you must have received my previous note. I am coming eastward in a month or six weeks, I hope.

How are you all? Give Mother my heartfelt love. I wish I had her strength, she is a true Christian. My health is much better, but the old strength is not there yet. I hope it will come some day, but then, one had to work so hard to do the least little thing. I wish I had rest and peace for a few days at least, which I am sure I can get with the sisters at Chicago. Well, Mother knows best, as I say always. She knows best. The last two years have been specially bad. I have been living in mental hell. It is partially lifted now, and I hope for better days, better states. All blessings on you and the sisters and Mother. Mary, you have been always the sweetest notes in my jarring and clashing life. Then you had the great good Karma to start without oppressive surroundings. I never know a moment's peaceful life. It has always been high pressure, mentally. Lord bless you.

Ever your loving brother,
Vivekananda.

CLVIII — DHIRA MATA

To Mrs. Ole Bull

1502 JONES STREET,
SAN FRANCISCO,
4th March, 1900.

DEAR DHIRA MATA,

I have not had a word from you for a month. I am in Frisco. The people here have been prepared by my writing beforehand, and they come in big crowds. But it remains to be seen how much of that enthusiasm endures when it comes to paying at the door. Rev. Benjamin Fay Mills invited me to Oakland and gave me big crowds to preach to. He and his wife have been reading my works and keeping track of my movements all the time. I sent the letter of introduction from Miss Thursby to Mrs. Hearst. She has invited me to one of her musicals Sunday next.

My health is about the same; don't find much difference; it is improving, perhaps, but very imperceptibly. I can use my voice, however, to make 3,000 people hear me, as I did twice in Oakland, and get good sleep too after two hours of speaking.

I learn Margot is with you. When are you sailing for France? I will leave here in April and go to the East. I am very desirous of getting to England in May if I can. Must not go home before trying England once more.

I have nice letters from Brahmananda and Saradananda; they are all doing well. They are trying to bring the municipality to its senses; I am glad. In this world of Maya one need not injure, but "spread the hood, without striking". That is enough.

Things must get round; if they don't, it is all right. I have a very nice letter from Mrs. Sevier too. They are doing fine in the mountains. How is Mrs. Vaughan? When is your conference to close? How is Turiyananda?

With everlasting love and gratitude.

Your son,
Vivekananda.

CLIX — DHIRA MATA

To Mrs. Ole Bull

1502 JONES STREET,
SAN FRANCISCO,
7th March, 1900.

DEAR DHIRA MATA,

Your letter, enclosing one from Saradananda only and the accounts, came. I am very much reassured by all the news I since received from India. As for the accounts and the disposal of the Rs. 30,000, do just what you please. I have given over the management to you, the Master will show you what is best to do. The money is Rs. 35,000; the Rs. 5,000, for building the cottage on the Ganga, I wrote to Saradananda not to use just now. I have already taken Rs. 5,000 of that money. I am not going to take more. I had paid back Rs. 2,000 or more of that Rs. 5,000 in India. But it seems, Brahmananda, wanting to show as much of the Rs. 35,000 intact as he could, drew upon my Rs. 2,000; so I owe them Rs. 5,000 still on that score.

Anyway, I thought I could make money here in California and pay them up quietly. Now I have entirely failed in California financially. It is worse here than in Los Angeles. They come in crowds when there is a free lecture and very few when there is something to pay.

I have some hopes yet in England. It is necessary for me to reach England in May. There is not the least use in breaking my health in San Francisco for nothing. Moreover, with all Joe's enthusiasm, I have not yet found any real benefit from the magnetic healer, except a few red patches on my chest from scratching! Platform work is nigh gone for me, and forcing it is only hastening the end. I leave here very soon, as soon as I can make money for a passage. I have 300 dollars in hand, made in Los Angeles. I will lecture here next week and then I stop. As for the Math and the money, the sooner I am released of that burden the better.

I am ready to do whatever you advise me to do. You have been a real mother to me. You have taken up one of my great burdens on yourself — I mean my poor cousin. I feel quite satisfied. As for my mother, I am going back to her — for my last days and hers. The thousand dollars I have in New York will bring Rs. 9 a month; then I bought for her a bit of land which will bring about Rs. 6; and her old house — that will bring, say, Rs. 6. I leave the house under litigation out of consideration, as I have not got it. Myself, my mother, my grandmother, and my brother will live on Rs. 20 a month easy. I would start just now, if I could make money for a passage to India, without touching the 1,000 dollars in New York.

Anyhow I will scrape three or four hundred dollars — 400 dollars will be enough for a second class passage and for a few weeks' stay in London. I do not ask you to do anything more for me; I do not want it. What you have done is more, ever so much more than I deserve. I have given my place solemnly to you in Shri Ramakrishna's work. I am out of it.

All my life I have been a torture to my poor mother. Her whole life has been one of continuous misery. If it be possible, my last attempt should be to make her a little happy. I have planned it all out. I have served the Mother all my life. It is done; I refuse now to grind Her axe. Let Her find other workers — I strike.

You have been one friend with whom Shri Ramakrishna has become the goal of life — that is the secret of my trust in you. Others love me personally. But they little dream that what they love me for is Ramakrishna; leaving Him, I am only a mass of foolish selfish emotions. Anyway this stress is terrible, thinking of what may come next, wishing what ought to come next. I am unequal to the responsibility; I am found wanting. I must give up this work. If the work has not life in it, let it die; if it has, it need not wait for poor workers like myself.

Now the money, Rs. 30,000, is in my name, in Government Securities. If they are sold now, we shall lose fearfully, on account of the war; then, how can they be sent over here without being sold there? To sell them there I must sign them. I do not know how all this is going to be straightened out. Do what you think best about it all. In the meanwhile, it is absolutely necessary that I execute a will in your favour for everything, in case I suddenly die. Send me a draft will as soon as possible and I shall register it in San Francisco or Chicago; then my conscience will be safe. I don't know any lawyer here, else I would have got it drawn up; neither have I the money. The will must be done immediately; the trust and things have time enough for them.

Ever your son,
Vivekananda.

CLX — JOE

To Miss Josephine MacLeod

1502 JONES STREET,
SAN FRANCISCO,
7th March, 1900.

DEAR JOE,

I learn from Mrs. Bull's letter that you are in Cambridge.

I also learn from Miss Helen that you did not get the stories sent on to you. I am sorry. Margot has copies she may give you. I am so so in health. No money. Hard work. No result. Worse than Los Angeles.

They come in crowds when the lecture is free — when there is payment, they don't. That's all. I have a relapse — for some days — and am feeling very bad. I think lecturing every night is the cause. I hope to do something in Oakland at least to work out my passage to New York, where I mean to work for my passage to India. I may go to London if I make money here to pay a few months' lodging there.

Will you send me our General's address? Even the name slips from memory now!

Good-bye. May see you in Paris, may not. Lord bless you, you have done for me more than I ever deserve.

With infinite love and gratitude,

Yours,
Vivekananda.

CLXI — RAKHAL

Translated from Bengali

To Swami Brahmananda

SAN FRANCISCO,
12th March, 1900.

MY DEAR RAKHAL,

I got a letter from you some time ago. A letter from Sharat reached me yesterday. I saw a copy of the invitation letters for the birthday anniversary of Gurudeva (Divine Master). I am frightened hearing that Sharat is troubled by rheumatism. Alas, sickness, sorrow, and pain have been my companions for the last two years. Tell Sharat that I am not going to work so hard any more. But he who does not work enough to earn his food will have to starve to death! ... I hope Durgaprasanna has done by this time whatever was necessary for the compound wall.... The raising of a compound wall is not, after all, a difficult thing. If I can, I shall build a small house there and serve my old grandmother and mother. Evil actions leave none scot-free; Mother never spares anybody. I admit my actions have been wrong. Now, brother, all of you are Sâdhus and great saints, kindly pray to the Mother that I do not have to shoulder all this trouble and burden any longer. Now I desire a little peace — it seems there is no more strength left to bear the burden of work and responsibility — rest and peace for the few days that I shall yet live! Victory to the Guru! Victory to the Guru! ... No more lectures or anything of that sort. Peace!

As soon as Sharat sends the trust-deed of the Math, I shall put my signature to it. You all manage — truly I require rest. This disease is called neurasthenia, a disease of the nerves. Once it comes, it continues for some years. But after a complete rest for three or four years it is cured. This country is the home of the disease, and here it has caught me. However, it is not only no fatal disease, but it makes a man live long. Don't be anxious on my account. I shall go on rolling. But there is only this sorrow that the work of Gurudeva is not progressing; there is this regret that I have not been able to accomplish anything of his work. How much I abuse you all and speak harshly! I am the worst of men! Today, on the anniversary of his birthday, put the dust of your feet on my head — and my mind will become steady again. Victory to the Guru! Victory to the Guru! You are my only refuge — you are my only refuge! Now that my mind is steady, let me tell you that this resignation is the permanent attitude of my mind. All other moods that come are, you should know, only disease. Please don't allow me to work at all any longer. Now I shall quietly do Japa and meditation for some time — nothing more. Mother knows all else. Victory to the Mother of the Universe!

Yours affectionately,
Vivekananda.

CLXII — MARY

To Miss Mary Hale

1719 TURK STREET,
SAN FRANCISCO,
12th March, 1900.

DEAR MARY,

How are you? How is Mother, and the sisters? How are things going on in Chicago? I am in Frisco, and shall remain here for a month or so. I start for Chicago early in April. I shall write to you before that of course. How I wish I could be with you for a few days; one gets tired of work so much. My health is so so, but my mind is very peaceful and has been so for some time. I am trying to give up all anxiety unto the Lord. I am only a worker. My mission is to obey and work. He knows the rest.

"Giving up all vexations and paths, do thou take refuge unto Me. I will save you from all dangers" (Gita, XVIII.66).

I am trying hard to realise that. May I be able to do it soon.

Ever your affectionate brother,
Vivekananda.

CLXIII — DHIRA MATA

To Mrs. Ole Bull

1719 TURK STREET,
SAN FRANCISCO,
12th March, 1900.

MY DEAR DHIRA MATA,

Your letter from Cambridge came yesterday. Now I have got a fixed address, 1719 Turk Street, San Francisco. Hope you will have time to pen a few lines in reply to this. I had a manuscript account sent me by you. I sent it back as you desired; besides that, I had no other accounts. It is all right.

I had a nice letter from Miss Souter from London. She expects to have Mr. . . . to dine with her.

So glad to hear of Margot's success. I have given her over to you, and am sure you will take care of her. I will be here a few weeks more and then go East. I am only waiting for the warm season.

I have not been at all successful financially here, but am not in want. Anyway, things will go on as usual with me, I am sure; and if they don't, what then?

I am perfectly resigned. I had a letter from the Math; they had the Utsava yesterday. I do not intend to go by the Pacific. Don't care where I go, and when. Now perfectly resigned; Mother knows; a great change, peacefulness is coming on me. Mother, I know, will see to it. I die a Sannyasin. You have been more than mother to me and mine. All love, all blessings be yours for ever, is the constant prayer of

Vivekananda.

PS. Kindly tell Mrs. Leggett that my address for some weeks now will be, 1719 Turk Street, San Francisco.

CLXIV — MARY

To Miss Mary Hale

1719 TURK STREET,
SAN FRANCISCO,
22nd March, 1900.

MY DEAR MARY,

Many thanks for your kind note. You are correct that I have many other thoughts to think besides Indian people, but they have all to go to the background before the all-absorbing mission — my Master's work.

I would that this sacrifice were pleasant. It is not, and naturally makes one bitter at times; for know, Mary, I am yet a man and cannot wholly forget myself; hope I shall some time. Pray for me.

Of course I am not to be held responsible for Miss MacLeod's or Miss Noble's or anybody else's views regarding myself or anything else, am I? You never found me smart under criticism.

I am glad you are going over to Europe for a long period. Make a long tour, you have been long a house-dove.

As for me, I am tired on the other hand of eternal tramping; that is why I want to go back home and be quiet. I do not want to work any more. My nature is the retirement of a scholar. I never get it! I pray I will get it, now that I am all broken and worked out. Whenever I get a letter from Mrs. Sevier from her Himalayan home, I feel like flying off the Himalayas. I am really sick of this platform work and eternal trudging and seeing new faces and lecturing.

You need not bother about getting up classes in Chicago. I am getting money in Frisco and will soon make enough for my passage home.

How are you and the sisters? I expect to come to Chicago some time towards the first part of April.

Yours,
Vivekananda.

CLXV — MARY

To Miss Mary Hale

1719 TURK STREET,
SAN FRANCISCO,
28th March, 1900.

WELL BLESSED MARY,

This is to let you know "I am very happy". Not that I am getting into a shadowy optimism, but my power of suffering is increasing. I am being lifted up above the pestilential miasma of this world's joys and sorrows; hey are losing their meaning. It is a land of dreams; it does not matter whether one enjoys or weeps; they are but dreams, and as such, must break sooner or later. How are things going on with you folks there? Harriet is going to have a good time at Paris. I am sure to meet her over there and parler fransaise! I am getting by heart a French dictionnaire! I am making some money too; hard work morning and evening; yet better for all that. Good sleep, good digestion, perfect irregularity.

You are going to the East. I hope to come to Chicago before the end of April. If I can't, I will surely meet you in the East before you go.

What are the McKindley girls doing? Eating grapefruit concoctions and getting plump? Go on, life is but a dream. Are you not glad it is so? My! They want an eternal heaven! Thank God, nothing is eternal except Himself. He alone can bear it, I am sure. Eternity of nonsense!

Things are beginning to hum for me; they will presently roar. I shall remain quiet though, all the same. Things are not humming for you just now. I am so sorry, that is, I am trying to be, for I cannot be sorry for anything and more. I am attaining peace that passeth understanding, which is neither joy nor sorrow, but something above them both. Tell Mother that. My passing through the valley of death, physical, mental, last two years, has helped me in this. Now I am nearing that Peace, the eternal silence. Now I mean to see things as they are, everything in that peace, perfect in its way. "He whose joy is only in himself, whose desires are only in himself, he has learned his lessons." This is the great lesson that we are here to learn through myriads of births and heavens and hells — that there is nothing to be asked for, desired for, beyond one's Self. "The greatest thing I can obtain is my Self." "I am free", therefore I require none else for my happiness. "Alone through eternity, because I was free, am free, and will remain free for ever." This is Vedantism. I preached the theory so long, but oh, joy! Mary, my dear sister, I am realising it now every day. Yes, I am — "I am free." "Alone, alone, I am the one without a second."

Ever yours in the Sat-Chit-Ânanda,
Vivekananda.

PS. Now I am going to be truly Vivekananda. Did you ever enjoy evil! Ha! ha! you silly girl, all is good! Nonsense. Some good, some evil. I enjoy the good and I enjoy the evil. I was Jesus and I was Judas Iscariot; both my play, my fun. "So long as there are two, fear shall not leave thee." Ostrich method? Hide your heads in the sand and think there is nobody seeing you! All is good! Be brave and face everything — come good, come evil, both welcome, both of you my play. I have no good to attain, no ideal to clench up to, no ambition to fulfil; I, the diamond mine, am playing with pebbles, good and evil; good for you — evil, come; good for you-good, you come too. If the universe tumbles round my ears, what is that to me? I am Peace that passeth understanding; understanding only gives us good or evil. I am beyond, I am peace.

CLXVI — HARIBHAI

Translated from Bengali

To Swami Turiyananda
SAN FRANCISCO,
March, 1900.

DEAR HARIBHAI,

I have just received a bill of lading from Mrs. Banerji. She has sent some Dâl (pulses) and rice. I am sending the bill of lading to you. Give it to Miss Waldo; she will bring all these things when they come.

Next week I am leaving this place for Chicago; thence I go over to New York. I am getting on somehow.... Where are you putting up now? What are you doing?

Yours affectionately,
Vivekananda.

CLXVII — JOE

To Miss Josephine MacLeod
1719 TURK STREET,
SAN FRANCISCO,
30th March, 1900.

MY DEAR JOE,

Many thanks for the prompt sending of the books. They will sell quick, I believe. You have become worse than me in changing your plans, I see. I wonder why I have not got any Awakened India yet. My mail is getting so knocked about, I am afraid.

I am working hard — making some money — and am getting better in health. Work morning and evening, go to bed at 12 p.m. after a heavy supper! — and trudge all over the town! And get better too!

So Mrs. Milton is there, give her my love, will you? Has not Turiyananda's leg got all right?

I have sent Margot's letter to Mrs. Bull as she wanted. I am so happy to learn of Mrs. Leggett's gift to her. Things have got to come round; anyway, they are bound to, because nothing is eternal.

I will be a week or two more here if I find it paying, then go to a place near by called Stockton and then — I don't know. Things are going anyhow.

I am very peaceful and quiet, and things are going anyway-just they go.

With all love,
Vivekananda.

PS. Miss Waldo is just the person to undertake editing Karma-Yoga with additions etc.

CLXVIII — HARIBHAI

Translated from Bengali

To Swami Turiyananda

DEAR HARIBHAI,

I am glad to hear that your leg is all right and that you are doing splendid work. My body is going on all right. The thing is, I fall ill when I take too much precaution. I am cooking, eating whatever comes, working day and night, and I am all right and sleeping soundly!

I am going over to New York within a month. Has Sarada's magazine gone out of circulation? I am not getting it any longer. Awakened also has gone to sleep, I think. They are not sending it to me any more. Let that go. There is an outbreak of plague in our country; who knows who is alive and who is dead! Well, a letter from Achu has come today. He had hidden himself in the town of Ramgarh in Sikar State. Someone told him that Vivekananda was dead; so he has written to me! I am sending him a reply.

All well here. Hope this finds you and all others well.

Yours affectionately,
Vivekananda.

CLXIX — JOE

To Miss Josephine MacLeod

1719 TURK STREET,
SAN FRANCISCO, CALIF.
April, 1900.

MY DEAR JOE,

Just a line before you start for France. Are you going via England? I had a beautiful letter from Mrs. Sevier in which I find that Miss Müller sent simply a paper without any other words to Kali who was with her in Darjeeling.

Congreave is the name of her nephew, and he is in the Transvaal war; that is the reason she underlined that, to show her nephew fighting the Boers in Transvaal. That was all. I cannot understand it any more now than then, of course.

I am physically worse than at Los Angeles, mentally much better, stronger, and peaceful. Hope it will continue to be so.

I have not got a reply to my letter to you; I expect it soon.

One Indian letter of mine was directed by mistake to Mrs. Wheeler; it came all right to me in the end. I had nice notes from Saradananda; they are doing beautifully over there. The boys are working up; well, scolding has both sides, you see; it makes them up and doing. We Indians have been so dependent for so long that it requires, I am sorry, a good lot of tongue to make them active. One of the laziest fellows had taken charge of the anniversary this year and pulled it through. They have planned and are successfully working famine works by themselves without my help.... All this comes from the terrific scolding I have been giving, sure!

They are standing on their own feet. I am so glad. See Joe, the Mother is working.

I sent Miss Thursby's letter to Mrs. Hearst. She sent me an invitation to her musical. I could not go. I had a bad cold. So that was all. Another lady for whom I had a letter from Miss Thursby, an Oakland lady, did not reply. I don't know whether I shall make enough in Frisco to pay my fare to Chicago! Oakland work has been successful. I hope to get about $100 from Oakland, that is all. After all, I am content. It is better that I tried.... Even the magnetic healer had not anything for me. Well, things will go on anyhow for me; I do not care how.... I am very peaceful. I learn from Los Angeles, Mrs. Leggett has been bad again. I wired to New York to learn what truth was in it. I will get a reply soon, I expect.

Say, how will you arrange about my mail when the Leggetts are over on the other side? Will you so arrange that they reach me right?

I have nothing more to say; all love and gratitude is yours; already you know that. You have already done more than I ever deserved. I don't know whether I go to Paris or not, but I must go to England sure in May. I must not go home without trying England a few weeks more. With all love,

Ever yours in the Lord,
Vivekananda.

PS. Mrs. Hansborough and Mrs. Appenul have taken a flat for a month at 1719 Turk Street. I am with them, and shall be a few weeks.

CLXX — DHIRA MATA

To Mrs. Ole Bull

1719 TURK STREET,
SAN FRANCISCO,
1st April, 1900.

DEAR DHIRA MATA,

Your kind note came this morning. I am so happy to learn that all the New York friends are being cured by Mrs. Milton. She has been very unsuccessful, it seems, in Los Angeles, as all the people we introduced tell me. Some are in a worse state than before the skin paring. Kindly give Mrs. Milton my love; her rubbings used to do me good at the time at least. Poor Dr. Hiller! We send him over post-haste to Los Angeles to get his wife cured. You ought to have seen him the other morning and heard him too! Mrs. Hiller, it appears, is many times worse for all the rubbings given; and she is only a few bones; and, above all, the doctor had to spend 500 dollars in Los Angeles. That makes him feel very bad. I, of course, would not write this to Joe; she is happy in her dreams of having done so much good to poor sufferers. But oh, if she could hear the Los Angeles folks and this old Dr. Hiller, she would change her mind at once and learn wisdom from an old adage not to recommend medicine to any one. I am so glad I did not write of old Dr. Hiller's alacrity in getting over to Los Angeles when he heard of this cure from Joe. She ought to have seen the old man dance about my room, with greater alacrity! 500 dollars was too much for the old man; he is a German; he dances about, slaps his pockets and says, "You can'th have goth the five hundred, buth for this silly cure!"

Then there are poor people who paid her three dollars a rubbing sometimes and now complimenting Joe and myself. Don't tell this to Joe. You and she can afford to lose money on anyone. So also the old German doctor, but the poor boy finds it a bit hard. The old doctor is now persuaded that some devils are misarranging his affairs of late. He had counted on so much to have me as his guest, and his wife righted, but he had to run to Los Angeles and that upset the whole plan; and now, though he tries his best to get me in as his guest, I fight shy, not of him, but of his wife and sister-in-law. He is sure, "Devils must be in it"; he has been a Theosophical student. I told him to write to Miss MacLeod to hunt up a devil-driver somewhere so that he might run with his wife and spend another five hundred! Doing good is not always smooth!

As for me, I get the fun out of it — as long as Joe pays — bone-cracker, or skin-parer, or any system whatever. But this was not fair of Joe — after having got in all these people to get rubbed down, to run off and let me bear all the compliments! I am glad she is not introducing any outsiders to be skinned. Otherwise Joe would be gone to Paris, leaving poor Mr. Leggett to collect the compliments. I sent in a Christian Science healer to Dr. Hiller as a make-up of Joe's misdemeanour, but his wife slammed the door in her face and would have nothing to do with queer healing.

Anyhow, I sincerely hope and pray Mrs. Leggett will be well this time. Did they analyse the sting?

I hope the will will arrive soon; I am a bit anxious about it. I expected to get a draft trust-deed also by this mail from India; no letters came, not even Awakened India, though I find Awakened India has reached San Francisco.

I read in the papers the other day of 500 deaths in one week of plague in Calcutta! Mother knows what is good.

So Mr. Leggett has got the V. Society up. Good.

How is Olea? Where is Margot? I wrote her a letter the other day to 21 W. 34, N.Y. I am so happy that she is making headway. With all love,

Ever your son,
Vivekananda.

PS. I am getting all the work I can do and more. I will make my passage, anyhow. Though they cannot pay me much, yet they pay some, and by constant work I will make enough to pay my way and have a few hundred in the pocket anyhow. So you needn't be the least anxious about me.

CLXXI — MARGOT

To Sister Nivedita

U.S.A.,
6th April, 1900.

DEAR MARGOT,

Glad you have returned. Gladder you are going to Paris. I shall go to Paris of course, only don't know when. Mrs. Leggett thinks I ought to immediately, and take up studying French. Well, take what comes. So you do too.

Finish your books, and in Paris we are going to conquer the Froggies. How is Mary? Give her my love. My work here is done. I will come in fifteen days to Chicago if Mary is there. She is going away to the East soon.

With blessings,
Vivekananda.

PS. The mind is omnipresent and can be heard and felt anywhere.

CLXXII — AMERICAN FRIEND

To an American friend

SAN FRANCISCO,
7th April, 1900.

... I am more calm and quiet now than I ever was. I am on my own feet, working hard and with pleasure. To work I have the right. Mother knows the rest.

You see, I shall have to stay here, longer than I intended, and work. But don't be disturbed. I shall work out all my problems. I am on my own feet now, and I begin to see the light. Success would have led me astray, and I would have lost sight of the truth that I am a Sannyasin. That is why Mother is giving me this experience.

My boat is nearing the calm harbour from which

it is never more to be driven out. Glory, glory unto Mother! I have no wish, no ambition now. Blessed be Mother! I am the servant of Ramakrishna. I am merely a machine. I know nothing else. Nor do I want to know. Glory, glory unto Shri Guru!

CLXXIII — DHIRA MATA

To Mrs. Ole Bull

1719 TURK STREET,
SAN FRANCISCO,
8th April, 1900.

DEAR DHIRA MATA,

Here is a long letter from A__. He seems to be entirely upset. I am sure a little kindness will completely win him over. He thinks that you want to drive him out of New York, etc. He awaits my orders. I have told him to trust you in everything and remain in New York till I come.

I think, as things stand in New York, they require my presence. Do you? In that case I shall come over soon.

I have been making enough money to pay my passage. I will stop on my way at Chicago and Detroit.

Of course by that time you will be off. A__ has done good work so far; and, of course, you know I do not meddle with my workers at all.

The man who can work has an individuality of his own and resists any pressure there. That is my reason in leaving workers entirely free. Of course you are on the spot and know best. Advise me what to do.

The remittance to Calcutta has duly reached. I got news of it by this mail. My cousin sends her respects and thanks, but she is sorry she cannot write English.

I am getting better every day, and even walking uphill. There are falls now and then, but the duration is decreasing constantly. My thanks to Mrs. Milton.

I had a little note from Siri Gryanander. Poor girl, she is so thankful to be trusted. That is just like Mrs. Leggett — good, good, good. Money is not evil after all — in good hands. I hope fervently Siri will completely recover, poor child.

I will leave here in about two weeks. I go to a place called Star Klon and then start for the East. It may be I may go to Denver also. With all love to Joe,

Ever your son,
Vivekananda.

PS. I do not any more doubt my ultimate cure; you ought to see me working like a steam engine cooking, eating anything and everything, and, all the same, sleeping well and keeping well!

I have not done any writing — no time. I am so glad Mrs. Leggett is much better and walking about naturally. I expect her complete recovery soon and pray for it.

PS. I had a nice letter from Mrs. Sevier; they are going on splendidly with the work. Plague has broken out severely at Calcutta, but no hullabaloo over it this time.

PS. Did you reveal to A__ that I have given over to you the charge of the entire work? Well, you know best how to do things; but he seems to be hurt at that.

CLXXIV — JOE

To Miss Josephine MacLeod

1719 TURK STREET,
SAN FRANCISCO,
10th April, 1900.

DEAR JOE,

There is a squabble in New York, I see. I got a letter from A__ stating that he was going to leave New York. He thought Mrs. Bull and you have written lots against him to me. I wrote him back to be patient and wait, and that Mrs. Bull and Miss MacLeod wrote only good things about him.

Well, Joe Joe, you know my method in all these rows; to leave all rows alone! "Mother" sees to all such things. I have finished my work. I am retired, Joe. "Mother" will work now Herself. That is all.

Now, as you say, I am going to send all the money I have made here. I could do it today, but I am waiting to make it a thousand. I expect to make a thousand in Frisco by the end of this week. I will buy a draft on New York and send it or ask the bank the best way to do it.

I have plenty of letters from the Math and the Himalayan centre. This morning came one from Swarupananda. Yesterday one from Mrs. Sevier.

I told Mrs. Hansborough about the photos.

You tell Mr. Leggett from me to do what is best about the Vedanta Society matter. The only thing I see is that in every country we have to follow its own method. As such, if I were you, I would convene a meeting of all the members and sympathisers and ask them what they want to do. Whether they want to organise or not, what sort of organisation they want if any, etc. But Lordy, do it on your own hook. I am quits. Only if you think my presence would be of any help I can come in fifteen days.

I have finished my work here; only, out of San Francisco, Stockton is a little city I want to work a few days in; then I go East. I think I should rest now, although I can have $100 a week average in this city, all along. This time I want to let upon New York the charge of the Light Brigade.

With all love,

Ever yours affectionately,
Vivekananda.

PS. If the workers are all averse to organising, do you think there is any benefit in it? You know best. Do what you think best. I have a letter from Margot from Chicago. She asks some questions; I am going to reply.

CLXXV — AMERICAN FRIEND

To an American friend

ALAMEDA, CALIFORNIA,
12th April, 1900.

Mother is becoming propitious once more. Things are looking up. They must.

Work always brings evil with it. I have paid for the accumulated evil with bad health. I am glad. My mind is all the better for it. There is a mellowness and a calmness in life now, which was never there before. I am learning now how to be detached as well as attached, and mentally becoming my own master....

Mother is doing Her own work; I do not worry much now. Moths like me die by the thousand every instant. Her work goes on all the same. Glory unto Mother! ... Alone and drifting about in the will-current of the Mother has been my whole life. The moment I have tried to break this, that moment I have been hurt. Her will be done! ...

I am happy, at peace with myself, and more of the Sannyasin than I ever was before. The love for my own kith and kin is growing less every day, and that for Mother increasing. Memories of long nights of vigil with Shri Ramakrishna under the Dakshineswar Banyan are waking up once more. And work? What is work? Whose work? Whom shall I work for?

I am free. I am Mother's child. She works, She plays. Why should I plan? What should I plan? Things came and went, just as She liked, without my planning. We are Her automata. She is the wire-puller.

CLXXVI — JOE

To Miss Josephine MacLeod

ALAMEDA, CALIFORNIA,
20th April, 1900.

MY DEAR JOE,

Received your note today. I wrote you one yesterday but directed it to England thinking you will be there.

I have given your message to Mrs. Betts. I am so sorry this little quarrel came with A__. I got also his letter you sent. He is correct so far as he says, "Swami wrote me 'Mr. Leggett is not interested in Vedanta and will not help any more. You stand on your own feet.'" It was as you and Mrs. Leggett desired me to write him from Los Angeles about New York — in reply to his asking me what to do for funds.

Well, things will take their own shape, but it seems in Mrs. Bull's and your mind there is some idea that I ought to do something. But in the first place I do not know anything about the difficulties. None of you write me anything about what that is for, and I am no thought-reader. You simply wrote me a general idea that A__ wanted to keep things in his hands. What can I understand from it? What are the difficulties? Regarding what the differences are about, I am as much in the dark as about the exact date of the Day of Destruction! And yet Mrs. Bull's and your letters show quite an amount of vexation! These things get complicated sometimes, in spite of ourselves. Let them take their shape.

I have executed and sent the will to Mr. Leggett as desired by Mrs. Bull.

I am going on, sometimes well and at other times ill. I cannot say, on my conscience, that I have been the least benefited by Mrs. Milton. She has been good to me, I am very thankful. My love to her. Hope she will benefit others.

For writing to Mrs. Bull this fact, I got a four page sermon, as to how I ought to be grateful and thankful, etc., etc. All that is, sure, the outcome of this A__ business! Sturdy and Mrs. Johnson got disturbed by Margot, and they fell upon me. Now A__ disturbs Mrs. Bull and, of course, I have to bear the brunt of it. Such is life!

You and Mrs. Leggett wanted me to write him to be free and independent and that Mr. Leggett was not going to help them. I wrote it — now what can I do? If John or Jack does not obey you, am I to be hanged for it? What do I know about this Vedanta Society? Did I start it? Had I any hand in it? Then again, nobody condescends to write me anything about what the affair is! Well, this world is a great fun.

I am glad Mrs. Leggett is recovering fast. I pray every moment for her complete recovery. I start for Chicago on Monday. A kind lady has given me a pass up to New York to be used within three months. The Mother will take care of me. She is not going to strand me now after guarding me all my life.

Ever yours gratefully,
Vivekananda.

CLXXVII — MARY

To Miss Mary Hale

23rd April, 1900.

MY DEAR MARY,

I ought to have started today but circumstances so happened that I cannot forgo the temptation to be in a camp under the huge red-wood trees of California before I leave. Therefore I postpone it for three or four days. Again after the incessant work I require a breath of God's free air before I start on this bone-breaking journey of four days.

Margot insists in her letter that I must keep my promise to come to see Aunt Mary in fifteen days. It will be kept — only in twenty days instead of fifteen. By that I avoid the nasty snowstorm Chicago had lately and get a little strength too.

Margot is a great partisan of Aunt Mary it seems, and other people besides me have nieces and cousins and aunts.

I start tomorrow to the woods. Woof! get my lungs full of ozone before getting into Chicago. In the meanwhile keep my mail for me when it comes to Chicago and don't send it off here like a good girl as you are.

I have finished work. Only a few days' rest, my friends insist — three or four — before facing the railway.

I have got a free pass for three months from here to New York; no expense except the sleeping car; so, you see, free, free!

Ever yours gratefully,
Vivekananda.

CLXXVIII — MARY

To Miss Mary Hale

30th April, 1900.

MY DEAR MARY,

Sudden indisposition and fever prevent my starting for Chicago yet. I will start as soon as I am strong for the journey. I had a letter from Margot the other day. Give her kindly my love, and know yourself my eternal love. Where is Harriet? Still in Chicago? And the McKindley sisters?

To all my love,
Vivekananda.

CLXXIX — NIVEDITA

To Sister Nivedita

2nd May, 1900.

MY DEAR NIVEDITA,

I have been very ill — one more relapse brought about by months of hard work. Well, it has shown me that I have no kidney or heart disease whatsoever, only overworked nerves. I am, therefore, going today in the country for some days till I completely recover, which I am sure will be in a few days.

In the meanwhile I do not want to read any India letters with the plague news etc. My mail is coming to Mary; either she or you keep them (you, if she goes away) till I return.

I am going to throw off all worry, and glory unto Mother.

Mrs. C. P. Huntington, a very, very wealthy lady, who has helped me, came; wants to see and help you. She will be in New York by the first of June. Do not go away without seeing her. If I cannot come early enough, I will send you an introduction to her.

Give my love to Mary. I am leaving here in a few days.

Ever yours with blessings,
Vivekananda.

PS. The accompanying letter is to introduce you to Mrs. M. C. Adams, wife of Judge Adams. Go to see her immediately. Much good may come out of it. She is well known; find out her address.

CLXXX — NIVEDITA

To Sister Nivedita

SAN FRANCISCO,
26th May, 1900.

DEAR NIVEDITA,

All blessings on you. Don't despond in the least. Shri wah Guru! Shri wah Guru! You come of the blood of a Kshatriya. Our yellow garb is the robe of death on the field of battle. Death for the cause is our goal, not success. Shri wah Guru! . . .

Black and thick are the folds of sinister fate. But I am the master. I raise my hand, and lo, they vanish! All this is nonsense. And fear? I am the Fear of fear, the Terror of terror, I am the fearless secondless One, I am the Rule of destiny, the Wiper-out of fact. Shri wah Guru! Steady, child, don't be bought by gold or anything else, and we win!

Vivekananda.

CLXXXI — MARY

To Miss Mary Hale

1921 W. 21 STREET,
LOS ANGELES,
17th June, 1900.

MY DEAR MARY,

It is true I am much better, but not yet completely recovered; anyway, the complexion of the mind is one belonging to everyone that suffers. It is neither gas nor anything else.

Kâli worship is not a necessary step in any religion. The Upanishads teach us all there is of religion. Kali worship is my special fad; you never heard me preach it, or read of my preaching it in India. I only preach what is good for universal humanity. If there is any curious method which applies entirely to me, I keep it a secret and there it ends. I must not explain to you what Kali worship is, as I never taught it to anybody.

You are entirely mistaken if you think the Boses are rejected by the Hindu people. The English rulers want to push him into a corner. They don't of course like that sort of development in the Indian race. They make it hot for him, that is why he seeks to go elsewhere.

By the "anglicised" are meant people who by their manners and conduct show that they are ashamed of us poor, old type Hindus. I am not ashamed of my race or my birth or nationality. That such people are not liked by the Hindus, I cannot wonder.

Ceremonials and symbols etc. have no place in our religion which is the doctrine of the Upanishads, pure and simple. Many people think the ceremonial etc. help them in realising religion. I have no objection.

Religion is that which does not depend upon books or teachers or prophets or saviours, and that which does not make us dependent in this or in any other lives upon others. In this sense Advaitism of the Upanishads is the only religion. But saviours, books, prophets, ceremonials, etc. have their places. They may help many as Kali worship helps me in my secular work. They are welcome.

The Guru, however, is a different idea. It is the relation between the transmitter and the receiver of force — psychic power and knowledge. Each nation is a type, physically and mentally. Each is constantly receiving ideas from others only to work them out into its type, that is, along the national line. The time has not come for the destruction of types. All education from any source is compatible with the ideals in every country; only they must be nationalised, i.e. fall in line with the rest of the type manifestation.

Renunciation is always the ideal of every race; only other races do not know what they are made to do by nature unconsciously. Through the ages one purpose runs sure. And that will be finished with the destruction of this earth and the sun! And worlds are always in progress indeed! And nobody as yet developed enough in any one of the infinite worlds to communicate with us! Bosh! They are born, show the same phenomena, and die the same death! Increasing purpose! Babies! Live in the land of dreams, you babies!

Well, now about me. You must persuade Harriet to give me a few dollars every month, and I will have some other friends do the same. If I succeed, I fly off to India. I am dead tired of the platform work for a living. It does not please me any more. I retire and do some writing if I can do some scholarly work.

I am coming soon to Chicago, hope to be there in a few days. Say, would not Mrs. Adams be able to get up a class for me to pay my passage back?

Of course I shall try different places. So much of optimism has come to me, Mary, that I should fly off to the Himalayas if I had wings.

I have worked for this world, Mary, all my life, and it does not give me a piece of bread without taking a pound of flesh.

If I can get a piece of bread a day, I retire entirely; but this is impossible — this is the increasing purpose that is unfolding all the devilish inwardness, as I am getting older!

Ever yours in the Lord,
Vivekananda.

PS. If ever a man found the vanity of things, I have it now. This is the world, hideous, beastly corpse. Who thinks of helping it is a fool! But we have to work out our slavery by doing good or evil; I have worked it out, I hope. May the Lord take me to the other shore! Amen! I have given up all thoughts about India or any land. I am now selfish, want to save myself!

"He who revealed unto Brahmâ (the first of the gods) the Vedas, who is manifest in every heart, unto Him I take refuge, hoping deliverance from bondage."

CLXXXII — MARY

To Miss Mary Hale

VEDANTA SOCIETY,
146 E. 55TH STREET,
NEW YORK,
23rd June, 1900.

MY DEAR MARY,

Many, many thanks for your beautiful letter. I am very well and happy and same as ever. Waves must come before a rise. So with me. I am very glad you are going to pray. Why don't you get up a Methodist camp-meeting? That will have quicker effect, I am sure.

I am determined to get rid of all sentimentalism, and emotionalism, and hang me if you ever find me emotional. I am the Advaitist; our goal is knowledge — no feelings, no love, as all that belongs to matter and superstition and bondage. I am only existence and knowledge.

Greenacre will give you good rest. I am sure. I wish you all joy there. Don't for a moment worry on my account. "Mother" looks after me. She is bringing me fast out of the hell of emotionalism, and bringing me into the light of pure reason. With everlasting wishes for your happiness,

Ever your brother,
Vivekananda.

PS. Margot starts on the 26th. I may follow in a week or two. Nobody has any power over me, for I am the spirit. I have no ambition; it is all Mother's work; I have no part.

I could not digest your letter as the dyspepsia was rather bad last few days.

Non-attachment has always been there. It has come in a minute. Very soon I stand where no sentiment, no feeling, can touch me.

CLXXXIII — SISTER

To Miss Mary Hale

102 E. 58TH STREET,
NEW YORK,
11th July, 1900.

MY DEAR DEVOTED SISTER,

I was glad to get your note as also to learn that you were going to Greenacre. Hope you will have much profit. I have been much censured by everyone for cutting off my long hair. I am sorry. You forced me to do it.

I had been to Detroit and came back yesterday. Trying as soon as possible to go to France, thence to India. Very little news here; the work is closed. I am taking regularly my meals and sleeping — that is all.

Ever faithful and loving brother,
Vivekananda.

PS. Write to the girls to send my mails, if any, at Chicago.

CLXXXIV — TURIYANANDA

To Swami Turiyananda

102 E. 58TH STREET,
NEW YORK,
18th July, 1900.

MY DEAR TURIYANANDA,

Your letter reached me redirected. I stayed in Detroit for three days only. It is frightfully hot here in New York. There was no Indian mail for you last week. I have not heard from Sister Nivedita yet.

Things are going on the same way with us. Nothing particular. Miss Müller cannot come in August. I will not wait for her. I take the next train. Wait till it comes. With love to Miss Boocke,

Yours in the Lord,
Vivekananda.

PS. Kali went away about a week ago to the mountains. He cannot come back till September. I am all alone, and washing; I like it. Have you seen my friends? Give them my love.

CLXXXV — JOE

To Miss Josephine MacLeod

102 E. 58TH STREET,
NEW YORK,
20th July, 1900.

DEAR JOE,

Possibly before this reaches you I shall be in Europe, London or Paris as the chance of steamer comes.

I have straightened out my business here. The works are at Mr. Whitmarsh's suggestion in the hands of Miss Waldo.

I have to get the passage and sail. Mother knows the rest.

My intimate friend did not materialise yet and writes she will come some time in August, and she is dying to see a Hindu, and her soul is burning for Mother India.

I wrote her I may see her in London. Mother knows again. Mrs. Huntington sends love to Margot and expects to hear from her if she is not too busy with her scientific exhibits.

With all love to "sacred cow" of India, to yourself, to the Leggetts, to Miss (what's her name?), the American rubber plant.

Ever yours in the Lord,
Vivekananda.

CLXXXVI — JOE

To Miss Josephine MacLeod

102 E. 58TH STREET,
NEW YORK,
24th July, 1900.

DEAR JOE,

The sun = Knowledge. The stormy water = Work. The lotus = Love. The serpent = Yoga. The swan = the Self. The Motto = May the Swan (the Supreme Self) send us that. It is the mind-lake. (This explains the design on the Ramakrishna Math and Mission seal, printed on the title page of this volume — Ed.) How do you like it? May the Swan fill you with all these anyway.

I am to start on Thursday next, by the French steamer La Champagne. The books are in the hands of Waldo and Whitmarsh. They are nearly ready.

I am well, getting better — and all right till I see you next week.

Ever yours in the Lord,
Vivekananda.

CLXXXVII — TURIYANANDA

To Swami Turiyananda

102 E. 58TH STREET,
NEW YORK,
25th July, 1900.

DEAR TURIYANANDA,

I received a letter from Mrs. Hansborough telling me of your visit to her. They like you immensely, and I am sure you have found in them genuine, pure, and absolutely unselfish friends.

I am starting for Paris tomorrow. Things all turn that way. Kali is not here. He is rather worried at my going away, but it has got to be.

Address your next letter to me care of Mr. Leggett, 6 Place des Etats Unis, Paris, France.

Give my love to Mrs. Wyckoff, Hansborough, and to Helen. Revive the clubs a bit and ask Mrs. Hansborough to collect the dues as they fall and send them to India. Sarada writes they are having rather hot times. My kind regards for Miss Boocke.

With all love,

Ever yours in the Lord,
Vivekananda.

CLXXXVIII — DEAR___

Translated from Bengali

To a Brahmacharin (Brahmachari Harendra Nath) of the Advaita Ashrama, Mayavati

NEW YORK,
August, 1900.

DEAR __,

I had a letter from you several days ago, but I could not reply earlier. Mr. Sevier speaks well of you in his letter. I am very pleased at this.

Write to me in minute detail who all are there, and what each one is doing. Why don't you write letters to your mother? What is this? Devotion to the mother is the root of all welfare. How is your brother getting on with his studies at Calcutta? The Sannyasin-names of those there escape my memory — how to address each? Give my love to all conjointly. I got the news that Khagen has now fully recovered. This is happy news. Write to me whether the Seviers are attending to your comforts and other details. I am glad to know that Dinu's health is all right. The boy Kali has a tendency to become fat; but this will all surely go away by constantly climbing up and down the hills there. Tell Swarup that I am very much pleased with his conducting of the paper. He is doing splendid work. Give to all others also my love and blessings. Tell everybody that my health is now all right. From here I shall go to England and from there to India very shortly.

With all blessings,
Vivekananda.

CLXXXIX — HARI

Translated from Bengali

To Swami Turiyananda

6 PLACE DES ETATS UNIS,
PARIS,
13th August, 1900.

DEAR BROTHER HARI,

I got your letter from California. So three persons are getting spiritual trances; well, it is not bad. Even out of that much good will come. Shri Ramakrishna knows! Let things happen as they will. His work He knows, you and I are but servants and nothing else.

I am sending this letter to San Francisco — care of Mrs. C. Panel. Just now I got some news from New York. They are well. Kali is on tour. Write in detail about your health and work in San Francisco. And don't be indifferent to the question of sending money to the Math. See that money goes certainly every month, from Los Angeles and San Francisco.

I am on the whole doing well. I am shortly starting for England. I get news of Sharat. Recently he had an attack of dysentery. The rest are all well. This time few got malaria; nor is it so prevalent on the banks of the Ganga. This year, owing to the scarcity of rain, there is fear of famine in Bengal also.

By the grace of Mother, go on doing work, brother. Mother knows, and you know — but I am off! Now I am going to take a rest.

Yours affectionately,
Vivekananda.

CXC — JOHN FOX

To Mr. John Fox

BOULEVARD HANS SWAN,
PARIS,
14th August, 1900.

JOHN FOX, ESQ.,

6 Dr. Wolf Street,
Dorchester, Mass, U.S., America.

Kindly write Mohin (Mahendranath Datta, younger brother of Swamiji.) that he has my blessings in whatever he does. And what he is doing now is surely much better than lawyering, etc. I like boldness and adventure and my race stands in need of that spirit very much. Only as my health is failing and I do not expect to live long, Mohin must see his way to take care of mother and family. I may pass away any moment. I am quite proud of him now.

Yours affectionately,
Vivekananda.

CXCI — BROTHER HARI

Translated from Bengali

To Swami Turiyananda

6 PLACE DES ETATS UNIS,
PARIS,
August, 1900.

DEAR BROTHER HARI,

Now I am staying on the sea-coast of France. The session of the Congress of History of Religions is over. It was not a big affair; some twenty scholars chattered a lot on the origin of the Shâlagrâma and the origin of Jehovah, and similar topics. I also said something on the occasion.

My body and mind are broken down; I need rest badly. In addition, there is not a single person on whom I can depend; on the other hand so long as I live, all will become very selfish depending upon me for everything. . . . Dealing with people entails constant mental uneasiness. . . . I have cut myself off by a will. Now I am writing to say that nobody will have sole power. All will be done in accordance with the view of the majority. . . . If a trust-deed on similar lines can be executed, then I am free. . . . What you are doing is also Guru Maharaj's work. Continue to do it. Now I have done my part. Don't write to me any more about those things; do not even mention the subject. I have no opinions whatever to give on that subject. . . .

Yours affectionately,
Vivekananda.

PS. Convey my love to all.

CXCII — HARI

Translated from Bengali

To Swami Turiyananda

6 PLACE DES ETATS UNIS,
DA FOREST P.O., SANTA CLARA CO.,
PARIS, FRANCE,
1st September, 1900.

MY DEAR HARI,

I learnt everything from your letter. Earlier I had an inkling of some trouble between the full-fledged Vedantist and the Home of Truth — someone wrote that. Such things do occur; wisdom consists in carrying on the work by cleverly keeping all in good humour.

For some time now I have been living incognito. I shall stay with the French to pick up their language. I am somewhat freed from worries; that is to say, I have signed the trust-deed and other things and sent them to Calcutta. I have not reserved any right or ownership for myself. You now possess everything and will manage all work by the Master's grace.

I have no longer any desire to kill myself by touring. For the present I feel like settling down somewhere and spending my time among books. I have somewhat mastered the French language; but if I stay among the French for a month or two, I shall be able to carry on conversation well. If one can master this language and German sufficiently, one can virtually become well acquainted with European learning. The people of France are mere intellectualists, they run after worldly things and firmly believe God and souls to be superstitious; they are extremely loath to talk on such subjects. This is a truly materialistic country! Let me see what that Lord does. But this country is at the head of Western culture, and Paris is the capital of that culture.

Brother, free me from all work connected with preaching. I am now aloof from all that, you manage it yourselves. It is my firm conviction that Mother will get work done through all of you a hundredfold more than through me.

Many days ago I received a letter from Kali. He must have reached New York by now. Miss Waldo sends news now and then.

I keep sometimes well and sometimes bad. Of late I am again having that massage treatment by Mrs. Milton, who says, "You have already recovered!" This much I see — whatever the flatulence, I feel no difficulty in moving, walking, or even climbing. In the morning I take vigorous exercise, and then have a dip in cold water.

Yesterday I went to see the house of the gentleman with whom I shall stay. He is a poor scholar, has his room filled with books and lives in a flat on the fifth floor. And as there are no lifts in this country as in America, one has to climb up and down. But it is no longer trying to me.

There is a beautiful public park round the house. The gentleman cannot speak English; that is a further reason for my going. I shall have to speak French perforce. It is all Mother's will. She knows best what She wants to have done. She never speaks out, "only keeps mum". But this much I notice that for a month or so I have been having intense meditation and repetition of the Lord's name.

Please convey my love to Miss Boocke, Miss Bell, Mrs. Aspinel, Miss Beckham, Mr. George, Dr. Logan, and other friends and accept it yourself. My love to all in Los Angeles also.

Yours,
Vivekananda.

CXCIII — TURIYANANDA

Translated from Bengali

To Swami Turiyananda

6 PLACE DES ETATS UNIS,
September, 1900.

MY DEAR TURIYANANDA,

Just now I received your letter. Through Mother's will all work will go on; don't be afraid. I shall soon leave for some other place. Perhaps I shall be on a tour of Constantinople and other places for some time. Mother knows what will come next. I have received a letter from Mrs. Wilmot. From this, too, it appears that she is very enthusiastic. Sit firm and free from worries. Everything will be all right. If hearing the Nada etc. does anyone harm, he can get rid of it if he gives up meditation for a time and takes to fish and meat. If the body does not become progressively weak, there is no cause for alarm. Practice should be slow.

I shall leave this place before your reply comes. So do not send the reply to this letter here. I have received all the issues of Sarada's paper, and wrote to him lots a few weeks ago. I have a mind to send more later on. There is no knowing where my next stop will be. This much I can say that I am trying to be free from care.

I received a letter from Kali, too, today. I shall send him a reply tomorrow. The body is somehow rolling on. Work makes it ill, and rest keeps it well — that is all. Mother knows. Nivedita has gone to England. She and Mrs. Bull are collecting funds. She has a mind to run a school at Kishengarh with the girls she had there. Let her do what she can. I do not intervene any more in any matter — that is all.

My love to you. But I have nothing more to advise as regards work.

Yours in service,
Vivekananda.

CXCIV — MADEMOISELLE

Translated from the original in French

6 PLACE DES ETATS UNIS, PARIS,
October, 1900.

MY DEAR MADEMOISELLE,

I have been very happy and content here. I am having the best of times after many years. I find life here with Mr. Bois very satisfactory — the books, the calm, and the absence of everything that usually troubles me.

But I don't know what kind of destiny is waiting for me now.

My letter is funny, isn't it? But it is my first attempt.

Yours faithfully,
Vivekananda.

CXCV — SISTER CHRISTINE

Translated from the original in French

To Sister Christine
6 PLACE DES ETATS UNIS,
PARIS,
14th October, 1900.

God bless you at each step, my dear Christine, such is my constant prayer!

Your letter, so beautiful and so calm, has given me that fresh energy which I am often losing.

I am happy, yes, I am happy, but the cloud has not left me entirely. It sometimes comes back, unfortunately, but it no longer has the morbidity it used to have.

I am staying with a famous French writer, M. Jules Bois. I am his guest. As he is a man making his living with his pen, he is not rich; but we have many great ideas in common and feel happy together.

He discovered me a few years ago and has already translated some of my pamphlets into French. We shall in the end find what we are looking for, isn't it?

Thus, I shall travel with Madame Calve, Miss MacLeod, and M. Jules Bois. I shall be the guest of Madame Calve, the famous singer. We shall go to Constantinople, the Near East, Greece, and Egypt.

On our way back, we shall visit Venice.

It may be that I shall give a few lectures in Paris after my return, but they will be in English with an interpreter. I have no time any more, nor the power to study a new language at my age. I am an old man, isn't it?

Mrs. Funke is ill. I think she works too hard. She already had some nervous trouble. I hope she will soon be well.

I am sending all the money I earned in America to India. Now I am free, the begging-monk as before. I have also resigned from the Presidentship of the Monastery. Thank God, I am free! It is no more for me to carry such a responsibility. I am so nervous and so weak.

"As the birds which have slept in the branches of a tree wake up, singing when the dawn comes, and soar up into the deep blue sky, so is the end of my life."

I have had many difficulties, and also some very great successes. But all my difficulties and suffering count for nothing, as I have succeeded. I have attained my aim. I have found the pearl for which I dived into the ocean of life. I have been rewarded. I am pleased.

Thus it seems to me that a new chapter of my life is opening. It seems to me that Mother will now lead me slowly and softly. No more effort on roads full of obstacles, now it is the bed prepared with birds' down. Do you understand that? Believe me, I feel quite sure.

The experience of all my life, up to now, has taught me, thank God, that I always find what I am looking for with eagerness. Sometimes it is after much suffering, but it does not matter! All is forgotten in the softness of the reward. You are also going through troubles, my friend, but you shall have your reward. Alas! What you now find is not a reward but an additional affliction.

As to myself, I see the cloud lifting, vanishing, the cloud of my bad Karma. And the sun of my good Karma rises — shining, beautiful, and powerful. This will also be the case for you, my friend. My knowledge of this language has not the power to express my emotion. But which language can really do so?

So I drop it, leaving it to your heart to clothe my thought with a soft, loving, and shining language. Good night, gute Nacht!

> Your devoted friend,
> Vivekananda.

PS. We shall leave Paris for Vienna on October 29th. Mr. Leggett is leaving for the United States by next week. We shall notify the Post Office to forward our letters to our further destinations.

CXCVI — JOE

To Miss Josephine MacLeod

> PORT TEWFICK
> 26th November, 1900.

DEAR JOE,

The steamer was late; so I am waiting. Thank goodness, it entered the Canal this morning at Port Said. That means it will arrive some time in the evening if everything goes right.

Of course it is like solitary imprisonment these two days, and I am holding my soul in patience.

But they say the change is thrice dear. Mr. Gaze's agent gave me all wrong directions. In the first place, there was nobody here to tell me a thing, not to speak of receiving me. Secondly, I was not told that I had to change my Gaze's ticket for a steamer one at the agent's office, and that was at Suez, not here. It was good one way, therefore, that the steamer was late; so I went to see the agent of the steamer and he told me to exchange Gaze's pass for a regular ticket.

I hope to board the steamer some time tonight. I am well and happy and am enjoying the fun immensely. How is Mademoiselle? Where is Bois? Give my everlasting gratitude and good wishes to Mme. Calve. She is a good lady.

Hoping you will enjoy your trip.

> Ever affectionately yours,
> Vivekananda.

CXCVII — MOTHER

To Mrs. Ole Bull

THE MATH, BELUR,
HOWRAH DIST., BENGAL, INDIA,
15 December, 1900.

MY DEAR MOTHER,

Three days ago I reached here. It was quite unexpected — my visit, and everybody was so surprised.

Things here have gone better than I expected during my absence, only Mr. Sevier has passed away. It was a tremendous blow, sure, and I don't know the future of the work in the Himalayas. I am expecting daily a letter from Mrs. Sevier who is there still.

How are you? Where are you? My affairs here will be straightened out shortly, I hope, and I am trying my best to straighten them out.

The remittance you send my cousin should henceforth be sent to me direct, the bills being drawn in my name. I will cash them and send her the money. It is better the money goes to her through me.

Saradananda and Brahmananda are much better and this year there is very little malaria here. This narrow strip on the banks of the river is always free from malaria. Only when we get a large supply of pure water the conditions will be perfected here.

Vivekananda.

Discovery Publisher is a multimedia publisher whose mission is to inspire and support personal transformation, spiritual growth and awakening. We strive with every title to preserve the essential wisdom of the author, spiritual teacher, thinker, healer, and visionary artist.

www.ingramcontent.com/pod-product-compliance
Lightning Source LLC
Chambersburg PA
CBHW080242170426
43192CB00014BA/2533